SHARING CARE

SHARING CARE

The Integration of Family Approaches with Child Treatment

By

Robert G. Ziegler, M.D.
with **Andrew H. Bush, M.D.**

Routledge
Taylor & Francis Group
LONDON AND NEW YORK

First published 1999 by
Hamilton Printing Co.

Published 2014 by Routledge
2 Park Square, Milton Park, Abingdon, Oxfordshire OX14 4RN
711 Third Avenue, New York, NY 10017

Routledge is an imprint of the Taylor and Francis Group, an informa business

SHARING CARE: The Integration of Family Approaches with Child Treatment

ISBN 978-0-87630-974-2 (hbk)
ISBN 978-1-138-00970-7 (pbk)

Cover design by Nancy Abbott.

A CIP catalog record for this book is available from the British Library.

Library of Congress Cataloging-in-Publication Data

Ziegler, Robert G.
Sharing care : the integration of family approaches with child treatment / by Robert G. Ziegler, Andrew Bush.
p. cm.
Includes bibliographical references and index.
ISBN 0-87630-974-0 (case : alk. paper)
1. Family psychotherapy. 2. Child psychotherapy. I. Bush, Andrew, M.D. II. Title.
RC488.5.Z54 1999
616.89′156—dc21 99-12989
CIP

Dedication

This book is dedicated to
the past and present
Adult Residents and Child Fellows

in training at the
Department of Psychiatry
at The Cambridge Hospital
Harvard Medical School

who ask too many good questions to be ignored

and the staff, personnel, and faculty at
The Cambridge Health Alliance
who have made a place
for those children and families in need of care.

CONTENTS

PREFACE

"I think my 6-year-old daughter hates me."

"My 15-year-old son has been in a juvenile detention center for three months and he is losing weight. I think he has a brain tumor. He is supposed to go before the judge next week."

"My 5-year-old son's poops have started leaking out of his pullups onto our living room rug. If I thought I would have to put up with poop on the rug, I would have gotten a dog. What can you do to stop him? Nothing we have done works."

"My 17-year-old son has terrible acne and is getting depressed. He actually said he wanted to talk with someone."

"My 5-and-a-half-year-old has been getting more and more anxious over the past eight months. He can't leave for school without crying; he can't go to the bathroom at school without his teacher going with him. He says he remembers when he wasn't worried all the time."

"My 16-year-old son is selling drugs and the housing authority said that if he didn't get treatment we would be evicted. Could you come in disguise? He runs away when we say we are going to bring him to see someone."

"We just saw a television program about attention disorders and we are worried that our 9-year-old son has that. Can you help us?"

"My 8-year-old daughter told her school counselor that her stepfather was abusing her after he grounded her, and now the Department of Social Services is in our life. Can you help us get them out?"

"My 8-year-old son doesn't listen to me, and it doesn't even matter when I whop him."

"The teacher said our son in second grade was slow and that he couldn't pay attention. We think he is fine, but the school said we had to have an evaluation. He's no worse than the other five we have—we think the teacher doesn't like him."

"When my son started fifth grade, his face just started jumping around and now he clears his throat all the time. The pediatrician told us to give it time, but we are still worried."

"My daughter is still having long temper tantrums and she is 6 years old. I'm a single mother who has to work and she just got suspended from her after-school program."

"Adjani's father died last year in Brazil so we had to bring him here. He won't go to school and says he misses being able to be in the bars at night. He told his aunt he had a 25-year-old boyfriend there."

"My son just got caught stealing from a department store. It is right before his bar mitzvah and he says he doesn't even care."

"Our 8-year-old son told us that he is hearing a voice that tells him to do bad things. He is always in trouble."

"Our 15-year-old daughter took an overdose and is getting discharged from the hospital in two days. Our insurance company said you were on our list."

This is just a small sample of the calls for help that can come across a child/adolescent and family therapist's desk in the course of a month. Each one raises different questions or fears in the mind of the therapist. Each call requires evaluating the child, the parents, and how they work together as a family unit. Information from home and school as well as medical, family, and developmental histories will need to be considered in a full assessment. Part I of this book will focus on a way to gather and integrate these multiple points of view. Chapters 1 and 2 will review some of the tools, techniques, and concepts that clinicians can use in the process of assessing the presenting dilemma. Four zones will be defined that represent the level of function in child, parent, and family. Each of these zones of care will lead to a specific approach to treatment. Part II will focus on the treatment of the current *DSM-IV* internalizing and externalizing disorders in children and adolescents and their treatment. The initial steps in either treatment plan will be reviewed in chapters 5 and 6. Short-term approaches (fewer than 20 sessions for child, parent, and family) will be reviewed as well as what some of the current literature suggests about implications for continuing care (one to two years). Issues of longer term care (over the course of years) will be discussed in Chapter 8. Guidelines will be offered to assist the clinician in identifying the various elements of care that lead to stabilization for children and families over the course of the child's development.

Throughout the text, the authors have attempted to develop useful clinical vignettes made up from a composite of their treatment experiences. Most clinical examples do not represent one child, adolescent, parent, or family, but are a creative blend of various clinical encounters drawn from practice over many years.

ACKNOWLEDGMENTS

The evolution of this text has been drawn from years of practice, teaching, and supervision. The first author has seen the extraordinary change that can be achieved in a single session, as well as the slow painful growth that has occured in some who manage the extraordinary impact of mental illness, adverse life experiences, or character problems. There have also been cases in which the way to make a helpful contribution was never clear. Even with the increased availability of new techniques and psychopharmacological options, I have never found a single silver bullet. The most powerful tool for treatment, in my opinion, has been a plan of care that enhances an individual's or family's recognition of their own strengths and patterns of coping, coupled with their sense of being understood.

This book was written with Andrew Bush, M.D. He has helped me understand how best to be clear about the various steps I have advocated in both diagnostic and treatment phases. He has helped me focus on the most common concerns that may come to the mind of the new therapist in facing the types of problems that are discussed here. His careful point of view, as a child psychiatrist who is both a child and family therapist, has made this work more readable and has challenged me to clarify the overall principles I wished to describe.

Dr. Ziegler is grateful to Drs. Giuseppe Erba and Valeria Cavazutti who conveyed the similarly complex issues in contemporary pediatric and adolescent neurology and neuropsychiatry during our years shared in the Division of Neurology at Children's Hospital, Boston. In this setting the uneasy hope for a silver bullet from another field was seen as what all clinicians and parents wish for—an easy answer. This is not available. My wife, Patricia Ziegler, who is a talented and pioneering psychotherapist and whose groundbreaking work in the treatment of borderline disorders at The Cambridge Hospital, Cambridge, MA, offered me the courage to value "plain speak" (rather than indirect metaphoric allusion) and cognitive–behavioral perspectives when they were still rarely used in treatment. Our daughter, Lisa, pushed the work along on this volume by helping to finish a number of details while always respecting and encouraging me; our son, Jeffrey, provided some needed humor and sense of perspective to make sure this book did not atomize family life.

All of my colleagues, past and present, at Boundaries Therapy Center in Acton, Massachusetts, where I have treated children, adolescents, parents, families, and adults for over 25 years, have been invaluable clinical resources and sources of friendship and support. These include Marc Berman, Bonnie Broe, Mady Drucker,

Laura Englander, Helen Frey, Bill Gresser, Peter Musliner, and Ellen Ratner. The support of the administrative staff at Boundaries—Jackie Mayer, Michele Roy-Curtis, Watcha Trim—kept us productive. At The Cambridge Hospital Department of Child Psychiatry, a core group of second year child fellows, Drs. Andrew Bush, Paul Hartman, Paula Martin, and Saiya Remmler, offered encouragement to this work in progress in 1996–1997; followed by Drs. Tina Ferrer, Kirk Lum, Lisa Nelson, and Gale Pasternak in 1997–1998. Judy Nathans created the cover art with Lisa and Jeffrey many years ago and it has retained its flavor of adults and children working together.

Andrew Bush would like to thank all of the teachers and role models who have offered so much along the way: Hugh Leightman and Harry Parad, for their dedication and generosity as codirectors of Wediko Children's Services, Boston, where Andrew worked as a child care worker; Petra Hesse, who provided an introduction to developmental psychology and who fanned the flames of an inquisitive spirit; Ed Mason, for the opportunity he provided to explore the world of documentary filmmaking; Shevert Frazier, for his warmth, infectious enthusiasm, and breadth of interest, which led to Andrew's decision to apply to medical school; Bob Waldinger and Pam Peck, who supported and encouraged Andrew during his early years in residency; Tim Dugan, who stood firm through some periods of doubt; Carter Umbarger, for an introduction to family systems work and his willingness to listen; Neal and Vicky Kass, who reminded Andrew of who he was and what he could be; and, of course, Bob Ziegler, who through his openness to hearing what another thought of his work was able to make this collaboration possible and for the friendship that grew out of the work. Most importantly, Andrew would like to acknowledge the help and support of his wife, Ruth Faas, with whom he has learned what matters most about raising children.

Both authors appreciated the help and suggestions of Bill Ackerly, Isabel Bradburn, John Cusack, Judy Howe, Lynn Holden, Devorah Meshoulam, Mary Reynolds Moussa, Ginger Phakos, Bob Sedgwick, Connie Taguiri, and Patricia Ziegler who read and commented on different parts of the text or offered suggested readings. The discovery and documentation of certain key resources was helped enormously by the work of Jennifer Lee at The Cambridge Hospital Library, Kate Benning, the Somerville Hospital librarian, and the generous sharing of Dr. Jim Beck's "Silver Platter" series on his computer. We are grateful for the time and encouragement of the staff at Brunner/Mazel initially Suzi Tucker, then the help of Laura Haefner and Toby Wahl who shepherded this book through production. We have appreciated the careful editing of Jean Anderson, whose laughter on the phone has made one more change less onerous.

INTRODUCTION

☐ The Foundation of Psychotherapeutic Care: Relationship and Knowledge

Although there is no one formulaic response that can address the complex questions that a clinician must consider in the care of children, adolescents, and families, this text is oriented toward helping the clinician use his or her resources in the most effective manner possible. Ultimately, therapists must exercise their clinical judgment, which has been shaped by training and experience. The text will emphasize that all treatments should be informed by the use of the bedrock of child and family practice: relationship and knowledge. These two elements are the foundation for all good psychotherapeutic work. Relationship to all members of the family will be stressed as a key element of care as well as current knowledge of child, adolescent, parent and family function and disorders.

Relationship is, to this day, one of the most effective psychobiological/neurobiological tools that is available in the therapeutic armamentarium of care. Relationship bathes and protects the central nervous system from the toxic stresses of everyday life, which have their own neurobiological components. Just as parents who are well attuned to the needs of their infant can help settle distress, well trained psychotherapists use attunement to form relationships with child and family, which will facilitate every intervention undertaken. Since all child treatment rests upon the foundation of the strength of family relationships, the therapist must routinely strengthen and enhance the ties between child, parents, and family in all phases of assessment and treatment.

To care for a child patient is to care for all family members involved in caring for the child; the therapist will focus on *Sharing Care*. The therapist will be helping parent and family best respond to the child's needs. The therapist must form an alliance with all members of the family and consider their needs for care as well. In the more severe cases, the care will be shared, not just by the family, but by agencies, state protective services, and schools. Multiple therapists may have to develop a shared plan of care.

In most cases, however, the therapist will be sharing the care with the family. In this era of managing care, the therapist must actively choose—among the competing needs and feelings of the child, parent, and the family as a whole—how to allocate the available resources (number of sessions and time within each session) to best address the problem to develop new family-based solutions. On top of that, the therapist must foster the positive aspects of the relationships within the family for the child to truly continue to heal. From patterns of compliance to the impact of pharmacotherapy, well-attuned relationships with all members of the family will enhance outcome. The therapist must understand, explore, and tolerate his or her own feelings and the complexities of relationships with the children and their families.

When therapists create a context in which family members can truly express and discuss their feelings toward each other, these exchanges lay the groundwork for the process of acceptance among family members as well as between therapist and family. Acceptance is a core psychotherapeutic component in establishing relationship and in developing the treatment alliance. The more the therapist struggles with being able to accept all of the family members, or feels imbalanced on the pathway of the care plan, the more this sense of risk is diagnostic. The relational stability among family members that is the foundation for most therapeutic interventions is not there. The therapist may have to reevaluate his or her expectations for the treatments.

In addition to relational sensitivity, there is a base of knowledge that child and family therapists draw upon. It comes from multiple fields of study. From developmental research and current diagnostic definitions, to an understanding of parental functioning and adult psychopathology, to a sensitivity and orientation to the principles of systems- and family-based practice, each component of a therapist's prior education and training may be utilized at some point in an intervention with children and families. This process can be an overwhelming task for a therapist, particularly in these pressured times. This book is designed to help a therapist continue to develop a comprehensive and integrated model of assessment and care that will lend itself to the further refinements expected by the explosion of knowledge in the various fields that influence child and family therapeutic practice.

The confidence that therapists have in the level of their knowledge interacts with the therapeutic relationship. Since the impact and stabilizing effect of therapeutic work rely upon the introduction of a calming influence (the therapist) into the entire system, therapists must feel settled with the plan of care that they develop. Thus, a therapist's countertransferential uncertainties can undermine the capacity to be a stabilizing and modulating influence in the life of the child and the family. The approach developed here will help therapists feel more secure with the various elements of their assessment and treatment plan. It asks the therapist to address as soon as possible potential complications to care. As the treatment unfolds, the therapist's knowledge of the various components of the problem will evolve along with that of the family.

☐ The Initial Assessment: Setting the Stage for Treatment

The assessment of the child or adolescent, the parents, and the way the family functions as a whole will lead to the development of a treatment plan that can be shared with all of the family members, separately and then together. Each person must understand his or her part in the problem and his or her role in the solution.

The child must know that the problem does not mean "I am bad." The parents must hear how their skills as parents, their emotional resources (with their pluses and minuses), and their connection to the child can help the child master the dilemma embodied in the presenting problem.

The family must be encouraged by the therapist to recognize that they, as a productive team, can work together to feel better. The fundamentally positive connections between parent and child must be strengthened. In the most difficult instances, the therapist must balance the treatment plan on the high wire of the family's declared (and undeclared) tensions, which interfere with the child's and parent's use of their natural abilities to resolve the presenting difficulties. Then the therapist must find out what resources can be used to find solutions.

The assessment of the presenting dilemma should lead to the therapist's understanding of the child, the parents, and the way the family interacts. The resulting diagnostic formulation, when presented to the family, buffered by the therapeutic relationship developed in the initial phase, lays the groundwork for the treatment plan. The relationship with the therapist will help both child and parents bear the pain of looking at, for example, family relationships that need attention or the presence of an anxiety disorder in parent or child, even when this news is not wanted.

Handling this highly charged negotiation depends upon the development of trust between clinician and family. This trust must be built on the therapist's honest feedback about the difficulties that are defined within each segment of the family. The alliance with the child must be developed, while acknowledging the child's "mistakes" or identifying areas of growth that must be addressed. The role of the parental assessment, the focus of chapter 3, should enhance the parental alliance. At the same time, the assessment will define the nature of the work the parent needs to do for the child. When an aspect of parental psychopathology (the parents' "mistakes") is uncovered that bears on this work, the therapeutic relationship should help the parents understand that their own treatment may be necessary. Yet another tension the therapist must balance is that of the alliance with the family as a whole. The family relationships may be complicated by issues posed by marital tensions, the family's style of interaction, or poor communication. Only after each of these assessments is completed can the therapist begin to define with the family the various ways that they can choose to begin to resolve their concerns.

At first, the treatment plan may only address the needs (or diagnoses or both) within one element of the system (child or adolescent, parent, or family). The focus will be on success. The classification of the zone of care, introduced in chapter 2 and expanded in chapter 4, will help the therapist identify where best to begin. When the clinician can classify the nature and level of difficulty in the function of the child, parents, family, or all of these, the family and therapist can more quickly direct his or her energies to the relevant problem area. The child and family's function, taken together, will fall into one of four zones of care.

Zone 1 is the zone of normal developmental progress. Here the parenting skills and constitution of the child are "good enough." Here a range of outpatient short-term, family-based approaches to child or family problems is often quickly successful. These are the children and families whose care has been "carved out" by managed care organizations (MCOs). These are people who have insurance through employment and most often have relationship skills as well as the many ego strengths and positive coping styles needed to work quickly in treatment.

Zone 2 is the zone of child despair. Here the child's family context is that of a severely dysfunctional family or adult impairment leading to parental failure. Here the treatment must direct itself to the search for resources that can support the child's health and resilience. Referrals for treatment of the parents are usually not implemented by them. Family contacts, or reports elicited from the child, may only lead to filing with a state agency for child welfare. A classic individually based therapeutic approach may not be possible in typical outpatient settings. Longer term therapies may be developed for these children in their school placements to help them deal with the intense affects of loss, trauma, and anger. This type of treatment, however, risks heightened loyalty conflicts for the child and, as a result, is often resisted by the child or is not consented to by the parent. In some cases, however, the treatment relationship may remind a child of the hope that there can be adult relationships that can be trusted where nonfamily-based issues can be addressed and solved.

Zone 3 is the zone of parental grief. In this instance, the child is affected by severe developmental, medical, or psychiatric disorder. Treatment of the "good enough" parents should help them mourn the loss of the healthy, normal child and help them search for ways to enhance the adaptive capacities of their child. Child-based therapies will be appropriate, depending upon the diagnosis and nature of the child's developmental compromises, at different stages of the long-term relationship with child and family.

In the classic *zone 2 to 3* switch, i.e., where a child is removed from a dysfunctional home and placed in one in which the parenting skills are "good enough," child treatment is often needed to address the past trauma. In the context of secure supports—with the simultaneous loss of the parent(s)—the child may become extremely symptomatic. The treatment can focus on these issues while helping the child consolidate the newly available relationships. The adoptive parents may need guidance and support in parenting meetings, while the "new family" relationships are supported in a family-based treatment.

Zone 4 is the "most at risk" zone. It consists of those children with seriously compromised function and their families who are most dysfunctional. The parental or familial dysfunction may lead to involvement of other agencies, but the child is not removed. Here the therapist is most at risk of feeling a sense of helplessness and hopelessness. This feeling represents the countertransferential mirror of both the parent, who feels helpless in the face of the child's behavior, and the child who feels hopeless about the help the parent may offer. Treatment must be directed toward mobilizing ancillary systems involvement (schools, child welfare agencies, and other outreach programs).

The model of the zone of care and the diagnostic formulation together will help the therapist prioritize the initial goals of treatment within the fiscal contract. The family must consider how to make these decisions with the therapist about implementing a treatment plan that lies within their financial resources (available insurance, self-pay, or other components). Since mental health benefits are so often limited, the therapist may need to help the family access sources of support that rely on other sources of funding: community activities that exist for children, school supports or agencies that help children access tutors, after-school programs, or summer camps.

Following the assessment, the therapist's skills will help the child and family identify which goals the family might most successfully tackle together with the therapist. This text will suggest how the initial diagnostic "homework" and the first treatment suggestions can be oriented to success and help prioritize the next objectives. The result of this first phase of the therapy should lay the foundation for any longer term goals, which may be reached through more continuous or more intermittent contact. The realities of most mental health plans often mean that the short-term plan may be all the family can afford if they must work within their insurance benefit.

Like much of the current literature and reviews of child and adolescent treatment, *Sharing Care* is oriented to the use of multimodal treatments for a wide variety of child/family difficulties. The ways to intervene with children and families often includes, even in a short-term intervention, a creative combination of individual play and dynamically oriented verbal therapies, parenting education and guidance, family therapy, cognitive–behavioral strategies, and psychopharmacological interventions. The authors will continue to emphasize that these are best contained within a family-based approach.

This treatment model asks the therapist to promote the child and parents' teamwork in problem solving while the therapy enhances the fundamental strengths of their relationship to one another. The therapist's knowledge of a wide variety of interventions can help the family members decide how to invest their energies and resources to support the best possible outcome for themselves. The reader will be referred to many of the key readings in child- and family-based assessments and treatments that complement the approaches defined here.

☐ Planning Short-Term, Intermittent, and Long-Term Therapies for Children and Families

The short-term aspect of the treatment plan should first be oriented toward trying to enhance the family's relationships, increase understanding of the problem to further active mastery (coping), and to ameliorate any presenting symptoms. Any success will lead to a continuing process of growth and development that permits new choices, an expanded emotional, behavioral, and cognitive repertoire, and the child and family's improved sense of relationship and exchange. Unfortunately, for some, the course of treatment may see the evolution of a more complex psychiatric disorder in a child, or more complex parenting problems or family dilemmas may become apparent.

When the child's or the family's development is challenged by forces and difficulties that do not readily yield to treatment, the role of resources, whether insurance or the family's ability to pay, will have a greater impact on what treatment may be possible. The effects of parenting difficulties, the severity of the child's disorder, any underlying psychopathology in the parents, or high levels of family conflict may demand more treatment meetings than are available. For some children, the type of resources that are needed are not those that standard outpatient mental health treatments can provide, such as a structured school program, a midnight basketball program, or parental and community solidarity about standards of drug or alcohol use. For other families, their difficulties may involve the lack of resources, which doesn't allow them to provide basic care for their child. These interventions require community support that is dependent upon the values and votes and dollars of a society.

Working with Families to Manage the Use of their Resources, Insurance, and MCOs

The intervention must take into account the complexities of the presenting problem, the players in the family, *and* the surrounding fiscal conditions (increasingly presented in the form of an MCO). Mental health funding is an enormous issue for American society. The existence of, as well as the treatment for, mental health and substance abuse disorders continues to be debated in political circles. From a clinical perspective, therapists face, with clients, the enormous pain and turmoil that mental and relational difficulties create. For those who work with children this is an even greater source of anguish since children are often at the proverbial bottom of the barrel in terms of resources (in spite of society's rhetoric).

This is amply demonstrated in the field of mental health for children. At the outset of a child and family assessment, the number of meetings needed to complete an initial diagnostic evaluation can be an issue. Even though each system within the family must be considered, clinicians are often given one meeting to complete an assessment. The extra time needed for child and family evaluation must be advocated for so that the treatment plan rests on a thorough understanding of child, parent, and family. Without this thoroughness, the treatment path is harder to find. Since the financial circumstances of most parents are limited, it means that therapists must consider and plan how to guide the family's choices about the use of their resources and how to advocate for themselves.

Treatment plans have always cost money. Therapists must deal with their own income. This income is based on a session and service rate that clinicians have established but that contracting insurers pay. These rates have declined as MCOs have developed contracts with providers even while burdening them with many additional, unreimbursed, administrative demands and treatment constraints. It is important to note that social workers' salaries have rarely been competitive with other master's level incomes. This is also true for Ph.D. psychologists and for the medically based psychotherapeutic providers, the psychiatrists, whose income is among the lowest of all doctors.

As therapists attempt to juggle the demands and costs of the treatment plan, as well as the relationship with the child and the family, the fiscal issues make keeping the therapist (and the working alliance) in balance a challenge. Therapists must be skilled and highly trained. Today's therapists are confronted with the "business" of mental health in even more stringent ways than other medical providers are. As a result, even with the wealthiest clients, therapists need to address fiscal issues. The task of managing money as part of a treatment plan is unavoidable. Even if Congress were to enact managed savings accounts as a way for families to deal with their own health care expenses, this same issue of the cost, as reflected in the number of sessions weighed against the family's perception of the benefit, would return to the family's decision making. The parents would then need to determine what they might spend on any psychotherapeutic intervention for their child (or themselves) from the first moment of care, rather than after some third party assistance.

Therapists have had a long tradition of managing financial choices in the therapy because mental health has been underfunded for so long. As a result, a child and family practice must orient itself to clarify and define the issues and the elements of the therapy *to parents*. There is no other way that a therapist can help parents become active in working with their resources or benefits. This can occur in the most direct possible way in the family-based approach defined here. In this context, the need for further sessions and their cost, or the forms of MCOs, can be used to help discuss the issues of care, the MCO's requirements, and the parents' choices that can be integrated into the clinical work.

As therapists struggle with these considerations, the countertransferential hate (Winnicott, 1958) aroused in some very demanding cases can make walking the tightrope of contemporary practice difficult. On the one hand, the influence and orientation of the MCO will have its weight on the fiscal tightrope openly acknowledged and so is an easy target for this feeling. On the other hand, the countertransferential hate can be directed toward the parent, since parents may elect not to accept treatment for themselves, may not address complicating family factors, and may resist additional expenses or needed care for the child, whether in the form of treatment, sports, or tutoring. They may fail to negotiate honestly with the therapist about money, or, in the final act, to pay off a balance.

This text is not designed to define or address the multiple concerns that exist in the financing of mental health treatments. Clinicians, as well as parents, need to be advocates for children in the national health care debate whose components are being written and rewritten. While much of a patient's pain and shame is not the focus of concern of these companies,[1] the ethical dilemmas therapists face about the privacy of the consulting room, how clients are helped to understand what information must be shared, their resulting decisions, or the way in which therapists have chosen to act, politically or professionally, is the subject of many other articles and volumes. However, fiscal concerns in treatment planning must be handled. As a result, the text will raise these issues throughout the case discussions, even while it is unable to finally solve them. There are times when needed treatment cannot be afforded and the therapist and family must share this pain together while they make "the best possible use of limited resources."

---

[1]Simultaneously, another element of concern for therapists is the continuously opening window allowing greater informational flow to insurers about their patients' lives.

PART

I

GETTING STARTED: AN OVERVIEW

Child[2] treatment is treatment of the family. First, the therapist must establish a respectful relationship with each member of the family and the child and family together. The therapist must be attuned to the child's individual needs while sensitively gauging the collective needs of the family and parents. Second, therapists who work with children and adolescents have to expect that parents also need to be treated as the therapist's patients: they too need to be understood. Empathy must be extended to their feelings as they face a dilemma with their child. The parents' psychological makeup must be assessed so that the therapist understands any contributing historical factors or symptomatic clusters in the parents that can impact on the recovery of child and family, or have contributed to the creation of the problem.

These primary relationships between therapist, parent, child, and family are established during the assessment phase. The therapist uses the initial contact to enhance the essential relational triad of treatment in work with the child, parents, and families (see Figure I.1). It is the connection between parent, child, and family through which the therapist must work. The family is the stage upon which the child readies his or her performance for life and the couple's relationship constructs the set (Lewis, 1998). These interwoven relationships become the platform upon which any future treatment plan must rest.

[2]The text will use the term "child" to represent a condensation of the term "child or adolescent" as a matter of convenience.

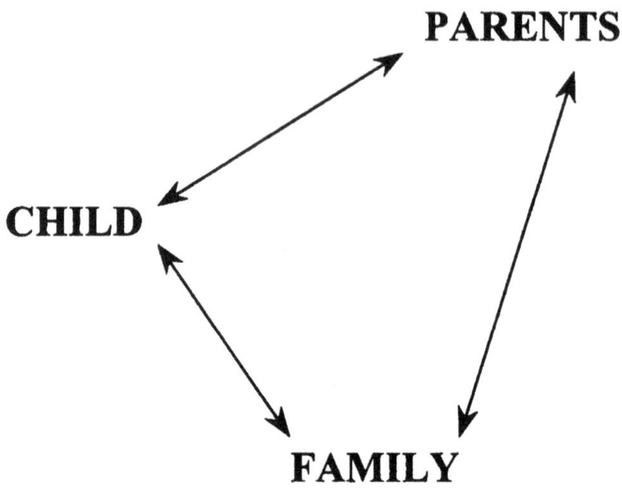

FIGURE I.1.

Any contact between the members of the family and the therapist should function to strengthen this triad of relationships. Each subset of the evaluation must be presented and conducted in a way that furthers the family members' care for one another. The therapeutic alliance is dedicated to reinforcing or strengthening the family members' sense of their positive connections with one another.

Whatever the origins of the dilemma the family faces, the implementation of the solutions should feel like moving toward a family victory. Treatment contributes to the further development of healthy parent–child–family relationships by increasing understanding, empathy, and communication. Where family relationships are strained, treatment may need, as a first step, to reestablish the bonds that have been stretched to breaking by a child or parents' symptomatology, developmental challenges, or environmental stresses. The parents must be able to understand and support the goals of the treatment or, at the very least, not undermine it.

Often, the more resources a family has, as well as its familiarity with the world of "professional advice," the more prepared it is to establish a trusting and active relationship with the therapist promptly, as illustrated in chapter 1. In the more challenging cases, an extended assessment phase may be required to lay a foundation for healing relationships before other work begins. As Dr. Herman says in *Trauma and Recovery*, "The belief in a meaningful world is formed in relation to others and begins in earliest life. Basic trust, acquired in the primary intimate relationship, is the foundation of faith" (p. 54). Even before the family can accept treatment, they must have faith to accept a therapist.

The child and family who have been disrupted by trauma need to find a way through the family's denial or blame in order to enter a treatment alliance. In chapter 2, a disadvantaged family is portrayed who may see the professional world through a lens of being blamed or shamed, and they mirror this process in their interactions with one another and the therapist. They defend themselves against any contact with the therapist. Their present interactions often perpetuate ongoing psychological trauma.

Limited resources and continuing family conflict both diminish a sense of hope and a sense of trust in caretakers or future success. These families often see professionals as adversaries. As illustrated in this case, the establishment of a working alliance involves a process that makes the assessment very time consuming. Contact may not be possible within the constraints of a common office practice. If the family engages in treatment, sensitivity, combined with "plain talk," will be needed from the therapist. Establishing "a safe place," in Dr. Havens' terms, is no easy task (1989). Too frequently, an impasse develops that requires the therapist to actively diffuse the critical or negative stance these families may project.

The therapist must establish a style of communication with the family that promotes trust. The child and family should feel respected in the process of coming to terms with their strengths and weaknesses as they face the problem or search for a solution. The family's efforts to problem solve must be positively framed. The therapist should convey that the only purpose of his or her psychological and developmental knowledge is to enhance the family's success, not to pass judgment. The assessment should confirm to the family that it has taken a healthy step to acknowledge a difficulty and solve it by entering the therapist's office.

Because of the varying levels of dysfunction that may exist within the child or family or both, therapists must have a way to classify the nature of the challenges before them. Chapter 2 will describe four *zones of care.* These zones will prompt therapists to examine both the level of distress and the dysfunction that may be presented by the child or the family or both. The parental assessment (chapter 3) is an essential step in determining the strength or vulnerability that exists within the family. Defining the zone of care will direct the therapist toward the initial therapeutic tactics that may be required as well as what resources that may need to be mobilized from other community systems (chapter 4).

In order to make these classifications, a child and family therapist's perceptions must be informed by a broad knowledge base and understanding. The work requires a background in *DSM-IV* diagnosis, psychodynamics, affect and defense, character structure, and character disorder for parent evaluations. The therapist must use his or her clinical training both to establish a working relationship with each member of the family and to assess the member's function. However, to understand each family member is not to understand the family as a whole.

The therapist must gain skills at working with family systems so the therapist is comfortable sitting together with the entire family and "seeing them in relation to each other" in preparation for charting the therapeutic course. In some cases, a child's symptoms have resulted from stress or conflict among family members or between the parents. The assessment may clarify the pathway through which the child has become symptomatic, so the family members can be asked to focus their efforts on change.

Besides understanding adult and family assessment and treatment, a child and family therapist is required to understand child development. The skill of playing with children is an essential component of communication with them and of being able to understand and translate the child's concerns. The therapist must tell the child that the therapist's "ideas," drawn from the exchanges with the child, will be reviewed with the parents separately or in family meetings, so that the child and family can work better together. The therapist must help the child understand that the alliance is with the entire family. The therapist must have the skill to talk "straight" with children that is respectful yet appreciates the dilemma posed by both their current behavior and their past history (Cotton, 1993; Glasser, 1965). This includes discussing in a forthright way the parents and family's involvement and the therapist's responsibility to use judgment about the disclosure of child or adolescent behaviors that involve risk.

Finally, the assessment phase concludes with the therapist actively considering where and how the family's initial focus of attention for treatment will be directed. As the therapist considers all the possible avenues through which a "child-focused" problem can develop, the assessment should have helped to specify the most germane determinants, whether they represent developmental disorder, psychological conflict, *DSM-IV* disorder, family pathology, a parenting problem, or a cluster of all of these. Whatever the origin (and it is often possible that one can feel some uncertainty here) a treatment direction that balances an element of each of the following triad of goals can be defined.

As proposed here, treatment requires the therapist to pursue a triad of goals (see Figure I.2) that is built upon the platform of the family's relationships. This triad of goals directs the family to understand (implicitly or explicitly) how the treatment will

1. support and further the development of healthy relationships,
2. promote active mastery (coping skills) of the emotional or situational challenges the child and family confronts, and
3. find methods that help to reduce symptoms.

It is no accident that two of the triad of goals defined here are those that Dr. Herman reviews in her discussion of resilience in the face of trauma. "Stress resistant individuals appear to be those with high sociability [relationship], a thoughtful and active coping style [active mastery], and a strong ability to control their destiny" (p. 58). This last factor, described elsewhere in the psychological literature as an "internal locus of con-

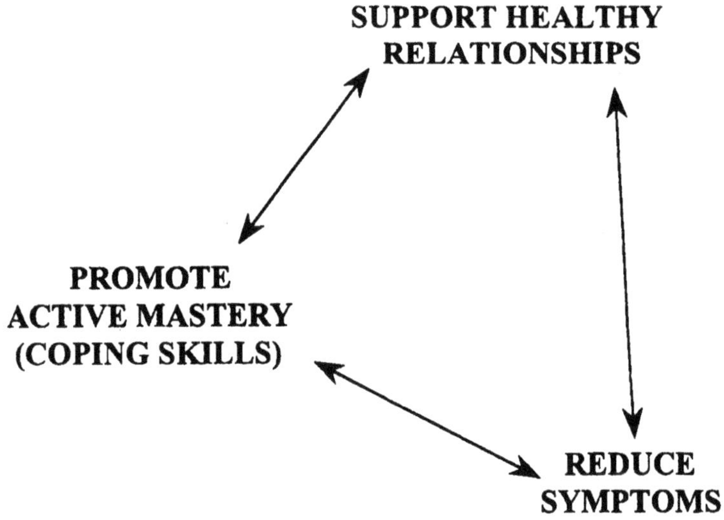

FIGURE I.2.

trol," is included here as the part of the treatment goal called active mastery/coping. Since both relationships and coping are undermined by the presence of active symptoms, the therapist must focus on symptom reduction as the third essential goal.

The therapist's own personality, way of working, and the variety of skills that a therapist will continue to develop will be drawn into this triad of goals in a flexible, everchanging way. The therapist's moves will be determined by the therapist's consideration of which focus may yield the greatest benefit. Several directions may be tested simultaneously. The goals, however, remain the same: to support good relationships, active mastery (coping), and to promote health (symptom reduction). Each move toward one goal can support the efforts to move toward the others.

Supporting Healthy Relationships. While the treatment will rely upon a working alliance between the family and the therapist, the family members' longer term success will depend upon their ability to continue in healthy relationships with one another. Optimally, all treatment efforts should promote healthy contact and problem solving between parent and child and in the family so that this outcome is supported. We will describe parameters the therapist can use to assess the various dimensions of the relationships within the family and between parent and child.

Active Mastery (Enhancing Coping Styles). The contact with the child and family should permit the therapist to understand how the parent and child cope. Broadly defined (Kottmeier-Leandro, 1995), the two major ways of coping are (1) by managing feelings and (2) by taking action. Women more often use coping techniques that manage feelings, whereas men are more likely to take action. Each coping style is more likely to work in different situations. Managing feelings is essential when no action-based solution is available, for instance, following the loss of a loved one or in increasing intimacy in relationships. Action-based coping techniques work better when there is the possibility to influence the outcome of a problem through "doing something." Being able to utilize both coping styles appropriately is optimal. Understanding the child and family's coping style can guide how the therapist promotes mastery of feelings and the active implementation of solutions.

Symptom Reduction. The reason symptom reduction is placed on an equal level with mastery and relationship is that many of the problems that therapists treat involve the presence of symptoms that can actively interfere with coping (e.g., depression) or relationship (e.g., irritability) or mastery (e.g., anxiety). Continuing assessment must identify and minimize any active symptom profile in the course of the therapy.

Assessing the degree to which coping styles are compromised, relationships are dysfunctional, or symptom levels are high, will, in turn, contribute to the therapist's assessment of the nature of the zone of the problem. Each aspect of the assessment helps the therapist gauge which factors may bear more weight in the definition of the zone of care. Establishing a zone of care can provide an initial direction for treatment as based in the broad outlines suggested in chapters 4, 5, and 6.

Note that most clinicians feel their clinical formulation guides their treatment planning. But, as Smith and Beck (1998) ask, "What do we make of the fact that clinicians with markedly different views all believe they make 'good' case formulations that will work for the clients they serve?'[3] We propose that however a clinician formulates a case, the successful treatment has, in some way, combined elements of restoring relationships, creating active mastery, and reducing symptoms.

Whatever the origin of the problem before the therapist, its persistence is often traumatizing for the child and family. An element of demoralization has set in. Part of the early "placebo" effect in treatment occurs when families again attempt active mastery by engaging with professional help. The therapist should attempt to heighten the child and family's optimism in the initial contact. The therapist can assess the level of the family's readiness to take action by the assignment of homework tasks. Further light will be shed on the ways that both parents and child begin to cope by reviewing their efforts to complete the homework task.

The family's faith in therapy as a way to find solutions will depend upon the therapist's ability to respect all members of the family and to establish hope for a positive outcome. It is important that the family be able to sort out that the therapist's work will not mean agreeing with each of the members all the time. While scorecards are often kept, when the therapist is dedicated to solutions that ultimately make everyone in the family feel better, the family will accept the therapist's shifting perspectives.

Even if *everyone* (parents, child, and other family members) must work a little harder to handle a problem, the therapist sets the stage for the family's success. It is not the particular details of each "therapeutic move" that will determine the outcome of each case. Rather, it is the therapist's respectful and persistent search for the strengths and special connections between the child and family that is what the family will hold in their minds in the long run. This value is what the family will use to find whatever victory there may be for them.

---

[3]According to Smith and Beck, "Most clinicians believe it is important to have a good case formulation to guide therapy. While comforting to believe, it is a proposition difficult to defend. What makes a case formulation good (truth, beauty, utility)? What do we make of the fact that clinicians with markedly different views all believe they make 'good' case formulations that work for the patient. Tension between the fragility of our clinical knowledge and importance (or use?) of formulation in directing treatment" must be acknowledged.

1

CHAPTER

The Initial Contact: Introductory Concepts

☐ Getting started: "The Perfect Case: Jessica"

The Initial Phone Contact: Setting the Stage

Mrs. Gardner has called and left a message asking if the therapist can call her to discuss some concerns she has about Jessica, her 9-year-old daughter. The therapist returns the call.

The therapist welcomes Mrs. Gardner. The therapist asks how she got the therapist's name and how she thought the therapist might be of help.

What the Therapist Is Attempting to Accomplish

1. Therapists should establish a sense of their referral sources for two reasons. The first is that it will help identify how the therapist is known in the community. A key part of building a practice includes the development of relationships with referral sources (whether the family ultimately gets to see the therapist or not). The second is that one comes to know the expectations and needs of different professionals in the community who refer.
2. A therapist offers a professional service. It has two key components: (1) a body of knowledge on child and family development that can be accessed to establish a working assessment of the problem and the skills used to treat the problem and (2) the relationship skills that permit a therapist to establish a "working alliance," i.e., one in which the therapist develops a partnership in which the parents' involvement will be key to the outcomes.

   Throughout the course of the diagnostic phase (described in Part I) and the treatment phase (Part II), the therapist will be constantly interweaving these two skills in the interaction with the child and family.

Mrs. Gardner says that Jessica has begun to pull tufts of stuffing out of her mattress at night, cannot get to sleep, and is complaining about all the other children in her class not liking her, in spite of her having several best friends.

Mrs. Gardner describes her family briefly. She is a computer programmer and her husband is a teacher. They have recently adopted a baby from China and her mother ("Nana") has moved into their home to help with the transition. She describes how Jessica was involved with all of the planning and was quite eager to have a new baby in the family.

The therapist's reactions:

- A treatable problem has been identified in a cogent way; the parent appears sensitive and attuned to the child.
- The therapist wonders about the parent's description of having Jessica "involved in the planning" and whether that represented a burden for the child or was done in a developmentally appropriate way. This question is noted for consideration within the context of the diagnostic phase since the therapist's pocketbook will not be well served by spending a large amount of time on the phone.

Even though the therapist is hearing a key description of the concern, the therapist must still reserve judgment about whether the "problem" is "*the* problem" or whether in the context of both family system evaluation and child diagnostic review the focus of treatment may be different.

At this point, the therapist cannot draw a conclusion; however, it is time to affirm what the therapeutic transaction includes:

(1) *Therapists offer knowledge.*
- The therapist can validate mother's concerns as reasonable and suggest that an assessment is indicated.
- Part of the assessment, the therapist explains, is to require that the parents fill out a variety of forms and checklists to make sure the therapist has the full range of information that will help her consider various issues in the assessment. The therapist can ask if they would like these to be mailed or if they would like to come to the therapist's office a bit early to do this work in the waiting room.

(2) *Therapists offer care in the context of the therapeutic relationship.*
- The therapist explains to the parent that she appreciates the parent has taken action on her daughter's behalf and that it sounds as if it is genuinely difficult for Jessica, as well as the whole family, at this time of change.
- The therapist lets the mother know that she can explain to Jessica that she will be coming to see a "helper" who knows about kids and about the many different ways to help them and their families when kids feel worried or unhappy. The mother should be told to let Jessica know that the therapist will meet with the family, with Jessica alone, with her parents alone, and then give them some ideas about making things better.

The third point in an intake call has to do with business.

(3) *Therapists offer a service within a contractual relationship.* Since this is a professional relationship, the therapist must introduce and explain fees and that the therapist works with many different insurers. Since there are so many different insurance programs (and mental health benefits are often more complex than medical ben-

efits), the therapist should explain that the parents should gather information about their mental health benefit, any authorizations needed, or other steps they may need to take. The therapist should explain to the mother that she and her husband can best access this information from their plan, since benefits vary widely depending upon their employer and the nature of the contract they may have. The therapist will also explain that the last few minutes of the initial meeting will be saved in order to allow the parents to report what they have discovered about their insurance coverage and how to create a plan together that takes into account their insurance benefit and their own resources.

Mrs. Gardner thanks the therapist for the information. She says she will speak with her husband about their benefit and will get the paperwork in order before they visit so that any insurance information or authorizations are obtained. She agrees to an initial visit in which all three of them, she, her husband, and Jessica, will attend. She reports that she feels relieved about what to tell their child.

By the end of this conversation, the therapist has set the stage for the parents becoming active partners in the assessment by asking them to participate in joining the initial visit with their daughter and then by filling out a variety of checklists and history forms. The therapist has also set the stage for the parents to recognize that, in some fashion, the therapist will be working together with their insurer and discussing resources for treatment.

The therapist has already established that the structure of the first appointment of the assessment process will have three parts. There will be an introductory family-based meeting, a child meeting, and a brief parent contact to get insurance information and plan the rest of the assessment. Depending upon the nature of the strengths of the family and child, these three components may be accomplished in a single meeting or may require other separate meetings. In a single meeting, approximately one third of the time will be devoted to the family-based meeting; one half of the time will be spent with the child; and one sixth of the time will be spent in a brief review with the parents. The therapist will set the stage for the parent evaluation session (chapter 3) and the family-based treatment planning meeting (chapter 4) to follow.

As a result of the therapist's phone call with the Gardeners, the first impression suggests that it may be possible to complete these three elements in the first meeting. The parent has been able to describe the concern cogently, clearly appears to have a positive relationship with the child, and enters willingly into a diagnostic process with the therapist. The parent also appears to be willing and able to assume responsibility for the fiscal contract in the professional relationship. In the less than perfect case described in the second chapter, we will be looking at the elements that might prompt the therapist to think otherwise.

The First Appointment: The Family Component

When a child is asked to see the principal or when parents are invited to a parent–teacher conference, there is often a worry about judgment, disapproval, or both. The initial family contact with the therapist needs to dispel these notions. For the child it is designed to establish that the parents have a concern about him or her. In the course of the consultation the child's behavior or some feelings may be reviewed, but the therapist will want to help the child see that the parents care and want to help the child feel better and do his or her best. There is an openness to the communication that the therapist can encourage. In most "good enough"[4] functioning families, the child is already aware of this. Most parents will attempt to describe or resolve those troublesome moments of distress in their children's lives in some way, and it is unusual when these efforts have not preceded the therapist's meeting with the family. The therapeutic contact exists along the continuum of the family's access to their own problem solving, and the parents can be reminded of the value of their efforts in the course of the initial description of the presenting problem.

The three main objectives in the initial phase of the focused family-based meeting, which takes place before seeing the child alone, are the following:

(1) To define the presenting problem(s) in a neutral and caring way that blames neither the child nor the parents. This will be the focus of the therapist's overt interactions with the child and family. Most families enter therapeutic consultation with a point of view about the presenting problem. This needs to be respectfully reviewed.
(2) In addition, the therapist must also rule out or define the symptom complexes that may be present and affect the child's function. Without attending to this potentially complicating factor, the parents will not have the full benefit of a diagnostic consultation with a developmental expert. (See Tables 1.1, 1.2, and 1.3.)
(3) Another, although more covert, objective is to establish an initial assessment of the nature of the relationships within the family by observing the nature of how the child and parents relate to each other as they describe the presenting problem. The therapist will see how they discuss the symptoms they are concerned about and how they interact with each other and with the therapist.

> Mr. and Mrs. Gardner come to the therapist's office at the designated time with Jessica. They have in hand a sheaf of papers. The therapist welcomes them and receives the checklists and insurance forms. The therapist explains to Jessica that one set of papers is about things her mother and father have noticed and the others are "business papers" that the therapist will discuss with her mother and father later.
>
> The therapist tells Jessica that she spoke to her mother about a week ago. The therapist asks Jessica if she knows why her parents have brought her to the office.

This question is asked in order to define:

(a) Whether Jessica recognizes what the problem is at her developmental level.
(b) Jessica's response will offer a clue about the level and nature of the parent and child communication.
(c) The therapist will observe how the child manages a "novel situation" and what her emotional and coping resources are.

Note: The therapist has also just told Jessica that she "knows her Mom" and that gives the child permission to begin to talk.

> Jessica begins to cry. Her mother waits a minute and then gives her a tissue. Her father says, "It's okay. Remember we told the therapist that we wanted to see somebody who helps kids and families. It's all right to talk to her."

---

[4]See D. W. Winnicott's (1965) article on "good enough" parenting for an important discussion of the parental contribution to child development.

TABLE 1.1. Medical screening form, past mental health history, and consent to communicate with primary care physician or pediatrician

1. List any current illnesses, allergies, or health problems.

2. Prior history of head trauma, neurological problems, or seizures.

3. Pregnancy, Delivery. Problems? Birthweight:

4. Developmental Problems
   Infancy (colic, problems with sleep, feeding, attachment):

   Milestones (identify late development or milestones of concern):

   Early problems with toileting/toilet training:

   Early fears, separation problems, nightmares:

5. History of exposure to traumatic events:
   Physical abuse, or sexual abuse, or both traumatic experiences:

6. Does your child have any current physical symptoms (e.g., complaints of stomachaches, poor sleep, ear pain)?

7. Is your child having any learning/adjustment difficulties at school?

8. Has your child had prior counseling or psychiatric treatment? With whom?

Hospitalizations for psychiatric reasons?
Where and when?

Psychiatric or behavioral medications?
Prescribed by?
During what period of time?

The mother agrees and asks if Jessica wants to know what the mother told the therapist.

Jessica nods.

Already the therapist has begun to discover these family interactions:

- The family appears to be supportive and emotionally responsive.
- They speak at the child's level and offer to help her.
- They indicate that they have had prior discussions with the child and, in the therapist's presence, reaffirm the plan for open communication and honesty in the relationship to the therapist.

Jessica's mother repeats what she told the therapist on the phone. The father moves Jessica over to his lap. Jessica nods, stops crying, and looks a little brighter. Jessica begins to describe her poor sleep and that she has bad dreams and doesn't want to go to sleep. She feels so "twisty" inside that she twists the stuffing out of the mattress from a little hole in it that happened when she moved to her own room a few years back. She says

TABLE 1.2.
Selected questions in checklists used to identify the presence of attentional disorders and hyperactivity for parents

- Denies mistakes or blames others
- Restless in the "squirmy" sense
- Restless, always "up and on the go"
- Difficulty learning
- Excitable, impulsive
- Childish or immature (wants help he shouldn't need, clings, needs constant reassurance)
- Distractibility or attention span a problem
- Mood changes quickly and drastically
- Easily frustrated in efforts
- Fails to finish things

Selected questions in checklists used to identify the presence of attentional disorders and hyperactivity for teachers

- Distractability or attention span a problem
- Restless in the "squirmy" sense
- Disturbs other children
- Demands must be met immediately
- Excitable, impulsive
- Easily frustrated in efforts
- Difficulty learning
- Childish and immature
- Fails to finish things that are started
- Restless, always "up and on the go"

nobody at school likes her anymore and when her parents ask why, Jessica says, "They don't make me feel good anymore."

The family talks on their own a bit about different aspects of these problems and the different ideas they had shared as a family to help Jessica.

The therapist now begins to actively explore the history and the prior attempts at resolution of the problem that has been defined. A brief history of the presenting problem is elicited, as well as the success and failure of various attempts at problem solving. The therapist defines how Jessica functioned before these changes and when these difficulties began. The therapist asks more about the child's relationships and recent family changes. What is Jessica's grandmother like? How has it been with *two* new people in the family? Finally, the therapist also asks what things Jessica feels proud of and what she likes about her family.

What the Therapist has Discovered in the Initial Family Contact. At this point the therapist has a sense of the presenting problem, its duration, any associated stresses that preceded it (if any), and has asked, indirectly, about the impact of the baby's and the grandmother's arrival.

The therapist has seen the family's exchanges, had a glimpse of the way they interact with the therapist and problem solve and has seen to what degree emotions are

TABLE 1.3. Selected questions in checklists used to identify the presence of other symptom clusters in various checklists

1. Oppositionality

Disobedient or obedient, but resentfully
Doesn't like or doesn't follow rules or restrictions
Wants to run things

2. Anxiety

Fearful (of new situations, new people or places, going to school)
Worries more than others (about being alone, illness, or death)
Somatic complaints } depressive concerns as well
Feelings easily hurt }

3. Depression

Basically an unhappy child
Pouts and sulks
Somatic complaints/sleep distrubances

4. Irritability (depressive equivalent) or Aggression or Both

Fights constantly
Destructive
Bullies others

5. Social–Emotional Peer Problems

Lets self be pushed around
Disturbs other children
Doesn't get along well with brothers or sisters
Problems with making or keeping friends
Cruel

6. Conduct Disordered Behavior

Lies
Steals

defined and accepted within the family. The therapist has a sense of the parents working together and being motivated to help their child cope with a problem.

In the last family-based question, the therapist has turned Jessica and her parents' attention to some positive experiences. The therapist hopes that Jessica has things she is proud of and hopes the parents will be positive about Jessica, too. A report about positive things in the family also helps to shift the emotional tone a bit away from the problem.

This sets the stage for the next small challenge in the developmental interview: asking the child to meet with the therapist alone and noting how the parents and child separate.

Jessica separates easily from her parents. They give her a kiss and remind her that she can tell "the doctor" anything she wants.

The Child Interview

The child interview is designed to complement the family interview. It gives the therapist an opportunity to assess how the child will discuss the problem, monitor the child's associated feelings, and probe the child's experiences in the family in the absence of her parents (e.g., with whom is it easiest to talk in the family, what does Mom or Dad do if the child makes a mistake). In addition, the therapist may have time to ask relevant mental status questions and explore school function. The therapist may use some basic child assessment tools, such as the Draw a Person test (Harris, 1988; DiLeo, 1973) or the Kinetic Family Drawing (Sattler, 1988), asking her to tell stories about feelings pictured on a feelings chart, administering parts of the Children's Thematic Apperception test (the child's TAT; Murray, 1943), or using selected cards from the Themes of Emotional Development (TED) (see Harris, 1988).

The therapist is going to attempt to establish through the course of this first interview

(1) a sense of the child's developmental level and any unevenness or potential difficulties in learning functions;
(2) a picture of the child's inner world of emotions, the range of people in the child's life and the child's feelings about them; and
(3) an elementary view of the child's coping skills and emotional defenses (his or her ego skills).

If the therapist is concerned about issues of risk assessment, it is important to let the child know that therapists *must* always tell someone when there is something dangerous going on.

The therapist tells Jessica her job is to be very curious about Jessica's problems and feelings, as well as having a time to play together. The therapist explains that she will talk with Jessica's parents about what the therapist's ideas are about Jessica's feelings and how to be of help. The therapist promises to tell Jessica her ideas.

Jessica moves to the dollhouse and begins to play with the play family. The play involves a mother and daughter spending time baking cookies while the baby is in a distant part of the house. After a period of time, the therapist asks Jessica to draw a picture of her family doing something together. Jessica includes the new baby in the picture but leaves out her grandmother. Then, when the therapist tells her they just have a few minutes left, she asks Jessica to tell her stories about two pictures. The therapist picks two pictures from the Themes of Emotional Development (TED) test (Sattler, 1988; Cohen & Weil, 1971), one that has a theme about a new baby and the other with a mother and daughter together. After listening to the stories, the therapist tells her she has to talk with her parents about seeing the child again to think about how to help her feel better and to talk about the "business papers."

The therapist's initial sense of the child's play will lead to a more directed assessment component in the diagnostic exchange with Jessica. The therapist uses dialogue, free play, and directed tasks (such as the Draw a Person test, a reading level card, or selected cards from psychological tests) to establish an initial formulation of the child's dilemma within her family, which can be placed in the context of a preliminary assessment of the child's developmental history. This formulation of the problem will guide aspects of the directed portions of the parenting interview. (See chapter 3.) The parent meeting will be scheduled for another appointment after the therapist and the parents have a brief meeting on "fiscal informed consent."

The Parent Meeting Component and Fiscal Collaboration

Part 1: Homework. The therapist, at this point, may have a good sense of the presenting problem and even have some hypotheses about what has contributed to it and some thoughts about changes that may help the family to help the child. The more experienced the clinician, the more readily will initial suggestions come to mind. For many problems, however, a simple way to illuminate the presenting problem further is to suggest "detective work" as part of *a homework prescription in the context of the initial formulation.* In Jessica's case, the therapist is concerned that the relational disruption of the new baby and the entry of her Nana into the family scene have been more than Jessica can bear. Jessica's anger seems to be directed toward her parents for bringing about these changes. For a child, especially with parents "so perfect," the therapist suspects that Jessica's anger is harder for the child to convey to her parents. As a result, it has been displaced into her view that her friends don't make her feel good, when, in fact, her family does not feel good at this time.

The therapist invites the parents to return to the consulting room and asks Jessica to wait outside. The therapist will remind the parents that they were right to come and they can be congratulated on their empathy and concern for Jessica. The therapist validates that Jessica is indeed stressed. The therapist tells the family that while Jessica appears to be happy about the new baby and the family changes, these changes are taking a toll. The parents can be told that the therapist will review the checklists and developmental forms before their next meeting. In the meantime, the therapist would like the parents to do the following homework task. To test the formulation, mother can be asked to set aside some time to count with Jessica the fun times she has with friends and to list the times that her friends have made her mad. The therapist reminds them that at the next meeting with the parents alone, she can give them a little more feedback and see how this relates to the family's impressions. She will also be using their time to review other family history, ask more specific questions about themselves, and then prepare for what they can do together to help Jessica.

The therapist also faces a *diagnostic task.* Does the child have any active symptoms? If so, do these meet criteria for any of the current descriptions of childhood psychiatric disorder, or is this an interactional problem or adjustment reaction? The therapist will be helped in this effort by reviewing the various instruments (checklists, medical and developmental forms, diagnostic child instruments) that the therapist has given the parents to fill out. (The use of checklists and brief homework assignments will also be discussed later in this chapter.)

The symptoms drawn from the checklists will be used to help consider any of the common presentations of childhood psychiatric disorder and the medical and developmental history that will contribute to the therapist's active questioning in the parent interview and assessment, which will take place in the next appointment. These checklists and information will help to define any *DSM-IV diagnosis* and highlight the need for other medical evaluations.

By defining the child's style, it will help the therapist understand the degree of the *match or mismatch between the parent and child*[5] as well as the particular stresses that the parents may experience in adapting themselves to help their child cope. For instance, the obsessive parent may have less tolerance for the hyperactive child, or a traumatized parent may find it hard to bear their child's anxieties. These issues will be actively explored in chapter 3. An active consideration of any concomitant psychopathology in the parent(s) on dysfunction in the family system and their impact on the child will be an important aspect of the separate parental assessment.

Part 2: The Fiscal Collaboration. In the foreseeable future, how a therapist's services are billed and paid for will continue to require an ongoing discussion between the therapist and the family in any therapist's practice. It is best to begin this discussion in the initial phone contact (see above) and then to continue it in the brief initial parent meeting following the child's contact with the therapist.

In order to move on to the fiscal discussion, the therapist needs to set a boundary around the use of the remaining time. After giving some brief feedback as noted above, the parents can be asked about what they have discovered about how their insurance or benefit works. The therapist may be able to supplement this information if the therapist has had other experiences with this benefit.

Use this as an opportunity to explain the therapist's practices and policies concerning no shows, telephone time, and other charges, like school meetings, which tend not to be covered by insurance. Much of this information is often best conveyed in a handout that the therapist can develop that also explains confidentiality issues. Explain to the parents that the therapist will be sharing clinical information with them and will guide them in the process of making decisions together about how to most effectively use their benefits to help them help their child. The therapist should prepare them for the fact that some choices may involve spending their own money, given the limits of certain coverages.

> The Gardners thank the therapist for meeting with Jessica. They explain that they do not have a lot of financial resources for other meetings, but they can handle their copayments. They have already decided they want to pay out of pocket for a school meeting, because that will help the therapist know Jessica better and help her teacher, too. They say they will tell Jessica how much the therapist liked her. They will explain to her about the "homework" job the therapist has given them.

As described above, the initial meeting has many different components. These will be discussed in more detail before moving on to consider the complex challenges that other families can offer. These will be illustrated in chapter 2, "the less than perfect case," where a complex mix of familial, parental, and child psychopathology is encountered.

Overview of the First Meeting

In the case described above, which will be discussed in greater detail in the subsections to follow, the technical aspects of the first meeting have included:

---

[5]This important concept was articulated in the groundbreaking work on child temperament in the work of Thomas and Chess (1977).

(1) An initial family contact: This has been used to provide an overview of key elements within the child–parent relationship. It should permit an initial appraisal of these key family ingredients:
- the degree of empathic attachment between parent and child,
- the level of the communication skills between parent and child,
- the nature of the developmental awareness in the parents.

Simultaneously, the therapist will be establishing his or her own foundation for a therapeutic relationship with child and parents.

(2) Checklists: To help the therapist begin to develop both a diagnostic and descriptive database, the use of parent and school behavioral (or symptom) checklists (see Tables 1.2 and 1.3) is recommended. Medical history and past treatment can also be initially surveyed with a form (see Table 1.1). The therapist can choose to either mail these to the family prior to the meeting or ask the parents to complete them when they are in the waiting room while the therapist is seeing the child alone. In those families where the parents resources are more depleted and their organizational skills compromised, all of the paperwork may need to be done in the office, and the therapist may need to be more actively involved in collecting information.

(3) A brief assessment of the inner world of the child: Basic child training should include mastering the skill of conducting a verbal- or play-based interview. There are also many tools for child assessment that a therapist may wish to have available.

(4) Homework: The therapist has set the stage for furthering the collaboration with the parents by underlining the importance of their role in the care of the child and by making some simple suggestion or defining an information gathering task or homework.

(5) Insurance: The stage has also been set for the active role the parents must take in paying for the treatment. They must deal with their insurance company or manage facets of how their insurer's MCO works. They must consider how their own resources will be involved to some greater or lesser degree depending upon their benefits and related fiscal issues.

When all of these elements are completed in the first meeting, as with the Gardeners, the treatment is off to a good start. An initial impression of child, parents, and family has been formed and the contractual professional relationship with the therapist has been established. In those instances in which the presenting problem is easily understood, the strengths of the child and parents and their relationship are readily perceived and validated, and the symptoms are clear, an experienced clinician who has consolidated the broad range of skills described above can often complete an assessment in one extended meeting.

Most cases require a standard three meeting evaluation. The more frayed the family relationships, or when there is a history of complex medical and developmental issues, concerns about parenting skills or parental psychopathology, issues of child comorbid conditions or a child's poor prior psychosocial adaptation or both, at least these three full meetings (family based, parent evaluation, child evaluation) are needed. Often school-based or system-based meetings (i.e., involving other professionals or other services involved with the family) are also required.

In some cases, the traditional three play-based visits with the child may be necessary in the context of an extended evaluation in order to gain a sense of the child's emotional concerns. Since children in difficult family situations—or those who have suffered abuse or trauma—do not reveal themselves readily, more time is needed. Even in these cases, the therapist must find a way to manage a family-based meeting since the therapist must help the child understand how the child's issues and needs will be discussed with the family.

While many MCOs still grant only one evaluation meeting, most are receptive to the need for a larger investment of time in child and family cases. If not, these issues and choices must still be reviewed with the family in terms of costs they can bear, what the process of advocacy may be, as well as the availability of other free care or community supported services.

The Initial Family Contact

If the therapist begins the work *within* the family system, then the therapeutic angle of perception is set to include the largest set of variables. Then, when the parent meeting follows, not only is a developmental history and fuller family history obtainable, but it is one that already is keyed to the significant issues. The therapist's concerns will have been flagged by having seen the parents in action where they have revealed both their emotional style and emotional connectedness and awareness of their child's inner life. The level of communication within the family and the developmental knowledge of the parents that is expressed by that interaction with the child is also gleaned in the initial family contact. In addition, a sense of the child's temperament, his or her ability to communicate and label feelings, as well as the strength of the child's bond to the parent, has begun to develop in the therapist's mind.

This section will elaborate a therapeutic perspective that helps the therapist gather a full range of data while reinforcing the positive relationship between parent and child. The basic tenet of *Sharing Care* is that the therapeutic challenge—often felt most acutely in the diagnostic phase of therapy—requires the development of an alliance with all parts of the family system. The therapist must balance one's affect, interpretations, questions, and remarks in an initial family contact so that each family member feels understood and respected. This interview should set the stage for the child and family to begin to have a sense that therapeutic contact can help.

Why an Initial Family Meeting?

The family meeting should permit the therapist to accomplish the following:

(a) It fosters a comprehensive alliance with the therapist. Child work cannot succeed without an alliance that walks the tightrope of building a relationship with child, parents, and the family system.
(b) It can be used to highlight the positive working relationship between parent and child.

In more challenging cases:

(c) The initial meeting is also oriented to detoxify any exchanges between parent and child that have become regressive and hopeless. The anger and discouragement that may exist can be diminished by the therapist's actions during the first contact.

(d) At the same time, the family meeting may highlight the risk factors associated with pathological relationships and the potential presence of child neglect or abuse within the family. Often, the less responsive the family is to the therapist's interventions, the more concerned the therapist may be with the implications of the parent's behavior. These interactions and these data are what may lead to filing reports with state agencies.

The purpose of beginning the evaluation in the family context has a subliminal purpose as well. This meeting alerts the parents to the fact that their involvement is a key part of the care plan. The parents must be ready to communicate honestly and in an emotionally supportive way. As mentioned in the introduction, the relationships among family–child–parent constitute the platform upon which a treatment intervention is based. If the parents have trouble within the relationship with their child, the stage is set for addressing this (or other) parenting-based issues in the parent meeting. The therapist will be better prepared to do an adult assessment in the parent meeting since the need for certain skills with the child will be clear as well as the particular vulnerabilities between parent and child that have been noted.

If the initial contact is made only with the parents alone, the treatment approach fosters the sense that the problem is "in the child." While this may be the case, often difficulties in children reflect problems in their relationships with their parents, or their parents' lack of emotional understanding or good parenting skills, or all of these. Even if the problem is a biologically based disorder "in the child," the child's management or recovery from the problem will depend not only on whatever resilience the child has, but also on the parent–child relationship. The parent must provide the support, guidance, and problem solving that the child will need reinforced over time in order to cope with any difficult life situation or a present, or evolving, psychiatric disorder.

With some adolescents, the therapist may choose to have a brief introduction with the adolescent first and then have a family meeting; the value of the contact with the whole family will still set the stage for the later work. This might be especially true in situations in which the parent has already communicated to the therapist that the adolescent is reluctant to enter into therapy. The therapist may find that the adolescent may be better engaged in the process of taking responsibility for his or her role in the treatment if he or she is introduced to the therapist first. Many supervisors suggest that all adolescents should be seen individually initially; however, there are many adolescents who are most easily engaged in the context of their struggle with their parents, rather than in the parents' absence. In some reviews, outcomes of adolescent therapy appear to be better in family-based (Mann & Borduin, 1991), group (Fine & Forth, 1991), or cognitive–behavioral therapy than in individual treatment (Brent, Holder, & Kolko, 1997).

Getting Started with the Family

Two basic principles about the therapist's approach during this initial contact are to:

(1) carefully explore the nature of the difficulty that is being presented from the point of view of the child, and
(2) gear language to operate at the simplest level. If something can be explained to a

> preschooler without condescension, the level and complexity of language and thought can be increased for anyone older. In some of the most difficult families, the emotional age and awareness of the family may be at a preschool level, too. If so, a side benefit of this approach is that everyone will be able to understand the therapist.

In order to begin an assessment, the first statement can be addressed to the identified patient, "how come Mom and Dad decided to have you (the child) come to the office to meet me?"

This phrase establishes that the therapist is a person who is oriented to children and adolescents. The child's experience, feelings, and knowledge are valued. In addition, the therapist is making a tacit acknowledgment that mother and father are key players in the room. They have arranged this meeting and the therapist is suggesting, indirectly, that part of their parental responsibility is to take part in reasonable and respectful communication with the child. The background assumptions within this simple question are quite important. They establish a tone and a guideline that will be enacted in a variety of ways by the therapist during the family's contact.

In this first exchange about the problem, the basic tenets of a therapeutic approach to communication are being modeled for child and family. The therapist should wait attentively for answers to questions. An atmosphere of respect should be verbally and nonverbally extended to all family members in the office. When the therapist wants to guide the interaction, a sense of empathy should guide the manner and attitude conveyed.

A therapeutic conversation should develop out of the child voicing the problem. When the child does not respond, the therapist moves quickly to create a dialogue within the family. The first prompts by the therapist should serve as a model for the family. For instance, if the child does not respond to the question, the child can be asked to ask the parent about what the problem is, or the therapist can give a gentle version of it. When the therapist explains to the child that there has been information drawn from a phone contact with the parent, it is done in a way to preserve the self-esteem of the child and is considerate of the parent's perspective. Many parents will tend to highlight the problem without helping the child to see the visit as part of the way the parents are trying to care for the child. The therapist draws the family into an exchange in which the parents' concerns are identified as a response to a worry that occurs as part of their caring relationship. The visit is defined as a way that the parent expresses care and provides help to the child. The positive comments of the parents are underlined, as well as any indications of the child's closeness to the parents or phrases or behaviors that suggest the child welcomes the help from the parent. The empathy between the relationship of parent and child, and among family members, is underscored repeatedly. In most normal families in which love can be comfortably acknowledged, the therapist's emphasis on the positive relationship will enhance the readiness for the family to work together positively on the presenting problem.

If in the course of exploring the problem, the parent jumps in with a comment or a negative comment to get the child to respond to the therapist's question, the therapist must model both patience and respect by suggesting that the parent "wait, while Johnny thinks about what you told him because some kids are often nervous or shy." Alternately, the therapist can tell the parent and child that one of the rules of the office is that people can share difficult times and difficult feelings here, even when it takes a little bit of time. This also serves as a reminder that the therapist has rules and will assume a gentle authority in the meetings. After some moments, if the child still seems unable to describe the problem that has brought the family in, the therapist may ask the parents, in a respectful way, to tell the child what they are worried about or ask the child to ask the parents.

In prompting the initial basic exchange, the therapist should make some effort to use the kindest and gentlest hypotheses, ones that can normalize the stress in the context and offer parents some information about communicating with kids. The process of regard, respect, acceptance, and enhancing relationships is underscored in all interactions. Therapists must have ways to manage and confront difficult interactions, not retaliate. These must maintain empathy with everyone in the room. If the conduct of the interview is consistently empathic, it is rare that the message is missed by the family: "The rule in this office is to look for ideas and underline exchanges that facilitate emotional communication and understanding. No one is going to be stuck with the label 'bad.' " The therapist is going to be empathically open to the experience of each member of the family.

In therapy, there is no substitute for the essential component of being listened to and understood. This impact is magnified when all family members have the same experience in spite of their multiple and differing points of view and personal histories. To be able to establish a respectful connection with each family member requires that the therapist have an inner certainty that the quality of the relationship between everyone in the room and the child is truly relevant to the child's best possible outcome.

The training that therapists have in understanding nonverbal expression and relational exchanges is immediately called into play. Understanding the relationships among the family members requires observing the emotional and nonverbal cues that are part of the interview. The observation of the sequence of interactions can give further clues in the course of the assessment. After an awkward moment, does the parent jump in and explain that the child was never told about the meeting; or does the parent listen and watch the child attentively with a feeling of receptivity? On the one hand, the therapist will watch these exchanges and evaluate them. On the other hand, the therapist will smooth these exchanges to heighten rapport between parent and child and diminish the level of stress in the family.

As a result, it is always useful to begin the first meeting with the assumptions that

(a) there is positive love in the family, and
(b) there is a positive goal or solution that can be identified, even in the course of the first contact(s).

When the first therapeutic contact can affirm what is best about the child and family, it helps the family better manage the issues they face together with their child. This effect can be further magnified if the family can successfully follow through with even the simplest of homework tasks offered in this first meeting. The therapist's comments, which highlight the positive aspects in each of the family members, are often remembered and reinforce the best of the relationships within the family. Some families feel this first contact is sufficient and will not return for further treatment. Early therapists often fear that the family choosing not to follow up represents their failure rather than their success.

Evaluating Key Elements of Family Relationships

In the initial family contact, it is often possible for a therapist to define some observations about the nature of family life as well as to begin to formulate what clinical questions or tasks may further serve to illuminate the nature of the family. What the therapist will be looking for during the initial family contact will be the following four key elements of family function that particularly effect the child's function and development of symptoms and will suggest how the therapist may shape the treatment.

(1) Examine the nature of the *relationship* among the various family members. Is it supportive or hostile? Close or overclose? Emotionally attuned or misinterpreted? Warm or cold and distant? From another point of view, family system's theory approaches key family relationships through systemic concepts that influence the relationship between children and their parents. Are there triangulations and conflicts of loyalty? What is the nature of the boundaries between parent and child or among other family members?

(2) Assess the level of *affective life* in the family and the degree of emotional awareness. Is the emotional level of exchange subdued or vibrant? Can feelings be labeled and identified by each member of the family? Are emotional messages well articulated or covert? Is it a family that doesn't hesitate to criticize but has trouble saying loving and caring statements to one another, or vice versa? Do the nonverbal messages feel consistent with the verbal ones? Is there emotional turmoil, with the capacity to repair and reestablish the attachment, or repeated turmoil without resolution?

(3) Determine the nature and clarity of the *rules* that govern family life and the structure of family power. Can basic family rules be articulated? Is there a clear acknowledgment of how the process of power and decision making is handled? Does the parent claim authority appropriately, yet leave room for negotiation? How do the family members communicate? Are they clear with one another? Can they resolve a problem through discussion? Is there some consistency in their messages despite the parent's differences?

(4) What is the level of *developmental understanding* that the parents appear to have? Are their expectations consistent with the child's age or level of development? Do they adjust their behavior and expectations to support the growth of the child? Can they understand what their child can do realistically? How do they handle the issues created by having children of different ages? Are children's rights and responsibilities clearly defined so that the children understand the difference between a privilege that occurs when children are older versus a privilege that can be earned by the child?

As these questions play in the background of the therapist's clinical observations, what is continuing to happen in the room? What items will be entered on the therapeutic scorecard for further exploration and discussion? How will those questions be framed and tested in later interviews with the parents or child alone? In many instances, none of these questions can be fully settled in the initial evaluation and often will be refined in the course of therapy.

Many of the considerations described above relate to the degree of maturity of the parents and the nature of the relationship they have with each other and with the child. As a result, careful attention must to paid to the level and nature of the function of the parents themselves. (It is no surprise that the treatment plan for many children settles out to be couples therapy!) Chapter 3 will discuss the integration of the parenting meeting, the exploration of the developmental history of the child and family, and the evaluation of possible adult psychopathology or overt–covert marital conflict or both.

An Alternative Beginning: Meeting with the Parents Alone

There are many parents who would prefer to meet with the therapist alone before bringing in their child. Many of these parents wish to see if they can create a working alliance with the therapist; some may wish to make sure that the therapist stays focused on the child, rather than parenting- or family-based issues. The former requests are not unreasonable and the latter are often not fully understood until later in the diagnostic assessment or as the treatment evolves. (See chapter 7.)

This first parent meeting can serve as the platform for the three-part diagnostic intervention described here, as well as for treatment. The authors want to stress that this meeting, while it may provide some clues about the nature of the parents and their concerns about their child, does not truly function as the beginning of the diagnostic assessment. The parents often want the therapist to describe himself or herself, the therapist's background, training, and orientation, and get a sense of how the therapist may approach the assessment and treatment of their child.

This work falls into the category of relationship building, sharing knowledge, and forming the parental alliance, rather than diagnosing and assessing. In a world in which there continues to be severe limits on most family's mental health benefits, this type of session may be considered a luxury by MCOs but a necessity for some parents. The therapist must address these issues immediately by exploring how this meeting may have "used up" an authorized session or an available dollar benefit and the resulting implications for the family's costs. The benefit of this meeting for the therapist will be the extra time there will be to discuss the fiscal contract. In the authors' experience, the families who have this wish are often those who face fewer fiscal constraints about their benefits and are often willing to be self-pay clients.

It is often possible to engage the parent in a piece of further detective work or to give a suggestion about parenting as early homework. While the therapist will often not have time to explore the results of this homework until the parent meeting—which will serve to assess parenting skills, the parents' own family of origin experiences, and any adult psychopathology—it can be a good time to make a suggestion. (See homework section in this chapter.)

Parent and School Behavioral (Symptom) Checklists

Just as the therapist must attend to the nature and quality of family life, the child's overall level of behavioral function and possible symptoms or medical and developmental concerns must be considered. This is a tall order for a first interview. As a result, we recommend the use of some ancillary materials. A medical form (see Table 1.1) and behavioral checklists can highlight and help fine tune the therapist's questioning in the parent meeting. They save the therapist the arduous task of detailed and repetitive questioning, which can derail the interpersonal rapport created in the initial contact.

Checklists serve two very important functions: (1) they help screen for and identify symptom complexes that have a bearing on developmental and diagnostic issues; (2) they highlight areas that require further exploration without a time intensive (and somewhat boring) series of questions. As noted, most symptoms also interfere with coping and, as a result, the role that particular symptoms may play should be identified so their impact can be addressed in the treatment. In addition, the symptomatic data can be helpful if psychopharmacological consultation is considered. This early data will serve as a base line indication of the intensity of the presenting symptoms.

One example of a checklist among the many that are offered by various companies is noted below. It relies on the Conners scale (Conners, 1973). It was initially developed to screen for attention deficit hyperactivity disorder (ADHD). (See Table 1.2.) The Conners profile has 46 items, 10 of which are correlated with attentional disorders. Each item can be scored according to severity: not at all = 0, just a little = 1, pretty much = 2, very much = 3. (See Table 1.2 for the typical questions in the parent and teacher questionnaire that screens for ADHD.) In addition, other screening questions (Table 1.3) can be used to alert the therapist to concerns about social–emotional and peer issues, oppositionality, aggressivity, features of conduct disorder, depression, anxiety, or all of these. (See Table 1.3.)

Over time, the therapist will develop a feel for the clinical implications of the checklist, even without detailed scoring. The therapist will be able to distinguish those children whose profiles are quite specific—either mostly pointing to impulse control or acting-out symptoms (externalization) or those with a mixed picture of anxiety and depression (internalization). Some patterns seem quite mixed, yet areas of self-control or good function are still highlighted by the items that are marked "not at all" or "just a little."

In some populations, the forms may have a solid column of "very much" from top to bottom on every item on the page. This profile may indicate either high risk children or a high risk family or both. A further clue to whether parental psychopathology may be present is that these are often the same parents who respond to the question, "What do you like most about your child?" or "What is your child's major strength?" with a shrug. The impact of parental psychopathology on checklists will be discussed in chapter 3.

For a more detailed inventory, the use of the Achenbach Child Behavior Checklists (CBCLs; Achenbach, 1991a, 1991b) is suggested. These have been in use for a number of decades. The CBCLs come in different varieties. They include a form for children of preschool age, which parents complete, parent forms for children 4 to 16, and a youth (ages 11–18) self-report form, which early to late adolescents can complete independently. For this age group, a therapeutic family approach can be accentuated by the therapist's suggestion that parent and child do the checklist together, with the parent responding to the item *after* the adolescent has marked his or her rating. For early and midteens, this technique can help parents and adolescent develop a shared perspective, as well as clarify their differences. Discussion, rather than conflict, can be promoted by the instruction that each family member should use a different color pen to mark the form. Their task is not to develop a final "right" number but to share perspectives and record them.

In addition, the first two pages of the CBCL include a request to list social contacts and important activities, including sports, clubs, hobbies, and friendships. Family-based chores and sibling relationships are also covered. A brief academic review is included, as well as identifying any special academic needs or problems. In both the self-report form and the parent version, there is a specific question about what the "best things" are about the individual child. There is also another opportunity to identify concerns. This scale also has a version for teachers, which is four pages long. Additional technology can enhance the therapist's perspective, since there is a computerized scoring module that is available. When the CBCL is completed, a profile will be developed, like one that can be seen in various research articles that examine child profiles and change (Biederman et al., 1996). The CBCL gives a score on the following eight areas of adjustment: withdrawal, somatization, anxiety/depression, social problems, thought problems, attention problems, delinquent behavior, and aggressive behavior. These scales can show differences even within a group of children with the same diagnosis.

Since the CBCL is a four-page instrument, therapists may be concerned that it will be intimidating for some parents or children. Forms and checklists should be identified and used that the therapist feels are genuinely helpful and manageable. When these forms are integrated into a standard assessment protocol, any burden that child or parent may experience is diminished. In fact, most families often feel that the forms are a good way to identify and clarify their concerns. Checklists can heighten their sense of the seriousness of the therapist's concern and that their input is taken seriously.

In selected instances, the therapist, whose suspicions of an autistic spectrum disorder have been aroused, may wish to use a newly developed tool to screen for autism, called the Pervasive Developmental Disorder Screening Test (Siegel, 1996).[6] It can only be used with children older than 18 months.

Assessing the Inner World of the Child

Just as checklists enhance the perspective of the therapist and can focus the therapist's diagnostic questioning, there are tools that can be used within the child interview. The therapist will want to develop a sense of the child's inner life. There are many materials available to help a therapist. However, no materials can substitute for the therapist's ability to conduct a focused interview that relies on engaging children.

Understanding the child's point of view begins within the initial family component of the interview. Depending upon the conduct and exchange between parent and child during the discussion about the presenting problem, it is often possible to turn one's attention to the parent for a portion of time while instructing a child to draw a picture of a person. If this is completed quickly, the therapist may also ask the child to draw a picture of his or her family doing something together. The therapist has set the stage for the next portion of the meeting, which is to see the child alone.

In this individual meeting, what the child has listened to during the focused family exchange will influence the child's emotions, which are reflected in their art, play, and discussion. The child's play can lead to further questions from the therapist about the concerns that the therapist and child have heard in the family meeting. The therapist's

---

[6]This form may be obtained from Dr. Siegel at the University of California at San Francisco at the Langley Porter Psychiatric Institute.

assessment of the child's ability to handle further questions as well as how they respond to feedback about their family will give the therapist a great deal of insight into how the child can manage the stress of the problem as well as to anticipate the level of the child's motivation to solve the problem. By the end of this session, the child should have a sense of the therapist's concern and the therapist will have a sense of how the child may be able to cooperate with further treatment.

To help in the interpretation of the child's drawings (the Draw a Person test and the Kinetic Family Drawing), there are a variety of resources. In addition, there are many other types of semistructured interview materials and projective materials that are available to integrate into the child interviews. The therapist does not need to give a "psychological battery," but rather therapists can use these materials selectively to enhance their understanding of a child's inner emotional life and cognitive–emotional constructs, the nature of the problem, and how he or she views the world. Selected components of sentence completion tests, using cards from the TED or the Children's Apperception test or TAT, can complement the portion of individual free play meeting(s), combined with some directed questioning.

Not being direct does not exclude being directive in therapeutic assessment and care, and vice versa. Children often have a surprising capacity to answer direct questions simply and with full emotional awareness, as well as the ability to use play and metaphor to deliver the needed message. The fundamental techniques of play therapy with children are discussed in many other useful texts (Schaefer, 1976) and are foundations in the assessment and treatment planning for children and families.

Clinicians should be familiar with common developmental play themes as well as children's common management techniques in competitive games (cheating, rule changing) and how these change with maturation. Continued study of preschool children (Warren, Oppenheim, & Emde, 1996) suggests that play themes that are associated with distress and destruction can predict behavioral disorder.

Initial Homework Tasks in Treatment: Furthering the Collaboration with the Therapist and Enhancing the "Detective" Skills in Child and Family

From the preliminary assessment fashioned in the first contact, the initial clues and concerns that the therapist has identified can lead toward a tentative formulation and a homework task that may test that hypothesis further. The nature and strength of the relationship of the child and parent as well as the energy available to develop change can be assessed further through the use of homework. When a therapeutic suggestion or homework is assigned in the brief parental feedback component, the followup in the parent meeting can contribute to one's appreciation of the level of function of the family network and the degree of resistance or psychopathology or both that may be present. Knowing a variety of homework tasks can help the therapist make these suggestions (Schultheis, 1998).

When a parent is invested in the homework, a solution oriented focus can be useful (see Seleckman, 1997). Choosing tasks that the parent understands will address the problem also helps the parent maintain a perspective that mental health consultations are valuable, but that they also depend upon the compliance and cooperation of the family. Giving the parent and child a task that engages them productively together in problem solving can enhance their relationship and coping skills. The strength of the therapist's initial conviction that their assessment of the parent and child and the nature of the problem is correct is often directly correlated with the ease with which the therapist offers initial directives to solve the problem.

Especially for the beginning therapist, whose behavioral repertoire may be limited, first-step homework suggestions are best framed as "detective work." In addition, the therapist's hesitance to offer a specific directive may be part of a gut response that suggests some degree of discomfort with what has been learned within the diagnostic contact with a family. This countertransferential element should be tested to evaluate whether it should be respected. It may represent a not yet well understood or disguised deeper problem in the family interaction. Alternately, it may be recognized as a resonance that relates more to the therapist's own makeup.

In cases that arouse discomfort, it is often wise to restrict directives to those that will illuminate the times the problem presents, recording the problem when it occurs by parent or child or both, or simply marking a calendar with the frequency of the problematic behaviors and directing the parent to be alert to precipitants in the interaction with the child or to other factors, e.g., a child's easily triggered frustration. In this way, the therapist can test the resolve of the family to work cooperatively and not get involved immediately in a struggle over what is or isn't going to work.

Detective work is an approach to child–family problems that requires that child and parents attend better to the nature, timing, and presentation of the identified problem. The task should enhance parent–child communication as well as the sense that the parent and child are working together to feel better. It should diminish any possible alienation between them and enhance their sense of power. When the complaint is about anger or family fights, one simple homework task is to request that the parents put a mark on the calendar so that they know how often the fights are happening. It is often telling when the parents arrive for the parent meeting without the calendar and say, "Johnny didn't do it." For a family that might have more energy, writing about the fights—both the content of the conflict and the feelings aroused—can be suggested. Younger children can tell their parent the ideas and feelings, which the parent must write down. Often first and second graders can enjoy writing simple sentences about "being mad."

Many other homework tasks can be as simple as the following:

(1) Mark a calendar with a dot when the designated problem occurs.
(2) A task for a parent: Go to the school to meet with the teacher to have the checklist done and ask where/when/how your child is most successful.
(3) A task for a child: Make a special book where you can draw pictures to show that sad feeling we talked about.
(4) Write down what time you tell Sally to go to bed, the time she goes to her room and gets into bed, and the time that she falls asleep. Each morning make a yellow circle when she wakes up in a good mood and a red circle when she wakes up in a bad mood.

Other tasks that may engage the larger family network in helping the child and parent manage a difficult situation can be the following:

(1) When Johnny gets mad, make sure he and his father talk over ideas about mad feelings each night.

(2) Have Johnny's grandmother bake cookies with Johnny on Saturday so the parents and the other children can do another activity.

Simple behavioral interventions that rely on recommending clear language that can be used consistently can be as simple as a trial of using a code word to help a parent organize his or her limits. For instance, "Stop!" "This is your second warning to stop." "Now you must stop and take a time out." To help the child state feelings, rather than act out the problem, the child may say, b"This makes me mad!"

While the above examples pertain to the younger child, adolescents can be engaged in a similar fashion in coming to know themselves and their behaviors and the expectations of their parents.

Each task should further the knowledge about the problem or help move to some resolution through increased understanding and rapprochement between parent and child. The assessment of each task will further define the ability of the system to utilize suggestion and direction. Often, the focus does not have to be on the problem. The clinician can suggest the parent and child write down all the fun times they have had in a week. Or, as in a workbook for parents of oppositional disorders, the initial suggestion can be that parent and child set aside a specifically planned time for play each night (Barkley, 1997).

The Fiscal Planning or MCO Planning Process

The last few minutes of the meeting should be reserved for the discussion of the preliminary treatment plan taking into account the resources available to pay for the intervention. The therapist may use statements such as the following: "There are tremendous numbers of health plans in our state at this point—each one has different rules and different benefits. Each one has different requirements. Just as we talked about the detective work on Jessica's problem, you will need to investigate what number of visits your insurance may cover and what aspects of the treatment are not covered (like phone meetings or school visits). We will need to discuss what you might pay for directly or if you feel we must work within your benefit. I believe you were right to seek help for Jessica and that we can identify how treatment can be helpful. Knowing how many sessions we have to work with will remind us to focus on which aspect of the problem is the most important. We will review the homework and the insurance information next time we meet (in the parent meeting)."

The issue of sharing this responsibility and placing a major part of this in the hands of the parents cannot be underestimated. Many people do not understand a great deal about their insurance or the intermediaries their insurance company hires (MCOs) to manage benefits. Therapists must explain to the families that they are not the MCO. The therapist and the family must form a team to work with an MCO regarding choices, forms submitted, and any appeals process that there may be. Without sharing this work, the therapist may quickly burn out or be in danger of having his or her countertransferential feelings toward the MCO be displaced onto the patient.

Therapists must clarify with the family what their benefits are so the alliance can be built around an understanding of guidelines that are established by the outside system. If the therapist works within the MCO, there are different challenges. Different systems of care create different issues, which are the source of much discussion from a legal and a clinical point of view (Gutheil, 1997).

In the perfect case, the therapist has been able to cover a tremendous amount of ground in just one meeting. There is a positive alliance that has begun, a good sense of both the child's and the family's function has been obtained, and the fiscal collaboration has been initiated. The stage is well set for the second visit, the parent meeting, and the third meeting with the child and family to establish the treatment contract.

The real world will present the therapist with some more lively challenges. In the next chapter, the less than perfect case will be described to see how the assessment can be confounded by the possible presence of severe developmental disorder in a child or a disorganized and compromised family system (often including severe parental psychiatric disturbance) or both. The reader will be introduced to two additional key concepts that can be used in treatment planning: *The Zone of Difficulty of the Case* and *Challenging Children: Zebras versus Horses.*

2

CHAPTER

Challenging Children: Challenging Families

Getting Started: "The Less than Perfect Case: Jennifer"

The basic elements of the first phone contact—setting the stage—and the first diagnostic meeting have been reviewed in chapter 1. Whether the case is "perfect" or "less than perfect," the objectives, assessment components, and overall plan are still the mainstays of the diagnostic phase and will be similarly attempted.

> Mr. Weed calls late in the day and asks for the therapist to call back soon. He seems short tempered in the message and does not leave a telephone number. Later in the week, he calls during the day and complains to the secretary that the therapist has not been responsive. The receptionist was prepared by the therapist about his call on the tape and explains that he had not left his number. He replies that he thought Dr. Faithful, his child's pediatrician, had called the therapist to tell her "all that stuff." The receptionist takes his number.

The First Red Flag

The therapist is unable to begin a systematic approach to the care plan. The initial work is complicated by the parent's style and raises concerns. The therapist's next phone contact will need to establish the early alliance in the face of the family's suggested disappointment.

The referral source is revealed inadvertently amidst the assumptions that the parent has about the referral process. Since the pediatrician is not familiar, this fact will need to be discussed in the next phone contact.

> The therapist calls Mr. and Mrs. Weed back. This time Mrs. Weed is at home. She explains that their 9-year-old daughter, Jennifer, is having "lots of troubles" and her pediatrician referred them. Mrs. Weed says she works and her husband is at home on disability so that he sees more of Jennifer's behavior. She thinks that Jennifer has always been

> a fussy child so she doesn't know "what the doctor is aggravating them about," and sounds as irritable as her husband. The therapist asks when they can have an initial family meeting and Mrs. Weed says it has to be in the evening because "I work and am the sole support of this family." The therapist, in her wish to engage the mother, says her role as head of the household will make it even more important for her to be present. The therapist asks if she can send papers for the parents to fill out about Jennifer and explains that the family will have to investigate their medical insurance. Mrs. Weed says she will check into it. When the therapist attempts to explain what to tell Jennifer, Mrs. Weed cuts her off. Mrs. Weed says, "you've given me more than enough to do."

When the therapist asks how to be of help, in order to establish the role of therapeutic service and form an early alliance, the tactic fails. Neither parent particularly appears to desire help, and the primary concerned party is identified as the pediatrician who has not made any contact.

Typically a referring doctor wants either a consultation about the nature of the child or family's difficulties or hopes the therapist will be able to intervene. In this case, it is not yet known what the pediatrician's question is. If the therapist chooses to take on this case, enough of an alliance with the family will need to be formed in order to complete an evaluation.

To develop a working alliance with the parents, the therapist will have to work hard to join with them in whatever concerns they have for themselves as well as their child. It looks like an uphill climb. It is also likely that if the referral source wants the therapist to be a change agent, there maybe disappointment about the therapist's inability to "control" or shape a better outcome for the child.

> The family does not come to the scheduled appointment. The therapist calls the family's home and leaves a message on the answering tape. Mr. Weed calls the office an hour later and says they had car trouble on the way to the office and wishes to reschedule. The therapist sympathizes with the family's difficulties. She asks if she can call Dr. Faithful. The therapist reiterates the components of the first meeting emphasizing again how this contact can help the parents and Dr. Faithful with their concerns about Jennifer. The therapist says she will send forms and checklists for them to fill out before the next meeting. She reminds the father as well that they will need to gather insurance information. The father seems to ignore much of what is said and reports they "have other thing to do besides this," but does give permission on the telephone for calling Dr. Faithful. They accept an appointment for the same time the following week.

Other Red Flags

The two key components of the initial contact (knowledge and acceptance) are not readily established in this case.

(1) *Therapists offer knowledge.*
- The parents do not seem to share the concerns of the pediatrician. In fact, the pediatrician may already have strained the alliance with the parents by pressing his concerns about their child. The permission to contact the pediatrician (which some parents refuse) does mean that their initial interactions with the therapist and the therapist's impressions of the family can be shared with the pediatrician. It is likely that these will be concerns that the pediatrician has noted.
- The various components of the assessment process need to be explained several

times. The therapist infers that the parents have a limited ability to manage the requirements of the evaluation as well as to maintain a concern about their daughter. The parents' involvement needs to be reinforced in order to "discover" what the problem is for Jennifer.

- While things may be genuinely difficult for Jennifer, the parents feel her behavior is another way the child bothers them. Furthermore, mother is pessimistic that the therapist's knowledge can offer help since Jennifer's emotional reactions reflect "the way she is."

(2) *Therapists offer care within the therapeutic relationship.*

The therapist attempts to appreciate the parents' efforts in taking action on their daughter's behalf, but these actions seem irrelevant to the family. The therapist's suggestion to create a bridge between parent and therapist to offer care and concern to the child has led to immediate resistance.

The parents appear to be more absorbed by their own stresses. The therapist is not perceived as caring but as intrusive.

The third point in an intake call has to do with business.

(3) *Therapists offer a service within a contractual relationship.*

The therapist is pessimistic that the parents will gather information that is needed about their benefits. Even if they try, they may get little (or only confusing) help from their insurer about what they need to do. In this case, it is unlikely the family will even place a call.

In cases like this, the therapist needs to keep in mind that they may not be paid. Therefore, the therapist should identify for themselves the name of the insurance company and how it works.

Therapists who work with children in trouble must be prepared for families who are trouble. Unlike adult clients who feel they are doing something for themselves in seeking therapy, certain parents may experience their child's distress as "one more thing they have to do," or "another manipulation." They may fear that the therapist may attack an already vulnerable ego by exposing their failures to care for their child, or worse, by reporting them to a child welfare organization.

> The therapist can now call Dr. Faithful. This physician and the therapist have not worked together before. During the call, the doctor reports that he feels that Jennifer often appears anxious and unhappy. The family interactions seen thus far by the therapist are described, which leads the doctor to report that he has faced similar difficulties. He is glad that they have called and that someone else can help this child. Dr. Faithful checks their insurance and names the company, where "you are on their list of providers."

The therapist anticipates the next meeting with anxiety. No additional information can be gathered about the insurance without the family's data.

The First Appointment: The Family Component

> Mr. and Mrs. Weed come to the office a half-hour late for the designated appointment with Jennifer.

The therapist realizes that it will still be important to develop, albeit briefly, a sense of this family, have a brief contact with the child, and then meet alone with the parents to clarify the insurance issues.

The parents begin the interview by complaining about how uncooperative Jennifer was in getting ready. Jennifer appears not to hear them.

They have in hand a sheaf of papers. The therapist welcomes them all into the office and accepts the papers. She explains to Jessica that one set of papers is about things her parents have noticed about her and the others are "business papers" that the therapist will need to discuss with her mother and father later.

The therapist tells Jennifer that she spoke to her mother about a week ago and has also talked to Dr. Faithful. The therapist asks Jennifer if she knows why her parents have brought her to the therapist's office and "if it was hard to come here." Jennifer immediately looks anxious and begins to cry.

The therapist has modified the traditional "how come Mom and Dad brought you here" with an addendum. The therapist is trying to build a bridge to Jennifer by redefining the parents' complaint. The therapist does not wish to challenge the parents' interpretations immediately but does not wish to sacrifice the child to their attitude. Without promptly attending to these exchanges, the family interview can rapidly become a session focusing on blame and one in which the child retreats from contact with the interviewer.

Her mother looks disdainfully at Jennifer and says, "don't put on a show. Tell her that we're late because you were having a tantrum about not getting dessert because you didn't finish your plate." And then Mrs. Weed glares at her husband. "There she goes again; I thought you told her what this was about." Mr. Weed roughly tells Jennifer to "stop crying and speak up. Since your mother is never home for you anyways, now you can tell her."

More Red Flags

In order to manage a family meeting in which the parents manifest negative reactions to the child so quickly, as well as barely conceal the conflict between themselves, the child therapist must have a broad range of techniques and tactics to handle these issues.

This chapter will review a variety of initial strategies for working with families as well as for interacting with more difficult family styles.

Jennifer haltingly tells her mother that Katie, her baby sister, is "mean" and breaks all her toys. Mr. Weed looks at his wife and says, "I tell her all the time: 'what does she expect from a 4-year-old?'" Mrs. Weed says, "if you got off your ass instead of just watching television all the time maybe you wouldn't have to yell so much." Jennifer gets out of her chair and goes to the play area. The parents ignore her and look at the therapist while saying, "Jennifer has always been moody, overactive, and had a short attention span." They laugh and say, "We hope she doesn't show you one of her tantrums." The therapist asks if Jennifer has these same difficulties at school and the parents look anxiously at each other and say yes. They then report that Jennifer has been evaluated at school and there is a contact person there. The therapist tells the parents Jennifer having some school support is wonderful and expects that she and the parents will need to work together as a team. Before she sees Jennifer, however, she asks if there has been any trauma that Jennifer might have experienced when younger or currently. Both parents say, "Jennifer has had a golden life—she has gotten everything we never had." They then look at the therapist and say, "Now what?"

The therapist feels anxious, aggravated, and uncertain. The interaction of this family is very negative, and there has not been a consensus established about a problem or a way to work together. Concerned about the time, she decides to proceed with her plan to separate the parents from the child and see the child alone.

The therapist, before making this suggestion, glances at the papers the parents have brought in and sees they are not filled out. She suggests the parents go to the waiting room and fill out the papers and she will spend some time alone with Jennifer, explaining that her time is limited by the family's lateness and this will help them use their time as best as possible.

The use of behavioral and symptom checklists is still important in any diagnostic evaluation, even difficult ones. However, as will be discussed in chapter 3 on parental psychopathology, the parent's psychological state may influence the data that are recorded.

The Child Interview

Jennifer plays silently, moving from toy to toy with little engagement. She does not answer any of the therapist's questions. The therapist tries to use a puppet as an intermediary. Jennifer grabs the head of the puppet with an alligator puppet and tries to pull it off the therapist's hand. She sees the dollhouse family and quickly rips off their clothes and then bends them in half, trying to break them. As the therapist defines the office rules for play, Jennifer glares silently at the therapist and moves on to another activity. As the therapist moves a little closer to observe, she also tells Jennifer that they have "five more minutes to play." Jennifer drops her toy and says, "I'm done" and leaves the office.

The therapist is understandably alarmed by Jennifer's relating style and the primitive and aggressive nature of her play. Her poor concentration and limited ability to communicate raise many diagnostic concerns. The nature of her underlying cognitive capacities (a common comorbidity in child behavioral disorders) must be evaluated. The therapist cannot tell if she is dealing with the relatively common symptoms of an attentional disorder (a "horse") complicated by the family's care pattern and the child's defensive relating style or a more problematic diagnosis. Because the parents have described a history of tantrums and mood swings, she even wonders if there might be the uncommon presentation of an early bipolar disorder (a "zebra"). She worries about a history of trauma, or the presence of abuse, or the continuing impact of a very stressed family with many immediately visible negative interactions with their child. She feels she must share her alarm with the parents and ask for permission to gather information about Jennifer's function at school. She realizes that she can only focus briefly on the fiscal informed consent given her sense of urgency about the other clinical matters.

The Parent Meeting Component and Fiscal Collaboration

The therapist invites Mr. and Mrs. Weed back into the consulting room. They have not completed the checklists, since there were a large number of items about which they had different opinions. The therapist explains that their homework will be for each parent to fill out a set of checklists so that she can understand each parent's perspective better. She says that she was quite alarmed about the level of distress she felt Jennifer was communicating and will need to see her further to help make a treatment plan. She asks them to sign a release of information for the pediatrician, the school, and a previous contact they had with a community mental health center. She says having the school contact person fill out checklists will be very helpful, too. The parents say little. They sign the papers. She wonders if the next meeting might take place at the school, since she imagines that the school has been just as concerned as the parents.

With one minute left in the hour, the therapist asks the mother about whether she has gotten authorization from her company for the visit. The mother says "no" and that she did not even know she had to do anything. She says, "Dr. Faithful takes care of all that. The therapist asks for the family's insurance card and photocopies it. She explains to the mother the number the therapist will call for an authorization. The parents agree to meet after hearing from the therapist what information she can gather from the school.

The therapist sees that Jennifer's symptom level is high, as is the level of adversity in the home. This child and her family are "most at risk." This type of case makes the therapist feel a sense of helplessness or hopelessness. Therapists need a way to address these issues, rather than succumb to the temptation to ignore this high risk family. In this chapter we will describe a way to rank the level of child-based or family-based pathologies into one of four different "zones." Specific therapeutic approaches are related to each of these four zones. In the case presented above, severe compromises appear within both the family and the child's development, which places this case into zone 4.

In zone 4 cases, the first question is to evaluate the level of safety. Is the level of adversity such that as a mandated reporter the therapist must file a report with a state child protection agency? In this case, she has no data that can permit her to file with the state agency that will not be "screened out." In other words, while these emotional exchanges are very troublesome, neither basic care nor the child's safety is compromised. Having this family engage in treatment would be the best option.

Keeping in mind the limitation of the family to engage, the zone 4 therapeutic approach will be on the development of a systems plan for the child. A further evaluation of the parenting system is needed, with the hope that this meeting may promote further engagement. The therapist will hope to be able to assess the level of parental function, as she suspects that father's disability may be psychiatric and mother's ability to attach to her child may be compromised. She will need to take a thorough family history. If the mother and father have therapists, their involvement may be helpful in defining a treatment plan. Because the therapist is concerned that the parents may not readily return, the second task (calling a systems meeting) will be discussed with the parents to see if they will agree to have this meeting next.

The second task, taking a broader systems perspective, requires releases of information that the parents have given, although meeting with the parents alone may identify other involved professionals. Since she knows that this MCO does pay for systems meetings, she decides to move ahead. While an investment of time is required to coordinate such a meeting, she decides that, whether the parents come or not, she will convene a meeting with people at school. She will invite the parents to come there to meet the other professionals who are involved in this child's care, invite the pediatrician, and then explore in the follow-up parent meeting if there are (or have been) other agencies involved with the family.

At this point, the therapist knows she will be paid for the session she has just provided because she will be obtaining her own authorization, as well as one for the case conference and parent meetings to follow. Fortunately, this family's insurance will reimburse for a case conference; however, many do not. In terms of planning her further involvement with the family, she worries about the rate of no shows for which she may be able to bill but is unlikely to collect. She will be limited in terms of what therapy she can provide by both fiscal constraints and the parents' collaboration. In zone 4 families, a standard therapeutic intervention may yield limited results. As a result, her experience has led her to begin by investing her energies in looking for other forms of support for the child.

The therapist has made a commitment to the systems meeting. If the parents attend, that will be a major step forward in planning for the child's needs. Since the therapist has also planned a parent meeting to follow immediately after the systems meeting, she can then convey her initial impressions gently but directly. She should be prepared to tell them that she sees them as a family laboring under intense stress. Both mother and father should be asked further about the stresses that exist for each of them. Then the therapist must clarify that since their daughter's ability to change either her feelings or her behavior depends so much upon them, parent-based treatment must be the first step.

In addition, a discussion of *fiscal informed consent* must be fully reviewed for at least half of this meeting (given the therapist's sense of how long it takes these parents to absorb information). With a family like this, the therapist must discuss the financial inability of the therapist to implement treatment with many no shows. Since the therapist cannot pretend that the no-show bills are likely to be paid, given this family's fiscally precarious situation, the therapist must spell out how many missed appointments will be tolerated before the treatment is terminated. In addition, the therapist already knows the family does not understand its insurance. The work with the insurance company must be incorporated into the parent meetings so that, in a very concrete way, they understand what their insurance company will and will not do.

While many therapists might feel that this focus on the parents represents an abandonment of the child, it actually represents an effort to have *the parents not abandon the child.* (The parents are the most important people in this child's life since everything she experiences is filtered through her care by them.) The reality of therapy is that in cases like these, the parents determine whether the child will have any consistent contact with a therapist. There should be a grave doubt in the therapist's mind that this is likely. The therapist who plans child-based meetings at this point will present the child with another model of the inconsistent availability and unreliability of adults as a result of erratically kept appointments. If Jennifer's parents persist in the parenting work, a reliable child therapy and family-based treatment may then be possible.

Given her experience this far, the parents do not come to the systems meeting, the therapist can clarify the great likelihood that this family will not be able to comply with treatment. To pretend that they will be able to do so is foolish. For a therapist to believe they can do the impossible does no one any good, since a fragmented pattern of care is unlikely to produce reliable change. When the therapist is clear about this, it may also permit the school to provide other resources, lead the pediatrician to file with a child welfare agency, or for other actions to be taken. When the therapist indicates that the impossible may be accomplished, the other professionals are less Likely to be proactive. The therapist is the one they will expect to solve the problems!

☐ Dealing with Difficult Children and Families

At this point, the reader has a sense of how the different elements of an initial child and family assessment are brought together. However, the "less than perfect case" brings up the importance of three other elements that will be discussed in this chapter: techniques for managing difficult family interactions, the zone of difficulty of the case, and, finally, distinguishing between the common presentation of child problems and the more rare diagnostic entities ("horses versus zebras").

The therapist must be prepared for the difficult initial family interview. Without having a set of techniques to try to nourish a more appropriate family interaction, the therapist will have a harder time clarifying what the premorbid relational picture may have been like. Similar presentations can have different causes. A child's persistent symptoms can erode a parent's caretaking, or a child's function can be compromised by becoming the focus of family blame or distress. The section to follow will present a variety of techniques that help diminish the level of tension in the family so that the family assessment can proceed.

In the most difficult cases, therapists may begin their evaluation with a certain degree of worry about the adequacy of the family environment or other risk factors in the child's life. Children are abused and neglected. Many children have symptoms as a result of terrible experiences. Many children can have psychiatric disorders, as may other members of the family.

However, to begin an evaluation using a positive attitude toward the elements of success in adaptation, communication, and emotional connection between parent and child does not require ignoring red flags of either *DSM-IV* disorder or maltreatment. In being positive, the therapist does not give away a concern or suspicion of abuse or serious developmental disorder. The therapist, in looking for the best, does not lose the ability to identify the worst as presented by serious risks within the family or to notify relevant state agencies.

The key to all of these techniques is to find the positive core in the relationship between the parent and child. A central component of child and family therapeutic work is relational. In child and family problems, the key relationship is between the child and the parent. When it can be restored to a functional level in which the parent can support the positive growth in the child and the child can become more secure, behavioral symptoms are likely to diminish.

The same three techniques, which Les Havens (Havens, 1997) refers to as the "analgesia" needed to explore the state of pain in an individual mind, can be used in the family interview. First, he suggests, the therapist must protect the patient's self-esteem by being able to both celebrate and admire the patient. Second, the therapist's understanding is needed, not for a brilliant insight, but to grasp the patient's point of view. Finally, he feels the treatment must provide a "future," a sense that "the world can be made better for them." These can be challenges in an individual interview and they multiply in the contact with parent and child.

The variety of techniques described below should both help create the analgesia needed for each family member to participate in the interview as well as help the family explore a difficult problem. The reader should note that in the case of Jennifer as initially described, the case was chosen to illustrate one of the more frustrating clinical encounters. Even if the therapist was armed with all of the techniques described, there might still have been a disappointing and worrisome outcome.

☐ Techniques for Dealing with Family Interaction

Therapeutic Tactic 1: Underscoring the Empathy between Family Members

When the therapist can underline the positive regard the parents and child have for each other, the treatment is off to a good start. In more difficult cases, however, the spirit of helpfulness between parent and child has been eroded. However, even in the most difficult cases, the parent has still gone to the trouble and effort to bring a child to the therapist. It is still an act of concern even when the parent is frustrated with the child. This is what can be pointed out as the therapist works to control the impact of the anger expressed between parent and child. The way in which the child counts on and cares about the parent should also be identified. Even when a child angrily reacts to a parent's comments, the therapist can point out that the parent's attitudes really matter to the child. Love may be as difficult a topic to discuss for some families as anger is for others.

As a result, even when there are difficult signals from the first contacts with a family, as in the case of the Weeds, the therapist can still use the traditional opening gambit to explore the problem. The therapist must be prepared for the fact that there appears to be little indication that there is a working alliance available between the parents and the therapist. The therapist will be testing the level of the available alliance between the parent and child. In those cases in which there are rapid indications that there is a failure of empathy on all fronts, and little indication of a working alliance with the parents that can help the therapist draw the family into a positive collaboration, the therapist must be prepared to switch tactics. However, the therapist should continue to be alert for signs of a positive relationship that can be reinforced.

For example, in another case, the therapist has suggested that a boy's trouble speaking up is caused by the unfamiliarity of the office setting; some parents may disagree, feeling that the therapist is indulging in misattributions." A parent's comment like, "Doc, my kid hasn't ever been shy," can be met with a response that still conveys empathy to the child's dilemma while responding to the parent. To do so, the emotional tone of the parent must be read. If it reflects subtle pride, it can be greeted with a response like, "Wow, that must be wonderful to have a youngster who can stand up in difficult situations, even if this one seems harder." On the other hand, if the parent's emotional tone conveys negativity and a put down, the therapist can respond with a comment like, "It is hard to have a kid who has such of mind of his own, but it's good to see that he can be different." In either case, the therapist's tone conveys a gentle empathic regard in order to begin to move the family exchange toward thinking of each other's feelings and responses in a more positive way. For any intervention to succeed, the parents must support the health of the child as well as the alliance with the therapist.

The Case of Jennifer. Finding empathy within this family is impossible in these first exchanges. The therapist also faces the challenge of maintaining openness to a relationship with the family when the early exchanges have not led to an initial sense of trust. Both the parents and the child have immediately manifested difficult behaviors. As noted above, part of the technique of identifying empathy among family members in a system that does not display any may require the therapist to model it.

Once in the room, the opening gambit used by the therapist leads to a response where the parents immediately place blame. They define the child's behavior as the reason they are late. They go on to follow up with a series of exchanges in which each family member places some form of blame on another. As a result, the therapist can move to empathize with each of them. The first effort of the therapist in empathy ("understanding" in Havens' terms) may be as simple as reminding the parents, especially since they have shared this information, "that this is a very busy family and sometimes everyone may feel rushed and possibly irritated. I know that many children worry a great deal about a visit to a therapist and it often makes it harder for them to get going for the doctor's visit." In the use of this tactic, the therapist has expressed concern for the parents, has offered psychological information about a child's behavior, and has accepted the fact that all the members of the family are stressed. The family's arrival is an act to be celebrated.

Therapeutic Tactic 2: Translate Behavior into Feelings

As in the first brief exchange of the Weed family, the rule that empathic communication be emphasized is often undermined by the abrasive behavior and communication on the part of the child or the parent. The therapist's first message, Empathy!, can be easily overruled and ignored.

The therapist must be alert and active in modifying the difficult exchanges in these initial high stress moments. For instance, the parent may quickly proceed to derogate the child, if the child still remains silent: "Don't act so stupid, you know I told you what this was about in the car." Then, turning to the therapist, the parent will continue: 'That's the way he is–sullen and dishonest. He always makes me look bad." The therapist's response must find a way to redefine the parent's behavior as reflecting their feelings as well as doing the same for the child. For example, the therapist might then turn to the parent and say, "Wow, Johnny already has a terrible reputation with you–it seems like you may have felt overwhelmed for a long time. I hope Johnny isn't terribly discouraged, too.

There is another point here. In responding to the parent first, the therapist acknowledges the family hierarchy. The therapist understands that the parent has a great deal of power and responsibility and reaffirms the wish to develop an alliance with the parent. Were the therapist to turn immediately to the child, the parent could be affronted, believing that their concerns were going to be ignored, and that therapy will just reinforce the child's tendency to be an "ungrateful brat." When the therapist can reinforce the parent's authority, it may allow the parent to accept new interpretations of the child's behavior as an expression of feeling about something, rather than ingrained "badness." This tactic may help both parent and child move from anger to acceptance.

Alternatively, the therapist might offer to the child a comment on the parent's remark: "Mom sure seems mad at you. How does that make you feel?" This statement is coupled with a diagnostic probe. Immediately, the child learns that the therapist has noticed a striking emotional interaction and that rather than focus on "facts about his badness," the therapist will, for the moment, empathically attend to how he is feeling as well as the concerns of the parent.

The Case of Jennifer. In the next set of exchanges, the therapist can more actively intervene by letting everyone know that all the family members appear to be feeling angry. It might even be possible to suggest that people get most angry when "nothing seems to go right and everyone has more to do than it seems they can get done." The feeling of blame might be identified. Mother blames Jennifer for being late; Mother blames Father for not communicating with the child; Father blames Jennifer for not speaking up; Father blames Mother for not being home; Jennifer's distress may be a form of blaming everyone. The therapist can then identify that blame happens when people feel that too many things are going wrong.

Therapeutic Tactic 3: Plain Talk about Realities

Clinicians are aware of how much more kids know or sense about what is happening in a family than parents can initially accept. For instance, can the parent speak about a conflicted divorce in a way that is respectful and empathic to the child's tie to the other parent? Or, does the parent allow the marital conflict to impinge on the needs of the child, focusing on how bad the child is as "a result of the father allowing the child to be wild" whenever they visit each other? Does the parent wish to talk about how the child seems to be depressed but does not wish to discuss the conflicts that occur each weekend as a result of a parent drinking? Can the parent, who suspects that the child may have a learning disability talk about those concerns while being considerate of the child's self-esteem? Another example is one following a phone intake where the parent tells the therapist about family secrets and then says, "But that's not the problem and Johnny doesn't know."

The Case of Jennifer. The therapist has begun to lay the foundation for plain talk about realities by underscoring in the previous communication that "everyone has too much to do." The mother has identified herself as the sole support of the family; the father is struggling with some form of disability and its impact on his function and sense of self-esteem; and the child has appeared overwhelmed to the pediatrician. All of these initially observed, simple realities need to be underscored as an active part of the dilemmas that face this family. On the one hand, they may serve as an excuse for bad behavior; on the other hand, they lay the foundation for identifying areas of stress that may have some potential solutions and be part of the treatment contract. They become one of the ways the therapist can begin to "provide a future." Using the information and countertransferentia experiences from in the initial phone contact, the therapist is able to convey her attention to detail and focus on the therapeutic process.

Therapeutic Tactic 4: Speaking to the Parent through the Child and Speaking to the Child through the Parent

When an anxious parent has just finished reviewing a child's neglect of parental guidelines in an angry way, the therapist can begin to talk to the child about how often their mother or father worries about them. While the therapist is also changing behavior into feelings (tactic 2) the therapist is addressing this to the child, not the parent. The message says, indirectly, to the parent, "I know you are worried as well as angry." This prepares the parent for the fact that the therapist will focus on all sides of the family's emotions without a direct confrontation. The therapist may want to refocus the family meeting on a discussion of how much the parent means to the child. An aspect of this restructuring can include mini role plays in which the child or parent is asked to politely inquire about different feelings in their experience with each other.

With an adolescent who is difficult to engage, a conflictual situation can be diffused by speaking to the other family members in the room. One old family therapy rule of thumb is "never pursue a distancer" (Bowen, 1978). The way in which the therapist engages the parents may create a context that is irresistible for the child or adolescent. A parent's comment will spontaneously make the adolescent jump in. We must remember to not call attention to this engagement that in any way suggests there has been a therapeutic victory. Often, the adolescent's comment may be simply to contradict or put down the parent, but the engagement has begun. Since tactic 1 stresses empathy, the therapist can say, "It is really great to hear that you have different ideas. This is a place for different people to check out the different ways that everyone remembers something." Or, to use tactic 2 to counter a put down (translating behavior into feelings), "It sounds like you didn't like what Mom or Dad was saying. Could you tell them that it made you mad?"

The Case of Jennifer. Another way to approach the initial exchange between the Weeds is to use the comments of each family member as a way to convey empathy, identify inappropriate behavior indirectly, or try to open other avenues of communication.

When the mother attacks Jennifer for making the family late and for not finishing her meal, the therapist might pursue this exchange by elaborating on it in another way. The therapist might choose to tell Jennifer that her mother really cares about Jennifer having good food. The parents have a tough job: taking care of kids, helping them get healthy bodies, and just having a lot of other jobs to do. The therapist can use that foundation to identify that when parents have too many jobs to do, sometimes parents just get mad all the time and then kids get "mixed up" about whether the parent really cares. In this exchange, you are telling the mother that her remarks may in some way be related to concern or love, but the message that is getting through is all about anger. It may be easier to let the mother know this through your talk with the child, rather than to confront mother directly especially in an initial interview.

Using this tactic with Mr. Weed, who has just finished saying to Jennifer, "stop crying and speak up. Since your mother is never home for you anyways, now you can tell her." The therapist can first turn to Jennifer and say, "Dad really wants you to be able to be strong and tell people and your family all about your ideas." Then, turning quickly to the mother, the therapist can say, "It sure seems like Dad knows how tremendously important you are to Jennifer."

Therapeutic Tactic 5: The Use of "Sometimes"

The therapist can label the frequency of difficulties as occurring *sometimes,* rather than always. Modulating extreme labels, such as most black and white thinking, can promote more healthy initial family transactions. Like the internal constraints posed by "must" or "should" or "I'm awful" and "no good," negative roles can lock in certain thought patterns and actions in individuals. When a child "always' does something, their behavior locks into the parent's perceptual filter as well as decreases the child's motivation to do anything else. "So, I'm bad no matter what I do. Who cares?"

The use of "sometimes" can have powerful mediating effects in family-based treatment. Broadening interpretations of how someone 'always acts" diminishes the trapped feeling that many members of a family have when they first come to therapy. Each intervention that makes room for variety and flexibility also creates a space for health and new opportunities in coping. Cognitive techniques have been defined to disrupt an individual's negative thought patterns (see Beck, 1972; Burns, 1990). But when behavioral sequences have become part of a rigid pattern of interacting with others, novel ways may be required to engage the family and community (Aponte, Zarski, Bixenstine, & Cibik, 1991).

The Case of Jennifer. The use of "sometimes" could occur throughout the opening exchanges. When mother tells Jennifer not to put on a show, the therapist can say, "sometimes kids don't know what else to do." When mother speaks of Jennifer not finishing her meal, the therapist can observe that, "sometimes kids have trouble finishing things." When the father tells Jennifer to speak up, the therapist could mention that "sometimes that is very hard for kids to do." When both parents are conveying their aggravation, the therapist might remark that, "sometimes parents lose their patience."

Therapeutic Tactic 6: Highlight Transactions and Similarities, not Individual Behaviors

As the initial family interview continues, the therapist may be better able to say things like, "you two really set each other off" to begin to focus on the circularity of certain interactions rather than focusing on the bad behavior of a particular individual. It is also possible, in a low key way, to identify similar emotional styles within the members of the family: "This is sure a feisty group of people." This comment suggests that the therapist admires this attribute as long as it is not making everyone in the family miserable. If it is, the family members need to readjust their view of themselves or tone down the style they may be highlighting as negative in one member of the family. Again, in the initial interview, these are also test comments. One can see how the family handles them and if they have any impact on the interactional repertoire. This tactic will serve as a bridge to the use of techniques that may be needed for even hotter interactions.

The Case of Jennifer. The therapist may have already attempted to highlight transactions and similarities by labeling everyone as angry. Because the initial exchanges are so sparse in the brief family contact, this is a harder tactic to use. Often it is most helpful after a number of similar interactions are noticed especially when the therapist's active management techniques do not create a shift in the family's interactional pattern.

☐ Techniques for Managing *Toxic* Family Relationships and Enhancing the Focus on the Problem

Therapists are at their best when their knowledge, clinical judgment, and empathic emotions determine the approach, rather than a set formula. For the beginning therapist, there are times when it is difficult to determine what has most influenced one's judgment. For instance, the new clinician is still learning the difference between the "gut" countertransferential experiences that are diagnostically useful versus the countertransference that flows from the therapist's own unconscious emotional experiences. Countertransferential responses are heightened in most family meetings, leading some clinicians to avoid meeting with the difficult family. However, if the only meeting format used in child work is the one that offers the clinician the most comfort and control, i.e., the one-to-one meeting, valuable information and opportunities for intervention can be lost. As a result, child therapists must feel comfortable entering into the cauldron of difficult family interactions.

Even if the therapist is familiar with the first techniques described above, she must still be prepared for the worst, as illustrated by the Weeds. The therapist must be prepared to encounter emotional storms between the parent and child, accusations on the part of the parent, and sullen withdrawal or acting out on the part of the child. If the contact is going to explore the interactional, emotional, and historical information required in an assessment, the therapist needs to detoxify some of the difficult exchanges within family meetings.

Remember, red flags of behavioral or psychiatric disorder within the child (as will be identified in the symptom or behavioral charts the parent and school fill out) will not be ignored. If the therapist fails to confront these toxic family-based behaviors, a cause or contributing factor to the child's problem can be missed. When the terrible communication that is being revealed is the baseline of the family, it is best to know this up front and then to be able to shape the treatment accordingly. Parents need to understand that they may be part of the problem, but they must be involved in the creation of a solution.

Each of these tactics assumes that the interaction the therapist is seeing represents the impact of multiple stresses that may have eroded a positive spirit between the parent and child. This initial assumption prompts interventions that look on the bright side of exchanges. The therapist attempts to reign in any toxic communicative patterns. When these efforts are effective, the therapist will be better able to assess the potential future level of function in the family.

When the toxic patterns continue despite the therapist's efforts, the termination of the family interview may be required. Even the experienced therapist may not be able to predict which meetings will have to be ended prematurely, but often the cues exist in the multiple misattributions, projections, and misreadings made between the child and parent. If the miscommunication and negativity cannot be diminished, the therapist must be prepared to terminate the family interview.

Detoxifying: Tactic 1: What You really Mean to Say is. . . ." Neutralizing Terrible Comments Made by Parents and Children

In difficult families, the parents may use "bad parentese," a language that alienates, diminishes, and negates the relationship to the child as well as the child's positive attempts at coping. (See Table 2.1.) The children in these families often have a behavioral repertoire (both verbal nonverbal) that negates the parent's care, authority, or values, called "bad childese." (See Table 2.2.) For example, when the parent looks at the child and says, "You never pay attention," the therapist can look at the child and say, "Mom and Dad really want you to do good listening." Here, attention is turned to the nature of the parent's goal, rather than focusing on the misbehavior. The therapist is also telling the child that the parents may have an empathic wish for the child to learn a skill, rather than simply sink the child in bad feelings. Similarly, when the child turns to the parent and says, "You are so stupid, I really hate you," a negative spiral of interaction is heightened. The therapist needs to have a way to translate the child's feelings into a wish or goal, using a comment that does not define blame, such

TABLE 2.1. Bad Parentese

Bad Parentese	**Therapist's Translations**
1. *Vague complaints*	Make concern specific/translate feelings/identify goals
You are so bad. I don't like what you do.	*To child*: Mom really wants you to listen to her. She wants you to be proud (looking at parent). *To parent*: Can you tell Johnny what makes you so mad? *To child*: Do you know what mistakes make your Mom so mad?
2. *Use of global negative attributions*	Break all or none frame.
You *never* listen to me!	*To child*: Are there some things that Mom tells you that are easier to do? *To parent*: All kids sometimes have trouble listening. We need to find out what makes it harder for Johnny.
3. *Toxic affect*	Gauge depth of affect—confront as serious risk and concern—use modifier as a trial
Do you think I can love you?	*To child*: Mom is worried that she isn't able to love you. Have you been feeling that Mom doesn't love you anymore? *To parent*: Are there still moments when you know how important/special your child is to you?
4. *Toxic Relationship*	Use therapeutic authority.
This is most often indicated by many nonverbal cues; interruptions, and nonsequitors; and a global lack of affirmation, even with the therapist "working the crowd" with translations, etc.	*To all*: Kids and families count on people caring about each other and learning how to talk things over and solve problems. It looks like there is a lot to learn here.
5. *Threats of abandonment*	Take seriously. Make a plan.
I don't want you in the house!	*To parent*: It's gotten so bad you're not sure you can take the right kind of care of your child. We can talk about who/what can help. *To child*: Even when there are lots of fights in a family, I know kids get very scared/worried about parents not wanting them, even though sometimes everybody is so upset they say they don't care and can't live together. How do you feel? (Although this is said to the child, it is a message to the parent. The therapist should monitor the parent's reaction.)
6. *Vague complaints coupled with toxic affective consequence*	Identify toxic affect. Clarify treatment as solution driven.
Stop acting like that, I can't stand you (I hate you, you are no good).	*To child*: Boy, Mom is really mad—those things she said can really hurt. Does she always say she hates you (can't stand you, feels you are worthless)? *To parent*: Has saying that to him/her really worked to help out?

TABLE 2.1. Continued

7. *Inappropriate consequences*	Affirm treatment goals.
If you keep acting like that, you can't visit your Dad (go on the field trip, have dinner).	*To all*: One of the things I'm going to be doing is to help you all think about *good* plans that help the family work better together.
8. *Denial of child's emotional reality*	Treat as red flag. Identify potential abuse issue. Explore separately and in family meeting.
Stop complaining. Nobody treats you bad. Don't tell those lies about people touching you. Doctor, you should see her when she hangs out in the neighborhood—she's such a tramp.	*To parent*: Why do you think your child would lie to you? *To child*: This is a place where kids and parents can talk about hard things. Would you ask your Mom if you can tell the doctor whatever you are concerned about?
9. *Neglect of child's needs (for attention, limits, or more work)*	Another red flag. Focus on communication. Identify parental responsibility.
I forgot that you failed the last quarter.	*To child*: Wow! Is Mom often so forgetful? *To parent*: Being a parent is like taking care of two people. You have to remember everything that is on your list to do and everything on your children's. We will try to figure out what to do with this, be cause therapy is more work for everyone—especially a parent.

as, "Gee, it sounds like you really wish things weren't so hard." When the therapist can neutralize either the parent or child's hostile comments, it has both diagnostic and prognostic meaning.

The translations noted in Tables 2.1 and 2.2 are used to facilitate a harmonious interview. At the same time, these translations should bring down the level of emotional negativity in the family or diminish misunderstanding or both. They should support positive emotional exchange and understanding. When emotional sparring or persistent misunderstanding and misattribution occur in the interview, the family may conclude that therapy is "no use; this is just like home."

The therapeutic interview should be *enough* like home so that the therapist can understand the emotional atmosphere and exchange, but it should make an initial contribution to assure that each party feels heard and accepted by the other family members, as well as by the therapist. Remember, since the family goes home with each other, their sense of acceptance of each other is as important as that which they may feel toward the therapist.

Detoxifying Tactic 2: Changing the Subject: Selective Ignoring of the "Old Conversation"—Shifting the Agenda

When the family continues to pursue negative interactions, instead of continuing to interpret or reframe, the therapist can take control of the interview. The family may

TABLE 2.2. Bad Childese

Bad Childese	Therapist's Translations
1. *Toxic Emotions*	Identify feelings. Explore structures in family for exchanges. Identify as wish for better feelings.
I hate you. Nothing you say is true. You're so stupid.	*To child*: You sound so mad. Can you tell me what makes you so mad? *To parent*: How does that make you feel when he says that? What are the rules in your family for how people tell each other about when they disagree or get mad?
2. *Denial of parental authority*	Clarify parental mandate.
You can't tell me what to do.	*To child*: Mom's job is to help you learn things—to remind you of your jobs and what you need to do. But I want to know what you are mad about so we can help your family work better together (message is also to parent).
3. *Denial of problem as disqualification of concern*	Identify therapeutic task. Identify treatment concern.
All you do is complain. You don't really care.	*To parent and child*: We're here together because we care about straightening something out. At the end of our meeting we'll make a plan to make sure we find out more about this problem and how often it happens.
4. *Globalization*	Redefine extremes. Focus on positives.
You never think I do anything right.	*To parent and child*: Everybody does some things right and some things wrong. I think we need to notice right things a lot more. *Exercise*: Tell parent to give three compliments a day. Write them down for the next therapy visit.
5. *Vague complaints*	Make concerns specific. Validate the child's emotions.
You never help me. You just don't understand.	*To child*: I'm glad you want help and want to be understood. This is just the place to get started, so you can say your feelings and we can all listen.
6. *Disengagement/denial of relationship*	Attempt to revitalize.
I don't care about you. So what? Yeah, yeah. You don't matter to me. You're not my mother/father (common to stepfamilies, adoption).	*To all*: Sometimes it's hard to care because nobody seems to have a good idea about how to make things better. *To parent*: Are you as discouraged as he/she is? When are the times when you all connect and things seem to work?

TABLE 2.2. Continued

7. *Severing connectedness*	Evaluate risk.
You can't talk. You don't know anything about me.	*To both*: I always worry when kids feel like they can't talk or be honest with their parents. It means something is really wrong. Parents are the people whom kids should be able to count on most.
8. *Threats of abandonment*	Clarify reality; i.e., attempt to derail parental authority or failed relationship. Explore success.
I want to live with Grandma. You don't really love me.	*To child*: Mom and Dad can still love a kid even if their rules are hard. So we need to figure out where things are better and why. *To parent*: You looked upset when Johnny said that–is that true? How is it that Johnny does better at Grandma's?
9. *Acting out*	
Running away. Missing curfew. Taking money for drugs.	Evaluate risks. Treat as communication. Treat as comment on relationship. Treat as avoidance of normal developmental tasks.

have some complaints and conversations that quickly seem so stuck, "the old conversation," that it is not worthwhile to follow them. In these most difficult families, their style of communicating about problems compounds their problems. This tactic in the family interview involves engaging the family in a kind of restructured exchange that does not follow *their* rules. Remember, it is surprising how little need most families have to follow logically the points that other family members have made, so that the new therapist need not worry about potentially alienating the family.

Highly structured questions are useful. It is often useful to begin by asking if there has been a time in which the problem has not existed. If there has never been a less troublesome period in the family's history, especially when their interactions appear to be ominous as well as locked in, the therapist should make sure to cover high risk behaviors (trauma, suicidal or aggressive acting out) before turning to other details. The therapist can gather developmental history, review other mental health issues in the family, or discuss other treatments that exist or have existed.

The Case of Jennifer. The therapist, in reading the emotional atmosphere of the parents, could decide to quickly move the focus of attention from the child to the parents' needs by exploring a phase in family life when "things were different" to see if they can recall a more positive and functional time of family life. The therapist could choose to explore whether the family had any support network or what it was like for the parents as children themselves. The therapist could discuss the major role shift the father might be experiencing from a worker to a full-time househusband and sympathize with the tremendous changes that the wife may be experiencing as well. In these efforts, the therapist is setting aside the current family interactions in order to build an alliance based on potential family strengths. As in the presentation of most difficult families, the therapist makes sure to ask about the presence of potential trauma.

Detoxifying Tactic 3: Why Labels are not Always Bad: The Use of Labeling (Pesty Brother) in Common Family Dilemmas

When a therapist can identify a common challenge in the course of the child's or the family's development, it can be helpful to label it for the family. The therapist's externalization is in the service of placing the noted behavioral concerns as part of predictable patterns of interaction or difficulties that relate to normal development. The use of these labels should help to enhance a sense of positive acceptance of normal family challenges. Even when parents are overwhelmed by other stresses, the developmental challenges of their child may still mobilize their attention and love. Hopefully, the therapist can use this concern to help the parent identify and recognize other stresses that could be modified.

Although there are times when these "reframes"[7] may seem reductionistic, therapists must remember that using these does not eliminate clinical judgment. Developmental stages bring along their pluses and minuses, which parents may not understand. The stress and behavioral difficulties experienced by parents become readily accepted after pediatricians explain "the terrible twos." In the initial family contact and assessment, there may be an opportunity to quickly identify normal stresses that occur within the family context. These can be helped by a psychoeducational approach and clear instructions that utilize some of the therapeutic tactics above.

The Case of Jennifer. In this case, although the 4-year-old sister is identified as a trigger to some of Jennifer's more troublesome interactions, the therapist has already noted the system of blame that the family uses. As a result, normalizing the problems of "pesty sisters" (or brothers) would perpetuate this unfruitful perspective. It might be valuable to see if a label could be used to help externalize this family's stress to other systems. The therapist might explore the "terrible" disability system for the father or the way employers make such poor accommodations for working parents, like mother.

Detoxifying Tactic 4: When Enough Is Enough—Stopping a Family Meeting

Once some heated family exchanges begin, the initial therapeutic tactics may be of little avail. Despite the best efforts of experienced clinicians, some family interviews need to be discontinued. When the decision to stop a family interview is made, a therapist might be tempted to blame herself. This response would obscure the power of the family dynamic and blind the clinician to potential opportunities for the family. The decision should be viewed as a clinical choice and not as a defeat. In announcing the decision to the family, the therapist should highlight the destructive cycle in which they have engaged. The therapist, as a witness to the horrendous enactments that

[7]Reframes can be used in a wide variety of clinical contexts. See LaClave & Brack, 1989; Gerber, Reiff, & Ginsberg, 1996; Himelein & McElrath, 1996; Morse, 1997.

have brought the difficulty of the home immediately into the office, must be centered enough to hold that information. Then both the parents and the child must be confronted separately and, perhaps, be comforted by the therapist's knowledge of how "serious" the problem really is.

In order for a clinician to choose to stop a family meeting, some mental preparation for the kinds of difficulties children and families enact is necessary. The security a therapist may have with the decision to stop a meeting is associated with a number of parallel questions that test a clinician's sense of "therapeutic authority" in the office: Whose responsibility is it if the child begins to make a mess or act rude? What if the child has a tantrum? What if the adolescent storms out of the office and disappears around the comer? While these are not everyday events, they do occur. They are always experienced more acutely when therapists do not know what to do and are uncertain about the value, meaning, or nature of their own position and sense of responsibility. A sense of therapeutic authority may not be achieved easily, but it is one of the more important developmental challenges that therapists face.

What a therapist may choose to do is also influenced by the nature and type of physical space the therapist occupies. How preoccupied will the therapist be by the impact on other people nearby of the child's screaming? When the child storms out of the office, is the surrounding neighborhood safe; does the child know how to get home, or does the child have to hang out in the parking lot of a suburban office? Is there a reasonable space indoors where the child can play while the parents are seen alone? All of these ingredients will need to be considered as part of the background of the clinical decision.

☐ Disturbed Attachment: Unavailable Emotional Connections

The techniques described above have focused on those difficult families whose behavior is out of control in the therapist's office. The family may be focused on what is wrong with their child, or be hostile or degrading, but they are there. The families who never bring their child to therapy present an often greater dilemma to other systems of care, such as schools, as well as challenging the mental and physical health of the child. The techniques noted above are irrelevant. The parent is unlikely to ever bring a child to an evaluation!

The vacant, abusive, unavailable, or emotionally neglectful parent is often impossible to see, so engagement falls to someone else in the child's world. At the point at which another agency becomes involved in the child's life, that agency may request an evaluation. These presenting problems fall into zone 2, just as the case of the Weeds introduced the reader to a zone 4 dilemma (see below). Treatment planning must be altered accordingly, as illustrated in the case below.

> Sally, a 7-year-old first grader, was brought for an evaluation by her school counselor. The school counselor explained that the school was requesting an evaluation because Sally was often caught up in her own world, sometimes was unpredictably aggressive, and seemed to need constant one-on-one attention. The child came to school daily, was always well enough dressed, and had never reported any physical punishment or activity that could have led the school to report concerns to the child welfare agency.
>
> When there were problems at school, the attempts to reach the parent were often

stymied. The parent's phone had been disconnected. A neighbor would be called and there was no information on the whereabouts of the parent. When the mother was reached, it was reported that "she sounded out of it." The counselor reported that one year ago there was a period when Sally came to school looking dirty and disheveled and was often late to school. A report had been filed. There had been a home investigation and no finding was made. Shortly thereafter, Sally looked better cared for again.

In the interview with Sally, she rapidly engaged in play. She soaked up the examiner's attention and was eager to sit on the examiner's lap in order to complete the drawing tasks that were given. She talked about how much she wanted to be a rabbit. She said she had had a bunny but it was now in Bunny Heaven. All of her drawings at school were about bunnies and she had to have her stuffed bunny with her every day.

As the details of her day were explored, it was evident that a great deal of her care was rendered by her big sister. She reported that her big sister had gone to college last year, but she came back home after "some trouble," which Sally could not explain. She talked about her mother's friends who came to the house a lot and that they all "took medicine."

She knew that her mother's medicine required her mother to go to the hospital every morning. As a result, her big sister, and sometimes her aunt in the apartment above, helped her get ready for school. She mentioned that sometimes her mother was so busy she forgot to make supper but that when she went and yelled at her, her mother remembered.

Sally appeared quite dejected when the interview was over but said she was happy to return to school. Her teacher was one of her "favorite people," and she felt really mad when they had to have a "stupid substitute."

The school counselor had gone to the mother's home during the interview to bring the mother back to the office so that the mother could receive the therapist's feedback as well as the counselor's feedback. The mother was not at home when the counselor arrived. Sally's sister did not know where her mother was.

In this clinical vignette, a traditional outpatient treatment is not possible. Mother is barely available for Sally's care and less so for treatment. The therapist infers that the mother was in the town's methadone maintenance program. Without this information being acknowledged, or mother being present to sign a release (were she willing), the therapist could not even explore the possibility of a parenting program for Sally's mother within the recovery program. The therapist may be able to support the programs that will help Sally adjust as best as possible within her school. Other after-school programs or opportunities for healthy peer-based activities can be supported but a family-based child therapy is, at this point, impossible.

The most severe later outcomes in cases of physical or sexual abuse are associated with the failure of emotional empathy and emotional neglect during childhood (Herman, Perry, & van der Kolk, 1989). Even a child's abuse can be ameliorated by the presence of the child's experience of caring and attentiveness through consistently supportive relationships. The nature of the child's relationship with the nonoffending parent is as critical as the safety intervention that protects the child from the offender. This knowledge should prompt child and family therapists to develop their treatment plans around the way healthy connections are established.

The crisis of abuse often triggers a protective agency's intervention when there are clear signs of physical abuse, severe neglect, or concerns about sexual trauma. The signs of a failed parent-child attachment may be more subtle and deserve as much attention. The treatment must plan to promote the long-term recovery of the child's ego strengths and emotional equilibrium. These depend upon the child's relationships that provide love and limits and understand the child's experiences.

When the child's primary relationships within the family do not respond, ancillary relationships need to be cultivated. The value of mental health consultation to teachers and other child care providers should help them maintain their connection to a child whose care can be emotionally demanding. In some cases, the providers must also be helped to bear the frustration of witnessing the impact of a family's failure, while being as powerless as other agencies to change it.

☐ Identifying the Nature of the Challenge: The Zone of Difficulty in Family and Child

The insurance-based practices of most clinicians means that the populations they see tend to be characterized by families whose parenting skills are reasonable and children who, although they may have some symptoms, exhibit many other strengths. However no office practitioner fails to see those children or families where significant difficulties appear. In order to appreciate the different levels of function that may characterize the family or the child, it helps to begin by visualizing the normal distribution of strengths and weaknesses that exists within any culture's population of families and children. The bell shape of these normal curves suggest that 2 to 3 standard deviations out, there are serious degrees of compromise that can be imagined within the child or in family dynamics or parental functioning.

We have presented two very different families, in the cases of the Gardeners and the Weeds. The initial contact in each case should have given the reader a sense of the level of function of the child and the parents and the way the family functioned together. The reader probably began to formulate the nature of the problem and the issues contributing to the presenting difficulty. Before the clinician can shape the treatment plan, the level of severity of the dysfunction in the child and the parents must be weighed. Without identifying the level of severity, the therapist will not be able to communicate, either to a parent or a distant insurance reviewer, the rationale for the resources needed.

A way to conceptualize the interaction of the level of severity (or functionality) will help the reader develop a sense of some broad principles that can be applied to treatment planning. This point of view does not require the clinician to determine causality but rather represents a clinical judgment about the current strengths and deficits displayed. This process of assessment is one that is parallel to the clinical formulation: for treatment planning both are needed. There are troubled children who come from healthy families, as there are children without active symptom profiles–and who function relatively well in the community and their schools–who come from very dysfunctional families. Similar formulations, depending upon level of severity will require very different treatment plans.

For instance, we know that many children with uncomplicated ADHD can be simply treated in a pediatrician's office. A therapist's consultation may help establish the diagnosis and the treatment may be tailored to enhance the skills of the parents by suggesting which popular and useful books on the nature of the disorder, techniques of behavior management, and parenting strategies may be most in order. The child may also benefit from an opportunity to discuss with the therapist and in family meetings what it means "to be hyper" (as some parents say) so that the child's self-esteem can be supported. The pediatrician may elect a course of pharmacotherapy, either with or without a pediatric psychiatric or neurological consultation. On the other hand, some children with ADHD have diagnostic presentations that are complicated by other comorbidities in the child, tremendous environmental challenges (social class, access to supportive education, opportunities for constructive afterschool programs), and family dysfunction. The nature of the parental psychopathology and surrounding adversities will exert considerable influence on what treatment plan can be developed. Intensive individual treatment for the child may need to be combined with recommendations for parenting skills training (where individual treatment to address the adult psychopathology may need to take place before the parents can utilize this suggestion) as well as family therapy. In these cases, much systems work, school consultation, and case management will be vital for the child's well being. Other agencies may need to be brought in to supervise the child's care within the family.

Figure 2.1 shows that the increasing severity of the dysfunction in the child or the family will define different regions of functionality, which create four different "zones" of care. (See Figure 2.1.) Depending upon the zone in which the child and family fall, the treatment approach to family and child will need to vary in nature, emphasis, or degree of intensity. The first instance, an uncomplicated and mild case of ADHD where the child functions relatively well and good parenting capacities exist, falls into zone 1. Here treatment can be focused and is readily assimilated by both the parents and the child. On the other hand, the second case requires a very different treatment approach and falls into zone 4. The way these four different zones of care modify treatment planning will be discussed in greater detail in chapter 4.

What follows is an introduction to the four zones.

Zone 1. The Zone of Normal Developmental Achievements and "Good Enough" Parenting

Here the capacities of both the child and family fall within the realm of "good enough." The background level of competency is such that the chief complaint can often be focused and usually affects isolated areas of function. The concept of "good enough" has been drawn from Winnicott's early observations of the wide range of parenting behavior that could be associated with children's success (Winnicott, 1965). Some studies have determined that a variety of parenting behaviors and family styles can support children's positive development. In addition to the strengths that exist in family life, the children in zone 1 are also considered "good enough." Their learning, temperament, and emotional adjustment is adequate. They exhibit expected age appropriate developmental achievements and concerns.

In zone 1, the symptomatology or the problems that are the focus of the referral represent challenges, which follow simple trauma, adjustment difficulties within the family or child, repairable relational-interactional difficulties, rectifiable problems in parental skills or understanding, and the mild range of "difficult" temperamental issues or mild to moderate symptoms of identifiable *DSM* disorders.

While some "good enough" families may need some intermittent support over the long-term developmental course of their child, they use the tools and understanding

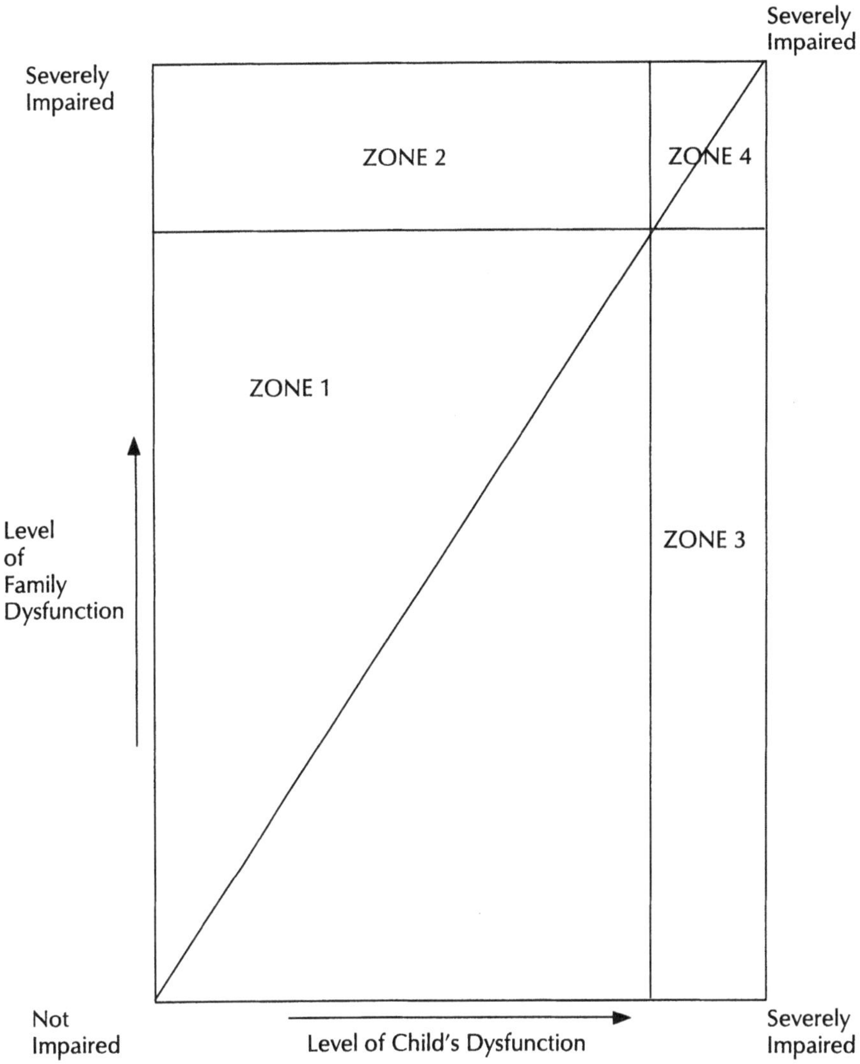

FIGURE 2.1.

the therapist offers readily. They adjust their emotional reactions or refine their parenting techniques. The child's "good enough" development of ego skills also permits the therapist to help the child process affect, manage symptoms, and further develop social-emotional problem solving, which keep the child's development on a healthy course. Most mild to moderate symptomatic presentations of psychiatric disorders in the child lend themselves to straightforward treatments.

Most MCOs assume their patient populations are zone 1 problems. This is most often the case. Since people who receive insurance through employer programs tend to have the ego skills required for work, they also often have regular support systems, communication skills, and healthy family relationships. The structure of the workplace and fiscal security help people function at their best. All of these serve to strengthen health and coping. In addition to mental health, studies have shown that overall health and longevity increase as a worker's income level and power and control in their job increase.

Of course, not all workers have the same level of social and emotional skill as the healthiest members of the workforce. In some cases, their partners may have significant mental health issues. These deficits may not be immediately apparent. Often the subtle character problems (narcissistic or borderline features), poor interpersonal skills, or lack of respect for a partner or another family member will intrude on the straightforward resolution of the problem area. The seeming zone 1 family may be close to the margin of zone 2. In divorced or openly antagonistic marriages, the children are often triangulated into relationships and internal emotional conflicts, which undermine their function. While these impacts are often hidden in the family's presentation, they can powerfully affect the resolution of a child's difficulty. On the one hand, the continuing negative attitude of a parent that can be based on projections from the parents' own past may take some time to uncover. On the other hand, the child's symptoms may become more serious and begin to suggest a zone 3 problem. These cases will be discussed in Part II, chapter 7.

Zone 2, The Zone of Child Despair: The Search for Resources that Support the Child's Health, Well Being, and Development in the Face of Parental Failure

In these instances, the child's adaptive and cognitive–emotional capacities fall within the normal range, yet the family's function is severely compromised by parental, familial, or environmental disturbances. The child's emotional turmoil is appropriate within the context of the parenting failure. As in the case of Sally, the family's failure may not have progressed to the point that she is removed from the home, but the continuing adversity takes its toll. However, the child's intellectual and emotional resources are "good enough" and the child may even be considered "resilient." In this zone, an affect of despair may characterize the referred child and may be prominent in the therapist's countertransference.

Treatment is focused on helping the child process the affect associated with the family's disruption and the child's losses. Therapy should also facilitate the child's connection to other current caretakers. More often than not, these families will not bring these children to therapy. Therapy may be provided in a school setting that recognizes the child's emotional needs. Other family members who continue to care for the child will also need support in understanding the child's responses if they are accessible to the therapist. The therapist's role as advocate for resources and ancillary community opportunities that promote healthy experiences will be needed.

As a result of the preexisting family turmoil, the family may not have medical insurance. Unlike the families in zone 2 who have some access to a mental health benefit, much of these children's treatment will depend upon the nature of state resources designed for underinsured or uninsured children. The child may have a Medicaid benefit that is the result of the child being placed in the custody of the state. Many states are now developing managed care programs for administering these benefits.

Zone 3. The Zone of Parental Grief: The Search for Ways to Support and Foster the Adaptive Capacities of a Moderately to Severely Compromised Child

In this zone, the parent's functions are not compromised. It is the child who presents with a significantly impairing developmental, psychiatric or medical disorder.

Therapy, or ancillary interventions, focuses on building and enhancing the child's adaptations. Treatment helps the parents advocate for and provide appropriate resources for the child. The major work in therapy with the parents is working through the grief that the parents may experience and reexperience in each new developmental stage. The treatment will also work to foster the parents' understanding of how best to manage their child. As these children mature and gain insight or perspective on their handicaps, they too must manage a grieving process.

Before the onset of grief, the parents must contend with the process of accepting the diagnosis. Parents may wish that their child has some disorder other than that defined by the therapist. For instance, some parents may come to child and family clinicians with an often unconscious hope that the clinician will define a "learning block" rather than some degree of retardation. Some parents may travel from clinician to clinician rather than face the emotional burden that the parent may feel by facing some psychiatric or medical disorder. To complicate matters, some parents may feel some diagnoses are more blaming of them than others are, or they may respond to a diagnosis with tremendous guilt.

One parent, a computer programmer, brought a child for assessment because he was not playing well with the plastic ball and bat he had decided to use to engage his son. He was furious when the clinician clarified the child had an autistic spectrum disorder and there were no easy answers about getting his child to play like a "real boy." In this instance, the parent wanted the "horse" of a motor planning problem, not the "zebra" of autistic features. Especially in the parents of an only child, a sense of perspective is more difficult to establish. On the other hand, some parents can adjust themselves more easily to the difficulty being "within" the child, but they balk in altering their parenting style to accommodate the child's cognitive or emotional style. There is also considerable work that needs to be done with handicapped children to promote their best possible outcome.

The "zebras" of childhood disorder include the most severe of the internalizing or externalizing disorders (see chapters 5 and 6), the unusual developmental disorders (autistic spectrum disorders or mental retardation syndromes), or the rarer and more serious psychiatric disorders in childhood (bipolar disorder, early onset schizophrenia, or unusual delusional disorders). All of these disorders place severe strains on parents and families: There are severe medical disorders or malformations that place children in zone 3. Many cases of severe psychiatric disorder as well as severe medical illness may require long-term therapy with the individual and family.

There are children who suffer traumatic treatment or neglect and initially present in zone 2, because their presentation may superficially appear adequate under the cloak of apathy and fear. Following placement with intact and well-functioning parents, they may develop severe behavioral and psychiatric impairment. At this point these children would be classified as zone 3 (the zone 2 to 3 switch). As a result, ongoing psychotherapy is indicated to help resolve the past trauma and to promote a better adaptation within the current supportive relationships. Psychopharmacological management of the child may be indicated for some of these disorders.

By definition, zone 3 families are those where the parent is likely to be employed and where the parents function well. These children with severe disabilities are often covered by an MCO under their parents' mental health benefit. Because the therapy for the child may vary in intensity or type, the family's benefit may often be exceeded. In addition, the treatment may require other resources besides the child and family therapy. Advocacy for specialized school programs, the development of adaptive skill building activities, and respite care may be needed. While this advocacy and case management function is required from the therapist, it is often not reimbursable through most insurance companies. These issues must be discussed in the development of the treatment plan and a fiscal agreement.

In some cases, the child's psychiatric or medical disorder may permit the family to access funds managed by departments of mental health or specialized programs even when their insurance coverage is not exhausted. These funds may support interventions that are not traditionally insurance reimbursable and vary from state to state. This is another reminder of the basic principle that fiscal discussions need to take place early in the treatment planning process. "Zebras" can consume tremendous resources, and families should develop a sense of what resources they can commit without becoming overburdened by debt.

Identifying Horses, Knowing about Zebras: The Rare Disorders that Constitute the Spectrum of Difficulty in the Child in Zone 3. Therapists, for the most part, deal with the "horses" of human experience, i.e., those problems that most commonly present themselves. However, given the wide range of children who are referred for help, cases with complex symptomatology will arrive at a therapist's office. Therapists need to be familiar with symptom complexes whose red flags alert the concerned practitioner to the rare, but serious disorders that occur in childhood, the "zebras" of child psychiatric disorder.

The "zebras" on the landscape often require intensive treatment where gains may be slow and where the disease may continue to erode the child's adjustment. This painful reality must be reviewed in developing the treatment plan with the parents. Diffuse behavioral control problems are the early presentation of many serious disorders in childhood that often look like ADHD. The severity of the symptoms, and their variety, is often a cue that a more serious disorder may evolve. While the therapist can clarify the hope that both therapist and parent may have for a "horse" as the child's problem, more serious diagnoses should be discussed. The therapist will need to be clear that the treatment will benefit the child by enhancing coping skills, increasing emotional awareness, and developing appropriate behavioral controls and better social problem solving, which will serve the child well even were symptoms to worsen. While troublesome symptoms may persist, or others develop, this focus is still germane. When the presence of multiple symptoms (comorbidities) continue to raise red flags, a therapist should encourage the family to prepare for and facilitate additional diagnostic psychiatric consultation, hospitalization, or pharmacotherapy when appropriate.

Clinicians must be able to consider that behind the current horse of an attentional disorder, there may lurk a zebra, an affective disorder (either depressive or bipolar) or an emerging complex anxiety disorder. Most of these diagnoses unfold with time.

One way to approach this perspective results from "playing the numbers." Therapists may know that the incidence of a "difficult temperament" in children in the preschool era is about 10% (Thomas & Chess, 1977). The incidence of ADHD is 3%–5%, although some authors suggest up to a 10% incidence or more, but this diagnosis accounts for 50% of child psychiatric clinic referrals (Cantwell, 1996). The incidence of early presentation of bipolar disorder is probably greater than 1% (Lewinsohn, Klein, & Seeley, 1995). In other words, clinics will most often see only about 10%-15% of the overall population of children in a given area; most of those children with externalizing disorders will have a diagnosis of ADHD. However, some small percentage of those children with an ADHD diagnosis will go on to develop a more severe disorder (Biederman et al., 1996).

Clinicians also know that a child's functional level is strongly affected by other familial or school-based stresses. A child who has a mild attentional problem without learning disabilities can manage well with good parenting supports. He or she may only come to our attention when a comorbid anxiety disorder evolves. However, in the presence of learning disabilities or severe language problems (receptive or expressive), the child's function may be dramatically worse. The therapist must be able to consider when neurological consultation or psychological testing (including neuropsychological consultation) or both should be used (Dinklage, 1994; Leimkuhler, 1994). Each clinician in different areas of the country may have different practice patterns, as well as very different access to these consultations.

Clinicians must be prepared for these unusual cases. In addition, the therapist must be prepared for the parent's reactions. Since the therapist will be giving feedback about parenting skills and family issues that may have a bearing on the child's outcome, the work of continuing care may be as stressful as the experience of initially imparting the diagnosis.

Zone 4. The "Most at Risk"—The Zone of Therapeutic Despair

This is the zone in which the therapist often feels a sense of helplessness or hopelessness. This feeling is often a countertransferential mirror of both the child's and the parents' feelings. The parents feel helpless about getting the child to behave and the child feels hopeless about the nature of family life. In these cases, severe compromises appear within the family's and the child's development. These deficits are expressed by emotional, behavioral, and learning compromises in both parent and child. The parent's disability may include severe addiction, psychosis, and may be associated with the neglect and abuse of the child. A combination of psychiatric, developmental, behavioral, and learning disturbances are also present in the child.

These cases often require a full spectrum of services to support both the child and the family. Acute care services for children may be accessed repeatedly. Treatment is often crisis intervention since these families often have little consistent followup on their aftercare plans. Parental psychopathology may lead to repeated filings to a child welfare agency. Family turmoil may create intense and confusing symptoms in any family member. Many different agencies may be involved. High levels of coordination and case management are required. Specialized programs have been developed to work with this population.

Zone 4 patients are much less likely to be covered by managed care. While there are increasing efforts throughout the country to develop managed care programs for the

Medicaid population, these cannot easily address the multiple types of problems these children and their families experience. Specific programs are developing around the country that fund interventions for the severely emotionally disturbed (SED) child or adolescent and their family using combined monies from school systems, child protective agencies, and the courts. Some discussion of the management of the presentation of zone 4 families will be found in chapter 4.

The authors feel that the challenges presented by the care and management of zone 2, 3, and 4 cases (once the diagnostic is completed) are substantially different from those of most zone 1 children and families. As a result, a separate volume will be dedicated to the potential treatment techniques for zones 2, 3, and 4. Treatment of these zones will be noted where the potential seems to exist to move the child or family's function toward zone 1 by the therapist's intervention. Once the child or parent's level of function has improved, the other general principles of treatment described here will apply.

The implementation of most treatment plans will depend greatly upon the strengths of the parent. As a result, the next step in the evaluation phase is the full assessment of the parents. In all but the simplest of child problems, where the family's strengths are immediately apparent and can be evaluated in the first contact, a parent evaluation should be completed. The level of parenting functions and any comorbid adult psychopathology should be assessed. The parameter of this assessment is the subject of the following chapter.

CHAPTER 3

Assessing Parental and Family Function: Psychopathology in Parents That Can Undermine Children's Development. The Impact on Treatment Planning

Simply put, for children to succeed (whether in therapy or life) they need their parents' love, parental guidance, and limits, and they need their parents to understand and appreciate their "real life" struggles, feelings, and temperament. Successful treatment requires parents to accommodate to the needs of the child; clarify, set, and reinforce behavioral expectations; and follow through on the tasks required to support the child's social and emotional development. As a result, the therapist needs to gauge the parents' ability to provide this care and then to evaluate the parents' capacity to make changes in their own behavior to meet the child's needs.

The first step in the assessment, as discussed in the first two chapters, should have revealed to the therapist the way the child and family approach the presenting problem together, the parent's interactional and emotional style with the child, and prominent symptoms or troublesome behaviors in the child. These last cues should have been gathered from the data from the behavioral checklists and initial child contact. Following this initial child and family contact, the second step requires that the therapist meet with the parents separately. The meeting will serve several functions: to further engage the family, to explore the parent's level of function, as well as share some initial ideas about treatment. A further review of the history of the problem can take place. The meeting can define the child's strengths and weaknesses. Any medical concerns can be further clarified. In addition, the meeting permits the parents to disclose any information the family might not have wanted to raise in front of the child. Privacy also allows the therapist to review any family vulnerabilities, a history of mental or emotional symptoms in the family, or other problems. During this meeting the therapist will be evaluating the strategy the therapist will use to engage the parents in the necessary changes that the family will have to make for the benefit of the child. In chapter 4, we will discuss the third, and last, step of framing the treatment plan with the child and in the family-based meeting to follow.

The treatment will rely upon how the parents understand their own emotional responses so that they can consider how to create the best possible fit with their child's needs. If that behavior can be fostered in the course of the parenting component of the therapy, it will continue to help the child thereafter. For example, the therapist can explain that anxiety can be contagious, so that anxious parents with an anxious child may need to change their own reactions. A good balance between support and limiting the impact of the child's anxiety on necessary activities, like going to school or visiting friends, will need to be struck. As another example, parents who must set limits on an overactive child need to develop some detachment so that they are not feeling constantly angered or frustrated with their child's impulsivity. Some emotional distance can help them work with their child in a consistent and caring way. If the mother is patient, while the father is reactive and physically punitive, this difference needs to be addressed.

In the parents' meeting, the therapist is laying the groundwork to help the parents understand why some investigation of their life history, their relationship to each other, and possible symptoms in their own lives is necessary. Since the original presentation of the problem is about the child, the therapist can convey that how the child affects the parent and the nature of the parents' responses will influence how the therapist balances child, family, and parent meetings to achieve the best outcome. Questions about the marriage or other family relationships should be focused through the therapist's reminders that changes in the parenting style or family may help the child function better.

The best way to begin the parent meeting is to use the shared experience from the initial family contact, as well as to review the results of the initial homework. The initial homework suggestions serve to further evaluate the parents' ability to put into action their connection and concern for the child, no matter what barriers the therapist may have suspected. The homework will concretize the parents' motivation and reliability or the obstacles they experience. The therapist can also provide concrete examples to the parents about the child's style and the observed reactions of the parents.

In the "perfect" case (a zone 1 child and family), the homework suggestion was to count fun times the child had with friends as well as the times her friends made her mad. When the parents bring this information to the parent meeting, the therapist will better understand how the parents and child work together. The therapist will use this information to test how the parents might respond to the child being angry with them. In the "less than perfect case," the parents' ability to cooperate will be tested by whether they each do their checklists and whether they can attend and engage in the school-based systems meeting. This experience will set the stage for the discussion about treatment compliance with the Weeds in the parent meeting to follow.

Where significant parenting handicaps exist, as in the "less than perfect case," parents will be angered by a child centered therapy which does not resolve the problem. Unless the therapist quickly addresses the importance of the parents' responses and what the parents need to provide for the child, the parents can disengage further from their responsibilities. An unconscious conclusion that some parents draw is that "the therapist knows it's Johnny's problem since he's the one getting to play." Parents who are vulnerable in this way will also be angered by the demands the therapist begins to place on them later in the treatment plan. When the treatment does not secure a parental alliance, the outcome will be poor in any event. When, during the course of a child-based therapy, the failure of the parents to commit to the work that they need to do is noted, the focus of treatment is best moved to the family. It is better to ascertain this complication sooner rather than later.

Whenever possible, potential obstacles in the parenting or family makeup should be anticipated and quickly identified in the parent evaluation. When there are characterological, symptomatic difficulties or an emotionally charged history in the parent, the therapist should educate the parent that the work on behalf of the child may activate potentially painful emotional experiences, conflicts within the parent, or increase the parent's symptoms. A fairly straightforward example follows.

> A 4-and-one-half-year-old preschooler, Danielle, was referred for therapy following a car accident in which she was struck in a crosswalk and her leg broken. She developed a phobic, post-traumatic response that led to her refusing to leave her stroller anywhere outside of the home. Her mother was anxious and fearful about both her only girl child's traumatic reaction as well as about the "risks in everyday life" that she could neither protect her child from nor control. During the parent contact, the mother revealed her own history of a panic disorder but felt she had learned how to manage it. Her symptoms were no longer active. She felt she could implement a behavioral program for her daughter and work with the therapist to make a book for Danielle about the accident.
>
> A desensitization program was begun following the opportunity to use play and family dialogue about the accident and the attendant feelings, further supported by the bookmaking technique (see chapter 6) the mother had begun. This therapeutic combination prompted rapid progress until the phase of crossing the street was to be reinstituted. When mother reported Danielle's extreme reluctance, mother noted her own anxiety level was heightened as well.
>
> The therapist requested that the rest of the meeting be spent with the mother alone during which time the mother revealed aspects of her own traumatic history as well as the onset of another series of panic attacks (which she had reported previously) whenever she came to the crosswalk with her daughter. The mother, in the initial parent meeting, had revealed a history of panic disorder but had not wanted to discuss her prior history of trauma. As the work with the therapist had progressed so well, the additional element of professional trust permitted her to describe this complication in her daughter's care so it could be reviewed in a way to permit the treatment to go forward.

In this case, as in many others, the therapist's familiarity and skill with adult treatment modalities are quite important. In a family-based treatment, which is based on respect, understanding, and acceptance, the therapist is more likely to be able to develop a parental alliance and partnership that includes all family members. A therapist may be tempted to discount certain parents, but our recommendation is to work with a level of acceptance of even some troublesome, but not devastating, parental behaviors. Often this can be done in the context of a family-based treatment (Minuchin, Montalvo, Guerney, Rosman, & Schumer, 1967; Minuchin & Fishman, 1974). This alliance will enable the parent to reveal extreme feelings and then to work with the therapist to contain and manage them. Often the therapist may need to do a period of work with the parent to facilitate the treatment plan. Since the success of the treatment depends upon the cooperation, compliance, and ability of the parent to follow through on treatment recommendations, parents must be treated.

While the mother in the case reported above had reported her prior history of panic disorder in the course of the review of the family history in the initial parent meeting, treatment had proceeded because the mother did not feel her prior symptoms would be an active barrier to participating in the treatment of her child. The mother reported no active symptoms and denied any experience of current anxiety in working with the plan the therapist had defined. The mother's current anxiousness, she explained, was associated with her fears about the potential impediment to her daughter's development that her daughter's reactions might pose. It was only at the point in the desensitization process that the mother became fearful and guilty that she would be retraumatizing her daughter that her own history of trauma became a problem for her.

At the point at which a parent's symptoms are activated, as part of the work with the child, the therapeutic alliance and original parent evaluation should facilitate the further exploration of the impact of the problem and the additional complication that is revealed. The therapist will be able to consider with the parent the potential value of any intervention, from a behavioral to a dynamic or relational treatment to a medication intervention. In addition, treatment for the adult's symptoms is another facet of working with a family's resources or the way they access their insurance benefits. Depending on the level and nature of the parent's past trauma or symptoms, the therapist can assess with the parent their choices. The parent should understand the importance of resolving the difficulty so that the barrier that has developed in the work with the child can be removed. A referral to a colleague may be necessary.

☐ Balancing the Parental Alliance and the Parental Evaluation

Although the parent meeting is only the second meeting in the evaluative phase, it creates a new tightrope for the therapist to walk. The alliance must be secured while casting an objective eye on the nature of the parents. Not all parental difficulties are easily confronted or lend themselves readily to treatment. The major characterological difficulties, addictive disorders, or masked major mental illness may create enormous challenges in the treatment of children. When these are present, the therapist's definition of the zone of function of the child and parents will lead to how the treatment plan may need to be constructed. It is necessary to define as early as possible if a parent is unwilling to be treated or if the child's care and protection are at risk so that the process of filing a report with the state's child protective agency is addressed.

The authors are all too aware that the field of child or adolescent therapy has had a reputation for "parent bashing." At times, the difficulties of the child were simply blamed on the nature or attitudes of the parent. The most serious examples of this behavior in the field of mental health were enacted during the early years of the study in the 1940s, 1950s, and 1960s of childhood autistic and psychotic disorders. Parents were described as too cold (Rank, 1955), too close (Boszormenyi-Nagy, 1962), or the authors of a "double bind" for their psychotic family member (Bateson, Jackson, Haley, & Weakland, 1956). During this period of the early years in the study of serious mental illness and childhood disorder, the investigation of parental impact on a child's development was an understandable avenue to explore. It led to many other valuable ideas and interventions. The overzealous attitudes of the past should not now prompt a retreat from the fundamental need for parent evaluation or treatment. The central role parents play in shaping their child's emotional adjustment and coping skills along with the opportunities they provide for new experiences cannot be minimized.

Currently, the impact of children on parents is better understood, too. The attitudes and emotions that difficult children induce in parents continue to be studied in the field of child and family psychology. Since parents' own emotions and defenses are aroused by the behavior and experiences of their children as they parent, these important interactional elements must be considered. In the field of schizophrenia, this consideration is discussed in the multiple studies on expressed emotion (Butzlaff & Hooley, 1998), i.e., the measure of the level and intensity of expression of affect and conflict in the family. This concept has recently been extended to the study of parents with children with anxiety disorders with similar results. In these studies, relapse or higher levels of symptoms are correlated with high levels of expressed emotion (Hirshfeld, Biederman, Brody, Faraone, & Rosenbaum, 1997a). Parents and family members must develop new ways of managing conflict and communication. Finally, the study of childhood conduct disorders has shown that a central component of treatment and prevention is for parents to work on their disciplinary style as well as to engage their child in more prosocial activities.

Even in the "perfect cases," therapists may underestimate the degree to which their formulation of a child's difficulties may trigger new anxieties and fears in parents about their child's outcome, or, even in the first example, how guilty the "perfect" parents may feel about having in some way inhibited their child's ability to express anger. These concerns may be allayed in the course of the psychoeducational component of the treatment plan.

No matter how expert the therapeutic advice or how comforing the therapist may be, the parent will always face one irreducible fact: more work. If the child's temperament is sensitive or easily emotionally affected, whether as a result of a developmental issue or of symptoms of an anxiety disorder or depression, the parents' emotional attunement to the child and style of child management may need adjustment. When the problem involves family systems issues, for instance, conflict between parents, the alienation of one parent or another from the child, or marital tensions that are expressed through concerns displaced onto the child, the intervention exposes the emotional issues the parent was avoiding. It is difficult to grow a healthy child in the face of continuously troubled family relationships. How therapists understand the work of parents, parenting skills, and the relationship between these skills and adult psychopathology is the focus of the rest of this chapter. The three key components in parenting are love, limits, and real life.

Love

The first, and most important, element of parenting is the nature and expression of the parents' love for their child. The therapeutic assessment must consider the ways in which the parents experience and express their love for their child. The concept of "love" can provoke a wide-ranging discussion of philosophical, psychological, or relational issues. The clinical definition of love that will be drawn upon here is that of Harry Stack Sullivan (1953). He suggested that love is the ability of one person to treat another with the same importance that one treats oneself. The failure of parental love can have devastating consequences for the child's development.

> One New York Park Avenue mother brought her child for therapy because she experienced her child as oppositional. Gradually, the therapist came to understand that the mother had an untreated character disorder (for which she rejected treatment) that contributed to her vitriolic denunciations of her daughter. At various moments, she would look at her daughter and scream that she could not understand why she had been "cursed with this child. She was a shrimp; she would never be tall and elegant as she should have been. She should have been aborted." The tirade of anger and hatred would overcome the little girl. Mother acknowledged that these tirades would occur but would deny their frequency. In addition, if asked to discuss these with her daughter, she would minimize them or focus on the girl's bad behavior as their trigger.

This clinical situation, described by Dr. Clarice Kestenbaum (1997), is where the parent has wealth and lives in a society and culture that supports child therapy. In this zone of childhood despair (zone 2), the treatment had to focus on individual child therapy as the resource to be mobilized. Dr. Kestenbaum had to help this little girl understand that her mother had a mental illness. She analogized the little girl's mother to the wicked stepmothers of fairy tales in which artists depicted mothers with toads, snakes, and horrible creatures pouring out of their mouths. The little girl continued in a play therapy in which she could work through her despair. She created scenes of wicked witches, violent families, and a little girl's triumphs. As she did so, she was better able to avoid struggles with her mother and accept going off to play when her mother was in a "bad mood." In this case, neither insurance nor an MCO posed limitations on the treatment. There was no recommendation from a reviewer to focus on a behavioral treatment when a dynamic therapy was indicated. Unlike so many children who become victims of a parental mental illness, this child was able to be engaged and supported in an ongoing individual therapy that helped her master the emotions and questions aroused by the failure of her mother's love in this terrible dilemma.

The way in which this mother's love did not fail, however, was that she chose to provide a relationship for her child to help her cope. Her motherly love could not prevent her from disrupting the development of her child's secure *attachment*. The mother's *attunement* to the child's distress did lead to the search for treatment, although not a modification of her own style since her defenses prevented this. Her *commitment* to the child allowed the mother to draw on her resources to provide the finances for the therapy and to make sure the child could get to the appointment. These three concepts, attachment, attunement, and commitment, can help therapists evaluate the nature of parental love. (See Table 3.1.)

Attachment

Since evolution could not just depend upon a spontaneous outpouring of parental affection, mechanisms of early care were hardwired. Bowlby (1971), a seminal contributor to attachment theory in the field of child psychiatry, suggests a neurobiological element in the workings of attachment. Self-preservation might suggest that leaving the child in the path of the predator for a quick snack would permit the parent to escape (and later develop another hatchling), but the survival of the species took another turn. Bowlby's pioneering studies and review described what ethologists have called a "retrieving behavior."

TABLE 3.1. Parental love

Child's name
DOB:

Parent Evaluation: Love

1. How does the parent offer the child warmth, support, and love? Is it offered clearly in both verbal and nonverbal ways?

2. What does the parent feel are the child's needs? Are there problems with resources so that the provision of the basics of care (food, shelter, cleanliness, support, or education) are affected?

3. Does the parent appear attuned and receptive to the child's emotions and nonverbal signals? Can the parent listen attentively and positively to the child's concerns? Is discussion of feelings encouraged?

4. Does the parent understand the need for structure in the child's life? What are the ways that the parents use to create structure to help the child use those patterns in daily life?

5. Are there appropriate child centered activities? How does the parents' commitment support their use? Which activities?

Limits

6. How does the parent discipline or limit the child's troublesome behaviors? Does the child understand the parent's values?

7. Is the parent able to communicate about and resolve problems with the child?

Real Life

8. How does the parent understand the child's developmental level and the child's behavioral or tempermental style? Has this understanding existed at other developmental periods?

9. Does the parent understand any current stresses in the child's life?

10. Does the parent understand any *DSM-IV* diagnoses the child may have?

11. Is the parent well informed about the role of the child's medication (if any) in his or her life?

12. Is the parent able to comply with the demands of medical followup (e.g., meetings with the doctor, blood tests, other medical evaluations like EKGs, etc.) and regular administration of the medicine?

13. Does the parent have any *DSM-IV* diagnoses that affect the above? What challenges do they present to parenting?

This evaluation can be done with the parent. The therapist can use this discussion to focus the parent–therapist collaboration. It does not need to be done "on" the parent.

The neurobiological mechanisms that Bowlby suggested are manifested in evolutionary time by those species that, when threatened, gather the young into the nest or result in their being brought in close proximity. Attachment behavior results in how a mother will "gather [an infant] to her in conditions of alarm [which] clearly serves a protective function" for the species. The end result resonates with what Sullivan described as love; the infant's safety and well being is treated with equal regard by the mother. The child is also the trigger for the parents' love. Some studies have suggested that more positive emotional experiences seem to be elicited by babies who are evaluated to be cuter (Mischkulnig, 1989). The attachment system is probably closely connected to the dopaminergic reward system that is hypothesized by researchers (Hyman, 1996) that is short circuited in addictions.

> Joey was noted to be apathetic and ill nourished in his one-year checkup at the neighborhood health clinic. While the mother held Joey, she neither stimulated him verbally nor appeared particularly engaged. The nurse practitioner recommended a closer followup, recommended changes for the baby's diet, and referred the mother to early intervention. When the mother seemed neither concerned nor eager to accept the nurse's plan, the nurse practitioner was alarmed. She tried to engage the mother in a discussion about her own health, inquired about environmental stresses, and wondered if the mother was depressed. Jane, the mother, denied all problems. The nurse scheduled another appointment for the next week to monitor the mother's compliance and to follow Joey more closely.
>
> When the mother failed to come to the appointment, the nurse called to reschedule and found the family's phone had been disconnected. She contacted the housing project manager and found that several neighbors had reported that Jane's older child, 3-year-old Betty, had been wandering the project late at night asking for food. One neighbor had called the department of child welfare the day before.
>
> The nurse clinician called the department of social services and filed a report for medical neglect. Eventually the clinic was informed that mother was unable to follow the department's treatment plan, including the treatment of her own addiction, and the children had been removed and placed in foster care in another community.

In this instance, the mother's love of her drug came before the love of her children. Her attachment to her children had been destroyed. Without active treatment for her addiction, her ability to be attuned to the needs of her new infant and daughter, to follow through on the work of parenting (the commitment to the necessary tasks of care), could not be completed. No intervention for either the infant or 3-year-old could be useful without actively addressing the parental psychopathology that hampered the children's daily care and protection. The therapist must classify this presentation as a zone 2 problem.

Addiction has a broad impact on all spheres of parental behavior. The neurobiological processes that underlie attachment are destroyed. Even the perception of physical or emotional consequences on the safety or well being of the children could not alter this parent's behavior. In this zone 2 problem, the zone of childhood despair, the intervention requires mandatory treatment for the mother, or the removal of children, or both. These alternate resources can only be accessed through the Department of Child Welfare. The mother had to receive a court order to engage in a treatment plan. In the absence of her compliance, she would lose her children. In order to regain her children's custody, she would now need to establish her sobriety and work toward a recovery that permitted her to establish a context in which she could respond to her children's needs.

Another threat to child development is posed when the father has a severe and active problem with an addiction or alcoholism. The toxic effects of this zone 2 problem are futher exaggerated when the father has sociopathic features that heighten the exploitation of the child or lead to unpredictable explosive disciplinary behavior.

> Jimmy had just begun Head Start at age 4. His teachers became concerned by the nature of his startle reactions. Whenever an adult approached him from behind, he would flinch and move away. Occasionally he would have a bruise that his teachers would notice. When he was asked about what happened, his eyes would open wide and he would be silent. Because he was an extremely active child, and often fell on the playground, the teachers accepted his mother's reports that he ran into things in the home when he was playing chase with his older brother.
>
> He was brought to the school each day by his mother, appeared to separate easily, and seemed well cared for. When he had to return home, however, they noted he appeared anxious. Often, when his mother came to pick him up, he ignored her and resisted physical contact. As the mother's relationship with the head teacher developed, she accepted the teacher's recommendation that she come to school twice a week to join activities at the center with Jimmy. The teacher found this to be helpful to Jimmy and his mother. She learned that the mother waitressed in the evening while her husband, who was unemployed, watched the children.
>
> As Jimmy continued in day care, the teacher noted that he was also prone to unpredictable outbursts. Sometimes he would have an extended tantrum when he could not get the marker that he wanted; other times he appeared to have little concern about this type of frustration. On the playground, he was likely to run up to children and hit them as his greeting. He would often call his classmates "stupid" and used swear words the other children did not. He seemd to regard this vocabulary as natural.
>
> As the head teacher's relationship with Jimmy's mother increased, she shared these observations. She asked the mother to meet with the Head Start social worker. Mother was reluctant to do this, but since she had often met the social worker at the cener, she finally accepted a referral. After Jimmy came to school with a particularly bad bruise, the mother told the social worker that she worried that her husband was "rough" with the children. He had had a problem with addiction that she thought was "being treated."

These situations are often extremely difficult to approach clinically. They require resources from multiple agencies and legal protections. A potential for domestic violence may exist. A history of domestic violence needs to be explored empathically and the safety of the mother and children established. The engagement of the parent in developing a safety plan is extremely important. Laws about domestic violence are different (when they exist) from state to state. The access to resources for women and children varies tremendously as well. Often approaching these situations via a child welfare agency referral may only lead to the children being removed from the home and their attachment to the nonabusing parent ruptured.

Parental addiction, aggression, and domestic violence (in combination or separately) are zone 2 problems that threaten children's development through many avenues. The child's lack of safety, the potential identification with the aggressor, and the formation of pathological models of relationship are all possible. Behavioral symptoms are common. Furthermore, many fathers with sociopathic features may not only use unpredictable and harsh discipline but may reward the child's own aggressive behavior. Not all addicts or alcoholics are as severely compromised. Among those with heroin addictions, there is a considerable percentage of working addicts. For one portrait of such a father, Susan J. Miller's *Never Let Me Down* (1998) portrays her experiences as the daughter of a man who worked as a window dresser but was a jazz loving, Jewish junkie. Paternal patterns of alcoholism have also been much discussed (see Woititz, 1983) and have led to the inclusion of children of alcoholics meetings as a part of the AA and Alanon network of community meetings that support recovery.

The attachment mechanisms that have biological triggers in the mother are complemented by the way the child responds to attachment. The child's establishment of proximity during periods of distress can enhance internal mechanisms whose aim is to diminish anxiety. The work of Ainsworth, Blehar, Waters, and Wall (1978) suggested four styles of infant attachment behavior, which include the "Secure" attachment, which is reflected in the way the infant can use the parent for effective comforting. An "Ambivalent" style of attachment is described in which the infant seems to demand comforting but appears unable to use it. "Avoidant" attachments are those in which states of anxiety (as measured physiologically) are reflected by behavioral patterns of distance or "playing it cool" rather than seeking the comfort of the parent. There is a final "disorganized" style in which the infant has no consistent strategy.

The impact of a mother's major mental illness on children's attachment styles has been the subject of recent research by S. J. Miller (1998). Her study suggested that the patterns of infant's attachments were negatively influenced by the presence of the mother's illness. Only 9% of the infants of mothers with mental illnes had a secure attachment. Seventeen percent were described to be insecure and avoidant. These infants were noted to be affected by rebuffing parental behaviors. Another 4% had insecure ambivalent attachments associated with the mother's inconsistent behaviors. Another 35% were disorganized in their attachment, determined by both the mother's intrusive care-taking behaviors and documented histories of the infant's abuse and neglect. A startling percentage (35%) of the infants were described as having no attachment; i.e., there was no relationship apparent between the mother and child as a result of the impact of multiple separations and placements.

Some of the early work by Ainsworth has been extended by Main (1994; see Table 3.2) in which the mother's past experience of attachment and loss (rather than illness per se) are correlated with the type of attachment displayed by the infant. "Longitudinal attachment studies are beginning to identify aspects of parent and infant behavior predictive of a spectrum of later psychopathology, including role reversal in parent–child relationships, aggression toward peers of school age, and dissociative symptoms in adolescence. These early infancy predictors include unresolved parental fear, parental affective communication errors, and disorganized infant attachment behaviors" (Lyons-Ruth, 1997).

In the case that follows, the mother was able to make an attachment to her son, but his secure attachment was undermined by the mother's inability to function consistently.

> Gwendolyn had a paranoid schizophrenic disorder that was now manageable with medication treatment (which she took intermittently when she was "anxious") and with the support of her mother who kept the household organized. Gwendolyn had had a son as a result of a brief relationship and she and her mother had raised Eli together. Gwendolyn was on disability so that she felt she contributed to the household, but she was often angry that her mother controlled the finances.
>
> Gwendolyn's psychotic disorder had not led to the child welfare agency taking custody of Eli. They had noted in their periodic followups that his attachment to his mother was "constrained." Throughout his first four years, during mother's psychotic flares, she often became preoccupied with toxins and her political letter writing campaigns and was

TABLE 3.2.

Infant Strange Situation Category	Strange Situation Behavior	Adult's Experience
Secure (B)	Shows signs of missing parent on separation (often cries), greets parent actively (usually seeking to be held), then settles and returns to play once more.	**Secure/Autonomous (F)** Valuing of attachment but relatively objective regarding any particular event or relationship. Coherent and plausible regarding life experiences whether favorable or unfavorable.
Avoidant (A)	Fails to cry on separation from parent, actively avoids and ignores parent on reunion. Focuses on toys or environment throughout procedure.	**Dismissing (D)** Dismissing of attachment-related experiences and relationships. Normalizing and idealizing or (rare) devaluing.
Ambivalent/ preoccupied (C)	May be wary or distressed even prior to separation. Preoccupied with parent throughout procedure, may seem confused and angry or passive. Fails to settle and take comfort in parent on reunion, and fails to return to exploration.	**Preoccupied (E)** Preoccupied with or by past attachment relationships or experiences, and is often seemingly confused or overwhelmed. Preoccupation with parents is angry, passive, or (rare) individual shows fearful preoccupation with attachment-related traumatic events.
Disorganized/ disoriented (D)	The infant displays disorganized or disoriented behaviors in the parents' presence during the Strange Situation, suggesting a lapse of behavioral strategy. For example, the infant may freeze with a trance-like expression, hands in air, or may move away from the parents to the wall, turning the head away while crying.	**Unresolved/disorganized (U/d)** During discussions of loss or abuse experiences, subject shows striking lapse in the monitoring of reasoning or discourse. For example, individual may briefly indicate a dead person is believed still alive in the physical sense, or may lapse into a lengthy passage of eulogistic speech.

Note. Reprinted with permission from Mary Main, *A Move to the Level of Representation in the Study of Attachment Organization: Implications for Psychoanalysis*. Annual research lecture to the British Psycho-Analytical Society, London, July 6, 1994.

consequently unavailable for Eli. At those times, the grandmother, who was both rigid and cold, cared for him.

A further complication was that Gwendolyn was unable to set limits for him at times leading to the harsher reactions of his grandmother. Following one of these events, the mother would often undermine the grandmother's behavioral expectations for the boy. Both of these factors contributed to Eli's insecurity in his attachment to both his mother and his grandmother.

> A major complication occurred after Eli began Head Start. He delighted in the peer interaction, which had been severely limited by his mother, and was amazed at the playspace equipment where the style of the teachers allowed a great deal of free play and exploration. His favorite teacher was warm, consistently available, and clear about her behavioral expectations. Eli developed quite a warm attachment to her.
>
> When Valentine's Day came, he reported to his mother that he wanted to buy his teacher a Valentine's Day card. He had already, he told her, been working hard on one for her and for Grandma. Gwendolyn became paranoid and obsessed by this request.
>
> She could not believe that her child would want to do this for anyone but a family member. She became preoccupied by her son's relationship with this teacher. She suspected the teacher was sexually abusing her son. She often hovered outside the playspace to identify any signs of misconduct. When her voices confirmed that Eli was being sexually abused, she reported the school to the Department of Social Services.

Major mental illness can pose dilemmas that are expressed in various ways. This mother was capable of offering love and care to her child, especially with her own mother's support during her periods of illness. She was incapable of being consistent in her availability or in her limits. She was also capable, it turned out, of collaborating with therapy after the child welfare agency mandated it. She was able to bring the child for regular appointments, listen to the therapist's advice, and accept the child's relationship with the therapist. However, the therapist must address the mother's vulnerability by continually reinforcing the respect the therapist had for the mother, and accentuate the child's appreciation for his mother in the parent meetings.

While the child-based therapy helped the boy accept that his mother "worried a lot about other people," a major focus of attention was the parent work. The therapist was able to collaborate with the mother's psychiatrist and advise additional meetings when she began to relapse. These were relapses she would never have reported on her own. However, as a result of the mandate of the child welfare agency and the therapist's reassurance that her symptoms did affect Eli, she was more attentive to her own care. The parental treatment served to help the mother accept that her child would need to have other attachments in his life.

Attunement

Attunement is that component of "love" that refers to the parent's ability to read an infant's states or needs and the developing range of the child's emotional and cognitive responses. Attunement requires the use of those perceptions by the parents to adjust their responses to the "otherness" of the child. Parents who wish to be emotionally available to their children may have to modify the nature and range of their own characteristic responses. That said, most infants and children can still accommodate to the large range of parental behaviors that have been observed and still thrive.

The innate flexibility of most infants is illustrated in another way by the evolving research about fathers' styles with babies. The differences that have been captured between mothers and fathers in their early exchanges with their infants are described in *Fathers* by Ross Parke (1981). "Most fathers seem to present a more playful jazzing up approach. As one watches this interaction, it seems that a father is expecting a more heightened playful response from the baby. And he gets it! Amazingly enough, an infant by two or three weeks displays an entirely different attitude (more wide eyed playful and bright faced) toward his father than to his mother. The cycles might be characterized as higher, deeper, and even a bit more jagged." However, these very differences alter when the fathers are primary caretakers rather than secondary caretakers. Primary caretakers who are fathers actually behave more like mothers in their use of a range of high pitched vocalizations, more smiling, and more imitation of the babies' facial expressions. The infant appears to have no difficulty with this range or variation in parental behavior.

The impact of significant deficits in the expression of attunement, as a result of parental psychopathology, can lead to disturbances in child development.

> Amelia was brought to the clinic at age 4 by her mother as a result of mother's upset about Amelia's tantrums and oppositional behaviors. The mother's fears about her child's development were complicated by the concerns that since mother had been a slow learner and had had to be placed in special classes throughout her education, she hoped Amelia would not experience the same difficulties.
>
> In the initial family-based interview in the playroom, the mother explained at great length the reason Amelia was visiting the therapist and then, while Amelia was attempting to take off her jacket, interrupted her. Mother told Amelia to speak to the therapist. She reminded Amelia that mother had taught her to be polite.
>
> Amelia began to resist her mother's directives and the interaction began to miscarry. The therapist intervened by thanking the mother for helping Amelia get ready to play. She said, "first things first" and let Amelia take off her jacket.
>
> Simultaneously the therapist asked the mother to select three potentially interesting toys to help Amelia play "while we all talk together."
>
> During the course of the interaction, the mother shared that she was in treatment in a nearby clinic and that Amelia was in Head Start. The Head Start teacher confirmed that Amelia was doing very well in the classroom and reported seeing numerous instances of the mother's poor timing and misreading of Amelia's cues. These lead to increasing levels of distress on the part of the child.
>
> When the therapist requested the mother's record, it was notable for the presence of an anxious obsessiveness. Because of her perseveration on certain topics in therapy and her history of educational difficulties, a neuropsychological evaluation had been requested. The test report documented mother's mild mental retardation coupled with right hemisphere processing problems that affected her ability to respond to social cues.

In this instance, neither the mother's emotional attachment nor her commitment wavered. There was no doubt in the clinician's mind of the mother's *love*, or her attachment, for and to her child. She was able to be consistent and available. The mother's capacity to read her child's state and to adjust the emotional timing of her own behavior was compromised. The nurse practitioner who had followed Amelia during her early infancy reported that the mother had been consistently attentive, even if a "worrier" but that she had met Amelia's needs well and followed the principles of care the nurse had defined for her.

The nurse reported that more difficulties emerged in their interactions when Amelia was closer to 2 or 3 years of age. Mother's *attunement* to her child's behavior was affected by her poor social–emotional perceptions. Her dedication, however, as well as her own capacity to imitate the therapist's interventions in the initial family-based interview, suggested that a dyadic-based treatment model could be helpful. Amelia's autonomy was also reinforced by the mother's ability to access alternative supports (Head Start) and an afternoon playgroup that Amelia had available.

In this case, the adult psychopathology and limitations in parental function became more prominent as Amelia reached a developmental period in which her autonomy, emotional expressiveness, and knowledge of her own wants were more prominent. The mother's formulas for developmental care lacked flexibility, and the neurological impact on her attunement to her child's cues impacted her ability to smooth this developmental period. The mother was, however, still able to be empathic when the therapist could help Amelia define her different feelings and plans and engage her mother in listening. Failures of attunement that are psychologically based may be even more malignant than this one. The failure of empathy (love) in some cases can be profound. Attunement flounders as a result of the failure of the parent to relinquish the primacy of their own wants and needs. These deficits in parenting can be especially evident in borderline or narcissistic personality disorders in parents. Amelia's mother's had the ability to confirm Amelia's emotions and continued to support a healthy attachment. There was no doubt that Amelia felt very loved by her mother.

In another child problem, the impact of another axis I disorder in a parent, depression, had an evident impact on her parenting. Her "double depression," the alternation of episodes of major depression with a chronic background dysthymia, periodically exerted more dramatic effects on the adjustment of the child.

> Sally, now 4 years old, was seen for her annual checkup in the health clinic with her mother. The nurse practitioner knew that the mother had needed treatment for a chronic depression that had antedated the birth of this first child. The mother had never followed up on the nurse's recommendations for either psychotherapy or medication trials. The nurse practitioner recalled that the mother had confided that she hoped this baby would "light up" her life the way nothing else had.
>
> The mother felt a chronic sense of emptiness that she hoped her baby would fill. She managed the pregnancy well, the delivery was uncomplicated, yet mother remained depressed and anergic. Sally was a "good baby" yet always appeared slightly inactive and apathetic herself in her well-baby checkups. She had never been especially symptomatic, nor had she posed a "problem" to her mother. While Sally had seemed like a somewhat inhibited child, she had never shown signs of an anxious temperament.
>
> At this checkup, the nurse practitioner noted that Sally appeared somewhat depressed. But when Sally was asked how she felt she said, "good" to each question the nurse asked about herself, friends, and her playschool activities. When the nurse called the day care, the teachers reported observing these same changes. The nurse again referred the mother and child for treatment and was able to prepare the mother for the fact that her own treatment might be recommended to help her daughter.

In this instance, the parent's attunement is constricted, rather than absent, as a result of depression, which narrows the mother's range of emotional experience. Here the dyad is attuned, yet to a diminished palette of emotion. As neurobiological research continues to examine infant–parent behaviors, the clinical study of the depressed mother infant dyads reveals striking neuropsychological findings. In one study, infants of depressed mothers showed reduced activation in their electroencephalographic studies in the left frontal lobe (Dawson, Frey, Patagiotides, Osterling, & Hessl, 1997). This pattern is similar to that of their depressed mothers. It is not demonstrated in normal controls. It is hypothesized that the left frontal lobe is specialized for the expression of positive emotions that are affected by depression. The later difficulties of children of depressed mothers, which can include social, academic, and attention problems, may be related to this early lack of activation.

Free, Alechina, and Zahn-Waxler (1996) demonstrated that children of depressed mothers showed a decreased ability to recognize a range of emotions in comparison with controls. In the study context, children and their mothers were shown a range of pictures of infants manifesting different emotions. Both depressed mothers and their children demonstrated more inaccuracy of labeling, particularly of negative emotions. They were more likely, for instance, to label a picture of sadness as anger. Here both parent and child's attunement to and labeling of their emotional experiences are diminished. Another study (Lumely, Mader, Gramzow, & Papineau, 1996) suggested that mothers who use more emotion-focused coping were more likely to have children who were better able to identify and communicate their feelings. Children with less exposure to emotion-focused coping skills were more likely to be seen as alexythymic, i.e., having trouple understanding, differentiating, and describing emotions. The lack of a full range of emotional awareness can impair children's interactions and impede their development of emotional problem solving.

Paternal depression exerts its own effects. The impact of the "invisible father," whether the result of depression, workaholism, or diminished interest in relating, may be as psychologically compromising as the impact of paternal absence. Most single parents (mothers) do an extraordinary job of being both mothers and fathers for their children. Their use of their extended family network and other intimate relationships for children helps extend the role models children have as well as offers them additional supports. Many children suffer, however, from their psychological longing for a paternal figure. Herzog (1995) has described this syndrome in his papers on "father hunger." This need can be further intensified even if the father is in the home but remains secluded, unavailable, and is not attuned to the child's needs.

While the examples above suggest the impact of the diminution of parental attunement, therapists understand that there can be an impact of too much of something as well as too little. The process of overattunement may also complicate some aspects of a child's development.

> Vanessa's mother requested a child evaluation as result of her fears that 4-and-a-half-year-old Vanessa had "spells." The mother requested an initial parent meeting and she also wished her mother to accompany her. Both her mother and grandmother reported Vanessa's tendency to have extended temper tantrums when something did not go the way the child wanted or was frustrated or threatened in some way.
>
> The grandmother's anxiety was heightened by her own history of night terrors and problems with a serious panic disorder that emerged when she was an adolescent. Vanessa's mother was also anxious, and both the mother and grandmother wanted to prevent Vanessa from having to struggle with similar symptoms. They carefully described how Vanessa would perseverate in screaming and crying about what she wanted, how these episodes would last for up to an hour, and how they could not leave her alone because she might run from the house or damage something.
>
> Vanessa had already seen one child psychologist who provided a play-based therapy that mother terminated after four sessions, because it "was no help" and Vanessa's tantrums continued. The child psychologist reported to the current therapist that Vanessa's mood, interaction, and capacity to relate were well within normal limits. Reports from her preschool confirmed her precociousness and her good relationships with other children. Vanessa had only had one or two briefer tantrums at school.

In this case, the mother's *over* attunement to her daughter's distress prevented her from disengaging enough to get perspective. While her daughter screamed and cried, she continued to attend to her and attempt to comfort, distract, and half-heartedly limit her. Mother's own traits of perfectionism, anxious overcontrolling style, and fears of Vanessa either hurting herself or damaging many of mother's own or Vanessa's loved possessions, made it difficult for the mother to develop an alternative stance.

It is often easier to treat "too much care" than not enough, as the above cases suggest. Containing parental anxieties often permits parents to use other suggestions. Treatment can provide concrete direction in how to reassure a child while accepting the process through which they can "get their sad and mad feelings out" and detaching from the rest of the tantrum. The parent can tell the child that the parent will be available for a more productive exchange later. Many other techniques can be used to contain unsafe behavior. A system of positive rewards for shorter tantrums or the use of time out are possible. Most child therapists can learn to develop all these treatment plans.[8] Helping parents connect and comply is often the key task. The parent-based meeting is essential for that process. Treatment plans, and their followup, are just like the child's development in the long run. They depend on the parents' attachment and attunement motivating the parents' involvement. Finally, they rely upon the parents' commitment. (See Table 3.2.)

Commitment

A parent may be both attached to his or her child and attuned to his or her needs. Nevertheless, there may be cases in which the parent finds it extremely difficult to make the commitment to respond to the child's needs for appropriate activity and supports.

> A Little League coach had spoken to Arthur's mother about her son's increased expression of irritability, frustration, and discouragement. He also noted that Arthur often came late to games and even had missed some games. That had never happened before. He asked why he had seen so little of her lately.
>
> She explained that she had returned to work now that their youngest was 7 and that the only job she could get that would permit her to be home after school also required that she work many weekends. Her husband was now faced with organizing the kids' activities on most weekends and was having trouble rising to the challenge.
>
> She became tearful as she explained that she always knew her husband had ADHD but that he was a wonderful father and a sensitive husband. However, he had often lost jobs as an auto mechanic and service manager because he became especially disorganized with stress or criticism. In spite of her making out schedules and trying to help him manage these new burdens, he was having a difficult time and often blamed his difficulties on Arthur—who had ADHD symptoms himself—for not being ready on time or helping enough with the two younger children.

Other more severe parental disorders come to a therapist's attention only as the result of the natural course of the child's development, which creates new demands and additional commitments. These cases often fall into zone 2, depending upon the nature and severity of the parental compromise, one that is not always established by a psychiatric diagnosis alone.

Medical problems can limit the parents' ability "to keep up with the child" and to enact their commitment to the child's needs. Those referrals may come from primary care providers who are concerned about parents with heart, lung, or weight prob-

---

[8]The use of behavior shaping plans will be discussed in chapter 6. The articles and books suggested at the end of the chapter will direct the reader to resources that guide therapists in developing these plans.

lems, which make it difficult for them to manage aspects of their child's care. These may be complicated by other forms of parental psychopathology.

Olivia was referred for parenting consultation after she complained that her 4-year-old was running away from her. "There is nothing I can do about it because he can run faster than me," she explained as she described the impact of her obesity. She said he was particularly uncooperative in food stores and often embarrassed her and caused her to leave without all of her purchases. She said she often did not bring him to preschool because it was too far to walk and she did not want to ask her neighbor.

After listening patiently to the different ways in which Olivia felt angry, defeated, and helpless, the therapist directed Olivia's attention to how she and her son were connected. What were their best and most fun times? After reemphasizing the strengths in their relationship, the therapist then encouraged Olivia to talk about what she had done to become a loving mother to a little boy who was more and more interested in exploring the world. How, in other situations, did she set limits?

The therapist also began to explore the nature of Olivia's general anxiety and depression and her own history within her family of origin. Olivia revealed the traumatic nature of the way her parents disciplined her and how she had vowed to "never be angry" with her child. She realized that she tended to hold grudges, which often prompted further depression and withdrawal in her own family. She was now beginning to act out the same pattern with her son and her commitment to his activities had begun to suffer.

In this instance, the dilemma of the axis III (medical) disorder was only a part of the complex picture of issues, past history, and character problems that were impacting on Olivia's management of her preschool son. In order to focus the intervention in an adult therapy, the therapist needed to do some further work. The youngster had to be prepared to respond to the necessary changes in Olivia's style of parenting. The family meeting was also used as a forum in which her son could share his worries about Mommy's eating and weight and be reminded that the doctors and therapists were working to help Mommy be healthy, no matter what.

As the therapist determined that he appeared to be well adjusted in preschool and in many facets of home life, the therapist could begin to focus her work on a combination of adult psychotherapy and attuned parental guidance. The focus of treatment was set to address Olivia's health management issues, to help her with her self-assertion, and to continue to use these as part of her parenting skills in setting limits. Once she was less angry, she was better able to mobilize her commitment to his additional needs for activities with peers.

Love is the foundation of the child's care and even in the absence of other parenting skills the child's outcome may still be quite positive. When the parent's love is "good enough," the parent will find the way to make the needed commitments to support the child's growth. Another central parenting task is the establishment of limits that support the values of the family, the integrity and respect for the relationships therein, and that ultimately extend to supporting the limits within the child's school and community.

Limits

Limit setting is the second key function of parenting. Limits work best when the child has a clear sense of the parents' love, expressed through a healthy secure attachment, attunement to the child's needs, and commitment to provide for the child. Love contributes most to good outcomes for children. Even in the context of difficult child-based or interactional difficulties, where the family function is good, the long-term outcome of most children is more positive, whether in instances of child sexual abuse (Oates, O'Toole, Lynch, Stern, & Cooney, 1994), parent treatment of preschoolers with ADHD (Pisterman, McGrath, Firestone, Goodman, Webster, & Mallory, 1992), or in the outcome of traumatic brain injury (Max & Lindgren, 1997). Barkley (1997) stresses the importance of the child's sense of the parent's attachment in his many discussions of ADHD and oppositional defiant disorder. He recommends that the parent play with the child consistently each day. The love between parent and child needs to be consistently affirmed so that it is the background against which disciplinary or limit setting actions are placed.

Parents set limits in a variety of ways. Seven types of responses are most commonly seen on the part of parents in a wide variety of circumstances. Although none of these techniques may be consistently applied, the hodge podge of these typical parental limit setting responses tends to help most children develop prosocial behaviors. A therapist can evaluate the nature and range of these common responses to assess their efficacy and may suggest possible alternatives.

1. **Emotion.** Heightened emotional reactions (usually anger but often mixed with fear or dismay) to a child's behavior that violates issues of safety, the parent's own space or personal tenets, or interferes with social interaction. For example, "If you ever run into the road again, I'll kill you." "It makes me feel so bad to find you going through my pocketbook." "Can't you see that your father and I are talking?"
2. **Structure.** The demands of daily living, which require that the child conform to some degree of structure within the family. These structures are repetitively reviewed with most children. For example, "You know it's dinnertime so that you need to turn off the television, wash your hands, and come bring your plate to the table."
3. **Modeling.** Parental behavior models both social skills and the social norms of the family's culture. For example, during an angry exchange a parent will model what degree of volume, the tone of voice, or which words or actions may be used. Clinicians know that children copy these behaviors, although as they age they are able to modify them. Many adults report that they made a commitment to never treat their children as their parents treated them and still find themselves doing so. Of course, parents are not the only models that children have.
4. **The law of natural consequences.** Many parents allow their children to learn by permitting them to suffer failure, embarrassment, or disciplinary actions from others. For instance, some parents may not nag their children about their homework but will wait for the child to receive a bad grade so that the child will be more receptive to help. Contrariwise, there are instances of parents who alter the law of natural consequences by using their influence with authorities in the community to prevent a teen from receiving a ticket or to protect them from a driving while intoxicated conviction.
5. **Values.** The consistent promotion of the parents' set of values is affirmed through periodic discussion. Many parents define limits by advocating for what they see as ideal behavior. When children fail to meet these standards, they discuss and explain why and how they want their children to behave. The parents' disappointment may also become a motivating factor for most children.

6. **Monitoring behavior.** Many children respond to a sense of being watched. Here, community neighbors and family connections often serve to remind children that people both care and look out for them while monitoring any misdemeanors. This observation also reinforces both parental and community standards of behavior.
7. **Classic rewards and punishments.** Children earn treats and opportunities as well as get deprived of them on the basis of their behavior. Allowance, trips, food, and special events are used by many families to draw out desired behavior from their children. The consequent loss of privileges or disciplinary reactions may range from grounding (for adolescents) or time outs (for younger children), to spanking.

For those children with externalizing disorders (see chapter 6) a more consciously and consistently elaborated set of techniques is often needed. Most often, these are refinements of the use of rewards (reinforcements) with occasionally elaborated plans for discipline ("overcorrections"). Clear and consistent family structure and predictability is also emphasized.

In the context of a well-established relationship with a child, the parent must develop the skills needed to set limits. The parent must be able to bear the loss of connection and relationship with the child when the limit is set. Parents may need help in seeing that their limits are indeed an extension of their love, as expressed in valuing the child's ability to "do the right thing." Their children's success is often correlated with their children's ability to manage respectful relationships with adult authority. By extension, parents must recognize what the period of adolescence may hold for their child. If the child cannot come to terms with compliance with parental authority, especially in some communities, children's later involvement with gangs or dangerous activities will threaten their survival.

> When Jane had entered recovery and complied with the demands of the social service agency treatment plan, Joey and Betty were returned. Two years later, when Joey was 4 and a half, he was referred to the neighborhood clinic again as result of severe aggressive behavior and tantrums in the Head Start program. Jane was now employed as a school bus driver and was very involved with her children. She spent many months resisting the Head Start director's suggestions until she saw Joey deliberately pick up a stick and hit another child on the playground.
>
> When she was referred to the clinic social worker, she immediately began to cry. "I have just put them through so much, I can't stand it when I have to reprimand them. Betty is easier though, but Joey just falls apart and is in so much pain. I can't bear either his pain or my own. He gets so upset and then he won't talk to me. He goes in his room and it seems like he sulks for hours. How can I hurt him again? I just know he'll grow out of it by kindergarten."

Here, the mother's ability was limited by her intolerance of the rupture in this reconstituted relationship, which she perceived as fragile and still easily damaged. She believed that to acknowledge Joey's misbehavior would destroy the relationship she had worked so hard to reconstruct. During the active phase of her addiction, she was unable to motivate herself to act constructively. Now in remission, she was confronted by considerable pain when she had to face the temporary loss of her relationship with her child by setting limits. This same interaction may also be seen in depressive disorders. Here, parents lack the energy to follow up on their limits or are overcome by the intense emotional reactions their children display and so the parent fails to follow up on the limit.

From the point of view of adult development, the process of setting limits on a child draws upon an adult's sense of parental authority. This psychological factor, based on concepts of personal authority, draws upon the adult's sense of relationships as expressing both autonomy and separateness (Horner, 1978). Love, as an expression of connection and dependency, is expressed in "yes," while autonomy and separateness are evoked in the relationship when the parent or child says "no." The psychosocial task of an adult's feelings about separateness and issues of personal authority emerge in the parenting relationship as the parent is called upon to set limits (Englander, 1994). This process confronts parents with what they like and don't like about themselves and their children, with differences that may be hard to understand, accept, or tolerate. Therapeutic approaches to the failures of limit setting, which consider both the nature of the child as well as the psychological makeup of the parent, are essential in helping adjust the limit setting process toward the "right stuff."

While appreciating the dilemmas in the limit setting process for parents, it is also important to have a keen sense of the evocative psychological processes of having a child or adolescent. There is a degree of personal grief that parents may experience as their child ages and separates. This may be expressed by anger and irritation directed toward the peer culture's music or dress, as well as by devaluing the initial attempts of children and adolescents to explain their choices and values. We must listen carefully to the nature of parental responses to adolescent dialogue and distinguish these from the process of setting limits. One popular study suggested that in taped dinner table conversations between parents and adolescents, the rate of sarcastic remarks on the part of parents toward the child far outnumbered the sarcastic remarks of the adolescent. Reiss et al. (1995) confirmed this observation further by noting, "almost 60% of the variance in adolescent antisocial behavior (in boys) and 37% of variance in depressive symptoms (in girls) could be accounted for by conflictual and negative parental behavior directed specifically at the adolescent."

In another case, the child's anxiousness prompted an overly attuned parent to shy away from limits because she did not want to make her child "more fearful."

> Charlie clung to his mother and wouldn't look at the therapist when she brought him into the office. She kept rubbing his back and reassuring him that he would be okay. She was sure that this nice man wouldn't make him feel bad. Mother tried to mouth suggestions to the therapist that Charlie couldn't hear so that the therapist would help Charlie in the right way. Charlie was invited to look at the toys in the playroom at mother's suggestion but, in response, he bit his mother's arm and called her "stupid." Mother redoubled her efforts to console Charlie and ignored his attack on her. She said she knew his worries had "acted up" but that he could whisper in her ear what he wanted so that the man wouldn't hear what he said.

The tyranny of a child's anxiety disorder can be manifested in the demands the child makes for the parent to refashion reality to eliminate the source of their concerns. Children believe fervently that the anxiousness is out there—not a part of their own emotional responses. For instance, children may demand that they never have to go to *that* school, or face *that* game, or be exposed to *that* food that should never be brought into the house. This insistence seems more realizable to them than managing a new level of emotional mastery. As in the case of oppositionality, anxious children may react as fiercely in their wish to have the world orchestrated to avoid their discomfort or enhance their perception of control. As a result, parents must be able to both reassure and limit a child in order to enhance a positive outcome.

Even if a child has difficulty accepting limits, the parents must still contend with ways to develop a sense of discipline in the child. Some children react so severely to the parent's limits that the parent may feel more burdened by the limit setting exchange than by simply accepting the child's troublesome or defiant behavior. In this pattern, children with impulse control disorders may be more prone to the elaboration of oppositionality into conduct disordered behavior. They learn not to expect parental interference with their wishes.

> Anton first came to the clinic when he was 5. He had severe temper tantrums and was oppositional both at home and at school. The mother was poorly compliant with treatment, felt he was her special and "only" son, and gave in to most of his demands. The clinician recommended a behavior shaping program that the school could implement and advised the school support team that they could expect little reinforcement from the home.
>
> When Anton was 11, he was brought to treatment as a result of a neighborhood store filing charges against him for shoplifting. Apparently Anton had been doing this for some time and the storekeeper's discussion with his mother had never led to any action that he could perceive, so he reported Anton to the police. The juvenile hearing officer recommended that Anton be seen in the court clinic.
>
> After the initial family meeting, the clinician met with the mother alone and Anton was told to wait in the waiting room. After the meeting was over, the clinician discovered that a window in another part of the clinic had been broken during the time of his appointment with Anton's mother. The mother attended treatment with Anton for the required amount of time, although there was little indication that she implemented any of the recommended disciplinary limits.
>
> When Anton was in his second year of high school, the school filed a truancy report with the court. Whenever he was stopped in the halls and found to be without a pass, he told his mother he was picked on and "everyone at school had a bad attitude about me. They ignore the really bad kids." He had been reported to be involved with adolescents who were dealing drugs around the perimeter of the high school. In addition, Anton has another court charge following a drunken brawl on one of the neighborhood playgrounds. He had begun to stay away from home at night.
>
> Mother had become extremely anxious about his not being at home but continued to deny that his other behavior was a problem. She fought the charges as false and felt that he would attend school if the teachers treated him right. In the clinic she demanded medication for his attentional disorder since she now felt that this was the cause of his staying out overnight.

From a developmental point of view, many children without disruptive behavior disorders can come to limit their own behaviors. With the normal foundation of a good relationship, the child will become attuned to the parents' emotions. When the child behaves in ways that are difficult for the parents, even in the absence of their having a clear pattern of limit setting, their distress will be noticed by the child. The child's guilty feelings, which represent his or her awareness of the violation of the relationship between parent and child, eventually begins to modulate those behaviors for most children. Children with impulse control disorders, many of whom may also have poor social and emotional awareness, do not readily self-modulate. The child's failure to register clearly the emotional responses of others complicates the development of empathy. The child's awareness of his or her parents' distress and the child's knowledge of a very predictable pattern of parental reaction needs to be heightened and consolidated.

The complex interface between parental skills in setting limits and adult psychopatholgy is of special concern in the interface between child and adolescent externalizing disorders. Failure of limit setting is most evident in working with children with oppositional defiant disorder or conduct disorder. In the field of child treatment, approximately half of all child psychiatric services are mobilized to treat conduct disorder and its comorbidities. The incidence of children reported to have conduct disorder ranges from 5% to 10% in the United States. This represents 3.5 to 7 million children. Often these children come from homes where there has been domestic violence, parental problems with alcohol or drug abuse, or depression.

Parents in these homes have special problems with limits and often begin to set a limit but ultimately reward the child's troublesome behavior. For instance, a child will be limited, have a tantrum, and the result is that the parent backs off and rewards the child in order to distract him. The essential lesson is that the child learns that bad or disturbing behavior can "win" in these sequences. In order to treat these children, programs directed toward parent training are vital.

Just as the therapist must have a sense of the parental ability to love, the therapist must develop a sense of the parents' use of limits. Limit setting behaviors can range from erratic or nonexistent limits to ones that are punitive and physically abusive. In addition, cultural factors must be considered. Whether these relate to the way in which the Haitian culture accepts and uses physical limits (Stewart, 1996) to the degree of tolerance that Japanese culture (Vogel, 1996) manifests in response to a child's misbehavior, the therapist must develop an appreciation for these issues in working with any cultural or class configuration within the United States.

Real Life

Love and limits establish the foundation for the child's development within the family. The parent must then contend with the nature, temperament, and challenges that life has presented to the child and then commit their time and resources to meet the needs that may result. The parents' knowledge of the issues in their child's life will help them respond appropriately to the various stages of development, the common concerns of different age groups, and the emotional responses that most children may have. This is the stuff of the child's "real life." It reminds all parents that while children are part of them, they are separate beings who may face challenges over which parents have little control. Further adjustments in their parental style, additional demands for a child's treatment or support, or many remedial activities may be required. The therapist must be able to help the parents understand these demands as well as the parents' emotional responses to them.

One way to evaluate the parents' ability to appreciate the real life of the child is to ask the parent to talk about their child for five minutes (L. Miller, 1998). The therapist is testing the nature of the parents' internal representation of the child. Most parents can speak comfortably for this period of time and share many anecdotes and descriptions of their child. Normal representations should reflect some degree of concordance with the child's temperament, feelings, and needs as assessed independently by the therapist. Significant impairments in the parents' internal representations appear in truncated, sparse descriptions or ones that are highly skewed or schematic with little of the lively details that convey the "real life" of the child that helps therapists understand the parents' appreciation for their children's style.

Some parental vulnerabilities may be most manifest during a particular developmental stage. They may occur in response to some aspect of the child's emotional experience at home or in the world of school or play. The intersection of both a developmental stage and the nature of the child's emotions on the life and management skills of a parent can be seen in the challenges posed by a defiant 2-year-old. Some parents fear their own rage or acting out in either retaliation or a retreat, which may be expressed in various ways. What behavior the child's tantrums may activate in the parent will depend upon the parents' level of emotional control, the nature of their defenses, or their own life histories. Some parents are fearful of their own reactions, concerned about either a rageful retaliation or emotional withdrawal.

Some parents may bring their child for therapy because "my child doesn't listen." The issue of primary concern may be the parents' fears of harming their child, which may be connected to their own past experiences of abuse—a common case in parents who refer themselves to Parents Anonymous—or some parents who reach a phase where they would prefer to retreat from their child rather than be abusive. If, on the other hand, their affect is repressed through the use of denial, they may appear for treatment independently of their child for the "unexplained" onset of an anxiety disorder. Anxieties may also be triggered for some parents at different points in the process of separating from their child.

The natural stresses in the developmental course of childhood include the very nature of children's uncensored emotional or behavioral responses. It is not a kind and gentle phase of life. Whether expressed by the natural inclination in the preschool age to discover all the different ways a living creature may stop moving to the aggressively self-protective and acquisitive expressions throughout the developmental course starting with the 2-year-old's shriek of "Mine!," to the way in which children may treat one another, all can place new and evolving demands upon a parent's emotional life. Depending upon the constellation of their defenses or the nature of any axis I or II disorder which may be activated, unhealthy consequences for the parent and the adjustment of the child can begin to unfold.

From a family systems point of view, many of these developmental challenges relate to repeated dysfunctional interactions in the family that may be triggered around central themes in the expression of love, limits, or real life. These recurring themes, expressed in different ways at different developmental periods, pose challenges for the youngster's management of his or her own emotional life. The recent work of Peggy Papp (Papp & Imber-Black, 1996) as well as earlier naturalistic research (Ziegler & Musliner, 1977) has reviewed the impact of these naturally occurring, and inescapable, interactions in the course of a child's development within a family system from an intergenerational and cultural point of view. Each individual within a family system can be challenged by the course of the central dilemmas within the family. The emotional reactions to disappointments, frustrations, losses, or reversals of fortune or expectations, trigger a subconscious narrative as part of the coping mechanisms of the family system.

> Walter's mother sought consultation because she was fearful that her child had an evil nature, "just like his father's father," whom she saw as sadistic and uncaring. As she observed Walter in his playground interactions, she noted the way he was drawn to little girls but would often react aggressively to their failure to follow his play plans. As she noticed this, she became increasingly anxious. These concerns were clearly underlined in her endorsement of many symptoms of externalizing problems in Walter that were not correlated with the data gathered from the school reports.
>
> She recognized she had always been quite anxious and depressed herself. She had had

> a period in which she was agoraphobic for two years following the delivery of her second child. This little girl was colicky and difficult. She explained that she had been much closer to Walter because he had been such a soft and cuddly baby.
>
> She felt it was very difficult to know what to do with Walter. Whenever she discussed him with her husband, he dismissed her concerns as overreactions. He said Walter was a normal boy. Since the birth of the children, Walter's mother became more aware that her husband had never wanted to discuss the behavior of his own father or his own family life. He visited his parents rarely and when they did, the visits were short and never appeared to be very warm. He did not like to discuss emotions or what he thought of Walter's development.
>
> The mother was one of three girls in her own family. As a result, she felt insecure about her judgments about her son. Her feelings were compounded because her own father had abandoned her family when she was 5. Her anger and resentment about this abandonment was strongly defended against, which further diminished her interest in this discussion.
>
> The event that had led to her making an appointment followed her observation of Walter hiding behind a tree in the last snowstorm and packing his snowballs with gravel and then making them wet. He explained to her, quite naturally, that then they stung better and there was going to be a big snowball fight later in the afternoon between the boys on the block, and the big boys always made up one side and dominated Walter's peer group. He hoped he could really hurt Mel who had been mean to him in the past. Mother felt inarticulate, became dizzy, and had to go into the house to lie down. She felt she no longer knew what to do since her loving son had become "an evil, nasty boy."

The dilemma of this anxious and depressed mother is echoed and compounded by the nature of her relationship with her husband, her thoughts about this man's attitudes and emotional beliefs, the histories of their own families, and the balance of power between them. Helping her work with her child would create a disruption of a system that had been in effect for quite some time.

The way in which she learned to mobilize her own anger (which she rarely experienced) as well as how she asserted her value system with her child affected her view of the child and, like other mothers with a history of psychiatric difficulties, she reports more externalizing symptoms in the checklists (Chilcoat & Breslau, 1997). However, the openness and special affection between Walter and his mother were very evident. She was both well attached and attuned to him, and he reciprocated with his trust and sharing of his experiences.

Another of the most common presentations of the dilemma presented by the impact of real life challenges is seen in therapy when a child develops a sudden medical illness or suffers a serious injury. The elements of traumatic reaction and grief apply to the management and treatment of the parent whose child has suddenly become "abnormal" or endangered. The parent who has witnessed a child struck by a car, a mother whose child has had his first epileptic seizure, a parent who has discovered an incident of abuse by a neighbor or activity leader: all these parents must deal with grief, loss, rage, and anxiety.

A parent's reaction can include "overprotection" or a degree of fearfulness when faced with permitting their child to return to a normal round of activities (Holden, 1985). Often their affect is contagious so the child becomes more anxious and constricted as well; in other cases, the child struggles against the parent's restriction of her activities and develops a pattern of denial that affects her reasonable judgment so that she is more likely to make an inappropriate choice.

Charlotte, age 10, had a grand mal seizure for the first time on her school's playing field in the fall. She was in the midst of the her second field hockey game and had high hopes for continuing to improve her game so that in the spring she could become cocaptain of the team. The resulting workup revealed a central nervous system tumor. Surgery was completed, recovery was rapid, and Charlotte began taking antiepileptic medication. A psychosocial assessment at the time of the surgery confirmed the family's many strengths and the many supports available to help her adjust upon her return to school. A psychoeducational interview was conducted with the parents and Charlotte's siblings to prepare them for some of the common issues in the postsurgical course.

The mother returned to see the hospital staff in the late winter of that year. They had had their followup meeting with the neurologist and neurosurgeon and both had told Charlotte she could go skiing.

The mother was unable to tolerate her own anxiety and fear about a head injury, a potential seizure on the slopes, or Charlotte getting lost. Charlotte had already agreed to a buddy-up system for skiing and agreed, reluctantly, to wear a helmet on the slopes, as recommended by her doctor. Mother still felt she could not agree to this activity and the father's position was, "it's up to your mother."

The mother could not tolerate the degree of conflict this had created between herself and Charlotte. In addition, she was extremely sensitive to her daughter appearing "abnormal" so that wearing a helmet on the ski slopes embarrassed her. The mother felt she could not deal with the conflicts with Charlotte or manage her own ambivalence triggered when things were not the way "things should be." She became extremely anxious when she could not control or order life within the family.

This parental struggle may mobilize the therapist's own countertransference issues. The therapist may either overempathize with the parent's concern or accept the child's denial. Rather, a studied and solid minimization is needed in these instances. Appropriate minimization provides a psychologically helpful protective response while permitting an appropriate degree of activity and engagement with the world.

A balanced attitude is key to developing a therapeutic plan that can manage natural anxieties about certain activities while cultivating appropriate awareness about health and self-care. In the natural course of adolescent development, a parent faces these concerns as adolescents begin to drive. One knows a fender bender may lurk in the near future, but appropriate discussion and choices about speeding, drinking and driving, and the permissible behavior of peers need to be reviewed. The adolescent's bland denial, "It'll never happen to me," needs to be challenged to help cultivate thoughtfulness even while they experiment with some of life's dangers.

In other cases, the developmental difficulty of a child may heighten parental uncertainty and confusion about their management skills for their child. One parent who was well educated about the special needs of her child would often say, "Well, now that I've gotten my first six children out the door (referring to her special needs 6-year-old son), I can help the other two get ready." Often parents do not have the exposure or training to help them develop this sense of perspective about a child's behavioral disorder and its implications for parenting. Self-blame, confusion and resulting anxiety are not uncommon. Sometimes the therapist may have trouble identifying which aspect of the system (the parent's skills or the child's self-control) has failed.

Billy, now 12 who looked like a budding preadolescent, cheerfully greeted the therapist in their follow-up meeting. Billy and the therapist had worked together for six years since his ADHD had been identified following difficulties at school. The family and parenting component of his treatment had focused first on limits and structure. Gradually, the problems of the father's alcoholism and the mother's sometimes anxious paralysis about both her husband and Billy's behavior were uncovered. For the past three years the family had been doing relatively well, although Billy still tended to be a difficult and stubborn child.

Billy continued talking in the session about his father's attendance at recovery meetings and his own good report cards. He updated the therapist on his continuing involvement in community sports, a recommendation the therapist had told the family was an essential part of Billy's care, and his occasional arguments with coaches and teammates. When mother joined the meeting, she looked at Billy and said, "Well did you tell him?" Billy looked dismayed and stared at the floor while mother reported the increasingly severe fights between herself and Billy each night over his completing his homework.

The mother expressed dismay and confusion about what to do with Billy and rejected every therapeutic suggestion or complained that they had been tried and did not work. The mother appeared more anxious than she had been in some time. However, the therapist also knew that the mother was always much more anxious whenever Billy had any extra degree of difficulty. Billy confirmed that what his mother was saying was true about his homework, but then he launched into an attack on his father's immaturity and stupidity that distracted him from his work.

The mother reported that there had been little change in the father's baseline—which continued to be intermittently immature and somewhat intrusive, related to his own severe ADHD—but that he was continuing to manage work and home life well. The mother and Billy left with a new behavioral contract to support his completion of his homework. A separate parent meeting was scheduled to discuss management issues for Billy and to review the success of the behavioral contract.

The therapist also wanted to review, in Billy's absence, the level of family tensions. In this context, Billy's medication management was also discussed. The family was reminded to follow up with the psychopharmacologist. In the next meeting scheduled with Billy and both his parents, all reported a better degree of adjustment since Billy's medication was adjusted to include an early afternoon dose.

In this instance, the therapist found it very difficult to determine the origin of this cycle of family dysfunction. Billy appeared to be continuing to psychologically mature, while his mother appeared overwhelmed and uncertain of her parenting responses. His father's behavior was erratically difficult and might be stimulating further anger during Billy's preadolescence. In the family meeting, the father and mother both agreed that while Billy and his father could get very angry with one another, they continued to have a close and active relationship. The main issue of poor control appeared at the "homework period." Once Billy's medication was adjusted and Billy's behavior changed, his mother became less anxious and more focused. Further discussion about changing behavioral contracts as well as what to anticipate as Billy's adolescence progressed was possible.

The impact of children with learning disabilities and ADHD on issues of family control and the experience of parental anxiety needs to be reviewed as part of the therapist's openness to consider alternate hypotheses and to recognize that symptomatic expressions may be generated at any level in the family system. Margalit and Heiman (1987) reported that both anxiety and family climate were affected by the presence of boys with learning disabilities. *A free expression of feelings occurred less frequently in these families.* The families avoided conflicts about structures and concerns about achievement. In comparison, families were less affected either if their children were mentally retarded or had no learning disabilities. The authors hypothesize that the erratic and uneven responses of the children with learning disabilities generate an atmosphere of unpredictability, which heightens both parents attempts to structure the family and the experience of anxiety. In all of these cases, the impact of the child's "real life" struggles on the parents' adaptation must be considered as part of the treatment plan.

In other cases, a parent with a well-compensated axis I difficulty like depression, anxiety, or an attentional disorder may have her overall adjustment disturbed by the particular way the real life struggles of the child may effect her. Whether it is expressed in the child's behavior, or by the demands the child places on the parenting system, or by the psychological reactivation of past traumatic events in her own life, these impacts complicate a parent's efforts to contain her child and help her child cope.

> Alfred was referred to a behavioral therapist as a result of continuing problems with toileting at age 6. He was intermittently encopretic and the pediatrician had just placed Alfred on a diet and suggested a structured program of sitting. He had only partially responded, and the pediatrician felt the mother would need more support in implementing the program. The therapist reviewed the pediatrician's recommendations. After reviewing the program, the therapist asked the mother to share the charts the pediatrician had recommended and how the timing of the child's program fit in with the family's routine.
>
> Mother revealed that she had done the program for three days but then found it impossible to maintain because "there were so many things going on and besides I get completely distracted, especially in the mornings." The mother reported her history of an attentional disorder that had never intruded on her life since the completion of high school. She felt depressed and disturbed about her inability to consistently follow up with the program. The therapist contacted the pediatrician to review possible modifications in the timing of the stool softeners and laxatives to better accommodate the rhythms of the mother's day so her compliance could be more successful.

The therapist must understand the implications a child's trouble has for the parent. Certain disorders may exaggerate the impact of the parent's weaker skills. The structure the parent may be able to offer may not be enough. The child's developmental difficulties may make it difficult for the parent to communicate with the child. Often, where child therapy is not indicated, the best treatment is parental support and guidance. To develop a treatment plan that is based on parenting work, the therapeutic evaluation must take full advantage of the parenting meeting to enhance the parental alliance and to evaluate parental skills and potential psychopathology.

Not all parents are willing to commit to this kind of work. In addition, there are still a large number of families in which the father sees all child-related work as "woman's work." These fathers may be particularly difficult to involve in the family or parenting component of the child's treatment. Fathers who have narcissistic disorders may be especially difficult to engage. Their defenses often do not permit them to understand the impact of their behavior or their expectations on the child.

> Barney, 15, had become involved in a fringe group of drug-using and nonconforming teens at his elite private high school. His previous accomplishments, both academically and athletically, had fallen by the wayside. His mother brought up these concerns in the initial family meeting. Barney minimized them all. His mother described that his girlfriend of the past six months had refused to see him. Barney denied any distress. He

boasted that he now had more girls than he knew what to do with. He said he didn't want to be "tied down."

During the family component of the first meeting, he reported that his father measured success by sexual conquests and there was no reason he shouldn't. His mother made a feeble attempt to deny that was not his father's attitude. He gave his mother a look that made further exploration extremely uncomfortable. He then commented to the therapist, "If Dad ever agreed to waste his time here, he'd knock your socks off."

In the individual component of the meeting, he agreed to see the therapist "just to please his mother." He sarcastically commented that his father would think the therapist's office was "shoddy," but later remarked that he hoped his father would be getting a big bill for this. He minimized his drug use but admitted that he had to attend therapy as a condition to continue enrollment at his school. He also admitted that he didn't want to get "booted from the school," but "who could tell what would happen."

In the parenting meeting that followed as the second step of the assessment, Barney's mother described her husband as a high powered lawyer who was more often in New York or Washington than at home. He had continually ignored Barney's accomplishments. Father compared Barney negatively with the sons of his other colleagues. Nothing Barney did "measured up" to his expectations. As a result, he expected Barney to "look good" in public meetings and seemed not to care what else Barney did.

Mother felt Barney was learning how to "put on a show" and did not believe in himself or his potential. She suspected her son was quite depressed. She did not believe that her husband was willing to come into treatment, although she said the therapist could "give it a try."

The impact of the parent's narcissism, self-involvement, and competitive minimalization of others, including his child, is highly destructive. Children often abandon their talents in order to see if their parents can truly pay attention to them when they are in trouble. Since the attention the children gain with their successs seems to be owned by the parent, they may engage in highly self-destructive behaviors to defeat the parent. Too often the defeat is theirs alone. The destructive impact of one father's narcissism on each of his three children is one aspect of Richard Rayner's novel, *The Elephant* (1992).

The parental task—in loving the child—involves the struggle to "see" the real life child and to avoid placing too much emphasis on a parent's own history as the parent makes hypotheses about a child's behavior. The push toward projective forces between a parent and child can be heightened during a particular phase of development such as adolescence, or in some cases when a parent is more vulnerable, they can occur throughout the child's life. The works of Winnicott (1965) and Laing (1965) discuss the evolution of the true self and the false self as the child's response to the parent's behavior as the child reveals certain aspects of the child's developing self-system. The complex psychological interface between parent and child can assume significant proportions in the treatment of some adults who have had narcissistic parents (Miller, 1981).

Fiscal Informed Consent. When issues are identified that impact on the parents' ability to offer love, limits, or accommodate the real life issues of their child, parenting treatment becomes an essential component of the treatment plan. Part of the work may be focused on enhancing or developing particular parenting skills to match a child's areas of need. At other times, treatment may focus on the parents' own emotional experiences, which have blinded them to the needs of their child or created impediments to being emotionally available or able to work on social and emotional issues. There are times when a clear *DSM* diagnosis requires treatment so that the adult's overall function can improve to permit parenting work to be developed.

The parents will need, depending upon their insurance, to obtain the same kind of authorization that they accessed for their child, but in their own names. Alternatively, the therapist will need to explore how best to use a limited dollar amount of a mental health benefit. The therapist may need to identify what other resources the parent may have to pay for treatment. The role of the parent's treatment, how it is paid for, and its bearing on the symptoms of the child must be reviewed clearly with the parent. This review will also prepare the parent for the discussion of forms that may need to be filled out for the insurer about the parent and his or her diagnosis and past history.

☐ Broad Compromises in Parental Function: The Impact of Psychopathology on Love, Limits, and Real Life

From the other examples cited above, the clinician should be able to consider the implications of any *DSM-IV* disorder on parental function. (See Table 3.3.) The issue in some of the most difficult child and adolescent cases is that of the parent who tends to swing between the two poles of dysfunction in the ability to love (from symbiosis to neglect) and limit (from lax to overly punitive). (See Tables 3.4 and 3.5.) These cases most often involve axis II or character disturbances. The commitment to implementing basic recommended activities or interventions for the child is not followed through to completion. Most often this failure is associated with character pathology in the parent and may be associated with the parent's own traumatic history.

> Peter was brought for a developmental evaluation by the school department. He had exhibited multiple school difficulties, including outbursts of anger in the classroom. During earlier school conferences, the mother always denied her son's difficulties and blamed the school, often storming out of teacher conferences in front of her child. When the school had continued to pressure the mother to participate in home-based behavioral programs to reinforce the school's expectations, she reported she did not want to get

TABLE 3.3. The effect of parental psychopathology on parenting behavior

	Love	Limits	Real Life
Axis 1			
Axis II		Each aspect of parental	
Axis III		functioning can be affected	
Axis IV		uniquely by pathology at any Axis	
Axis V			

TABLE 3.4. Love's impact on nature of relationship

Parental Levels of Love, Attachment, Attunement, and Commitment	Relationship Behaviors
Overinvolvement	"Hypersensitive" parenting Symbiosis Projections from parent to child Blurred boundaries
"Good enough"	Fit with child Adequate attention and care Secure, positive attachment
Underinvolvement (None/withdrawal)	Poor commitment—poor attention to child's needs Poor empathy or attunement—inability to read child's clues Poor knowledge of child's developmental needs and issues Neglect

> him angry with her: "It's not my job how he behaves in class." Since his mother felt "he never had these difficulties with me," she thought the school should just meet his needs better.
>
> At this point, Peter was in fifth grade. He had become much less compliant with any expectation she had for him at home. He acted "like there was a wall between us." Difficulties in the neighborhood, including theft from the corner store, more fights with peers, and drinking on weekends, had come to mother's attention. All of these she excused by saying, "boys will be boys" and expected he would grow out of it. However, as Peter continued to withdraw from his relationship to her and placed more and more impossible demands on the relationship, the mother agreed to an evaluation to help him "at school." Although she refused to attend the initial visit, she told the school counselor that she hoped it would lead to her child being placed in a smaller, more structured classroom so that "Peter could learn to be nicer to me again."

The consultant was able to recognize the mother's borderline and narcissistic personality disordered features that had led to a disruption of her attachment, attunement, and commitment to her child. Even though she proclaimed how much she loved Peter, her love was flawed.

Sullivan's definition of love suggests that successful parental love draws upon the empathy that permits a parent to have "a sensitivity to what matters to another person." It is the foundation for the parent's commitment to the child's needs. However, love is also the pathway two people travel toward each other. Between parent and child, a complication exists since the initial behavioral, emotional, and need-based cues the parent receives from the infant or child can be unclear.

As a result, the developing child is a powerful screen upon which unconscious projections, reenactments, and reminiscences can be replayed. These issues surfaced repeatedly in the interactions between Peter and his mother. Her parenting was powerfully affected by her own psychological needs, just as other traumatized or sexually abused mothers may confront issues of separation from their children. Her fears of loss and abandonment interfered with her ability to provide a consistently secure attachment. Peter's mother's fears were triggered by the risk of the loss she perceived

TABLE 3.5. Impact of limits on nature of relationship

Nature of Limit Setting	Relationship Behaviors
Punitive limits	Abusive physical punishment Abusive emotional reactivity Rigidity
Comfortably structured guidelines	Normal development Family connections
No limits*	Lack of structure Positive responses to misbehavior Confused or contradictory responses

*Most troublesome in context of poor attachment/attunement

she would experience, which stemmed from her child's autonomy or involvement in other relationships. His anger could trigger aspects of her own trauma when she set limits (Hooper, 1992).

When Peter's mother was stable, she could be available. However, her rapid swings in mood and attitude led to Peter's sense of insecurity within the *attachment*. As a result of her unstable inner sense of self, her *attunement* to his many needs was uneven. Her ability to perceive him was affected by her response to her own projections. Her ability to make a consistent *commitment* to help him was unpredictable. In addition, her intense sensitivity to her child's negative emotions toward her could eradicate any affection she felt toward him. Her commitment to reasonable activities, peer or sports plans that fostered his growth, could be abruptly cancelled. As a result, Peter tended to shy away from supervised after-school activities.

Peter soon learned the parameters of their relationship. The mother vacillated between being overly responsive to his wants and needs and psychological abandonment. Peter's coping skills were affected by her continually bringing her child into her bedroom to settle his "night terrors," the term she used for whenever he (or she) awoke in the night. Her attachment, in terms of her ability to draw her to him for his safety, resonated only with her psychological need for his engagement. The impact of this vacillation distorted Peter's sense of expectations in relationships and his experience of separateness. He was always aware that his mother, when hurt, could withdraw in a hostile rage.

She rapidly disengaged from any interaction in which he appeared to be resistant. Her *limits* were inconsistent and capricious. She would never struggle with him to limit the choices he made that imperiled his safety or threatened the healthy course of his development, because the confrontation impacted her sense of safety of Peter's attachment, or her own self-esteem. Peter described her temper tantrums about his behavior. He told school personnel that she said if she had to do "more work" with those "stupid people at school," she was going to move. She constantly complained to Peter that other people were always expecting too much of her.

In addition, Peter's mother's sense of closeness was often ruptured when she felt he had slighted her in some way in spite of her awareness of the *real life* nature of child forgetfulness. She experienced his forgetfulness as an assault. She felt it was therefore appropriate to manage her reactions to Peter with the dictum "don't get mad, get even." Peter reported the time that he had not gotten her cigarettes at the corner store because he was pulled into a baseball game. When he returned home, he found she had thrown all of his toys out of his second story bedroom window. Her reactions were rarely connected to the limits that Peter needed to shape a successful and appropriately contained behavioral repertoire or an understanding of the real life events of childhood.

In cases like Peter's, the active engagement of the parent in long-term therapy is often essential to the improvement of the child's function, and it is also often impossible. The individual therapy of the parent needs to be pursued by someone quite conscious of the adult psychopathology's impact on the parenting function. The child's therapist must be patient with the pace of change for a parent, yet must feel assured that the parent's therapist is clearly addressing the issues in the way that they affect the child's development. There are some therapists who are gifted in their abilities to walk the tightrope of maintaining an alliance both with the parent and the child in these cases and conducting both therapies. Here the specialized skills of managing character pathology is key (Gunderson, 1984). In addition, the work with the family's resources in these instances adds another tension.

The tension is intensified by the child-trained therapist's natural identification with the child's needs. Most child therapists can quickly comprehend the enormity of the pain and confusion experienced by children whose parents swing between these extremes of contact and care or rejection and negation. Jackie Lydon, in *Daughter of the Queen of Sheba* (1997), captures the child's inner experience (her own) in relation to the stepfather, the Doctor, who was about to enter her life who behaved with these extremes.

> Out on a drive with the Doctor, I didn't know whether he'd buy me a soda or call me stupid, or quite possibly both. Both could happen in the same moment, yanking from polite calm to terror, so that I felt witless, drugged, a million miles away. I felt guilty for making him hate me so much. Just as suddenly I'd go weak with relief that he seemed to like me, pals, smiling while the two of us yakked it up. (p. 57)

> And anyway, I knew he did not love us because whatever love was it could not be a place where a wrong word was a trapdoor and a false step meant oblivion. (p. 71)

In most cases, the child's ability to perceive the flaws in the parent's attachment and limit setting functions is only partial. While the child's secondary gain in the "good moments" prompts denial, the complexity of the triggers of the parents' vacillations or attacks does leave the child "witless." It all can appear to the child as the child's fault. There is a high risk for the child to begin to develop character problems and have poor defenses.

An even greater threat to the child's development is created when sexual violation of the child is part of the parent's mistreatment of the child. In this sense, sexual abuse represents the violation of love, limits, and the real life of the child by the parent. It is a pervasively and invasively destructive force. Most often the child is a girl and is the victim of a male's behavior. The range of sexual violation—from inappropriate sexual boundaries to molestation and rape—has different prognostic implications for the development of the child depending upon the nature of the sexual behavior, the relationship between the victim and the abuser, and the duration and degree of threat utilized by the perpetrator. The work of Dr. Judith Herman (1992) and others reviews the subject of father–daughter incest as well as the later treatment of the problems that emerge in the trauma survivor's life.

The destructive impact of child sexual abuse on boys and girls is uncontested. The terrible prepoderance of girl victims is well documented. The treatment of the problem legally and socially, the use of family-based treatments, the evaluation of male pedophiles, and the treatment of victims is described elsewhere, although many issues remain unsettled. Intrafamilial child sexual abuse is a zone 2 problem. It requires intensive and coordinated clinical, social service, and legal resources, which are often unavailable.

When the therapist is confronted with a zone 2 problem, the parent by definition is not easily engaged in therapy or is unable to respond to treatment productively. Often there is neither the commitment nor the willingness to bring the child to therapy. In other cases, the restriction of resources defeats treatment efforts. Sometimes there is not the degree of neglect or abuse that requires school personnel or pediatricians to file with a child welfare agency. The therapist must manage the feelings evoked by continuing to work as closely as possible with the family despite (and because of) their doubts and concerns for the childs welfare. When a certain threshold of horror is exceeded in a case, a child welfare agency, empowered by state law, can mandate a care plan with which the parents must cooperate or lose custodial rights.

For any short-term or long-term treatment plan, the parenting system must be fully assessed for its abilities to love and limit and whether the parents can commit their energy to doing the work of meeting the real life needs of the child. Any underlying parental psychopathology must be understood as well as the historical and psychological (dynamic) forces that may affect the parents' abilities to ally with the child's needs. In these cases, the therapist's understanding of the parents' needs can help sensitize the way the therapist can advocate on behalf of the child. A partnership between parent and therapist is the model upon which the work on behalf of the child is founded.

4

CHAPTER

Finding the Treatment Plan in the Zone: Preparing the Short-Term and Long-Term Plan and Working with Available Resources (Including MCOs)

The therapist has now conducted the initial family contact, which included a brief child-based meeting, gathered checklists, and met with the parents. The parent meeting should have established the parental alliance and evaluated parental skills. Any adult psychopathology that may be present has been identified that may affect parental function. Financial resources, the role of insurance, or managed care should have been reviewed further. The background data of the problem, medical and developmental data, and the family history should now be clear. Any complicating tensions or difficult interactions in the family have been identified. In addition, the therapist has defined the "zone" of care. The third meeting is the point at which the therapist can review with the child, the parents, and then, together, what the treatment approach will be. If resources are limited, discussion with the parents must occur to determine what are their main objectives. Certainly this was underscored in the initial parent and child meeting with its focus on the reason for consultation. This active dialogue, begun in that first meeting and continued in the parent meeting, finalizes what the child and family want to solve and heightens their awareness of what they must do. (See Table 4.1.)

The definition of the zone of care will help the therapist focus on how to prioritize the elements of an initial approach to the presenting problem. In zone 1, a wide range of techniques can be helpful in resolving most problems. (See Table 4.2.) Assessment should have defined what treatment is indicated, choosing among a specific child and family intervention, a focus primarily on the parents' needs, case management, or multimodal therapy. The therapist should know, at this point, whether a therapeutic approach would be valuable or whether the treatment approach should integrate work

TABLE 4.1. Overview of tasks and assessments during first three meetings

		Information Collected	Tasks Given	Assessments Made
Session 1	Family interview	Observation of family interaction		Nature of family interaction
	Child play interview or Adolescent interview	Observation of the child	Checklists done by parents during play interview	Adaptive skills of the child Tentative diagnosis
	Parent check-in		School information to be collected "Detective work" Insurance task	Initial zone of care
Session 2	Parent meeting	Social–emotional–developmental–medical history Parental history Parental style of love, limits, real life Information from school reviewed Insurance planning review	Continue "detective work" or enhance emerging solutions	Rate child symptom severity and duration Confirm diagnosis Parental diagnostic Level of parental capacities rated Zone of care finalized Comorbid school problems identified
Session 3	Child/adolescent interview	Response to treatment plan Willingness and ability to follow treatment guidelines		Prognostic indicators Change in symptoms Definition of balance of therapeutic components: child, parent, family
	Family meeting		Continue solution-oriented steps	

with other systems of care, as is the case in all other zones. In zones 2, 3, and 4, the therapist must have a frank discussion about the severity of the problem and the limits of "fixing" the problem; rather there is the need to "manage" it, or to turn to other resources.

If the therapist has determined that the child's symptoms constitute the bulk of the problem, an axis I diagnosis can be made and the work may focus solely on symptom reduction, with the belief that enhanced relationships and active mastery will follow. Chapters 5 and 6, in Part II, will define the child and family treatment approaches the authors recommend for most *DSM-IV* internalizing and externalizing disorders presenting in children and adolescents. If the family is unable to work together on the presenting problem as a result of the parents' inability to understand and help the child's symptoms, this interaction must be addressed. The treatment plan must include parent and family meetings to help them understand the impact of the child's symptoms and begin to discover how, with the child, they can more successfully re-

TABLE 4.2. Zone 1: Treatment Planning

Child Component	
Enhance relationships	Integrated child and family therapies Psychoeducation Focused dynamic therapies
Active mastery/coping	Cognitive-behavioral interventions Skill specific group therapy Supportive-directive emotional problem solving or solution-focused therapies
Reduce symptoms	Cognitive-behavioral therapies Psychopharmacology
Parent Component	
Enhance relationships	Focused enhancement of the parent-child relationship through parent guidance or child-based family therapy Psychoeducation
Active mastery/coping	Parenting group Parent training Parent support organizations
Reduce symptoms	Individual adult psychotherapy or marital therapy when needed
Family Component	
Enhance relationships	Family-based treatment to increase social-emotional communication and to promote understanding and mutuality
Active mastery/coping	Family-based problem solving
Reduce symptoms	Family supports
Outside Component	
	State and national organizations that educate and support parents about disorders

solve the presenting problem. If, on the other hand, the therapist concludes that the child's symptoms follow as the result of a problem with the parents or in the family's interaction, the treatment focus should move to a family- or parenting-based approach, always looking toward simultaneously prompting the three key treatment elements. These were described in the introduction to Part I as follows:

enhance relationships,
active mastery/coping, and
symptom reduction.

The therapist should have a good sense of the ability of the parents to collaborate with the treatment plan, since treatment cannot occur without the parents following through. Two aspects of the initial exchanges (the initial family component and the parent meeting) have tested the parents' compliance and the level of the early alliance: Have the parents been able to reliably complete the therapeutic tasks so far, and how has the family faced questions about their own interactions, strengths, and weaknesses? How have they completed tasks related to the management of fiscal/insurance issues?

Several questions need to be considered that define the family's approach to the therapeutic tasks and where, along the continuum of severity, the child and family lie. These questions are different from those that were reviewed in chapter 3 about parental skills. Here, the focus is on the willingness, implementation, and responsibility shown by various members of the family in response to early aspects of the treatment contract:

- How have the child and family responded to early homework or structuring assignments? Was the first homework assignment lost, forgotten, or incomplete?
- Have there been no shows? How have these missed appointments been handled?
- How has the child or adolescent responded to the initial contacts? Have symptoms settled or escalated?
- How have the parents handled the process of the investigation of sensitive areas in the preceding interviews? How defensive or reflective are they? Has there been a feeling of honesty and comfort in the initial exchanges?
- Can the parents appreciate and understand the therapist's instructions and feedback? Do they understand the therapeutic process or accept the nature and meaning of the problem?
- Have the parents collected the teacher's checklist and scheduled a teacher's conference to find out the teacher's assessment of the youngster's behavior, emotional reactions, or interactions in the classroom?
- Have the parents promptly begun to advocate for further school-based evaluation or community resources if necessary?

Fiscal issues are raised in the course of discussing the potential intervention; these should have been discussed further with the parents in their meeting. Most insurers do not cover the collateral work that is often needed for child evaluation and treatment. The therapist must explain fees and how time intensive the work may be and ask the parents to decide what they wish to pay for. In some instances, the charges for this work can be diminished when the parents are interested in seeing what information gathering they can do. This process is the first exchange in addressing the potential additional costs of child treatment. The way the parents and therapist come to agreement about these issues will prepare the therapist for what to expect were therapeutic complications to occur. Areas of interest include the following:

- What issues were raised as the therapist explained that more meetings together would be needed to focus the work together?
- Did they find out the extent and nature of their insurance coverage? Do they know what their copayment is, for example? Do they pay it when the therapist requests it?

The third family-based meeting will have a portion devoted to child, parent, and family, in which the working treatment plan will be presented to each family member. Aspects of the shape of any possible treatment pathways have been explored in the first and second meeting. Drawing upon the above information will permit the therapist to refine the approach to the problem that will be suggested in this meeting. (See Table 4.1 for a schematic of this process and the associated steps.) It is worth noting that for some zone 1 families, these three meetings may constitute the entire intervention. The review of the child's problems, the feedback through the homework assignment, and the many suggestions and reassurances that are offered in the family and parenting meeting may well result in the third meeting being one in which the child and family declare success. Problem solved: the symptoms are gone, coping is enhanced, and relationships among family members are stronger!

In this chapter, a core problem will be used as the theme in different clinical situations. Symptoms (nightmares and disrupted sleep and play) develop in a 4-year-old boy. Each child will be called Johnny, *but each case represents an entirely different child and family*. Each case presents a different etiology with different surrounding family circumstances. The first four cases all fall in zone 1. The case presentation shows how the same tactics—initial family and child meeting, followed by a parent meeting, and ending with a planning meeting with the child and family—lead to different conclusions. The reader will come to see how the initial focus of treatment was defined within the recommended evaluation format.

Four other cases will follow that illustrate the impact of the zone of care. The implications of a zone 2 problem, a zone 2 to 3 switch, a zone 3 case, and a zone 4 case will all be reviewed. These issues are then addressed, in treatment planning, with all the members of the family. How the treatment plan must be adjusted according to the zone of care is reviewed.

What does it mean when 4-year-old Johnny awakens in the middle of the night screaming?

- Is this a normal developmental phase?
- Did Johnny's last toilet training session that included the "flush" lead to fears of loss and disorganization?
- Is his mother pregnant?
- Has Johnny just started preschool?
- Has his father changed jobs?
- Have his mother and father just finished fighting?
- Has the parental system become destabilized in some way so that Johnny needs midnight attention and reassurance that parental care is still available in the middle of the night?
- Has his mother just started dating a new boyfriend?
- Is this a signal of the early manifestation of an abuse incident or a trauma?

☐ Zone 1: The Zone of Normal Developmental Abilities and "Good Enough" Parenting

Case 1: A Psychodynamic Issue

Johnny had begun preschool three weeks prior to the onset of his nightmares. Mother and father were both concerned. Even though Johnny settled easily with their appearance at his bedside and accepted their comforting, he kept awakening. Unfortunately, after three weeks they were beginning to get exhausted. Janine, their 1-year-old, had begun awakening as well and then she would cry intermittently throughout the night. They went to their pediatrician asking if they could use more Benadryl to help Johnny get back to sleep. The pediatrician was concerned about their level of distress and referred them to a mental health specialist.

In the initial family visit, both the mother and father were attentive. They encouraged Johnny to play with the therapist. Although they told the therapist about their level of frustration, they had continued to be able to soothe Johnny when he awakened and had talked with him a lot about his new school. As they discussed this, the parents appeared quite able to work with each other cooperatively and empathically managed the new demands their child's troubles presented. Johnny said that he liked his teachers at his preschool and they reported he had no trouble separating when he was dropped off. He had friends in his preschool and rarely got into trouble. He had been excited about being a big brother, although the parents felt that lately he had become less playful with Janine than previously.

Both mother and father were able to help Johnny talk about his nightmares with the therapist. He was able to describe with pride how his new big bed did not have the bars "like Janine" had to have. He could describe what his nighttime routine was. He was very proud of how he had learned to get into his pajamas by himself.

During the interview, the parents expressed interest in Johnny's play choices and the other things in the office that caught his eye, but rarely labeled his feelings. They were tolerant of his exploratory behaviors and encouraged Johnny to play with the therapist after the initial family component and went readily to the waiting room to complete the medical history form and the behavioral checklists.

During the play session, Johnny gravitated to the dollhouse. After playing for awhile, he took the babydoll to the bathroom and kept sticking her head in the toilet. When the therapist inquired about what was happening, Johnny became anxious and changed the focus of play. Before the end of the visit, the therapist invited the parents back into the office and made arrangements for the parent followup.

The parents had secured an initial authorization for the mental health consultation and told the therapist that it was for three visits only. The therapist explained that in the last meeting of the assessment, they would complete forms together to request the treatment meetings the therapist would recommend. Their insurer's MCO would need to review this paperwork before granting other visits. Before stopping the first meeting the therapist suggested some homework. The parents were instructed to find a calendar for Johnny on which he could put monster stickers when he had nightmares. In addition, they were given a simple checklist for the day care teacher to complete.

Because of a change in the father's work schedule, only the mother could arrange to attend the followup parent meeting. The checklists and medical history form were reviewed and further family history was taken. The therapist focused questions on the relationship of Johnny and Janine, as well as on how both mother and father felt the siblings' relationship should be handled. The therapist outlined the basic family genogram in the mother's and father's respective families and evaluated the style of caretaking, limits, and accommodations that were made to their needs while they grew up. The presence of any current symptoms in the parents and a family history of psychiatric disorders was taken.

Because no red flags were uncovered in the symptom-based and medical history checklists, the therapist turned the discussion toward a reexamination of the onset of Johnny's difficulties. At this point, the mother realized that right before Johnny had started having nightmares, Janine had started walking. As a result, she had suddenly been able to get into Johnny's private play area and had broken one of his toys. He had thrown a block at her and been severely reprimanded. The therapist felt this was further confirmation of the source of Johnny's anxiety. The therapist explored further the mother and father's feelings about Johnny's reactions of anger in other contexts. The mother felt that she and her husband could accept Johnny's dismay and anger about the impact of the new baby but thought he should be able to "not be violent." The therapist realized the parents would need support were she to help Johnny display some of his anger more openly.

The potential red flags the therapist had noted in the case described above were as follows: (1) the parents' request to medicate their child, (2) the seeming last minute change in the father's work schedule, and (3) the pediatrician's concern about the parents' level of stress. These areas of concern, noted by the therapist, were diminished by the parents' openness and encouragement of Johnny, their completion of the tasks at home, and their reported feeling of comfort with the initial contact. Other positive prognostic factors included the fact that Johnny's symptomatology was focused in a sleep disturbance. There was no history of trauma, and there were no other signs or symptoms of other anxious, depressed, or acting-out difficulties. The parents had a positive relationship with Johnny and with each other. There was no family history of psychiatric problems and no evidence of severe parental psychopathology. They were willing to comply with treatment and accepted the responsibility for working with their MCO.

Although Johnny's sleep disturbance was not immediately resolved, the mother noted an increased sense of confidence after the first meeting. This meeting had prompted the parents to think through where Janine's crib was placed, and they had moved it even though that had no immediate impact on Johnny's nightmares. The problem, as the therapist formulated the case, was that Johnny's nightmares represented Johnny's anger with his sister, which made him anxious. This may have been heightened by his mother's overreaction to his normal aggressive response. The family was one in which feelings were not readily identified or discussed, but the mother suggested both parents would be receptive to increasing their skill.

The third meeting was set to review the treatment plan with all members of the family. The therapist met with Johnny alone, followed by meeting Johnny's mother and father briefly, before talking with them all together. The therapist played and talked with Johnny about her plan to help Johnny's mother and father help him learn how to have "a good night's rest." The therapist explained to Johnny that they would have five meetings to play with the doll family and other things he liked in the room. She told Johnny she also wanted his mother and father to check with him about the things that made him mad and they would all talk about that together. As before, Johnny looked away and his play theme was disrupted. The therapist felt her hypothesis was confirmed and that Johnny would need at least those five sessions and a reasonable amount of support from his parents to both identify and communicate directly about some of his anger.

In the parent meeting, the therapist reassured the mother and father that his sleep difficulties should respond quickly to a two-part intervention. Since his "monster dreams" related to his anger, one part would rely on Johnny's playing out his feelings with the therapist. The other part would involve the therapist helping the parents allow Johnny to be more comfortable in communicating about his anger in the family-based meetings. These meetings would also be able to identify if further behavior shaping plans could help Johnny with his sleep pattern. Behavioral programs would be discussed briefly with Johnny, but separate parent meetings would allow the therapist to help the parents understand and implement them.

The therapist took out the insurance company's clinical intervention form to fill out with the mother and father. She wanted them to be informed about the procedures required by their insurance company. The therapist requested five play sessions with Johnny, each with a brief family component and three separate parent meetings. She explained that when their company responded, they could schedule the next treatment meeting. Mother did not want to agree to the possibility of an extra charge, and the therapist wished to avoid taking the risk of a late authorization, so both agreed to wait. Now, the therapist said, we can review this plan together with Johnny.

During the final family portion of the visit, the therapist asked Johnny if he could remember the plan they talked about. He said that the therapist would help the bad dreams go away and then stopped speaking. The therapist continued for him by saying she had spoken to his mother and father and they too wanted the monster dreams to go away. She said that his mother and father had also told her that they wanted to know about the things that made Johnny mad, even if he was worried about them. The therapist explained that everybody in the family can get mad; even Janine screams when something happens that she doesn't like, and his mother and father feel this is okay. Johnny looked away. Although they needed to be prompted, his parents reassured him. The therapist said she would be calling the family to let them know when she could schedule their next meeting.

In zone 1, the capacities of the both child and family fall within the range of "good enough." In this case, as with many others that a therapist may decide fall into zone 1, there is often a clear connection between the symptom or problem in the "identified patient" and clearly acknowledged developmental problems, family problems, or external stresses. For instance, problems like a simple trauma, such as Johnny having had an accident at preschool on the day that his mother got to the day care center late; some adjustment difficulties within the family; or a change in life circumstances can disrupt the child's comfort. From a developmental perspective, current school demands, for instance, or issues about toilet training at home that might exceed the child's capacity to respond could be triggers. A typical presentation of distress can follow the arrival of another child.

While dynamic issues of anger, inner conflict, and perception of failure within a child can prompt the symptom, the presence of a *DSM-IV* disorder does not necessarily place a child outside of zone 1. If Johnny's temperament was in the anxious spectrum, or associated with another mild symptomatic disorder such as ADHD, a focused treatment still could be an appropriate response combined with parent educational meetings to help the parents understand their child's responses and how best to accommodate to him. A child's developmental difficulty or disorder can generate issues for the parents that lead to a conflict between them, which then interferes with their ability to jointly support or limit their child. This impasse may ultimately escalate the child's difficulty.

These zone 1 cases also include those with a family-based origin: the child's nightmares could be the result of his mother or father's increased frustration, or a marital difficulty that led to some evening conflicts. Parental issues include those in which the parents must modify their style and expectations for the child. The parent's past life experience or their own needs may be the focus of attention. The treatment may be to help a parent manage stresses that are brought into the life of the family.

Treatment responsivity can vary in zone 1. Most zone 1 difficulties will respond to a short-term treatment with the parents and child. Treatment may end, but the therapist should consider follow-up meetings that ensure that the treatment has "taken." Some cases develop slowly, and there are other cases in which some complicating factor has not been revealed initially (the concept of a "masked deficit," which will be explored in chapter 7). Longer-term goals are identified when the child is ascertained to have a mild developmental or *DSM-IV* condition or complicating family issues have been identified where periodic checkins will help the child and family continue to progress.

Enhancing Relationships. Relationships begin to be enhanced as the therapist evaluates the family and child in a respectful, accepting, and nonblaming way so that the roots of the problem are uncovered and treatment steps aredefined. Families in the first zone of care often have positive expectations about therapists as knowledgeable resources and as professional people who can be trusted. The therapist should actively take advantage of these positive transferences in the therapeutic process through the way the therapist behaves and offers information. For example, during the evaluation, this effect is heightened if the therapist clearly identifies the strengths and positive aspects of child *and* parents as they are revealed in the past history and present context. The investigation is most therapeutic when the therapist gives active feedback about clear areas of positive function within the parent and child's relationship and the way the family works together throughout the assessment.

Active Mastery/Coping. Discovering the link between the presenting problem and the symptom allows the family to better understand their dilemma and mobilize their resources to address it. This is crucial work. All too often the authors have heard families describe a past contact with a mental health professional in which they cannot describe what the problem was that they were working on with the former therapist. Therapists need to translate the code words of their field–whether diagnostic, interactional, or psychological–into terms that parents can understand and hold. Next, the family needs to understand how what they are asked to do relates to the solution. Depending upon the family, this can be time intensive work. Given the health promoting resources that exist within most zone 1 families, this understanding may be enough to allow them to solve this problem with minimal treatment.

The element that escaped this family–which becomes one focus of the work–is the way in which they overreacted to Johnny's expression of his anger in throwing the block, but also had not helped him develop another way to manage his feelings. He then experienced more anxiety about his aggression and developed nightmares. In this case, when the therapist spelled out the chain of events, it empowered the family to examine this discomfort. The therapist also needed to clarify that the parents avoided feeling labels in their communication. Talk about feelings is a necessary ingredient in increasing the level of acceptance, understanding, and comfort the child has with feelings. The parents' ability to embrace this input allowed the therapist to more easily walk the tightrope of addressing the needs of the parents, the child, and the family system. The goal followed: Johnny could learn to be more expressive of his anger and other feelings in a family that could work to support the appropriate expression of his anger without punitive reactions.

As the therapy supports new adaptations within the child and family, treatment complications can emerge. For instance, in working with the core issue of anger, the exploration of how to handle a child's misbehavior or anger outside of the home may become a prominent concern. This may mean that the parents must reexamine their own anger, how they express it, and what techniques they have to support their child even while they set limits on him. The parent–child relationship and family relationships must be considered in order to establish a new platform of relational strength that can include anger within the relational system.

The therapist must continue to evaluate the strengths and weaknesses in the system. For instance, a problem with a parent's experience of past abuse may be revealed in the course of the work. Parent treatment may be indicated, or they may require more active reassurance that Johnny's behavior will not become abusive if the parents also use the appropriate limiting techniques the therapist is offering.

The therapist must quickly identify any feelings or obstacles that may interfere with the active steps or emotional learning process the therapist is offering. An active and useful therapeutic relationship must include honest communication about the efforts of the child and family. The therapist's skills "to stay positive" will be tested as an active evaluation of the family's response to any treatment suggestions is made. While clients may be sensitive to the therapist "grading" their homework, this review should enhance the parents' motivation to conquer the problem and clarify their relationship to what they perceive as their child's needs. For example, the therapist must follow up about whether moving Janine's crib changed the parents' attitudes about Johnny or led to a better sleep situation.

The therapist's efforts to *reduce symptoms* follows as the therapist allays any secondary anxieties or manages complications that may emerge in the course of the treatment. In this case, the therapist may anticipate that natural personality differences between mother and father, their own family backgrounds, and their differing relationship to the two children may be heightened as Johnny becomes more assertive. Mother may express fears about the safety of the new infant; father may be more accepting of physical aggression. Johnny may strike a child in day care and create a new round of worries. Alternatively, reviewing the parents' respective roles in the nighttime schedules may uncover a marital imbalance that is feeding the presenting problem. Although the family can benefit from the calming effect that results naturally from the therapist's nonjudgmental stance, active problem solving may need to continue on issues that are only revealed in the middle course of treatment.

In a shorter term treatment, the phases of consolidation and termination commingle. This process is a "welcoming" termination phase, one which invites the family to return but also confirms the fact that the parents have resources to solve family problems and the child has many strengths. As follow-up meetings are spaced out, continuing to investigate the results of the modifications the child and family function have made will support the changes in emotional learning. It is often useful to have the last meetings occur at least one or two months after the initial period of treatment. The degree to which the family has retained the solution-oriented directives the therapist gave will confirm the therapist's work. Since the problems in zone 1 often respond promptly to intervention, this treatment period may be the therapist's only contact with this family.

Working with a Family's Resources. The case material presents only one example of a type of managed care process that exists; these processes vary from state to state and from company to company. This case highlights, however, many common elements in this process. The first step is the initial authorization process. In this case, the therapist and parents are both clear that the authorization process requires the client to initiate the request with their outside company. The company then issues a confirmation (or authorization) number to the parents and a copy is sent to the therapist's office. The therapist receives the company's printout prior to the family's first appointment, and it includes a clear visit limit. The parent is given the same information.

Although the number of sessions is limited to three, both the parents and the therapist feel this is an adequate number of sessions to use to evaluate the child and family's problem. The therapist can smoothly incorporate the education of the parent about the MCO into the evaluation. In order to move to the next step of treatment, a form is to be filled out. This is the company's request form for treatment. It is brief, and is easily shared with the parent. The company accepts that the therapist will complete this form with the client. Once this treatment form is faxed, the company's response authorizing the sessions for treatment arrives within a week.

The therapist finds that the parent is well informed and accepts that there is a shared management role that therapist and parents must play about their insurance resources and their own money. The parent recognizes the difference between the therapist and the mental health MCO. The parents understand that their insurance company has assigned the mental health benefit to this MCO. They know that human resource people at work have clarified what they can to do help facilitate requests.

The parents are able to make active choices. For example, they decide to wait for the therapist to receive the next authorization for treatment visits. They do not want to risk spending their own money at this point. The mother and father accept this as their choice and the nature of their company's rules. The dilemma is not displaced onto the therapist. No anger is displayed about the therapist's wish to ensure payment for the treatment visits, nor the therapist's desire not to bear the risk associated with their MCO rejecting the bill were the authorization to arrive after the service was delivered.

While the therapist had to explain some of these procedures to the parents, the parents also felt they could access and receive information from other sources at work. As a result, the issues of working with their company was less time consuming in the treatment hour. They accepted the limitations of the therapist's control over the MCOs decision-making process and knew there could be a process of appeal. The therapist was seen as an ally in filling out the forms and following the required procedures but was not expected to spend unpaid time in advocacy.

The family is able to discuss how it may choose to spend its own resources and how that relates to the number of visits available for therapy that the MCO may grant. At the point the treatment plan is made, neither the therapist nor the parents know if the company will agree to the total of eight additional visits requested. The therapist has clarified that the treatment plan may not resolve the presenting problem as quickly as they may wish. The parents accept that they may be willing to pay for more sessions if they feel the treatment is going well, although more slowly than they might like, or their company only certifies a smaller number of visits. The parents are comfortable making choices and educating themselves. Not all fiscal discussions are easily defined, and for many clients, discussions about money and insurance plans may become complicated. Different forms of reimbursement patterns will be illustrated below.

Case 2: A Family-Based Issue

Rebecca appeared at the health center reporting that Johnny was awakening in the middle of the night. He left his crib and came into the parents' room and crawled into the middle of their bed. Rebecca did not mind this, but her husband was upset and did not want this to continue. The husband was not interested in a referral since he felt this was his wife's problem. The mother accepted a referral when the pediatrician explained that Johnny was establishing a bad habit for a child his age.

The pediatrician knew that Rebecca was mildly depressed and that in other follow-up visits for Johnny he understood that there was some degree of marital tension. Rebecca had only alluded to these difficulties and had never wanted to accept a referral before. With this background, the pediatrician thought this would be an excellent time to make a referral. The family's insurance plan had a limited benefit and no management component. The family could choose whatever therapist they wished who was licensed.

Rebecca came to the first mental health assessment meeting with Johnny. He was a lively and happy 4-year-old. His interactions with his mother were appropriate and they clearly were well connected and understood each other. They talked together about his "sleep problem," and he appeared as disinterested in this discussion as his mother, although she insisted that "Daddy wants you to learn to stay in your bed like a big boy." Johnny explained that Mommy helped him get to sleep and that when Daddy was mad, Mommy would come and lie down on the floor next to his bed so he could go back to sleep. He said he liked Mommy's plan and Rebecca broke in and said, "I don't want Johnny to feel alone in his room" and Johnny nodded.

The therapist met with Johnny who talked about his friends at preschool and his special fun projects and he drew some pictures the therapist requested. In the brief parent meeting that followed, a family genogram, family history, and his developmental milestones were quickly reviewed. The therapist asked Rebecca to come to a parent meeting alone so they could talk together about her feelings and her plans to help Johnny. Rebecca agreed, although somewhat reluctantly, saying she did not want to take "Johnny's time, since the referral was to help him."

In the parent meeting, the therapist began to explore the mother's own history, symptoms of depression, and the nature of the marital relationship. Rebecca was somewhat resistant but complied as the therapist explained that changing a child's sleep pattern demands a lot of energy and a lot of collaboration between the parents. Rebecca had already said that she did not think that her husband would come in. Given the pediatrician's information, he decided to not press this point immediately. Rebecca's style tended to be passive and avoidant rather than actively resistant. Rebecca did reveal a history of chronic dysthymia, although she had never had a major depression. She said her husband was very controlling but that he was a good provider and very nice with the kids. She said in a flat and unconvincing way that they loved each other. She brightened up as the conversation returned to Johnny and his daily schedule.

Johnny's routines all worked well. He was cooperative, cheerful in the morning, and not a management problem. There were no red flags on his developmental or symptom checklist done by both his parents and the teacher of his preschool. He did not take a daytime nap any longer, although Rebecca said, with a small smile, getting him to sleep is a bit of an ordeal. She explained that he took a long time to settle down. They had the following routine: she and Johnny began watching television at about 7:00 PM. He resisted going to his bedroom at 8:00 so she had instituted a "cuddle time" where he lay on her chest on the living room couch with the television on. About 8:30 or so he often needed to get up and have a snack and she let him choose whatever cookies he wanted.

He was then again restless and it took another hour usually before he fell asleep on top of her. Once she was convinced he was fully asleep, she would bring him to his bed and then go to bed herself.

The therapist's assessment was that the problem reflected a sleep pattern disturbance in which Johnny had not learned to get to sleep by himself in his own bed. He was quite accustomed to an elaborate ritual that had developed with his mother. Whenever he was aroused in the middle of the night, he did not readily fall asleep by himself and would look to his mother's companionship to help him return to sleep. Mother's mild depression and passive style meant that she was unlikely to struggle with him over this problem. In addition, the therapist inferred that this elaborate ritual also served her to distance herself from contact with her husband and satisfied her needs for intimacy. Depending upon the degree to which her depression, her character style, and the couple's conflict impinged on the treatment, a solution-oriented approach could well fail. (See chapter 7.) However, it required a trial. After thinking through these issues, the therapist decided on an approach to present to Johnny and his mother in the third meeting.

While the therapist had a number of concrete suggestions in mind, the possible difficulties in implementing them were such that a tactic of indirection was chosen. It was clear that Rebecca was not ready to challenge the marital relationship. It was uncertain whether she could give up the double secondary gain of Johnny's symptom (reaffirming her closeness to her son, aggravating her husband), so the therapist felt that if the evening routine could be restructured to continue to affirm the relationship between mother and son as well as help Johnny discover that he could get to sleep on his own, a positive step would be made. In addition, the absence of other separation difficulties or developmental symptoms meant that the therapist was not concerned that the relationship should be immediately classified as a dangerous distortion in parent–child care; it remained a zone 1 problem at that point. The therapist recalled that mother was able to set some limits on Johnny. The child responded well to the limits in the preschool and those that Rebecca was able to support at home.

In the third meeting, the therapist told Johnny he needed to meet with his mother first. He was asked to pick out a special toy and to wait in the waiting room right outside the therapist's office. Mother came in. The therapist explained that he did not have an immediate suggestion for mother but that in working together he felt they could discover the right approach. The therapist asked the mother's permission to explain to Johnny that his mother was Johnny's "main helper" and that she would be finding new ideas to help the sleep problem. Mother agreed. Johnny readily accepted this plan and asked what other toys he might play with. The therapist gave Johnny a set of Legos and invited the mother to come in to confirm the plan with Johnny. Rebecca did so and then the therapist and mother discussed when best to set meetings with her and how to deal with the fees for therapy.

Enhancing the Mother–Child Relationship. The first step was to engage the mother and child in a respectful, accepting, and nonblaming way while taking steps to change their routine so that both parent and child could feel a sense of success, without the mother feeling too much of a sense of loss. The presenting problem and the symptom were the same in this case (middle of the night awakening). The long standing bedtime ritual and its relationship to Johnny's difficulty with returning to sleep without a great deal of attention was the central problem. The mother could be sensitive to feeling blamed by this formulation. As a result, the "discovery" that Johnny did not know how to get to sleep by himself was presented.

The therapist went on to focus Rebecca's attention on the therapist's experience with television overstimulating some children, as do certain foods. He explained that a bridge needed to be built so that Johnny could feel that he "trusted himself" to go to sleep in his own bed. The therapist explained that she had done such a wonderful job with Johnny that Johnny did not need to be seen. What they discovered together in treatment would be a gift to Johnny. It would help him achieve an important developmental step as it helped him become more secure.

Active Mastery/Coping. The therapist decided to explore with Rebecca if she could find, in their meetings and her experiments at home, a way to reconfigure her evening ritual, the snack, and the way Johnny initially got to sleep. The therapist could have given Rebecca the steps but felt, from the parent evaluation, that a directive might generate more resistance. The therapist did not wish to engage the father in this process since Rebecca was sensitive to his controlling nature. Rebecca needed to feel that this change was "for Johnny," not her husband.

If the plan is successful, the therapist's hypothesis that Rebecca's secondary gain from Johnny inserting himself between herself and her husband would then be disrupted. The therapist felt that Rebecca, in the interest of Johnny's needs, might be willing to give up the middle of the night contact, as long as the extended evening ritual was not disturbed too much. If this was not the case, some more direct treatment of Rebecca's concerns might be needed.

If Johnny consolidates his new gains, there will be a shift in the system that may result in further revealing the marital conflict. If this conflict is further unmasked, the treatment plan will enter another phase with a different problem list. The therapist is then in the position to suggest longer term treatment for the mother to address her feelings about her husband, to refer the couple for marital counseling (if they are ready), or to begin other treatment as a continuation of the present work.

Symptom Reduction. To reduce symptoms the therapist must be attuned to Rebecca's underlying depression and secondary anxiety that might be triggered were her special relationship with Johnny to diminish. At the same time, the therapist had to discover how to minimize any secondary gain that Johnny received since the presenting problem had been established. Johnny might respond with a lot of distress. He might be able to endure this distress with appropriate rewards and consistent reinforcement, for example, receiving a special breakfast time with Mom every morning if he gets through the night in his own bed.

Working with a Family's Resources. Another type of mental health insurance is a fixed benefit. It often takes the form of a fixed dollar amount. Some state legislatures have mandated this limited mental health benefit as part of everyone's insurance package. In this case, Rebecca's insurance company had a $500 per year mental health treatment resource that could be accessed for each member of the family.

Together, the therapist and Rebecca decided to use Johnny's insurance benefit to complete the three-session evaluation. That meant the therapist had another three meetings that could be accessed in Johnny's name, given the company's rate of reimbursement. The therapist did not know if Rebecca could complete the changes in the routine in the next three meetings but did feel that two weeks would be needed between each session to evaluate how Rebecca was managing the plan that she developed with the therapist.

Rebecca was clear that they did not have extra resources to pay for therapy. The therapist suggested they could have an extended payment plan so that the bill could be paid off gradually were extra sessions to be needed. Rebecca explained that her husband would be angry about those bills and she was not comfortable with that plan. She would see what she could do in the time allotted by her coverage.

The therapist anticipated that a difficulty might arise were Rebecca's depression to worsen or her resistance to change to heighten. In that case, the therapist might ask Rebecca to access the insurance benefit in her name for evaluation and treatment. Here, planning must consider both the client's access to resources and her "readiness" for change. Were there to be more resources, a focus of treatment could approach the resistance and actively address Rebecca's ambivalence about her marriage or any underlying depression. In this case, the patient's priority was clearly creating a better sleep pattern for Johnny. Then later followup could evaluate if this change had helped create a context in which a better overall family adjustment occurred and if Rebecca herself were doing better.

Case 3: A Temperamental Problem—Early ADHD—A Biological Issue

> Johnny's parents were convinced to seek consultation when the preschool teacher threatened to suspend Johnny. For some time the family had been living with Johnny's difficulty getting to bed and staying there. They had previously discussed this, as well as his activity level, with their pediatrician who suggested that time would help. When Johnny was calm and cooperative during the pediatric examination, which was all completely normal, the pediatrician reassured the parents that "there was nothing wrong with Johnny."
>
> The day care center gave Johnny's parents a few names of therapists who they had worked with in the community. When they called the pediatrician for a referral, he explained they had to call their toll-free number on their card since their insurance company could tell them who was on their panel of providers. The therapists that the preschool center had given them were not on their list. When they called the therapist's office, they were already aggravated. As a result, the therapist decided to begin with a parent-based meeting in order to help the family understand the way their benefits worked and to explore with them their concerns in the absence of Johnny's distractions or need to play.

Note: While the authors have recommended the format presented in chapters 1 and 2, the rule of thumb is that clinical concerns always take precedence over a particular format. The therapist's judgment that the parents needed to be seen alone to begin a process of respectful engagement is supported by the authors. While this step may lengthen the first phase of the initial evaluation, the benefit of a more successful start to treatment took priority. The therapist could tell from the initial contact that the parents were unnerved by the concerns that the day care center had triggered and the apparently contradictory information that they received from their pediatrician. The fact that their insurance had made them take an "unpreferred" provider did not help.

The parents arrived a few minutes late since Johnny had had a tantrum as they were leaving. Since it was difficult to get babysitters for him since he was "a handful," they had to spend the time calming him down before they left. The therapist supported their decision and told them they had the last appointment of the day so that they could still have the full appointment. The therapist empathized with the difficulty of finding babysitters who were interested in playing with active kids, rather than just "sitting." The parents immediately began to describe that Johnny had a constant need for activity and stimulation. Unless someone was playing with him, he just went from one thing to another.

The therapist listened for awhile and agreed that they certainly had their hands full and that it couldn't be "just them," since an experienced day care center felt challenged as well. As the parents seemed to get more relaxed, the therapist felt it was time to talk about their MCO and their mental health benefit. She explained what an MCO was and how she was a member of their "panel." This did not mean she was a part of the company or that she was employed by them. Rather, she explained, that they had put her on their panel after one of their mergers since she had been part of a different company. In addition, she knew that their benefits were limited and did not cover visits to schools or phone meeting times and that they could expect "a bit of red tape."

She asked whom the day care center had recommended and she agreed they were excellent therapists with whom she had had other professional contacts. Their offices were closer to the day care center, so they had more contact with the center's children. She explained which day care centers she often worked with in their town. After another ten minutes of discussion about "health care practices of today." She gave the parents the checklists to do at home, asked them to sign authorizations for her to contact the pediatrician, and gave a checklist for the preschool teacher to complete.

At this point, the recommended format for evaluation could begin.

The therapist explained that she would see Johnny on their next visit and the purpose would be to explore what he understood about "what got him in trouble" as well as to give her an opportunity to play with him in order to perform a social and emotional assessment. She said she would start with a brief family meeting so she could reassure Johnny that both his mother and father wanted to help him have a better time at school. She explained to the parents that she would adopt a positive tone and explore his ability to remember troubles, ask him how he felt about different things, and then watch the play activities he chose and how he handled them.

In her meeting with the family and Johnny, the boy was able to talk a little about the trouble at school he had, but he was clearly restless and eager to get to the toys he saw across the room. He kept trying to pull his father to look at the superhero figures. His father eventually held him in his lap "until the lady told him it was okay."

During the following play session, Johnny was able to tell brief stories about different feelings but then began to tune out the therapist as he pulled things out of the toy box. Going from one thing to another, his play became more and more exaggerated and filled with conflicts, things blowing up, including the superheroes, and nothing worked to help the people get things fixed up without one more accident.

In the following brief parent meeting, the therapist felt prepared to give further initial feedback. She again asked for the parents' permission to contact the pediatrician and the day care center and explained there would be a separate charge for this service were the telephone meetings to be more than a brief contact. If the day care center asked the therapist to observe Johnny and consult, there would be another fee. The parents agreed.

The therapist felt the alliance now permitted her to schedule a parent evaluation. She began the parent meeting by explaining that she agreed with the day care staff that his

> temperament was more than on "the active side"; in fact, he met criteria for an ADHD diagnosis. The therapist reported that it was not unusual that children with ADHD have shorter sleep cycles and are sometimes disrupted by sleep disturbances, such sleep walking or talking.
>
> She said she was amazed that the parents had managed so well with Johnny getting up at 5:00 AM and needing constant supervision. The parents explained that they were both on the active side themselves and that the father had been diagnosed as hyperactive when he was a child. They said they were inclined to be patient. The therapist explored how they set limits and what kind of disciplinary experiences they had in their own families of origin. Both the mother and father had experienced disruptive family fights and physical punishment that "was normal in their town." A family history was taken that revealed a high incidence of alcoholism. The therapist was impressed that the parents had accepted her and related honestly and fully. The parents seemed to accept the information about their child calmly. The developmental history and checklists were reviewed. The parents did not react negatively when the therapist gave some initial feedback that Johnny might benefit from some more structure.

Now, the therapist must prepare to go ahead with the third formal meeting (in this case actually the fourth meeting) by contacting the other providers. She is also more prepared to discuss the diagnosis of ADHD with the pediatrician and the day care center. In that call, she discovers that the pediatrician felt the parents were somewhat reactive and that they missed the point of his reassurance. The doctor agreed Johnny was hyperactive but was attempting to relay to them that Johnny's temperament was not based on a "physical" illness. The pediatrician was prepared to confirm the therapist's diagnosis when he saw the parents again. The day care teacher's checklist also confirmed Johnny's symptoms, and she said they would be very happy to work with the therapist.

> In the third meeting, the therapist began by meeting with Johnny alone. The number of toys he could openly access was reduced, and Johnny was told that he could choose one toy at a time while the therapist and Johnny talked together. She explained that she was going to work with Johnny and his parents to help him be a "good boss" of his body and his choices so that he could be proud of himself and do "good listening" at school. She explained to Johnny that they would then talk together with his mother and father and come up with a plan that the teachers at school could use, too. Johnny agreed and his parents were invited to come in.
>
> The therapist explained her contacts with the pediatrician and day care center and said everyone actually agreed that Johnny's temperament was very active and he needed special structure and support. As Johnny played in the play corner, she explained that the treatment plan would involve parent meetings that focused on behavioral training, consultation with the day care center, and possible referrals for medication or other testing later. Because she had spoken so long, she then told Johnny he could make a new toy choice while she and his mother and father discussed the other arrangements they needed to make.

Enhancing Relationships. The treatment relationship had to begin by helping the parents accept the disappointment they had suffered, since their insurance did not permit them to access their own choice of therapist. Unless the therapist spent some time educating the family and addressing this dilemma, she felt she would be at a disadvantage. From the family's point of view, she was an "unpreferred" provider. (Managed care companies often call the people with whom they contract their "preferred providers.") Until this task was accomplished, the child's difficulties could not be explored. The therapist must be able to establish the triad of relationships to form the platform for the work. In this case, the first step involved forming an alliance with the parents.

Once the parents were able to engage with the therapist in beginning an evaluation with her, the initial family contact that included Johnny could begin. The therapist anticipated another difficulty. Since the therapist knew her diagnosis of Johnny would be ADHD, she needed to get the parents' permission to do some collateral work. Since the pediatrician seemed to not have made a diagnosis of hyperactivity, she would need to have phone contact with the physician. In addition, while the day care center clearly described the child as ADHD, she did not want the parents to get mixed messages. Everyone needed to be on the same page.

Following the initial family contact, she saw Johnny's hyperactivity. The brief developmental history laid further groundwork for the diagnosis. He had had an extremely active disposition since he had first begun to walk. As the parents said, he didn't begin to walk, "he began to run." She was able, as a result, to guide the parents to some further reading. She gave them a recent article that had been published in a parent newspaper about ADHD. It even explained that of children seen in one sleep clinic, 63% of them had ADHD compared with the 37% that had a variety of other diagnoses (Corkhum, Tannock, & Moldofsky, 1998). The education prepared the foundation for the parents' acceptance of a diagnosis and the resulting treatment plan that included parent education and training that would permit the parents' relationship to adapt to Johnny's needs and be successful.

Active Mastery/Coping. The parents' anxieties about what it would mean to raise a hyperactive child needed to be addressed. Their relationship with their child would be affected across the years since they now understood that this was not just a "preschool" phase. They wanted to be prepared to maintain a positive relationship. No other obstacles appeared to interfere with these parents taking on the challenges Johnny presented in an energetic and positive way. Fortunately, the parents felt their own "overactive" temperaments had advantages as well as disadvantages. The father was successful even though he knew he had had a lot of attentional problems as a child and teenager. Both parents had already found many ways to work with Johnny. Further psychoeducation would be needed both about Johnny's difficulties and the kinds of compensations in family life that should be created.

Symptom Reduction. Once the therapist's suggestions during treatment for modifications in child and family function and emotional learning have been implemented, the therapist can gauge the degree to which there has been some symptom reduction. Followup with the day care center revealed that Johnny was doing better and the parents reported that he had responded well to the changes they had instituted in their care plan. His sleep pattern remained unchanged. At this point the family felt prepared to have other diagnostic contacts. A referral to a child psychiatrist for diagnostic confirmation and pharmacological assessment was made.

Since the initial processes helped the parents accept the diagnosis and modify aspects of family life, the therapist felt it was time to identify parenting groups or national advocacy groups like CHADD that could continue to be supports for them. She identified other reading they could do on their own. The therapist identified that ADHD may pose other challenges at other points in their child's development. As a result, a long-term goal would be to continue to identify and discuss these in intermittent follow-up meetings. The parents agreed to have the therapist monitor Johnny's progress and work with the family over the course of the next year or two.

Working with a Family's Resources. Another type of managed care benefit grants therapists a certain number of sessions. In this case, the MCO had a standard eight-session benefit for therapists and there were no extensions. There are other companies who permit access to a greater number of sessions depending upon their judgment of "medical necessity" following the therapist's completion of outpatient treatment reports.

In this instance, the therapist also had to educate the parents about how to access psychiatric consultation. This company's panel of child psychiatrists was quite limited. The parents would have some wait, but one could be identified. The parents discussed with their pediatrician whether they could just work with him. He told them he wanted them to access psychiatric consultation. The parents, at this point, were able to access their company's policy, which granted a single session only for psychiatric consultation. They learned that their company limited their medication follow-up appointments to brief (15 minute) checkins. The therapist supported the parents in completing this consultation.

In this family, both parents felt their financial situation permitted them to use some of their resources for the other meetings the therapist had recommended. They discussed that if their insurance changed again they might pay the therapist directly so that they would not need to change therapists again.

Case 4: A Trauma-Based Issue in a Child with an Anxious Disposition

Johnny's nightmares had begun, as the parents explained in their initial phone contact with the therapist, after Johnny had been molested by a 12-year-old friend of Johnny's older brother. Johnny had only told them after he had been having nightmares for two weeks. The parents said that they had already had contact with a victim's witness program, which was sponsored by the court in their local community. As a result of that contact, they had been advised to bring Johnny to therapy.

In the initial family contact, the family reviewed with the therapist their plans to help Johnny. They were able to talk to Johnny, in a simple way, about all the different things they were doing. The parents told Johnny that they were worried about his nightmares and the therapist could help. They said they were worried that now he would only play in the backyard and shied away from older children. They told him that they wanted Johnny to feel better and have the fun he used to have. They asked Johnny to tell the therapist what had happened.

Johnny repeated the story he had told his parents about the big boy taking down his pants and pulling on his penis and asking Johnny to pull on his penis, too. He couldn't remember how often it had happened. They praised Johnny for being able to tell and reminded him that it was good to tell his parents about things that worried him. Johnny said he was scared his brother's friend would be mad at him and had told him he would give him a new action figure if he didn't tell. This boy lived only a block away from the family and was frequently seen in the neighborhood and had played at the family's house often.

The family continued by saying they said they had immediately reported the situation to the police who would help keep Johnny safe. The department of child welfare had been informed so that they could assess Johnny's report and have the other child evaluated. In addition, the parents promptly called their pediatrician. He performed a physical examination in the emergency room that day to assess if there was evidence of other types of sexual trauma. The doctor reassured the parents that there was no evidence of any physical trauma. The parents were educated further by this contact as to how they might tell Johnny about the visit to the therapist. The doctor wanted to make sure that Johnny did not get further confused and worried about being "to blame."

The therapist told Johnny it sounded like everyone was sad and mad about the abuse and that everybody was working together to make sure Johnny would be safe. The therapist asked the parents to clarify what the rules were for Johnny's brother's friend. They explained that this boy could not come to their house right now. Johnny's brother still saw him on the school bus and was on the same hockey team but said there were some new rules for Johnny's brother. They reassured Johnny that his brother knew it was his friend's mistake and Johnny had not done anything wrong. They told Johnny that his big brother wanted to help Johnny, too. The therapist then told Johnny they would have some time to play and talk together and that he would talk more to his parents in the next meeting they planned.

In the play session, Johnny went immediately to the fire truck. He explained that the fire truck was his favorite toy and he had one at home that had a giant hose. At first, he set up a toy village with the blocks on the therapist's rug, which had a design of a neighborhood. After 20 minutes of quiet interactive play in which he said little, he grabbed the fire engine, started making loud siren noises, and began to destroy the village. The therapist commented that the fire engine was having trouble stopping. Johnny began to run around the office, knocking papers off the therapist's desk and other toys and games from the shelves. The therapist needed to repeat the limits and rules about safe behavior in the office before Johnny appeared to be able to hear the therapist and contain himself. After he calmed down, the therapist again explained to Johnny that he would see the therapist again and they would talk about the rules for safe behavior and how Mom and Dad would continue to work on keeping him safe from his brother's friend.

In the next parent meeting, the therapist inquired about Johnny's temperament and his style prior to the assault. The parent's explained that he always had had a slow to warm up style and that he startled easily. These two characteristics were also noted in the child behavior checklist and antedated the supposed onset of the abuse. When something happened that Johnny did not like, he tended to avoid it and when he came into a new play space, he tended to cling to his parent until he got adjusted. He had many difficulties separating for nursery school when he was 3. (See chapter 5.) His mother reported it took over six months before he was able to transition comfortably and "it was only three mornings a week." In spite of this anxiousness, once he was comfortable he was bright and energetic. He was popular and asked on many play dates by peers and had little trouble in those visits. He did well with all the other members of the extended family they visited.

The family history was positive for anxiety on the father's side and depression on the mother's side. Neither mother nor father felt they had ever had many active symptoms, although father reported that he hated the public speaking that went with his job. They knew they were very angry about the abuse and each knew they would need to deal with this feeling. They were also worried about the perpetrator and his family. They wondered "why things like this happen."

Sadly, it was one of his older brother's friends who had molested Johnny. The parents wanted to spend much of the parent meeting thinking through how to handle the events that were all currently on the table. The parents had many intense and conflicting feelings over how to handle the situation, although for the time being they were simply able to comply with the recommendations of the police, the victim witness program for children, and the social service worker who had been involved. They had described many of these plans in the initial family meeting because they knew that it was important for Johnny to know.

The parents reviewed with the therapist the strengths they had seen in Johnny. He did well both at home and at his day care center. He had special friends, a quirky sense of humor, and his teachers all liked him. Once he got used to a new routine, he was able to hold onto it and build on it. Both of his parents appreciated him and enjoyed the many activities that they did together with him with their two older children.

The parents were fearful that Johnny might begin to act out sexually himself since the trauma and wanted to anticipate how to help him. They stated that the day care center had reported that he had been masturbating at naptime, which he had never done before.

Enhancing Relationships. Engaging the family and child in a respectful, accepting, and nonblaming way was most important in this case. Johnny's parents, Johnny, and his brother needed to understand that "bad things happen" and then everyone has to figure out what to do. The therapist knew that the family would require reassurance that they had not been neglectful or done something wrong as well as much concrete advice about managing trauma. A plan for Johnny's older brother and his participation in the meetings needed to be made. The parents needed an emotionally neutral place in which to explore and consider the many feelings the sexual abuse incident had aroused. The therapist would need to continue to document the play session and other material that might be forthcoming. Case consultation time would be needed to coordinate the treatment with the work of the police and social service department's victim witness program.

Unfortunately, the link between Johnny's symptoms (his nightmares and regression) and the traumatic event meant that Johnny and his family could not escape from the feelings and the reminder of what had happened. In addition, Johnny had begun to act out a bit already and the tendency toward reenactment had to be contained or managed appropriately if it occurred. Johnny's symptoms would be part of the pressure in the system to deal with the problem until it could be comfortably put aside.

There was much the therapist had to do to help the parents learn about supporting Johnny as he recovered from the trauma, and Johnny had clearly indicated his need for play therapy as a way to deal with his feelings about the abuse.

In the third meeting, the therapist met with Johnny to explain again that he understood that Johnny had a big boy make a bad choice to do "bad touch" and told him to "do the same." He explained to Johnny that they would have meetings with the therapist to play and talk about the bad things that had happened and to make sure that Johnny could be safe and make "good choices about good touch" himself. He told Johnny that he would be helping his mother and father continue to help him be safe and that he would talk with his mother and father about helping his big brother too. The therapist explained that they would be meeting every week and that there would be extra meetings for his parents. They would also meet together with his family so that Johnny could ask questions and talk about the other people who were helping.

The therapist then met with the parents alone to identify what their resources were, what insurance would cover, and how they could access funds that the state had set aside for children who are victimized. The therapist scheduled the weekly appointment for Johnny and one every other week for the parents. The therapist said they would plan together when they would have family meetings.

The assessment and treatment plan needed to be in concert with other agencies and state efforts. Therapy created a safe place in which the family could talk and share feelings about these traumatic experiences. Everyone in the family needed to be educated about the impact of trauma so that relationships could be preserved and strengthened within the family. Johnny needed to have the special time provided by play therapy that would permit him to access and resolve his fears and feelings about what had happened to him.

Johnny's brother needed to be included to help his brother also manage his fears and concerns. Johnny's older sister, the parents felt, could join one of the family meetings and the therapist could make further suggestions based on the assessment at that time. The therapist's understanding of trauma and its broad impact on the entire family system and the different needs of siblings, parents, and victim will help him create a balanced treatment plan that deals with all the subsystems of the family as well as the other agency involvement.

Symptom Reduction. This is a very important part of the treatment and is required to allay the secondary anxieties and manage the conflicted feelings that arise as the treatment continues. This component of treatment is important in instances of trauma. Whatever psychological issues have been aroused will need to be discussed and considered. This is time intensive work. This is especially the case in the care of young children. The course of treatment must be lengthened in children with some predisposition to anxiety.

Anxious children can have heightened arousal leading to avoidant reactions to difficult stimuli. In addition, they are often vulnerable to generalization and the spread of the phobic response to other stimuli. The desensitization may take some time. It needs to be sensitively attuned to the needs of the child, especially following a trauma.

Active Mastery/Coping. Active mastery/coping should be fostered by the therapist's suggestions during treatment. Active mastery is supported by modifications in the family's behavioral exchanges. Coping reflects the way the therapy promotes emotional learning. The therapist will need to follow the basic steps of traumatic crisis intervention for each member of the family in order to monitor the symptoms, conflicts, and feelings that are aroused for each of them. (See Segroi, 1988; Terr, 1990; Gil, 1991.)

Were the initial response to the trauma to be reasonably resolved, the therapist could "suspend" treatment while alerting the parents to other red flags of concern that could permit their prompt return to treatment. The therapist would also need to identify midterm or longer term goals to promote the continued healing of child and family. If the child's progress was not consistent, or if other developmental processes did not appear to be on track, the family should return to the therapist. Because of the diagnosis of the child's anxious predisposition, the therapist should also alert the family to other anxiety symptoms that could appear. Psychotherapeutic reassessment would then be appropriate.

Working with a Family's Resources. If the family has a flexible benefit plan, this would serve them well. If there was a fixed or limited mental health benefit, the therapist would have needed to engage the family in a discussion of the potentially extensive costs of treatment. As treatment costs could be quite high, the family would need to consider what they could afford, whether some of these charges might be covered by the court or other social service agencies, or whether the family could use funds from the victim witness program, a program which varies in availability from community to community and from state to state.

The steps of trauma intervention are often defined in the treatment manuals of most MCOs. Both the psychological and behavioral interventions are well recognized. There is an understanding of the variable course of progress that healing may take. In some companies, benefits managers are usually able to provide a maximum benefit according to the underlying structure of the plan. In instances like these, it is easy to document the level of need not only for the index patient but also for each member of the family, as well as the family as a whole.

Zone 2: The Zone of Child Despair and the Search for Resources for the Child. The Zone of Parental and Family Failure

As the authors described in chapter 2, children who live in a severely dysfunctional home are rarely brought to an outpatient mental health office. The therapist may have had contact only with those children who are suffering from abuse and neglect in the course of a consultation with a preschool, Head Start, or a day care program. A child such as our case illustration, Johnny, whose main symptom is nightmares, might not be identified at all by a staff at school. Children in zone 2, by definition, exhibit reasonably "good enough" coping skills—it is the family that falls into the category of severely impaired. Zone 2 children may carefully follow the rules in day care, not protest when their parent is late in picking them up, and offer help to other children. Their relationships to supportive adults may not make them stand out in any way.

If a day care center has had evidence of abuse or neglect, they need to file with a state agency. In a case where the child is still in the dysfunctional family but no documentation of abuse or neglect can be established, filing is not possible. In many cases of "poor care" the failings of the home may be marginal enough that the child welfare agency would neither have created a service plan nor had to remove the children. The staff may be concerned about the child because of their notice of occasional poor care or their difficulty in reaching a parent during school hours or later. There may have been occasions when the staff wondered if the parent was drunk or high. The staff might use a consultation to think about how to help Johnny or his family.

Case consultation can remind them of how important those opportunities are when they can provide extra support and comfort. They will need to support the child's cognitive abilities and emotional strengths by offering praise and reinforcement. The therapist might suggest that the staff plan to continue to monitor the child's appearance, be alert for information that may be received from other neighborhood observers, and begin to make active outreach efforts to the mother or family to make sure they are aware of resources that could help them make their own best efforts to help themselves. Often agencies must file with state social service organizations. (See "Treatment" Table 4.3.)

Many cases of zone 2 children are identified in the course of their pediatric follow-up visits. Slowly, over time, a child may be seen again and again for injuries. Well baby and regular appointments for vaccination or follow-up care may be missed. The child may be seen often in the emergency room for an illness that could have been treated more promptly. These children are often identified by primary care clinicians and require some investigation and outreach. (See the zone 2 case of Joey, chapter 3.) This outreach is beyond the ability of most office practices and represents another weak link in the care of the most vulnerable children and families in our country. At times, the most consistent care these children receive results from their enrollment in community day care centers or Head Start.

For these children whose lives hover on the edge of adequate care, when there are other community resources available to extend the child's time in day care, the staff

TABLE 4.3. Zone 2: Treatment planning

Child Component	
Enhance relationships	Long-term relationally based psychotherapy when possible (issues of parental consent). However, loyalty/fear issues may complicate this grief-focused treatment.
Active mastery/coping	Case consultation to other caregivers—cogntive behavioral plans to help increase social skills, express feelings, and solve problems.
Reduce symptoms	Cognitive-behavioral therapies Psychopharmacology (issue of parental consent)
Parent Component	
	Engagement of parent into parenting or adult treatment usually not possible. Encourage treatment for failed parenting when possible; refer for parent's primary mental or substance abuse disorder. Coordinate above with care of child. File when evidence of abuse or neglect.
Family Component	
	Usually not possible
Outside Component	
	Community-based recovery groups, e.g., Alateen or Alanon, for affected child struggling to understand parent's addictive disorder or other impairment. Involve systems (school, other programs) to enhance child's quality of life and opportunities for success—help train schools to use cognitive-behavioral interventions. Case consultation to other care givers. File with appropriate state agencies when child victim of active neglect/abuse.

should see if they could acquire these resources and support the parent in using them. If the day care staff can support Johnny's relationships with other children, then Johnny may have other opportunities for peer contact and possibly receive extra nurturing from these children's parents. The staff should also make their best effort to smooth any transition that Johnny may make to a new school so that he is understood and supported there.

☐ Zone 2 to 3 Switch

The zone of child despair and search for resources for the child constitutes zone 2. In the zone 2 to 3 switch, social service investigation has led to the child being placed in an adequate adoptive home. Consequently, the child's symptoms may increase. The child now is quite symptomatic, but the new family is "good enough" (zone 3).

> The initial family contact began after the grandmother had spoken with the clinic nurse about being worried about her grandson's bad dreams. The grandmother told the therapist that Johnny's nightmares had begun right after he was moved to his grandmother's house by the Department of Social Services (DSS). She explained that his older brother had been put in a specialized foster care setting as a result of his extreme behavioral disturbance. His younger sister was in another town with his aunt. The grandmother explained that no one in the family had the capability to take care of all of them. "Ever since his Mama started on that crack cocaine, there was no way for any of us to help out much. She just kept us away until this very end, when DSS called us to ask us if we could take the kids in."
>
> Then she looked at Johnny and said, "But, Johnny, if your whooping and hollering at night keeps up, I'm not sure I can take care of you. Your Grandma is just gettin' too old." The therapist said Johnny must be a wonderful little guy since his grandmother was trying so hard to help him. The therapist said she understood that even though his grandmother was very worried, it seemed she was also getting tired and grouchy. Johnny stuck his head under his grandmother's arm and she said, "There's no two ways about it, Johnny is pretty special."

The therapist decided to keep the entire first meeting family based. The most important concern appeared to be the enhancement of vital relationships. Both the grandmother and Johnny had been through quite a bit. The therapist felt that the trauma they had survived needed the therapist to actively support the current relationship between Johnny and his grandmother to contain his distress. By doing so, Johnny would share and reveal more of his feelings in the therapy assessment as he felt more secure with his grandmother. In addition, the grandmother would understand better what the therapist's approach would be to enhance their working together, if that appeared to be possible.

> The therapist began to work with Johnny and his grandmother by drawing a picture of summer, winter, and spring (which it now was) to review the good and bad things that had happened in each season. Grandma looked at Johnny and said, "Sure has been a lot happening child" and started to cry. Johnny climbed in her lap and hugged her. The therapist shared that love doesn't always stop bad things from happening and supported their care for one another. The traumatic events of the past year were labeled nightmares. Johnny had lived through them, although they were still present, for the moment, in his sleep cycle.

Johnny was able to gradually engage in the meeting with his grandmother and to talk about what made him mad and sad. The grandmother commented that he was a regular whippersnapper and always surprised her with what he knew. She said he was the one that "stayed at her house mostly," because sometimes she knew what was going on. "Besides," she added, "he had been born on her birthday." She described that every one of his teachers at Head Start loved him. He was learning his letters quicker than most of the other kids. He wanted to draw a picture of his family for the fall–winter–spring book and made a surprisingly detailed picture of his grandmother, himself, and his brother and sister. Johnny left the project of drawing the family picture when he got to his mother. He complained he was tired and the therapist asked him if he'd like to make another play choice. Johnny chose the Legos and began to work on making a house for the small cars he had brought. The therapist and grandmother used those last few minutes to clear up some other details.

The therapist made a rapid assessment that the family of origin was in the second zone of care. The child has been removed and now is in a "good enough" caretaking setting but one that is still quite vulnerable. In addition, while Johnny's symptoms are not overwhelming the grandmother, his history places him at high risk for further emotional and behavioral disturbance. Since she knew that grandmother had missed the first appointment made for Johnny and that the sooner there was some collaboration with other resources, the better, the therapist decided to focus the next part of the evaluation on the larger "treatment team."

Before the end of the meeting, the therapist reviewed that it would be important for the therapist to have a meeting with the grandmother and all of the current caretakers. The state agency for children, the day care staff representative, and the mother's therapist from the addiction program would all need to get together to share a sense of a short-term plan, what middle range objectives were, and what would constitute a long-term plan. The therapist explained that often there can be a lot of uncertainty and confusion in trying to be of help, and everyone had to work together.

The grandmother's ability to care was certainly "good enough," but her resources and energy were limited. In addition, the grandmother explained that her ability to bring Johnny to a regular office visit taxed her strength. It took a cab ride to pick up Johnny from day care to bring him and then another cab to return him and get back home herself. That was just too expensive and "the welfare people tell you they will give you cab vouchers, but they never come on time. And I feel embarrassed not giving the driver a good tip because he needs to run in to get Johnny and bring him back while I wait in the cab." After day care, the grandmother and Johnny would be too worn out. Clearly she was willing to advocate for Johnny to have additional supports, but she needed them to be readily accessible and not to drain her limited energy.

In this instance, the child's adaptive and cognitive–emotional capacities are within a normal range, yet the prior parent's function had been severely compromised by psychopathology and addiction. Here, the affect is despair. Both child and therapist recognize the powerful emotions associated with the ruptured relationship and past neglect that has affected the child and his siblings. In the day care consultation, the therapist learns that following his placement with his grandmother, Johnny has begun to manifest alarming symptoms there—hitting, manifesting a great deal of hyperactivity, and being less responsive to contact with the day care center staff. His symptoms appear to be escalating in their view.

There are two essential bright spots in this case: Johnny is emotionally present with his current family support, his grandmother. She has had a relatively consistent, nurturing, and loving relationship with him since his birth. While this does not diminish the pain of Johnny's loss of his mother and his family unit, it does mean that his emotions can be identified, labeled, and then may be connected to his life experience within the real emotional connection he has with his grandmother. While the current level of his impairment places him in zone 3, the therapist is optimistic that with the right treatment and support he will do better.

While the grandmother can clearly love and limit this child, she gives evidence that her caretaking abilities are stretched and that her commitment will require additional system supports. She was unable to get the child to his first appointment. In the interview, the grandmother briefly resorted to threats of abandonment, but she is capable of acknowledging anger and frustration and reassuring the child when she is supported. The therapist did not find that the grandmother's caretaking would place the case in zone 2, but her lack of resources complicates the access to therapy. Further individual evaluation of her emotional makeup and any coexisting psychopathology (just as one would pursue in a meeting with the parent) is important here. Because she is the current primary caretaker, her strengths and weaknesses in her parenting functions will need to be understood and managed as part of the treatment plan.

Resources that support the grandmother's function and Johnny's adjustment will be necessary as ancillary enhancements for this family's coping. This support should include opportunities for the child to process both his affect and the realities the family faces. The treatment challenge is to define a set of interventions that prevent dissociation, splitting, or the development of primitive defenses that would impair Johnny's relationships and his coping skills in the long run. (See "Treatment," Tables 4.4 and 4.5.)

A long-term relationship-based therapy is needed that consistently enhances the key relationships in Johnny's life. This child must deal with his current losses while being helped to engage in the grueling process that will relate to the visits with his mother with all their uncertainties. He will need help to understand what has happened to his brother and sister. Visits that keep active his family connections to his siblings must reaffirm and reinforce his relationships. Finally, the way Johnny understands his connection to the caretakers who will affect his life and that of his grandmother must be constantly reviewed. Who are the people in child welfare? What is their plan? How do they talk to his mother and brother and sister? Johnny has a lot to attempt to understand for his age.

Treatment is seen as a bridge to *enhance family relationships*. The therapist's work with the child must connect the therapeutic relationship and the child's other "real world, real time" relationships. The therapeutic setting must help absorb and detoxify the components of Johnny's reality experiences and help him manage his emotions. It is likely that an initial period of play therapy will diminish the presenting symptom, yet the therapist knows that this child's needs extend beyond that initial symptom reduction. A long-term, eventually intermittent therapy that is integrated with the caretaking system of the family and state social service agency is called for. The issue of the payment for the therapist's time, the desire to have a consistent therapist for this child, and the hope for finding another good school and afterschool supports are on the agenda. In the coming year, when Johnny leaves day care, transitional support will be necessary, so the role of the therapist includes advocacy and direction to supplemental resources that the caretaking environment may not be able to manage.

TABLE 4.4. Zone 3: Treatment Planning

Child Component	
Enhance Relationships	Grief-focused therapies (re: handicap or loss) when appropriate to reduce anger and sadness that interfere with bond between child and parents or other caregivers
Active mastery/coping	Support adaptive learning Define alternative skills and strengths where possible—self-acceptance through above
Reduce symptoms	Cognitive-behavioral therapies Psychopharmacology
Parent Component	
Enhance relationships	Psychoeducation to help parents learn how best to relate to and manage their child Parent grief work to promote acceptance and care
Active mastery/coping	Support parent advocacy to gain adaptive supports to address child's primary disorder Parent group treatment and parent training to increase understanding and management of child's condition
Family Component	
Enhance relationships	To help (a) maintain positive parental bonds to affected child and find channels of communication; (b) to help sibling relationships deal with affected child; (c) to decrease stresses associated with care plans. To support respite care from family's caregiving circle
Outside Component	
	Connection to local and national organizations for child's disorder: e.g., National Alliance for the Mentally Ill, the Epilepsy Foundation, National Association for Tourette's Syndrome, etc.

In many clinical situations like this one, even with a therapist's desire to give continuity of care to a child, the ability of child welfare workers to help children attend regular therapy visits is limited. In addition, the ability of the often fragmented and stressed family to manage these visits themselves is doubtful. What may result is the child having a treatment that echoes the abandonment of the family! Missed therapy appointments as a result of the mother's relapse or lack of followup on her own care and fragmented care plans will lend a sense of confusion to what Johnny imagines he can count on. For this reason, many contemporary social service systems have looked to providing these services in school-based clinics.

School counselors may help provide an alternative source of continuity. Unfortunately because school system funding has been reduced, many of the experienced staff can only provide acute intervention and referral. As a result, the school-based

TABLE 4.5. Zone 2 to 3 switch: Family treatment planning (for guardians or adoptive parents)

Enhance relationships	Psychoeducational component to enhance understanding of the child and increase the bond and caretaking Enhance relationships when possible with new family Help adoptive parents accept child's relationship with family of origin that is mandated Family-based treatments for family of origin (following parental recovery) (a) to permit contact between biological parent and child (supervised–therapeutic visitation); (b) to support appropriate reunification plans.
Active mastery/coping	Parent management training

In the zone 2 to 3 switch, the child-based treatment and outside components are the same as in both zones 2 and 3 as indicated.

clinics have become training sites for different agencies, and the turnover of therapists, whether interns or poorly paid professionals, has diminished the opportunity to provide long-term relationships. Given the turnover of personnel, treatment will be short term and therefore focused on problem solving. When children can be directed to discuss and solve a problem, an internal locus of control (Seligman, 1975) can result. If the caretakers can also help these children see other adults as helpers for specific difficulties, then children can ask for specific help and expect to receive it.

Enhancing Relationships. In this instance, the treatment plan needs to move in two directions. The therapy must help Johnny and his grandmother feel able to discuss the recent loss of his mother. Then, they must develop a routine to settle and reassure Johnny when he has the nightmares, which signal his loss and anger. The grandmother's ability to make and maintain changes must be assessed so she can feel successful and competent in her care of her grandchild without being exhausted. Her initial contact with the therapist must not, however, overwhelm her clearly limited personal resources and energy. The therapist is already walking the tightrope of meeting the child and the grandmother's needs and potentially is positioned to deal with any reunification program that might be put in place if Johnny's mother successfully completed treatment and stabilized (the longer term component).

The therapist's first step was to use the initial treatment interview as a forum to recognize the loss. Johnny's knowledge of what had happened was validated. His ability to recognize his emotions was supported as part of his past and current relationship with his grandmother. He was not pressed about his avoidance of drawing his mother in the first session.

To help this dyad succeed in their relationship, the grandmother's grief must be understood. She is a parent who is suffering the distress of the loss of her own daughter to addiction as well as the new burdens of full-time child care. Her consequent anger and confusion about her daughter's impact on her grandchildren must be attended to in the therapy. Her limits in what she can provide for Johnny, her possible regret about the other children, and any covert agendas about her daughter or the men in her life must all be explored. The initial step was to support her in just comforting Johnny each night and returning him to bed. Their mutual love and care needed affirmation and support.

Active Mastery/Coping. Given the fragility of the current situation, the grandmother was not asked to take either active investigatory steps or implement a new routine. The therapist might have asked the grandmother to keep a calendar of the number of nightmares that Johnny had each night, but she could sense that grandmother was getting slightly overwhelmed by the idea of meeting together with all of the different agencies. As a result, that step was deferred until the therapist could meet with grandmother and find other funding resources and agencies to make sure the intervention could be consistently supported.

Simultaneously, a general systems approach needed to be instituted. Psychotherapeutic treatment alone cannot help this family succeed in their care for each other without the mobilization of additional systems to support the child's function and to extend the grandmother's emotional resources. Optimally, transportation, respite care and financial aid will provide significant assistance.

Symptom Assessment and Reduction in the Caretaker and Child. In order to understand what new bedtime routines can be established to allay Johnny's distress, several aspects of the grandmother's functioning will need to be assessed in the parent meeting, including how the grandmother can respond and comfort him in the middle of the night, or whether the grandmother can use a consistent structure for his behavior. Her own level of depression, sleep deprivation, and her need for support must be actively considered. Johnny's treatment cannot be severed from his grandmother's needs or the resources that will help this newly constituted family unit survive. If he becomes more out of control at his grandmother's house, the behavioral programs that help him succeed must be put in place in the home. The grandmother will require further training and support in order to manage these. In addition, the consultation to the day care system will be essential to contain Johnny's symptoms that are emerging there.

Working with a Family's Resources. The therapist knew that Johnny could benefit from a long-term therapeutic relationship, but the concrete obstacles to his care needed to be addressed. The care of these children is time intensive, requires much work outside of the office hour, and office practices are rarely reimbursed for this work. As a result there are not only barriers to the care of these children but disincentives. Given the limited number of sessions of many MCOs, the cost of collaborative time, and an often changing court ordered plan, caregivers must examine other funding options that may exist within other state budgets.

Although the therapist had an office close to the grandmother's health center, and was a managed care provider for the department of medical assistance's new effort to get Medicaid recipients to join MCOs, the therapist knew that the nontreatment time, no shows, and complications of this case would require efforts for which most traditional MCOs do not reimburse. All of these issues would be on the agenda for the treatment team to consider, especially since the mother had not yet fully lost legal custody and was part of the department of social service's plan for reunification.

Were this to be a case in which the MCO did not reimburse for case management meetings, the clinical care dilemma would be confronted immediately. It must be noted that in most of these cases the parenting figure is already overwhelmed by the needs of the child. Their ability to deal with the complex interface posed by current structures of MCOs and the complex phone or paperwork requests cannot be assumed. Here, the work will fall largely to the therapist.

The therapist would need to be in touch with the state social service agency to explore their plan for reimbursements in cases like these, since it had become the child's temporary legal guardian. While many state departments of medical assistance are creating opportunities for new companies to take Medicaid recipients within privately managed companies, most MCOs are more oriented to serving the population that has more resources. As a result, the design of systems that pay for these complex child and family needs in therapy and provide other resources is still a new endeavor, in spite of society having faced these kinds of issues for generations.

☐ Zone 3: The Zone of Parental Grief and the Search for Adaptive Capacities in a More Severely Compromised Child

Johnny's nightmares had been going on for four months since the family's most recent move. The parents had read Ferber's book on sleep problems (1985) and followed the instructions in the behavioral program. While Johnny's sleep disruption continued, he did not seem too cranky, and everyone seemed to get back to sleep well enough.

Johnny had recently begun to speak even less than he had previously. Suddenly, he seemed more irritable. They felt he was changed in some way. Johnny was their only child, so that mother wondered if it was just a developmental change. His father was a bit distant, she explained in her initial call, so he didn't have much of an opinion. He never seemed too concerned about anything outside of work. He refused to come to the initial meeting because of his current work demands.

In the initial meeting that mother and the therapist arranged, the therapist welcomed Johnny and his mother to the playroom. Johnny appeared distracted, clung to his mother briefly, and then separated abruptly. He took out a fire engine which he began to roll repetitively back and forth in front of himself while lying on the ground. The mother explained this was one of his favorite activities and that he had a large collection of fire engines. She said in the summer that his favorite thing was to sit in front of the fan in the living room whenever he was upset. "I think he likes the noise."

The child did not establish eye contact with the therapist or engage in any discussion of his bedtime routine or sleep problem. The mother explained he was probably shy because they had never had him in a day care center. There were no brothers or sisters. She did feel he had gotten "worse" after their last move. It was the third in two years that was prompted by her husband's job. She explained that Johnny always seemed a little withdrawn. She "guessed he was like his father" and reiterated that his language was slow to develop. He had many repetitive habits and often had tantrums when a routine was changed. Sometimes she had seen him "flapping his arms" when he was 2. "That was just a phase, too," she remarked.

The therapist decided to test the waters of Johnny's ability to relate separately. He asked the mother to go to the waiting room to do some paperwork. The mother rubbed Johnny's back, explained where she would be, and gave him a kiss and left. Johnny continued to roll the fire engine. He did not seem to react in the least when she left, although he stared away from the truck for a few moments.

After many other attempts to engage him, the therapist made a fire engine friend for Johnny with bristle blocks, which seemed of some interest to Johnny. He came over, took it, and took it apart and returned to his fire truck. Since it was near the end of the visit, the therapist told Johnny they had five minutes before his mother would come back in. The therapist again welcomed the child to pick anything in the room that he liked. Johnny went over to the trunk with all the stuffed animals. He threw them all on the floor and got in and tried to close the lid. The therapist told Johnny that was a fun hiding place. The next time, the therapist explained, they could play hide and seek in the trunk and do other things, too. The therapist and the mother scheduled a follow-up meeting to review the checklists and to review Johnny's developmental history further. He asked the mother to sign a release to get the pediatrician's record from the family's previous location.

In the parent meeting the mother again came alone as the father continued to reject the idea of attending. The therapist used the developmental history and checklist to highlight the significant concerns that the therapist had. He assessed the mother's personality style and ability to understand the painful information about her child. The therapist set aside half the time in this meeting to talk about setting in motion the exploration of a school based evaluation for children with developmental problems. He suggested the need for child psychiatric consultation. This meant that it was important to fax a note to her MCO that informed them of the therapist's concerns about the child's developmental disorder. The MCO would need to approve other professionals' involvement and designate who on their panel the parents could use.

In zone 3, the therapist has concluded that parental capacities are not compromised or are not the major source of the problem. Although there may be issues, as in this family, where the parents have a relatively rigid role definition of parenting, it is not seen as the etiology of the problem. (See "Treatment," Table 4.4.)

Enhancing Relationships. There is a tremendous need for parent education about normal developmental steps, play, and relationships to help this mother prepare for maintaining a relationship with her child and preparing for the feedback she will receive as evaluations go forward. These difficulties have a bearing on the treatment plan. The mother must come to understand how serious Johnny's difficulties are. She will be the link to the father's understanding. The father's lack of involvement is of concern since the father must come to understand the need for a longer term supportive therapy. He will need to be informed about the child's condition and that the therapist will want his involvement with his wife to make joint decisions. He will be encouraged to go to reviews about Johnny's school performance or to supplement activities that are planned for the child. The costs and choices about treatment will need to be explained to him.

In the third meeting, the therapist wanted to see Johnny again to further understand the child's relating style and then begin to talk about the various diagnostic and treatment approaches that might be possible to pursue.

Evaluating Symptoms. When a child presents with a significant developmental, psychiatric, or medical disorder, the initial phase must focus on diagnostic efforts. An alliance with the parents needs to be formed to help them bear the stress and strain of various investigations and to complete them. A therapist needs to anticipate the possible grief and alleviate what guilt or shame that may be triggered in the process. Again, if there is a pattern of intrafamilial conflict in which the husband and wife blame each other over the child's condition, this must be addressed as well.

In this disorder, the therapeutic work for the autistic spectrum child is focused on supporting all efforts toward the establishment of relationships, developing the child's ability to define emotional labels, and enhancing any fragmentary social–emotional problem solving and communication that may exist. Family-based efforts are primary. In addition, the therapist will be a source of information and education for teachers and schools. These ancillary relationships will need to be supported as well. In many situations, mental health professionals are more likely to understand these developmental disorders than some teachers, given their low incidence.

Active Mastery/Coping. The design of a longer term plan for therapy should help promote the adaptive environment that the parents can provide to prepare for grounding the child's evolving efforts to relate and cope. The therapist can connect the parents to appropriate national resources, such as the autism group, in this instance, or to CHADD for children with attentional disorders. Treatment must help the parents be advocates as well.

The parents' mastery is supported by their learning and activity on behalf of their child. The major challenge to their coping will relate to the emotional processes of their grief and the way they can face some realistic acceptance of the child's developmental course.

Working with a Family's Resources. The therapy meetings must be planned judiciously, since the resources of the family must be geared toward the long haul. It is better to be able to define with the family a long-term working relationship. The treatment is oriented to building skills in the child and gathering incremental understanding of the child's style of functioning. The parents must be helped to understand how to promote their child's efforts. If the therapist provides a period of intensive services with many meetings after which no change is perceived, where the parent becomes exhausted or frustrated and the child gains little rapport with the therapist, the treatment plan will probably not continue. When a child is affected by an autistic spectrum disorder or severe cognitive or developmental problems, the therapist will want to discuss carefully with the parent the process of slow gains, the issue of time needed to establish relatedness, and how to build adaptive understanding in the child. The way the parent is involved in the process of decision making about the use of their resources is a key element of planning.

In this zone, as the parents gain and accept diagnostic and treatment understanding, they can be advocates for the needed intensive therapies. They may or may not be able to afford them. Depending upon the community or state in which they live, their continuing efforts with their insurer, the school department in their community, and their political efforts with support organizations will be part of the work the treatment can encourage.

Many MCOs have classifications available for long-term disorders and severe mental illness. These may open the gate toward an enhanced number of visits. Many MCOs may need education about the value of consistent and comprehensive work with the parents as an essential and continuing component of the care, which should permit the parents to gain access to their own benefits package and not just that of the child as the identified patient.

Enhancing Relationships, Coping, and Symptom Reduction in Other Severe Child Mental Health Problems. On the other hand, were the child to present with a severe emotional and behavioral disorder, severe ADHD with oppositional defiant disorder (ODD), a severe separation anxiety disorder, an early presentation of a bipolar or psychotic disorder, the individual child therapy appointments are the tools through which a stabilizing relational bridge to the child is built. The well-attuned therapeutic relationship must help the child reestablish trust and comfort in the world. The therapist must facilitate the child's reengagement with his or her parents. The child must use the therapy to understand that the parents efforts are *for* the child, not against the child. Often these severe emotional difficulties have ruptured, distorted, or impaired the parent–child relationship. The child has come to see the parent's limits or structure as the enemy. It is through the intensive individual work with the child that the health of the parent–child connection can be restored. Without this component, the ability of the child to begin to use the structure and behavioral supports that the parent is learning in therapy is compromised. The parent must be educated about the importance of this work.

Unlike the therapies in the other zones, the treatment focus is first on diagnostic understanding. No homework or tasks—other than careful observations of the child's patterns of behavior or emotional reactions—will serve in many of these instances. The parents need to absorb developmental information and to be directed to texts that describe these developmental disorders. The parent will need emotional support in this process and will need time for their many questions, the process their own grief or guilt takes, and managing the level of their denial. Often a parent will need to seek out many second opinions. The therapist needs to be able to support this process, while clarifying the importance of a continuing therapeutic relationship. The therapist must understand the parents' wish to search for an expert who may offer a cure or tell them that their child will be normal.

On the other hand, when there are fewer cognitive and relational compromises in the child, as in children who have developed the signs and symptoms of a more straightforward *DSM-IV* disorder without multiple comorbidities and without major functional impairments, or an acute and chronic medical illness, as in juvenile rheumatoid arthritis, the focus of treatment with the child is clearer. Their need for a therapeutic relationship is also clear. Depending upon the severity of the symptoms and the degree to which the parent–child relationship is intact, the therapy can mobilize adaptive coping skills in all three systems (child, parents, and family). Eventually the therapist can help the child understand what is happening to him or her. In the early presentation of many disorders, it is the therapist who can begin to help make distinctions between self and symptom (see chapter 7), which will serve the child and family over the long term.

Zone 4: The "Most at Risk." The Zone of Helplessness and Hopelessness for Family, Child and Therapist

Zone 4 is where the family feels helpless in the face of the child's symptoms and the child feels hopeless about receiving the parents' support. The therapist feels both.

> Johnny's nightmares were discussed in the monthly providers' meeting for the day care center. When his mother was told that Johnny was worried and had told the staff that he had nightmares, the mother said she hadn't noticed anything. "He might be telling stories again to get attention," she said. On other occasions, the staff reported that the mother would often come in complaining about the kids and when she did, Johnny appeared frightened. Sometimes after she left, he wet his pants. He did that on other occasions, too. Numerous suggestions to the mother to consult her pediatrician had gone unheeded. She said everybody in the family was a wetter, including herself and her siblings, some of whom still wet the bed to this day.
>
> The day care staff often felt that Johnny looked ill kempt and was always in the day care center's kitchen looking for food. Once he was seen eating chalk. He never revealed any form of abuse. One time the day care staff filed with the state agency about concerns about neglect. The staff were frightened and concerned when Johnny seemed sick, stuck his fist down his throat, vomited, and then lay down next to his vomit to lick it. The report about neglect was not substantiated, although the center heard that there had been other filings related to the other children. After the center filed the report, however, the mother had not brought Johnny to the center for two months.
>
> Johnny was hyperactive, had poor language skills, and often was unpredictably aggressive with other children. He could not sit still for the reading or coloring activities. When he seemed to listen, it did not seem that he got the point of the activities. His fine motor skills were poor, but he was able to manage to careen around on the Big Wheels with great ease. He had good control, although he often enjoyed running into other children and knocking them off his bike. When corrected, he would just yell, "I won! I won!" He would have a hard time saying he was sorry to the other child unless he was told he would have a time out. Often following these situations he would run away from the center with little regard for his own safety. He had sometimes come to school and said he wanted to die.
>
> The mother was known to the nurse practitioner in the adjoining clinic. She kept her distance and often failed to keep her child's health record up to date without constant reminders. She often seemed distracted in those interviews and was quite guarded. She denied any problems with the children. She was pregnant again by another man whom she refused to discuss. Sometimes staff had heard that she had presented to the emergency room of the neighboring hospital for "falling down the stairs," but no substantial information was ever developed about the possibility of domestic violence although it was suspected.

In these cases in zone 4, severe compromises are present within the family and the child's development. They are often expressed in multiple forms in the child: emotional, behavioral, and learning compromises. Often there is a suspicion of, or documentation of, a background of severe neglect or abuse. Such cases often involve severe parental addiction, family dysfunction, or major mental illness, which can lead to a combination of relational disturbances or psychiatric, neurobiological, behavioral, and learning disturbances in the child.

When staff at school or pediatric clinics or other people involved in supporting the lives of young people work with these youngsters, a profound sense of despair, anger, or confusion is triggered. Intense rescuing efforts, anger toward parents, distancing or detaching from the child, can be common responses. These responses are no less rare in the treatment community. There seems little that can be done. The sad truth is that is often the case. Where there is no evidence that permits the intervention of a state child welfare agency to mandate change in the life of the family, everyone's hands are tied. Referrals to child and family treatment fail. The school or community may mobilize supports for the child that are often actively undermined by the parents' behavior or opposed by them. When the pressure of different concerned people becomes too intense, often these families may move.

When abuse and neglect are documented, often the removal of the child still poses major treatment hurdles. When the children are already manifesting severe neuropsychiatric disturbances, their ability to remain in family-based placements is compromised. Work must take place that coordinates and develops treatment plans that cross the lines of multiple agencies and caregivers at schools, community programs, and in the available support network of the family. When these children's behavioral or emotional symptoms escalate, the supportive placements can fail. As a result, they may be moved from placement to placement. When residential treatment is established, their long-term outcome is still clouded by their experiences and their major symptoms. (See "Treatment," Table 4.6.)

Establishing the Initial Treatment Steps. These cases are most likely to come to therapists' attention when their practice includes consultation to day care programs or school systems. In these cases, the treatment is actually focused on helping the

TABLE 4.6. Zone 4: Treatment planning

Child component	
	Most traditional treatment not possible All possible interventions when indicated Specialized home-based interventions or outreach Case management with other systems of care
Parent treatment	
	Most traditional treatment not possible All possible interventions when indicated Specialized home-based interventions or outreach Case management with other systems of care
Family component	
	Most traditional treatment not possible Specialized home-based interventions Outreach Case management Family-based planning meetings when possible
Outside components	
	Mobilize school and community supports

currently involved system deal with their emotional reactions, to persist in their efforts to support the family and direct them to other resources, and to handle the emotional stresses that are associated with filing with the state agencies. These are cases that everyone may dread.

While these children's behavior may be very challenging in every setting in which they are cared for, often their level of function as measured by global assessment of function (GAF) or other tools employed is not what determines the intensity of the utilization of the services available. In a select group of patients treated in one of our local hospital and community mental health service agency home-based projects, it was discovered that the level of intensity (number of visits per week, length of visits, and need for additional services such as respite beds) and the duration of needed services was more correlated with the lack of parental resources (fiscal, lack of transportation, or washing facilities) and the lack of availability of the parent for emotional support than with the level of dysfunction in the child (Reinert, 1997, personal communication).

Working with a Family's Resources. Because these children and their families fall outside of traditional treatment patterns, working with the MCO or insurers is not possible given their structure. These cases have begun to receive national attention through the work of the Robert Wood Johnson Foundation, the Casey Foundation, and other institutions that focus on severe emotional disturbance in children and adolescents. These initiatives are attempting to coordinate and bring together the resources of many state and local agencies and resources to focus on the development of a spectrum of services that can be "wrapped around" the child and family to support their function. An extensive literature is developing in this field, and outcome studies are beginning to be reported (Stroul, Lourie, Goldman, & Katz-Leavy, 1992).

In spite of these children's needs, a therapist most commonly may have only brief contact with these children. Managed care organization's benefits are rarely designed to work for this type of family in which a great deal of the service may be case coordination, consultation to other agencies, developing treatment plans within a variety of settings, and supportive outreach to the family. The level of outreach and often-missed appointments makes the service expensive and requires a great deal of therapeutic flexibility. The family needs to be treated as aggressively as the child is. Traditional MCOs and insurers of all types tend to support only classic office-based visits and rarely reimburse for other needed efforts.

PART

II

INTRODUCTION TO THE TREATMENT OF INTERNALIZING AND EXTERNALIZING DISORDERS

The concept of internalizing versus externalizing predispositions has a long history in psychology (Eysenck, 1967). In Eysenck's review, an individual's *emotional responses* are directed inward or outward. Internalizing involves turning emotions inward, which, if symptoms result, leads to the development of either anxiety or depression. The other broad psychological category is that of externalization. Here, emotions are expressed through acting out or directing the emotions against the environment, as in oppositional or defiant behaviors. These predispositions, along with their related symptom clusters, continue to be investigated in the present day.

A recent longitudinal study (Caspi, Moffitt, Newman, & Silva, 1996) examined the differences between undercontrolled (externalizing) children and inhibited (internalizing) children. They found that these differences in style remained somewhat constant. In addition, the young adults in the undercontrolled group were more likely to exhibit conduct disordered behaviors, while within the inhibited group more individuals met criteria for a depressive disorder. Understanding this broader approach to temperament and the potential developmental trajectories associated with these different styles can be useful in treatment planning.

The categorization of internalizing versus externalizing responses is broad enough to permit a clinician to consider two important contributing factors. Innate temperamental variables (neurobiological and genetic factors, which was Eysenck's perspective) can be examined as well as how the individual handles his or her emotions, i.e., which defenses he or she uses and how these may be changed in treatment or whether they will mature with time and life experience (Vaillant, 1993). Neither perspective (the neurobiological nor the psychological) need exclude the other. Both defenses and temperament are actively influenced by family life and experience. These categories can also help parents understand the child's problem and can set the stage for collaborating with the treatment intervention.

The diagnostic process that was described in Part I should have guided the clinician through a family-based assessment. While strengthening the existing family relationships, the clinician weighed the various impacts of the family's function, the parents' function, and their relationship with the child. The role of the child's temperament and inner emotional world in the defined problem(s) have been considered. The structure of the diagnostic process has identified the zone of care and should have permitted the therapist to identify key problem areas.

Chapters 5 and 6, which follow, present a wide variety of clinical problems that are seen in zone 1. Chapter 5 focuses on internalizing symptoms (and the *DSM-IV* disorders that certain symptom clusters represent, such as generalized anxiety disorders or dysthymia). Chapter 6 discusses the externalizing symptoms and their representative diagnostic categories, such as attentional disorders or conduct disorder. While zone 1 case histories are presented as prototypes, certain cases will examine the implications for treatment when the severity of the child's or family's pathology moves the case classification closer to a zone 2 (zone of childhood despair, significant parental psychopathology), zone 3 (zone of parental grief, significant child-based disorder), or zone 4 (zone of helplessness and hopelessness, significant child *and* parental psychopathology).

Chapters 5 and 6 have been written so that they have similar formats. The manner in which the diagnostic and assessment process is woven together with the clinical maneuvers necessary to set the stage for the treatment intervention is described for a variety of presentations of child problems. *DSM-IV* diagnoses that reflect internalizing and externalizing disorders will be reviewed. Factors that affect the presentation of an internalizing or externalizing disorder will be discussed. These include considerations that have been drawn from current research on temperament, attachment, learning disabilities, parenting or familial factors, psychodynamic insights, and cognitive–behavioral techniques.

As in the assessment phase, the therapist examines the initial treatment plan as a way to *enhance healthy relationships* within the family. When the parent–child relationship is already strong, the way the therapist shares a knowledge base with the parents and child should reinforce the family's ability to work together. Furthermore, it should be clear that the therapist's work, on behalf of the parents and child, is to help them be successfully connected to each other. Since the therapist has actively asked the family and the child about the most important problem for *them,* they should be quite ready to comply with the therapist's recommendations. The active focus on their perspective enhances their collaborative relationship with each other and the therapist.

The therapist will ensure that the parents' participation directly facilitates the child's new efforts to find solutions or master new psychological learning. Family-based meetings should reinforce the parent–child team in managing the presenting problem. In those internalizing disorders that interfere with active mastery, such as school phobias, obsessive worries, or compulsions, the treatment should help the parent be more actively involved in setting limits on the power of the child's symptoms. The therapist must help the child understand that these efforts are directed toward the child regaining mastery and self-command.

The first phase of *active mastery/coping* includes an initial psychoeducational approach as the first step. Besides helping to reduce shame and blame and assist in restoring relationships, the therapist describes and frames the problem in a way that empowers the family. The focus is derived from the child and family's view of the changes they would most like to see. The therapist's activity is based on choosing what may most likely succeed and simultaneously enhance the child–parent–family relationship.

In the treatment of the internalizing disorders, active mastery includes a focus on the child's ability to develop better coping mechanisms in order to achieve *symptom reduction*. The clinician can focus therapy in the child's treatment by helping the child extend his or her emotional understanding and expressiveness while promoting the child's more active adaptation, rather than withdrawal or negativity. Psychopharmacological assessment and focused cognitive–behavioral interventions may be recommended as part of the symptom reduction plan.

In the treatment of the externalizing disorders in zone 1, after the psychoeducational phase, the therapist's energies must be focused on treating the parent and family. Since these children need their families help to contain their impulses, successful relationships within the family will depend upon the therapist helping the parents to develop limiting and containing mechanisms that minimize the child's acting out. To support the parent–child relationship, these are explained to the child in the family-based meetings as helping the child to "be boss of himself or herself" or to "make better choices."

In the externalizing disorders, the parents' attention is directed to helping the child's active mastery of self-control and more appropriate social or emotional expression. As the child's specific behavioral goals are defined and the therapist further assesses the parents' ability to take appropriate actions, the individual treatment with the child will be directed toward helping the child maintain an alliance with the family and the treatment goals. Varied treatment formats can be used. These include those in which half of the session is devoted to work with the child while the other half is devoted to the parent, regular full family problem solving sessions, or meetings that alternate the child, parent, and family meetings.

There are also presentations of child problems in which the child manifests both externalizing and internalizing symptoms. In these cases, the skill of the therapist will be tested. The therapist will need to define the way in which the parents must walk the tightrope between the child's uncontrolled behavior on the one hand and his or her overanxious or depressive responses on the other. The therapist must help the parents become "super parents" in that the parents must learn to use carefully balanced support and containment. Poorly balanced containment and support often sets in motion a negative spiral of maladaptation within the child and the family system. As system dysfunction increases, the therapist must reconsider the zone of care. Severe parental vulnerabilities, when they exacerbate all the child's misbehaviors or lead to symptom activation, will move this kind of case toward zone 4.

Whenever the child is more severely symptomatic, either through internalizing or externalizing expressions in the child (moving along the continuum of impairment to zone 3), the "good enough" parents' involvement must necessarily increase. The parents will be directed to create environmental accommodations that will promote the child's ability to contain his or her anxiety or acting out within the family, school, or other social contexts. Additional limits will be needed to diminish any self-injurious or suicidal behaviors while more active and appropriate social and emotional behaviors are encouraged in the child. Considerable therapeutic resources must be directed to the process of helping an acting-out child develop the ability to contain affect. In addition, his or her ability to maintain a positive relationship with his or her parents will be further tested as limits are set, and more intensive family-based treatment is needed to keep relationships working as well as possible.

On the other hand, where the parents' dysfunction is severe (moving toward zone 2), the treatment must simultaneously include a refined combination of adult and parental therapy when possible. In the most severe cases of parental compromise combined with severe internalizing or externalizing disorders in the child (zone 4), treatment resources may need to include hospitalization, residential services, or continuous individual and family therapy along with outreach services. For most outpatient therapists, treatment in zone 4 may finally look like a series of limited crisis interventions. These families do not and cannot use outpatient treatment resources on a consistent basis.

Chapter 7 of Part II will examine the complications in the course of treatment that obstruct the straightforward resolution of the presenting problem in what has appeared to be a zone 1 child and family. In these cases, the complication was not readily detected or foreseen during the diagnostic process. In some cases, the elements of the problem in the identified patient or the family are initially obscured or are only revealed with time. The treatment plan will take more time to implement, and more work must take place to involve the patient and family in appropriate steps to help them resolve the problem and work together. Often, unconscious conflicts or characterological elements in the child or parents complicate problem resolution.

In these cases, the zone of care may need to be reconsidered depending on the severity of the complication. Certain complications move the case along the continuum of severity from zone 1 toward zones 2–4. These cases include masked or more subtle elements of familial, parental or child psychopathology. Often, the information needed to define these elements during the diagnostic process was not disclosed. For example, when the parents' history of abuse (moving toward zone 2) blocks their ability to learn appropriate limit setting, additional resources for the parents' treatment are needed.

In other instances, in what has appeared to be a normal parent–child relationship, the therapist may begin to see more symbiotic elements that pose an obstruction to the problem's resolution. Dysfunctional family processes, such as scapegoating, triangulations, or hidden marital conflicts that have been displaced onto the child, may take a while to be revealed. Alternatively, more severe forms of child symptoms may not respond to treatment or the child's condition may worsen. Here, the case moves along the continuum toward zone 3, and other treatment approaches are needed.

The treatment planning for zones 2–4 will not be reviewed in depth in this text. Since these cases are less likely to be seen in the typical office-based practice, another volume will be dedicated to the current efforts to care for this difficult population.

5

CHAPTER

Internalizing Disorders: Anxiety and Depressive Disorders in Children

Internalizing symptoms in a child deserve professional evaluation when they do not respond sufficiently to support from parents, members of the extended family, teachers, or friends. Although depressive or anxious symptoms can signal the presence of a primary anxiety or depressive disorder, they are most often seen in the therapist's regular office practice as a result of circumscribed reactions to environmental stresses, developmental challenges, or familial conflicts that overwhelm the coping resources of the child. As a result, therapists will find that internalizing symptoms, whether anxiety or depression, frequently accompany children's presenting problems.

Part I discussed the way the authors recommend completing a diagnostic assessment that simultaneously establishes a framework for treatment. The diagnostic assessment, like the treatment which will follow, will promote an understanding of the problem between the child and the parents, any associated symptoms, and the diagnosis. Simultaneously, the therapist's actions should strengthen the family's coping style and relationship to the child. By the end of the evaluation, the therapist's understanding of the components of the problem should be relatively complete and be presented to the family. To review, the therapeutic aims are built on the relationships within the family, and the therapeutic formulation should help the family begin by affirming these relationships. The therapist will identify how the treatment will continue to strengthen these connections. In addition, during the diagnostic phase, the therapist has directed the child and family to work together to find ways to master the problem and to reduce any associated symptoms.

Assessment Phase

Enhance Relationships

- The family meeting has permitted the therapist to understand the strengths and weaknesses of the connection between parent and child as well as the quality of their emotional communication and problem solving skills. Throughout the diagnostic assessment, the therapist has directed attention to strengthening these connections.

Active Mastery/Coping

- The parent-based meeting should have spelled out the impact of any intrafamilial (or parental) triggers for the child's anxiety and depression, such as familial demands the child cannot meet, parental psychopathology, contributing familial vulnerabilities (e.g., favoritism of a sibling or marital or other intrafamilial conflict), or environmental contributions to the child's symptoms (e.g., a poor school placement). The therapist should have a clear sense of which of these, separately or together, should be modified in order to help the child and family regain a sense of control.
- The therapist's contact with the child should have led to an estimation of the coping skills and psychological defenses the child uses, a sense of the child's self-esteem, and an initial appreciation of the child's major emotional concerns. The therapist will have a sense of how to help the child manage feelings, deal with conflict, and promote the child's sense of success.

Reduce Symptoms

- The presence and severity of any existing symptoms have also been identified by the descriptions drawn from the parents, the behavioral checklists that have been used, and the direct questioning of the child or adolescent. Learning problems should have been identified in this initial screening. The *DSM-IV* diagnosis is established. Then the therapist can consider which cognitive–behavioral techniques to use or whether psychiatric consultation can help in diminishing these symptoms.

In the final child and family feedback meeting of the diagnostic phase, the therapist's evaluation of the problem and perceptions of contributing factors are shared with the entire family. The therapist may choose to meet separately with the child and parents to create an opportunity for discussion that speaks to their separate needs. If separate meetings occur, the structure of the treatment plan should be shared within the family context. The therapist must balance the needs of both the child and family to support their essential relationship with each other. Treatment planning is another opportunity to clarify the therapist's emphasis on the "therapist–family team approach" to change the presenting problem. Throughout the assessment phase, the groundwork for the basic treatment ingredients has been laid out.

Treatment techniques that help adults to contain anxiety or depression, such as the ability to express feelings, accept reassurance, and test reality, work as well for children as they do for adults. In internalizing disorders, whether expressed by anxiety or depression, situations and feelings are often intertwined. In zone 1, the first phase of therapy consists of a series of the following related steps that the therapist will actively pursue.

First Phase of Therapy

Enhance Relationships

- Treatment should extend the child and family's understanding of the problem and its relationship to the child's symptoms and enhance their sense of collaboration and care.

- The family's communication, emotional connectedness, and positive feelings for each other should be addressed.

Active Mastery/Coping

- Stress relieving distractions, activities that promote health and family connections, and other indicated supports, whether tutoring or an after-school program, should be suggested when indicated.
- Treatment should help the child manage emotions and emotional communication in the most constructive way.
- The intervention must occur at the child's level of understanding. (The use of child-focused techniques, such as play therapy and appropriately modified relaxation exercises, help the child use the intervention.)

Reduce Symptoms

- The child should be given ways to help manage anxious or depressive symptoms so that other emotional work can be done and relationships can be maintained.

In the zone 1 family, as the first phase of treatment begins, the therapist should see the restoration of healthy responses in the child and an increased ability to manage the emotional challenge presented by the problem. The family will quickly move to support or limit the child or to engage other supports. The parents will be receptive to learning about themselves so they can become as effective as they can be as parents. The family will acknowledge their successes and identify other issues without blaming or shaming. Even strikingly symptomatic presentations may quickly resolve.

As successful relationships are affirmed, active mastery increases, and symptoms are reduced, the interval between therapy meetings can then be increased. The therapist can monitor and support the child and family's increased coping skills. If a failure to cope with anxiety or depression occurs, the child, family, and therapist will be better able to understand whether it has been triggered by an identifiable challenge within the family, peer group, or environment. The treatment should have helped the child and family identify whether some emotion, be it understandable sadness, frustration, or disappointment, is the trigger. Those minor reversals that may occur during the intermittent therapy can actually improve the child or family's understanding and result in further confidence in their coping skills. A typical case follows.

Initial Parent Meeting

The parents of 10-year-old Claude requested an initial meeting without the child. The mother reported that they were uncertain about how to discuss the reason for the consultation with him. She felt he was having panic attacks. The mother also wanted to ask the therapist "a few questions" before beginning. The therapist reviewed with her what insurance she had available and she said it was a straightforward indemnity plan. She had been in treatment for a number of years, so she knew how her mental health benefit worked and was quite willing to pay directly for meetings since she knew the limits of her insurance benefits. An appointment was set.

The parents arrived on time. As they entered the office, the mother looked somewhat downcast and anxious. Her husband had a more cheerful and straightforward demeanor. After they selected their chairs in the office, Claude's father looked at his wife and raised his eyebrows. She looked anxious but began the meeting by asking the therapist what he thought of medication. The therapist chose to answer directly by saying he had a number of clients who clearly benefited from medication and a number who had not. He worked closely with a woman psychiatrist who he felt was quite well informed about current medications and was a warm and comfortable person.

The mother looked relieved. She then spontaneously described her history of depression, anxiety, and alcoholism. She reported that it had now been six years that she had been in recovery. She described how grateful she had been to her therapist who initially helped her into recovery and, she felt, saved her life and her family. She did not get into recovery until Claude was 4.

However, she reported, following her sobriety, her medication treatment had only begun after another person in Alcoholics Anonymous (AA) told her that he had been on medication for three years and it had changed his life as much as AA. He knew that she suffered from the same kind of pervasive anxiety and depression that he did from her talks in meetings. As a result, Claude's mother had gone to see a psychiatrist and was now on medication. She felt it had tremendously changed her ability to function.

Her inner anxieties had always been manifested in impatience with her kids. Although she always felt she loved them a great deal, she felt Claude had suffered from her reactivity. Neither she nor her husband felt there had ever been any neglect. The therapist clarified whether, during the time she drank, there had been any physical abuse as part of her reactivity. Both parents reported the mother's irritability had never reached that point and her drinking had never been such that she was completely out of control.

Since Claude now seemed to have panic attacks, just like she had, she wanted to make sure that he saw a therapist who did not feel opposed to medication and would recommend a consultation if needed. The therapist reassured her that he would and was pleased that she was able to be so forthright about her concerns. He reminded her that she had also asked about what to tell Claude about the consultation and wondered if they could describe what Claude was experiencing.

The parents, together, then described the gradual onset of anxiety and panic symptoms that had begun over the past few weeks. Claude, at this time, could not go to school unless he had a full schedule of his parents' whereabouts. He reported extreme anxiety and tearfulness if his parents were late to pick him up from his music and tennis activities or if their schedule was altered in any way. His anxiety had diminished considerably since his mother had gotten a cellular phone so that he could call her from school and that she could call him if there was any change of plan.

At this point his parents said they had stopped seeing their own friends, since they were extremely worried about the level of his distress. They had heard from his teachers that Claude spent time crying at his desk and was unable to concentrate on any of his work. Even though he had always been a top student, with a special interest in math, he had begun to refuse to go to school. Although they had made him go, mother let him stay home with her when she could. She noticed that the next day was always worse.

The therapist responded that it did sound like a major anxiety disorder and that Claude sounded a bit depressed too. But, he said, that would not be too unusual since Claude sounded like the kind of fellow who would know that he wasn't doing as well as he usually did. The parents agreed and both described his many activities and his friends. His father then described the last scout trip that they had taken, during which Claude could not stay in the bunk with his friend. He had to sleep on the floor next to his father, which made Claude very embarrassed.

Since the above exchange had taken only 10 minutes of the interview, the therapist decided the family was engaged with him. The therapist asked the parents if they wanted to continue with him. They nodded yes. He said that the family should tell Claude that it sounded like his worries had become his boss and the boss of his entire family, so that his parents wanted to see someone to help them all get back in charge of things. The parents accepted his suggestion and sank back a bit in their chairs.

The therapist then decided he could do a full parent meeting in the time remaining, given their level of responses and their ability to stay with his questions. He began to take a full developmental history, do a three-generation genogram, and inquire about the presence of any history of mood disorders, anxiety, nervous breakdowns, or drug or alcohol problems elsewhere in the family. He was able to quickly elicit a timetable of the mother's depression, anxiety, and alcoholism and the way the father had responded. The father described his wife's struggle in an empathic way and said that even when she was drinking she was still the emotional core of the family because she was so attuned to everyone. Everyone just knew when to "watch out" for her irritability.

They were both able to describe the frequency of her anger, its impact on each of the children over the years, and how they had talked with both kids once the mother was in recovery. The mother said she told both of the kids that she knew they could be mad at her, but neither one of them had said much. Claude's sister, Angeline, was much like Claude in terms of a high level of competence at school and engaged with many friends and activities.

As the end of the session came closer, the therapist again reviewed the financial issues and asked if they had any other questions about what to tell Claude. They said they felt comfortable. Given their overall level of function and the quality of their relationship with each other and with Claude, the therapist decided to tell the parents to ask Claude (using his interest in math) and his parents to make a bar graph on each day of the calendar that would describe the different levels of anxiety he experienced that day. The family agreed. An appointment for a family visit was set which would include a meeting with Claude alone with the therapist. They agreed to fill out the behavioral checklists and developmental history at home to make sure the information they had reported was complete.

The therapist has now completed the initial parent assessment. He has given an initial detective homework assignment as well as helped the parents prepare Claude for the interview later that week. Their successful relationship with each other has been identified and supported in the first contact. The parents' active mastery was underlined in the therapist's interview as he addressed past and present family problems. An important aspect of the initial therapeutic contacts is to make sure a level of understanding is shared between the members of the family and the therapist.

The parents need to understand the function of the checklists so that they will complete them. The therapist has elicited an extensively loaded family history of anxiety and depression on the mother's side and none on the father's side. He has estimated that the period of mother's alcoholism could certainly have affected the security of the children's attachment as well as the way they have managed their anger. All of the mother's *DSM-IV* diagnoses would be considered to be "in remission" with her treatment continuing (medication, AA, and therapy).

Even in the first contact, the therapist has begun the process of psychoeducation. He has confirmed the parents' description of an anxiety disorder. He has let them know that these are "symptoms" and that, as such, his focus is on diminishing their power in the life of the child and family. The parents, he has assessed, are able to read "between the lines" and understand this to be a suggestion that Claude's worries should not be "the boss." Other children and families may require more direct illumination of the meaning of a symptom and what it is that the therapist is suggesting. The book-making technique described later in this chapter will often be helpful to promote active mastery and will be used to establish symptom definition or control where concrete aids are needed.

In this case, it was notable that neither the patient nor his sister had any of the early temperamental features of children with anxiety disorders and no other early symptoms. The absence of other symptoms and lack of a long history of temperamental vulnerability is a positive sign. The family's cognitive function was good, and there were no learning problems identified in the child. This suggests that directed techniques may be quickly and easily utilized by the child and family. There had been no reported behavioral problems in day care, nursery school, or grade school. Although the therapist may conjecture that Claude's anger is one determinant of the clinical picture, this hypothesis will require more attention. During the child interview and in the child and family's interactions, the therapist can explore how they manage anger. Throughout the intervention the therapist can support appropriate self-assertion and communication about anger within the family.

The parents' ability to communicate emotionally with their children appeared good by their report. The therapist felt the source of confusion about "what to tell Claude" about counseling reflected the mother's continued guilt and anxiety, rather than a true problem with communication. The father is a substantial member of the family but is a more "laid back" person. He was the one who focused more on activities than on emotions. He seemed, however, to be ready to play an emotional role in this process with further guidance. As a result, the therapist offered a piece of "detective" homework at this point that could help test his sense that the family can observe problems, cooperate with each other, and use the therapist's directions.

Initial Family and Child Meeting

Claude arrived clutching a sheaf of papers as he walked through the door with his parents. The initial family meeting began. The therapist asked the traditional question, "What did your Mom and Dad tell you about today's meeting?" Claude appeared slightly flushed and anxious but did not hesitate to respond. "They told me that you were going to help me with my worries and asked me to make a graph of how I was feeling." He got out of his chair and brought his work over to the therapist. He had decided that a bar graph was not a good idea and had chosen instead to make a linear graph that represented the length of the day and the degree to which his anxiety rose and fell during it. The therapist listened attentively to his descriptions and engaged the family in the discussion of what they had seen and experienced. Claude and his parents communicated well about the issues and even talked together about the things they had tried to make things better and what they had done to make him more comfortable.

The therapist mentioned that Claude's parents were sometimes frustrated when his anxiety got very high, so that they could not complete some of their plans, such as picking up Angeline before they picked him up. At that comment, everyone looked slightly flustered but the mother said that was true and that Claude knew that. Claude admitted that he did and said he felt ashamed and embarrassed but he didn't know what else to do.

His father moved closer to him and rubbed his back and talked about when they had the camping trip where Claude had to leave his bunk. The father said the other kids were really nice about it, and it had made some things a little harder, but that didn't matter—what mattered was Claude getting better. Both parents did say that since they had met with the therapist they had been trying to be clearer about what they could and couldn't do and that Claude had grudgingly accepted that. The therapist reaffirmed that it was important for them to be clear and that could help Claude get better, "which is what this is all about." He asked if Claude was comfortable meeting alone. Claude said yes, and his parents went to the waiting room. Claude talked further about the symptoms he felt and the therapist inquired about other symptoms of anxiety or depression. Although Claude felt sad often about what was happening, he had no active symptoms of depression. He said his Mom had told him that she had attacks just like his and that therapy really helped. He also asked about whether there was a medicine that could help him. The therapist said there could be and that was the job of a doctor. If he wanted to meet with the doctor, the therapist could help make the arrangements and "your great graphs would really help the doctor understand."

The therapist told Claude he also wanted to ask him other questions about his feelings, his experiences in his family, and what things were like with his friends and at school. After the direct questions, the therapist asked Claude to draw a picture of a person and to tell a story from some feelings picture cards.

Before the end of the meeting, the therapist asked Claude if he could try to do another piece of homework as well as the graph. He reviewed how Claude had said that there were times when he had the worried feeling, when he was able to focus on the work on his school page. The therapist asked if Claude could remind himself that even while he worried, he could still do his work. Claude felt he could try. The therapist reassured Claude that it might not work all the time, but he could mark on his graph when it did work.

The therapist then asked Claude's parents to join them again. He told them that he felt that Claude did have a separation anxiety disorder. He said Claude mentioned his interest in medication and the parents looked very relieved. Arrangements for a psychiatric consultation were made. The therapist recommended that at the next meeting he would tell Claude and his parents about other ideas that he had that could help, but in the meantime Claude should keep working on his graphs and refocusing his attention when he was anxious.

The therapist had noted that Claude's anxiety levels had begun to drop as the week progressed. He wondered to himself if it was related to the parents' increased clarity about their limits and how that made Claude feel less embarrassed and more contained. He had noted Claude's ability to be assertive by changing the format for the graph and also by actively initiating discussion of it. The therapist had, however, promoted a psychiatric consultation actively so that neither the parents nor Claude would be disappointed. He felt it would promote their sense of control and self-assertion as well. Medication review seemed to be an important agenda for them. Having medication discussed as soon as possible, rather than in an emergency mode, seemed to make the most sense.

The therapist's interview with Claude confirmed Claude's strengths. He was able to discuss his frustration with his mother and was able to describe venting anger with his peers. But in the family meeting when his parents' frustration was noted, he avoided discussing his anger. While it was clear that he had a perfectionistic streak and was invested in control, his self-esteem appeared positive, as was his connection to his parents and sister. No red flags were raised by the Draw a Person test or the stories that he made up in response to the feelings cards.

The therapist felt that in the third diagnostic/treatment meeting he could continue to help the family understand the way in which the anxiety disorder had affected all the family members' responses and how everyone had begun to feel out of control. He planned to help the family identify their expectations for Claude and to gradually help them increase the amount of time, for instance, that he might have to wait for them to pick him up (a desensitization program). Their responses to instructions so far and the quality of their relationship with each other and with Claude suggested they were in zone 1. The therapist had confirmed they would collaborate with his instructions.

He also felt that Claude could learn a relaxation technique to help him distract himself and refocus when his anxiety began to rise. The therapist could build on his suggestion to Claude that he tell himself he was "having a worried feeling, but he could still do his job" at school. His graph making illustrated that his self-observation and awareness were good. The role of any residual anger that Claude was carrying about his mother's irritability, as well as the role of his own perfectionism as part of his stress, would wait for the next phase of treatment. The first steps would be to see how Claude began to use the relaxation program the therapist would describe. The therapist would define its interface with the parents' work by holding Claude to a limit that would require that Claude manage the stress of separations better.

The Third Meeting: Child, Parent, and Family Components. Defining the Treatment Plan

At the time of the third meeting, Claude reported how he had been working on being able to refocus his attention on the classroom work when he felt anxious. He reported he had been successful at times. The parents reported that they had gone out to a friend's house on the weekend, but Claude's reaction had been so severe they returned home. They had, however, been able to leave him with a familiar adult babysitter in spite of the fact that he had been crying when they left. The therapist decided that was a good time to meet alone with Claude to talk about his learning a relaxation technique that could be fun and could help him, too.

Claude and the therapist met alone to talk about the bad weekend and the relaxation plan. He reminded Claude that their deal was to make sure the *anxiety* was not bossing everyone around, so that he would be talking to Claude's parents about how they helped Claude and would be helping them with their schedule, too. He explained that while Claude liked the job they were doing together so far, Claude might get mad at him in the future about some family changes. He advised him that Claude might get mad at his mother and father when they followed the therapist's directions. The therapist told Claude he wanted to hear about his anger and to talk about it in the family meeting if Claude was ready to do this. Claude agreed.

In the separate meeting with the parents, most of the time was consumed by mother's discussion of how leaving Claude that night had really thrown her. She had an anxiety attack at their friend's house and was getting ready to leave when Claude called. The therapist reassured her that it was indeed hard to see Claude suffer but pointed out that he had already made some gains. He told the mother how he had told Claude about his plan to work with them to rearrange their schedule and he hoped to arrange opportunities for Claude to express his anger about the changes. The therapist recognized that the mother could collaborate with the plan but still needed some protection from Claude's anger and her own guilt. The therapist explained that their guilt, confusion, and anxiety would be the main emotions on the agenda for the parent portion of the meetings.

The therapist then brought the family together again to review the ingredients of the plan. He explained that the next meeting would be entirely Claude's meeting to learn a relaxation technique. The therapist had begun the process of defining a plan of treatment to balance the child's needs, the parents' needs, and how the family worked together.

Beginning interventions for children with anxiety and depressive disorders are built on the platform of the family relationships and move toward the following steps.

I. Enhance Relationships.
   A. Through psychoeducation. The clinician helps the child and parent understand the features of the anxiety or depressive reaction and the way it has impinged on the child's behavior, experience of self-image, function, and the family's relationships. As a result, Claude can feel less guilty for his worries and the way he has attempted to cope with his demands and control. Claude's parents will feel less to blame for this predicament and better able to balance their limits and their support.
   B. Through active parent treatment. Treatment helps the parents to support the child's emotional needs and to set appropriate limits on the child's behavior so that a cycle of avoidance or overreaction to anxious or depressive symptoms, for instance, does not get set up. The context must facilitate forward progress as the child finds new ways to express feelings and builds different defenses. This may include parent management groups or parent training. In this case, Claude's mother may need additional review to help her diminish her sense of guilt and to help her parenting be less affected by her anxiety and fear.
   C. Restoration (or further development) of healthier child and parent emotional connections and problem solving. The treatment plan should enhance the social and emotional understanding and problem solving within the family as a whole, as well as within the child's skills. Once the child's and family's abilities to identify symptoms are consolidated, they can work on which of their resources can be mobilized. Understanding symptoms or their development aids in appropriate future treatment should symptoms recur. Claude's case requires that the therapist keep attuned to the family's exchanges that involve anger or disappointment.

II. Active Mastery/Increased Coping. The clinician assists in strengthening the child's coping skills and management of the feelings of anxiety and depression. Identification of feelings so that emotions that may be contributing to these symptoms can be identified and other defenses supported. Helping Claude with his anger will remain a secondary agenda while the therapist gives Claude active suggestions about how to manage his symptoms. Claude needs to gain mastery over his anxious feelings, not his family's schedule or whereabouts.

III. Symptom Reduction. The child and family are educated about techniques to manage and minimize symptoms. When appropriate, psychiatric assessment or medication treatment is suggested. In this case, cognitive–behavioral work is begun with Claude at the same time a psychiatric consultation is requested. The parents want to support Claude's mastery, but they do not want any "helpful medication" intervention ignored.

In other families, the initial work should have helped the parents and child identify any target symptoms. They should understand any diagnosis the therapist may have made. Then, if a psychiatric (medication) consultation is recommended by the therapist, the child and parents will be well prepared to understand the psychiatrist's orientation to symptoms, past history, and diagnostic categories. The family will be ready to discuss the risks and benefits of pharmacotherapeutic interventions during consultation since they will have learned the concept of "symptoms" in the first phase of treatment.

If the components of the child and family therapy have helped to consolidate appropriate parent–child understanding and problem solving so that a negative spiral of anxiety or depression does not occur, all of the treatment recommendations can be reinforced. If, however, the problems are not readily identified so that the child's coping skills are overwhelmed and unmanageable symptoms of anxiety or depression appear, a reevaluation of treatment is in order.

These principles are most straightforwardly utilized when the family is in zone 1. The child's diagnosis will be clear; since the child's overall ego function and developmental level is good, symptoms will stand out. The parent and family's function has clear strengths so that interactional problems do not obscure the nature of the child's adaptation. Even in those cases described below in which the child has a major psychiatric disorder, e.g., obsessive–compulsive disorder (OCD) or major depressive disorder, which may indicate a zone 3 problem, when the strengths of the family and parent are good enough to contain the child, outpatient-based treatment can be a substantial part of the child's care. Often it is not the only part, since often pharmacotherapy, environmental modifications, and special school and community arrangements may be necessary.

☐ Currently Defined Anxiety and Depressive Disorders in Children and Adolescents in *DSM-IV*

Each of the *DSM-IV* diagnoses of anxiety and depression will be presented. Illustrative case histories will follow. The most common diagnoses of anxiety and depression are *adjustment disorder with anxiety* and *adjustment disorder with depression* in an office-based practice for adults as well as for children.

The *DSM-IV* defines two major anxiety disorders of childhood, *separation anxiety disorder* and *selective mutism*. *Generalized anxiety disorder, panic disorder, social phobia,* and various *phobias, obsessive compulsive disorders,* or *avoidant personality disorders* are defined in the *DSM-IV* sections under adult disorders. These occur in children as well. The anxiety disorders of childhood affect 3% to 5% of children (Livingston, 1991) with an approximate 9% prevalence rate during a six-month period when simple phobias, social phobias, and agoraphobia are included (Popper, 1993). These disorders have a tendency to overlap with one another as well as with depression. As with adults, frequently there is a cooccurrence of anxiety and depressive features in children (Bernstein & Garfinkel, 1986).

Agoraphobia, as defined for adult patients, usually meets the criteria for separation anxiety disorder when encountered in a child, although the onset of agoraphobia may manifest later in childhood. Indeed separation anxiety may be an important predecessor in adults with agoraphobia or panic disorder, as suggested by a recent study that showed a high prevalence of separation anxiety dreams in adults with panic disorder (Free, Winget, & Whitman, 1993), as well as the increasing incidence of panic disorder in teenagers who have had prior anxiety disorders.

The mood disorders, which include the various forms of depression as well as *bipolar disorder,* are all described under conditions of adults. Cyclic and *seasonal mood disorders* follow the adult criteria as well. The most common diagnosis of depression in children and adolescents is adjustment disorder with depressed mood. However, as more careful symptomatic histories are taken, it is becoming clear that a number of children suffer from a chronic dysthymia. There are other children who have clear *major depressive episodes.*

The prevalence of depressive disorders in children and adolescents is still in the process of being studied. From some reports of prevalence in children from European studies (Canals, 1997) dysthymic disorder in preteens is approximately 1%, whereas in teens the prevalence in girls may increase to roughly 8% and to 3% in boys. Major depression in preteen girls under 9 was approximately 2% with increases in adolescence up to 4%. The incidence in boys was less. In both diagnostic categories, the expression of depression is less likely to include appetite or sleep disturbance, although in adolescence hypersomnia (oversleeping) may be as common as sleep disturbances in depressed adults.

The length of the depressive episode in children may, however, be somewhat shorter than that of adults. Another important factor is that irritability may be as cardinal a symptom as depressed mood in children and adolescents. Follow-up studies are beginning to identify that children who present with an episode of depression may be at higher risk for the development of bipolar disorder (Kovacs, 1996). Thus, as in the case of anxiety-based symptoms, the therapist should prioritize teaching the child and family to identify depressive, manic, or other symptoms.

In depressed children, another identified problem is the existence of comorbid externalizing symptoms. According to a review by Fava, this occurs in 43% to 95% of this population (Fava, Alpert, Borus, Nierenberg, Pava, & Rosenbaum, 1996). The conditions include ODD, attention deficit disorder, and antisocial problems. From mild to major conduct problems may accompany the onset of major depression. Anxiety and depressive disorders can cooccur (Biederman, Newcorn, & Sprich, 1991; Plizka, 1992). In the children who have externalizing behavior disorders, the techniques described in the next chapter will be important for the therapist to integrate into the treatment plan.

Since internalizing and externalizing disorders may present concurrently, it is valuable when the therapist can assess whether the internalizing disorder or the externalizing disorder appears to be primary or secondary. A careful history of the development of symptoms will be helpful as well as an investigation of the child's early temperament. For example, in children with any kind of disruptive behavior disorder, secondary anxiety may result as children come to recognize their behavior as impulsive. Anxiety may heighten their wish to understand the risks of such behavior and to exert more self-control. This anxiety or depression should not be "treated" but reaffirmed as part of a healthy response to behavior that is out of control.

A full-blown anxiety state or severe depression can also represent the onset of *posttraumatic stress disorder* (PTSD) or signal a significant degree of otherwise concealed conflict or violence within a family. Anxiety and depression can be seen as one reflection of the V code diagnoses in *DSM-IV, parent–child problem.* The failure to respond to standard multimodal treatment of anxiety or depression should trigger a reevaluation to consider the presence of any concealed, but devastating, familial patterns. Posttraumatic stress disorder and *acute stress disorder* are also defined by the adult criteria.

With each additional comorbidity (just as when there is significant pathology in parent or family function) vulnerability is heightened, moving the case along the severity continuum to zone 2 or 3 or 4. The complexity and various components of the treatment plan must be multiplied. When planning treatment, the parents need to understand this clinical assessment, and the MCO request will need to highlight these issues.

Issues to Consider in the Course of the Diagnostic Assessment

All of these factors are reviewed to help therapists be aware of the many potential contributions that may complicate the treatment of the presenting problem. The more of these issues that the therapist identifies, the more severe the presenting problem in the child or the family. Their place in the zone of care continuum can be adjusted accordingly.

Biological and Temperamental Factors. A temperamental vulnerability may antedate the development of full-blown symptoms of anxiety or depression in children. When these antecedents are present in the clinical case the therapist is evaluating, the therapist may feel more secure about making the diagnosis. This history also helps the parents better understand their child's vulnerability. Considerable work has been done in recent years examining the biological underpinnings that may predispose certain children to the development of either anxious or depressed symptoms.

Anxious children has been the subject of Kagan's groundbreaking work, initially published in *Science* (Kagan, Resnick, & Sniedman, 1988), where he reported his findings about the reactions of a large series of children to novelty. Kagan and his colleagues stated, "A child's initial reaction to unfamiliar events, especially other people, is one of the few behavioral qualities that is moderately stable over time and independent of social class and intelligence test scores. About 10 to 15 percent of healthy 2 and 3 year old children consistently become quiet, vigilant, and subdued in such contexts lasting from 5 to 30 minutes. . . . Empirical indexes of a pair of related, but not identical, constructs in adults, often called introversion [which when exaggerated create internalizing problems] and extroversion [which can be associated with externalizing problems], are among the most stable and heritable in contemporary psychology" (p. 167).

Kagan found that children who demonstrated restraint in their exposure to novelty at age 2 tended to be socially avoidant and quiet even at 7 years of age when confronted with unfamiliar children or adults. It is possible for these children to then experience secondary anticipatory anxiety, which is prompted by the thought of encounters with these situations. This phenomenon can promote generalized avoidance of places where the child anticipates facing such encounters, not unlike the adult patients' secondary reactions and restrictions of activity and place following the onset of panic disorder, which can lead to agoraphobia (National Institute of Mental Health, 1993).

A vicious symptomatic cycle can develop. The child's easily aroused anxiety reactions lead to the child's subsequent internal discomfort. To avoid the feeling, the child avoids any anxiety-arousing stimuli. As a result of this avoidance, the possibility for the child to develop better coping responses to stressful stimuli is eliminated. Helping parents to understand this cycle helps the parents follow through on treatment suggestions that require the parents to gradually desensitize their children, i.e., expose them to situations that make them anxious.

Kagan and colleagues' research suggests to the clinician that the temperamental predispositions of children require appropriate supports to help them develop coping techniques. In addition, the persistence of anxiety symptoms makes a longer term orientation in therapeutic work with children and their families an important part of the psychoeducation. Parents must appreciate their child's need to adapt to future stresses and how best to support them in active engagement with new experiences, even while their child reports anxiety symptoms.

Studies of depression in children have failed to identify a similarly specific temperamental factor. Since studies have shown a clearly higher incidence of depression in children of parents with an affective illness, more attention has been focused on genetic factors. It is within the familial relationships that children learn to identify feelings, modulate their responses, and control their behavior (as well as to expand their behavioral repertoire). Depressed parents may be less able to facilitate the broad development of these abilities (Free, Alechina, & Zahn-Waxler, 1996). In the treatment of depressed children, therapists should help the family context identify emotions and help their children express them in the best way they can, so that one episode of depression may not lead to others.

Attachment. Discussing temperament as a predisposing variable to internalizing disorders in the absence of considering parent–child interaction is like considering a child's psychopathology in an assessment and failing to evaluate the parents and the family. The degree to which the parents are able to establish a comforting and secure relationship with their child, regardless of the child's initial temperamental style, has enormous implications for how the child begins to build responses to manage emotion and to establish meaningful and reciprocal relationships.

From a clinical point of view, the way in which the parent helps the child use the relationship to modulate internal states and emotion, how the child shapes his or her behavioral responses within the caretaking relationship, and how the child comes to see the world are all initially established within the family. The nature of the parent–child relationship is vital to any therapeutic undertaking.

On the simplest level, a clinician's evaluation of any preschooler must include relationship variables. Boris, Fueyo, and Zeanah (1997) suggest that the clinician be able to understand how the child has learned to show affection and manage distress. *How the child seeks comfort is a key variable to consider in establishing a treatment plan.* The degree of cooperation the child can show may reflect issues related to the modulation of autonomy, the ability to comply, and the child's security in experiencing dependency within the parental relationship. Boris's work suggests the reunion responses of a preschooler may be as telling as separation issues. Any clinician who has worked on an inpatient unit can observe this process with the adolescent population. The adolescent's uninvolved, resentful, or dismissive behavior toward his or her parent in the context of their reunion during an inpatient stay is a striking clinical indicator of the poor health of the adolescent's relationship to the caretaker and often indicates the poor degree to which the adolescent will be defended against the work and relationship with the therapist.

Continued study of attachment responses in infants will eventually help clinicians understand these variables. At this time, some of the early classifications of infant attachment have expanded to include secure, avoidant, resistant, or disorganized attachment responses. Recent research has emphasized the parental correlates of these relationship styles as autonomous, dismissive, preoccupied, and unresolved. Indeed, further research (Shaw, Keenan, Vondra, Delliquadri, & Giovanelli, 1997) continues to examine the complex relationship between parental vulnerabilities in caregiving as part of the parent's own history and psychological makeup. These effects may have a different impact on a child at different cognitive–developmental stages, be different for different infants, and depend upon the duration of these effects over time.

Normal Cognitive–Developmental Issues. Internalizing disorders require the therapist to evaluate the level of the child's cognitive understanding. When understanding is limited, a child can be easily overwhelmed. This is illustrated in the preschool era when the rate of phobic reactions can approach 50% (Popper, 1993). Coming to understand the world creates some risks. For example, one 2-year-old made the connection between teeth and biting (stated as a hypothesis: if an animal has teeth, then it can bite). Farm animals that had previously been a source of delight for the child became the source of a phobic preoccupation, repetitively discussed as "horsey bite." The child began to avoid not only animals but also even their pictures (an example of secondary generalization).

Another young child, upon developing the capacity to categorize things as "good" or "bad," became anxiously preoccupied about the goodness or badness of his own behavior. In the same developmental context, another child may feel sad and confused and avoid taking the risk of being bad, whereas another may say, "I don't care," and do anything. Understanding these normal developmental processes permits the therapist to help the child and advise the parents.

Helping a child to use and correct the misconceptions created by their immature cognitive abilities requires that a parent be able to patiently and repeatedly review the child's concerns. In contrast, one can imagine the complications posed for a child whose parent is either phobic of animals themselves, is depressed, or has rigid and punitive reactions to "good" and "bad" behaviors. The child's cognitive development occurs in a *context*. The context of the family can ameliorate dilemmas and extend developmental mastery or impede appropriate social and emotional learning.

These developmental challenges do not end in the preschool period, although that era is filled with rapid change. In early adolescence, their extended conceptual ability to compare leads to adolescent preoccupations associated with perceptions of self and other: identity, social acceptance, and conflicts pertaining to independence can lead to a great deal of anxiety. This developmental phase includes the period in which young women can become preoccupied with the culture's emphasis on "a look." Their body image, habits of eating, and vulnerability to symptoms of body dysmorphia, eating disorders, and problems with self-image are all possible and all can be exaggerated by cultural and familial factors.

As the preadolescent gains the capacity to take another's point of view, the opinions and judgments of peers take on a new importance. In addition, a potential link between "If I do this, then my friend(s) may choose to do that" becomes clearer. Preadolescents may then become anxiously preoccupied with their choices and their hopes for desired outcomes within their circle of friends or their hopes to be accepted by a new group (Cotton, 1994). The loss of a friend, especially during the period of separation from the family, may trigger depressive symptoms. The resultant view of the self can become blaming, negative, and perpetuate depressive symptoms.

Learning and Developmental Disorders. From a developmental perspective, a child's *learning disability* or mental retardation of various degrees may predispose a child to anxiety or depression. These symptoms can be precipitated when the child's abilities do not permit him or her to manage the learning tasks demanded of the child. A learning disability profile should be ruled out in the presence of a child exhibiting performance anxiety. Children can be quite sensitive to "difficult" tasks as a result of some developmental unevenness in their learning style, especially when some aspect of their learning comes quite easily. Performance anxiety and easily aroused frustration or oppositionalism also occur in children who have more *global delays*.

The clinician should also be alert for disorders in the *autistic spectrum*, such as Asperger's or relatively high functioning children with pervasive developmental disorders (PDD). Many clinicians have mistaken the eye contact avoidance and the catastrophic reactions to change as anxiety. These children may also have poor social skills and few peer relationships, which may be confused with a social phobia. This is another example of the importance of careful diagnostic skills and the usefulness of screens, such as the one suggested in chapter 1.

Right hemisphere dysfunction or nonverbal learning disabilities that affect social and emotional learning can also present with anxiety. These children may also be felt to be anxious or awkward. If the underlying disorder is missed, the child's treatment program will be affected (Dinklage, 1994). These children tend to play with children who are much younger or older. Real peer relationships are difficult for them to establish and, as a result, they may also appear lonely or depressed as well as anxious and avoidant. More often, they may be overtly bossy and unresponsive to feedback from peers because their ability to process social cues is so impaired. Appropriate diagnostic and therapeutic modifications must be made in their care.

Psychodynamic Factors. Just as children's cognitive capacities either can help them understand stresses or lead to confusion and further symptoms, the nature of their emotional reactions can make them more vulnerable. A child's inability to identify, tolerate, and resolve ambivalent feelings about matters of family, school, or peer experience can expose a child to anxiety or depression. When children or adults cannot process their emotional experiences or manage internal conflicts generated by reality challenges to their wishes and longings, symptoms can result. A child's sensitivities to a parent's reactions and feelings can diminish his or her own coping. In many instances, child therapists will see anxious or depressed children whose compliant, worried demeanors conceal underlying aggressive needs or competitive drives.

The nature of a child's defenses can help a child cope with anxiety or produce it. Denial and minimization can help a child manage stress, just as it does for adults. However, when it interferes with taking appropriate problem solving actions, it undermines adjustment in the long run. Defenses such as withdrawal, passive aggression, somatization, or inhibition can heighten internalizing symptoms. Vaillant's work (1993) on "mature" or "immature" defenses is now being extended to adolescents in research studies. (See Table 5.1.) The field of psychotherapy can anticipate that further research will focus on the development of defenses during childhood. Future research will help us understand how a child's cognitive development is associated with certain defenses, as well as which defenses are most common during certain developmental periods. Which defenses are used by children and adolescents with externalizing disorders will be considered in chapter 6.

In other instances, the conflict between regressive wishes and independent strivings produces an inhibited and anxious or depressed veneer. Issues associated with reac-

TABLE 5.1.

Defense Mechanisms
Immature
Projection
Regression
Passive aggression
Somatization
Undoing
Inhibition
Splitting
Acting out
Fantasy
Withdrawal
Repression
Denial
Prosocial
Altruism
Reaction formation
Mature
Humor
Suppression
Affiliation
Anticipation
Sublimation

Note: Drawn from "Defense Mechanisms and Adjustment in Normal Adolescents," by Erickson, S. J., Feldman, S. S., and Steiner, H., 1996, *Am J Psych, 153,* pp. 826–828.

Compare with the discussion of defense mechanisms in Vaillant's (1993) discussion in *Wisdom of the Ego.*

tions to prior loss that have become internalized and unconscious may trigger depressive reactions within the context of a child's relationships to peers or adults. For other children, the desire for total control becomes associated with a dread of loss of control, which is then projected onto the world, making it a frightening place.

Key emotional issues in the background of anxiety and depression are those related to anger (self-assertion) and issues of a loss of support or the family's inability to meet the child's emotional needs. Anxiety or depressive reactions based upon these and other internal dilemmas can be managed through a wide variety of play therapy or talking techniques (Schaefer, 1976). There are many other excellent texts that help therapists lay the foundation for well-attuned dynamic treatment. Continued supervision is a key to continued therapeutic excellence as beginning therapists learn more about their own emotional reactions to a variety of children and families as well as how to treat different problems.

Anxiety or Depression Associated with Medical Illness

Anxiety may be a significant component in certain neurologically based movement disorders, like Tourette's Syndrome, epilepsy, or Sydenham's chorea, as well as in postinfectious encephalitis (Swedo & Leonard, 1994). Behavioral relaxation training (Carlson, Figueroa, & Lahey, 1986) and behavioral methods (Gilham, 1990) have been used with children with seizure disorders. For an even greater number of children with epilepsy, early education of both parent and child can do much to diminish the associated anxieties in this disorder (Jan, Ziegler, & Erba, 1991). Other childhood medical disorders deserve a similar approach to help contain anxiety and enhance collaboration with medical treatment.

The parents who are most able to utilize these approaches without therapeutic support tend to be college educated and are often middle income or parents who are willing to become quite invested in the overall well being of their child. Research in the mother–child relationship in epilepsy has also indicated the importance of the parents' ability to use educational supports to enhance their child's adaptation, especially when the parents can support task completion, offer emotional support, and enhance the child's ability to be self-reliant (Lothman & Pianta, 1993).

Research on children with leukemia stressed that the adequate functioning of these children and families is associated with the type of "coping strategies commonly used by the children and their parents which include problem-solving, a positive outlook and good communication" (Brown et al., 1992, p. 495). The child must be able to manage the frustration and anger of repeated medical procedures without becoming depressed, so that techniques that isolate this aspect of the child's experience from all the other positive activities may promote better collaboration with a medical regimen and decrease depressive responses. While the therapeutic intervention may focus on the child's needs for support, the intervention must be tied into using the family's skills in order to assure the best possible long-term outcome.

Parental, Familial, and Environmental Factors

Since the parents of children with a temperamental predisposition to withdraw from novelty are more likely to have anxiety difficulties themselves, the possibility exists for the parent unintentionally to reinforce the child's anxious responses. If an anxious parent has an anxious child, the parent may be too easily aroused and overly empathic to the child's distress. An intrafamilial maladaptive pattern can be created that reinforces the child's withdrawal tendency. As a result, the child's opportunity to generate better coping skills through the parents' support in tolerating some exposure to the feared stimulus or separation is diminished (Livingston, 1991). The helpful or troublesome impact of the *match* between a parent's response and a child's temperamental predisposition should be assessed by the therapist and provides an important area for intervention (Tureki & Tonner, 1985; Thomas & Chess, 1977).

Follow-up research on the same group of subjects of Kagan and colleagues (Biederman et al., 1993) has emphasized the higher risk of behaviorally inhibited children to develop anxiety disorders. Higher rates of both avoidant disorder and separation anxiety disorder were seen in these children as compared with controls. In addition, 75% of the children with separation anxiety later developed agoraphobia. In contrast, only 7% of children lacking earlier behavioral inhibition and separation anxiety disorder later developed agoraphobia.

In the study of the parents of the children showing inhibition to novelty, Rosenbaum, Biederman, Bolduc, Hirshfeld, Faraone, and Kagan (1992) reported that the parents of inhibited children *with* anxiety were more likely themselves to meet criteria for diagnosis of two or more anxiety disorders. These findings emphasize the importance of the parent assessment meeting, which includes a diagnostic review of parental past and present symptoms. High levels of anxiety or depression within the parents or others in the environment can be overtly or covertly communicated to and expressed by a child. During the diagnostic family interview, an anxious parent's disturbing communications can be detected by the therapist. Such influence may not be the sole etiology of an anxiety state, but it can further complicate any innate anxious predisposition in the child. The parent's style needs to be rectified as part of the treatment plan.

As discussed in chapter 3, the level of parental criticism (another expression of the quality of the attachment) exerts enormous effects over time. Parental negativity has been studied as a variable in the expression of both adolescent depression and conduct disorder. The way the parent manages emotion—whether emotional overinvolvement or parental criticism—has also been examined within a sample of youngsters with behavioral inhibition. Preliminary studies (Hirshfeld, Biederman, Brody, Faraone, & Rosenbaum, 1997b) suggest that these types of parental styles (overtly critical or overinvolved) increase the incidence of negative outcome in the child as reflected by the level of either externalizing symptoms or separation anxiety. The degree to which the therapy can modify any tendency of the parent to respond in these ways will help diminish the presenting problem in the child as well as ensure a more positive long-term outcome.

The depressed parent's impact on the level of energy in the family as well as the available emotional communication and nurturing has already been discussed. The treatment plan for the depressed parent, as discussed in chapter 3, is an important aspect of the approach to the care of the child or adolescent. Both psychotherapy and medication should be advocated to address the parent's symptoms.

A child's anxiety may also represent the impact of a family member's illness on family life, which often includes increased stress on the child and the limited availability of support. For some children, anxiety and fear are part of their response to general familial stresses, such as the impact of divorce, the loss of a cherished grandparent, or temporary family financial problems.

While issues of a parent's emotional difficulties can lead to a child's internalizing problems, a recent study documented the impact of several related risk factors in low-income families. Researchers (Shaw, Keenan, Vondra, Delliquadri, & Giovannelli, 1997) found that multiple factors during infancy can predict internalizing problems in preschoolers. These include negative emotionality, disorganized attachment, negative life events, and exposure to child rearing disagreements. This is another documentation of the connection between child problems and exposure to high conflict. However, others (Goodyer, Herbert, Tamplin, Secher, & Pearson, 1997) reported that the severity and complexity of symptom factors need to be considered as well as relationships in the persistence of depression. Another research report documented both internalizing (appearing sad or frightened) and externalizing behaviors in children exposed to physical conflicts in the marriage (Garcia-O'Hearn, Margolin, & John, 1997).

For some children, their day-to-day experience brings trauma because of the unpredictable, angry, or violent behavior of family members. For these children, there is a double jeopardy. First, a high incidence of parental anxiety or depression, alcoholism, or major mental illness has been reported in families in which violence occurs (Kashani, Daniel, Dandoy, & Holcomb, 1992). Second, these children may manifest anxiety as part of a generalized post-traumatic response and may gradually need to learn to differentiate their fear and diffuse anxiety from their anger and disappointment.

Another important aspect of the child and family evaluation may require direct and repeated inquiries regarding physical or sexual abuse (Helfer, 1975). The identification and treatment of post-traumatic disorder in children, as the result of physical, emotional, or sexual abuse, is well-reviewed elsewhere (see Pfefferbaum, 1997) and will not be the reviewed in this volume.

Haugaard, Reppucci, and Feerick (1997), in a study of long-term effects of attachment in girls who have suffered from sexual abuse suggests that "how sexual abuse affects overall mental health in later life depends on the quality of the abused girl's childhood attachment. Girls with a secure, responsive relationship in childhood with their mothers or other primary caretakers have some protection against the long term negative effects that sexual abuse has on other college women who were abused as children." The ability of a parent to remain emotionally connected to his or her child through this process in an essential component in the establishment of healthy responses in their children. Wind and Silvern (1994) documented that the presence of parental warmth diminished the impact of child abuse on the appearance of symptoms of depression and low self-esteem but did not seem to affect the appearance of the acute symptoms of stress.

A Technique to Focus Treatment with Anxious or Depressed Children and Their Families

The treatment of internalizing disorders depends upon techniques that promote health, encourage understanding, and support family cohesion. Two examples will follow in which the authors use the technique of making a book with (or for) the child and family to begin treatment. The book can lay a foundation for good communication about the problem, which should enhance family relationships. It can establish ways to cope with and master the presenting problem. In many cases, other psychodynamic, cognitive–behavioral, and family-based techniques can be integrated with this technique. These books can identify symptoms, whether anxious or depressive responses, so the child and parent can begin to consider how these might be reduced.

The book can spell out the way that the child, with the help of the parent, can begin to establish new coping skills, communicate about feelings, or encourage problem solving. This same technique can be used in the establishment of the treatment plan in the externalizing disorders and will be illustrated in chapter 6. A book can define current stresses, lay out the elements of a behavioral modification plan, and enhance the child's self-control and emotional communication.

Three principles, used separately or together, that will help the therapist write a book for the child and family are as follows.

(1) The presenting problem can be described nonjudgmentally so that the child and the family can understand the difference between their feelings, the symptoms, and the problem.

Children often need an adult's help in getting the whole picture. Describing a situation can be the first tactic of a therapeutic book. Children cannot easily integrate the elements of "the story" or all the feelings they are experiencing. The overview provided by the therapeutic understanding in the book is enhanced by the patience and concern the parent manifests in reading the book with the child. This approach should always serve to enhance the relationship between the child and the parent.

(2) The child's behavior can be described *neutrally* to help the child begin to understand his or her situation better. The book can enhance the parents' understanding and help them accept the child's symptoms or his or her response to stress. These steps foster closer attunement between parent and child and support efforts that promote active mastery. In this way, as children read about a situation and their reactions, the stage is set for them to "discover" and label their feelings. This includes defining the psychosocial triggers of anxiety or depression as well as describing the situations, internal conflicts, or family stresses. Children's feelings are a big part of what they experience. Children's feelings are intense and often lead to immediate reactions (symptoms). This understanding can serve to further reduce the presence of symptoms.

(3) A general and empathic statement about the child's reactions, strengths, and problems can change black and white thinking to a more modulated response in the family. The book can help the family by using the term "sometimes" to help the parents and child see that the situation or the child's feelings are not "always" a problem. Decreasing an extreme or judgmental approach to the child's experience can create pathways for change. The book can go on to define and strengthen new coping techniques the therapist suggests that can be reinforced and supported by the parents.

This work is based on the first author's clinical work (Ziegler, *Homemade Books to Help Kids Cope*, 1992). It relies on the fact that children find making books a natural way to make explicit both the understanding of the problem and the way an intervention can be made. In certain instances, making a book for a child (and indirectly for the parent(s)) will also clarify the context and development of the child's difficulty. Thereafter, subsequent books can define and reinforce the coping techniques that the therapist suggests. Each book should be designed to describe the child's feelings or the situation in a low key, nonjudgmental way and set the stage for new steps of a behavioral program, relaxation exercise, or problem solving technique. By making a story, the therapist can create an affectively neutral cognitive perspective for the child and family. Children can use the assistance of therapist-made books to deal with their experiences, particularly experiences that families often feel confused about or afraid to address.

When the therapist creates the story, it can diminish the parent's reactivity as well as the child's. For instance, in the face of a loss triggering depression, the book can create a context in which the parent and child can grieve together. Often the parent may be afraid to share these feelings or is blocked themselves. As a result, the child may respond to a situation with both behavior and feelings that may appear to the parent as irritability, lack of cooperation, unwanted fretfulness, or stubbornness. *Acceptance* is the way to help children identify and understand their feelings. Of course, children can test the limits of a parent's ability to admit, accept, and describe behavior. The therapist must take an active hand in this process of understanding. Acceptance can be modeled in a book made for a symptomatic child by adding a general closing statement that expresses empathy for the child and encourages the parents' engagement with the child.

Psychotherapeutic books are not just for younger age children. Older school age children can participate at a deeper level in the process of defining and implementing the production of a book. They can follow up themes defined by the therapist more independently as well as illustrate their books themselves. For children with chronic illness, socialization and coping are supported when, for example, the book provides a base for use in the classroom as the child's science project. Duotherapy (Lyman & Selman, 1985) has been used to help children work together on their individual and peer problems. Making books about stresses can be adapted for duotherapy or group work with children who need to reflect and review the impact of their illness. Two 11-year-old girls worked together in therapy on a book entitled, "It's a Drag to Be Sick." One girl was in treatment for juvenile diabetes and the other for scoliosis and epilepsy.

For teenagers with anxiety problems, they can benefit from using a paper and pencil listing technique in which their symptoms can be reviewed and defined. Or as described in the first case history, teenagers can be involved in graphing the level of their symptoms and various triggers. Adaptations of the cognitive–behavioral strategies with adults can help children begin to list feelings, clarify what they think when these feelings occur, and, finally, make "thought corrections" that may result in better coping techniques (Barlow, 1992). These strategies are well defined in the adult literature (Burns, 1990) and elsewhere in this chapter. (See Table 5.2.)

Case 1: Adjustment Disorder with Depressed Mood

Lennie, age 4 and a half, was brought to treatment by his mother following another violent episode in the home, which Lennie had witnessed. Mother was able to talk with Lennie about the "big fight," but Lennie pouted as she described her worries about him. He asked where his Dad was and his mother described that he couldn't come visit anymore because he couldn't keep his temper. In the play session, Lennie was able to engage with some of the toys but appeared sad and withdrawn whenever he was ready to go on to another play choice.

The mother's review of the family history and her own development and adjustment did not raise any major red flags during the parent meeting. The mother reported that the father had been abusive periodically even before they had Lennie. He felt that if they only had a child that it would never happen again. After Lennie's arrival, the father did well and even cut back on his drinking for awhile. However, the pattern of abuse began again. When the mother had to stay home from work to wait for her bruises to diminish, she decided it was time to act. She felt she could not protect Lennie from seeing these things anymore–she felt he had seen at least two episodes and was beginning to worry that the father would not contain his temper with Lennie either.

The mother had finally asked the father to leave and, in the aftermath of the turmoil of the separation, Lennie was tearful and unwilling to go to school or to go outside to play. He appeared unhappy most of the time. He told his mother "Maybe, I should just stay in bed with my Teddy." At times he was irritable and oppositional although his mother described him as "just moping around a lot." Lennie's development was within normal limits. There had been no preexisting symptoms, therefore, ruling out for the moment a post-traumatic syndrome.

TABLE 5.2. Some cognitive–behavioral techniques to use in treatment with children and adolescents

1. Relaxation training—Teaches a child methods for self-calming and self-control that can be useful in managing uncomfortable affects, including anxiety or anger.
2. Systematic desensitization—Helps inhibit the anxiety response by teaching the child to reduce anxiety—for example, through relaxation training—and then to gradually increase the child's skill in maintaining the relaxed state in the face of exposure to anxiety-inducing triggers.
3. Cognitive procedures—Helps the child learn positive statements about the self (e.g., "I'm brave") or the situation (e.g., "snakes are funny animals") or provide mental statements refocusing the child's mind away from anxiety-eliciting self-statements (e.g., "I feel really frightened") to a pleasant rhyme or tune (a form of thought stopping and thought redirection). The "self-talk" used by children who are anxious or depressed can be defined and addressed in ways compatible with their developmental stage and interests.
4. Flooding or implosive therapy—Exposes the child to a highly anxiety-provoking stimulus until the anxiety response is extinguished; can be done in imagination.
5. Modeling—Shows the child examples of someone coping with a noxious stimulus or situation (e.g., showing a child films of children being prepared for a surgical procedure). Emotional problem solving, such as conflict resolution or self-assertion in the face of teasing, can be taught.
6. Reinforced practice—Gradually helps the child cope with a step-by-step exposure to the stimulus, with mastery at each step encouraged and supported. Used to develop new skills and expand social and emotional mastery.
7. Exposure—Involves introducing the child to a feared stimulus in imagination or in vivo.
8. Response prevention—Involves blocking the child's anxious or obsessive response to the anxiety-inducing or ritual-producing stimulus. In the treatment of OCD in children, exposure is linked with psychoeducation and response prevention (March, Mulle, & Herbel, 1994).

The therapist made a decision to focus the intervention on the child's sense of sadness, loss, and confusion. The therapist chose to make a book for the child that would be the focus of treatment. In the third meeting, he reviewed the plan and text with mother, before meeting to play with Lennie. Mother was agreeable to reading the book at home with Lennie during the coming week. She said, "I know he misses that man but I'm not sure I ever will, and I know he has strong feelings for his Daddy that I need to help him with."

In the following week, the therapist had Lennie and mother bring in the book for the meeting. They talked together about the story and mother was encouraged to ask Lennie if he had new questions. Then the therapist told Lennie that during their play sessions together, Lennie could draw pictures for each page of the book.

As the therapy progressed, more drawings were completed. In certain sessions, Lennie needed to move to other play choices and the "hard page" was talked about later. When the first half of the book was completed, it was brought home again so that the mother and child could read it together there. They were encouraged to add other pictures (including snapshots) as well as write in other memories. As the work continued, the boy's mood lifted and he began to engage in more activities at home again. He was able to talk more spontaneously about his father.

"A Sad Thing Happened in Our Family"

Page 1. Mommy and Daddy met one another and wanted to have Lennie.

Page 2. Mommy and Daddy are very happy to have Lennie. Lennie loves his Mommy and his Dad.

(The story opens to stress to the child that he was wanted, loved, and loved each parent in his own way. The platform of relationships is acknowledged.)

Page 3. Then Daddy started to yell at Mommy.

Page 4. Daddy hit Mommy.
Lennie felt scared
sad
mad
and bad.

(The problem of the trauma is simply acknowledged. The different feelings are listed and the child is engaged in elaborating the feelings or working them out as he colors and draws the blank pages adjacent to the story line.)

Page 5. Mommy left Daddy so that she wouldn't get hit by Daddy. Mommy and Daddy tried to make a good plan: NO MORE FIGHTS! Mommy and Daddy and Lennie lived at home together again.

(Problem solving is acknowledged in simple-to-understand ways. The child knows there was an effort to fix "bad behavior" that will be applied to other situations the family faces. Here mastery is directed toward making good choices and coping with the aftermath of problems.)

Page 6. Then Daddy hit Mommy again. Daddy hit Lennie too! Mommy said, "no more bad fights." Mommy left Daddy for good. Daddy could not make a good plan.

(The separation is clearly acknowledged. A distinction is made to help the child understand that when good plans are made, things can be worked on. This helps the child understand that there is not a threat of abandonment for his "mistakes" and that he and his mother do know how to make good plans.)

Page 7. Everybody felt all mixed up and different.
How did Lennie feel?
How did Mommy feel?
How did Daddy feel?

Page 8. Now Mommy and Lennie live in a different place.

Page 9. Sometimes Lennie misses Daddy.

(Nevertheless, there are still troublesome feelings that are normal. The book provides a context–with the mother reading it–to acknowledge that Lennie has sad feelings and misses his father, no matter what her own feelings may be toward her former husband. Permission for feelings can diminish active symptoms.)

Page 10. Lennie sometimes remembers living with Daddy and gets shy. He goes to his room and cries a little. Mommy says, "I know you are sad. When you feel a little better we can go play."

(The book ends with an affirmation that feelings can be accepted, and that coping skills permit other activities to be enjoyed.)

In this instance, because of the history of domestic violence, the clinician may be concerned that this is a zone 2 problem. However, the mother has had the strength to confront her husband, to leave him twice (the second time permanently), and to accept the feelings of her child for his father. As a result, the point at which this intervention is developed, the classification of this family is in zone 1. The residual feelings and future coping are the issue: the family trauma is no longer active. From Dr. Judy Herman's point of view (Herman, 1992), this treatment represents a stage 2 intervention: safety has been established so another level of psychotherapeutic work can proceed. Were safety issues to continue to be of concern, the work would be actively focused with the parent to help her establish a safety plan for herself and her family.

If the clinician faced this situation before the marriage had broken, the degree to which the father could have been engaged in treatment, the level of the severity of the conflict, and the degree of maternal depression or character pathology would need to be assessed. Where the parental and familial psychopathology threatens the safety of the child, addressing the child's symptoms in the absence of a family safety plan will continue to drive symptomatic and behavioral responses on the part of the child. Child-focused therapy cannot usefully address these real-life concerns. Protective steps must be taken.

If the case evolved so that Lennie's mother arranged for Lennie to have supervised visits with his father, further work would be needed. The father would need to be actively engaged in the treatment process, with the first step being a parenting assessment. Another phase of treatment could involve a new book about the new issues that would arise. The assessment of the father to communicate responsibly with Lennie would be tested through the process of creating a treatment book. While the therapist's prior assessment should have given some indication of the degree to which the father had accepted responsibility, these concrete acts test this resolve. It may become clear that the father must engage in his own treatment to gain parenting and communication skills.

Case 2: Adjustment Disorder with Anxiety

The parents requested an initial family consultation following their 8-year-old son's regression. He had begun having trouble separating for school, showed increased stubbornness about the tasks he had at home and school, and manifested a general sense of gloom, anxiety, and somatic complaints. The parents were quite certain that these reactions developed following the mother's return to work and her new unavailability for one of the weeknights. There was also an increased pace and pressure within the family. The diagnosis of an adjustment disorder with anxiety was made.

The therapist recommended making a book to help the boy with his feelings. However, since the parents' direct inquiries at home and in the interview led to the boy's denial of all feelings or reactions, an indirect tactic had to be adopted in making the book. As a result, the book was designed in the follow-up parent meeting without making reference to his feelings. It was directed at the details of the new routines to help him see the new situation more clearly and accept his own reactions. This was the book that the parents were able to make during the consultation.

"The Family's Week"

Page 1. Sunday is a day that our family is together. We plan a lot of different things to do.

Page 2. Monday, Mom brings Billy and Adam back to school. Dad goes to work and picks up kids after school. Mom comes home from work for supper.

Page 3. Tuesday is a new kind of day. Mom drops kids off at school, but she isn't home for supper. She has a new job. Dad makes supper with Billy and Adam. They eat supper without Mom.

Page 4. Wednesday both Billy and Adam go to karate after school. Mom brings them there and brings them home. Wednesday is Dad's late night at work so we have a snack after karate before we eat supper with Dad.

Page 5. Thursday and Friday are kind of the same. Work for Mom and Dad and school for the kids.

Page 6. Saturday is a busy day for everyone. Sometimes there are soccer games and sometimes we all go to the playground.

After reading the book together for two nights, Billy went off to draw in his bedroom with crayons and paper. He said he wanted to make a new cover for their book. He came back with this cover.

Cover Page: I Hate Toosday. His " I Hate Toosday" cover did two things. It clarified what he was mad and sad about. It also showed how the family's book had helped him to organize his experience so that he could share his feelings in a more specific way. Once that was accomplished, he became more comfortable and cooperative with the new routines.

Sometimes the therapeutic intervention can focus on the situation and clarify the feelings; at other times, understanding and describing the feelings helps the child understand the situation. Active mastery is promoted and symptom reduction may follow.

A book, designed by the therapist in collaboration with the parent, can help a child gain and *keep* a sense of perspective. This can be reinforced by adding a general statement or conclusion. For instance, Billy could add a page after he had made his cover saying, "*Sometimes*, there are days that are really tough for everybody," and then the whole family could make a page on the day of the week they hate most to reinforce the sense that "there are these bad days, one has to cope, and we're all in this together." Relationships are enhanced when feelings are openly acknowledged and shared together.

Often, with a zone 1 family, the enthusiasm and support of the parents for the intervention is felt immediately. They recognize that their new schedules have created a stress for the child; they are prepared to accept the child's symptoms without blame; and they are prepared to accept the responsibility to help address the child's response to this stress in such as way to allow the child to make a better adjustment. The mother, in this instance, is not so driven by guilt that she needs to hide from the "I hate Toosday" cover. The father is prepared to support the child and his wife in making sure the child receives extra attention on this hard day and is able to accept his son's feelings without forcing him to "tough it out." The child has positive function at school and with peers even though he is quite symptomatic at the initial presentation and, in the context of the intervention, he is eventually able to identify feelings.

Treatment Planning. Anxiety disorders and depressive disorders in children respond well to a combination of treatment techniques integrated to highlight the core triad of treatment values enhancing relationships, increasing coping, and decreasing symptoms. A multimodal approach based on a dynamic and psychobiological model can use parent guidance, cognitive–behavioral interventions that may be associated with free play interviews, and directed family interviews. When the child has a family that can respond constructively to the therapist's suggestions, the prognosis for most zone 1 cases is good. These parents can deliver both the needed reassurance *and* limits to manage the child's behavioral program. Relationships will need validation, not resuscitation. These families are able to honestly address family stresses and conflict. The family that prefers to sacrifice a child's well being, rather than to address parental behaviors, such as overt conflict or extremely negative reactions to the child, falls into zone 2. Zone 2 cases will not comply with treatment recommendations (or attend the therapy), and the therapist must identify other resources of support for the child in the school, extended family, or community.

In this era of managed care, techniques that help define a problem and focus interventions are increasingly sought. The more dynamically oriented clinicians will find that they can integrate their skills with the concreteness that some MCOs demand (and many families need) by focusing on the three central treatment values. Spelling out the treatment plan through a book, or identifying concrete tools to diminish anxiety and depression, is, paradoxically, quite liberating for the child and family. The techniques help them focus their efforts toward more effective self-help and better relationships. It often frees them to better express the emotions that had been inhibited. The child and family will be more able to handle explorations of any feelings that were related to the original problem.

Neither of the cases described above required a psychiatric assessment for pharmacotherapy, given the prompt decrease in symptoms following the intervention. However, if the symptoms were more severe or unrelenting (as in some of the cases to follow), a psychoeducational approach can help both child and parents learn what symptoms are. A book could prepare the family for a psychiatric referral, if one were needed. The abililty of the parents to clearly describe the therapist's treatment plan will also help the psychiatrist know what else is being done.

☐ The Treatment of Anxiety and Depressive Disorders in Children and Adolescents

Case 3: Simple Phobia

One of the earliest descriptions of a childhood phobia was written by Freud at the turn of the 20th century when he described his patient's child, Little Hans, who was later used as a case illustration for *DSM-IV* (Spitzer, Gibbon, Skodol, Williams, & First, 1994). Little Hans had a phobia restricted to horses, which led Freud to speculate about the phobia's association with the boy's concurrent interest in his "widdler." A decade later, the behaviorists began to explore the nature of conditioned responses and set the stage for the cognitive–behavioral techniques that can be used with children, adolescents, and adults. In Watson's case history of Little Albert, he demonstrated that an anxious child could be made to have a simple phobic reaction to a rabbit, which could quickly spread to other animals and then even to a wide range of furry objects (Watson & Rayner, 1920; Jones, 1924). Many anxious children are vulnerable to having their anxiety generalize to many other stimuli, situations, and even other internal emotions.

Most simple phobias do not come to the attention of therapists. When they do, it is likely that either the child's distress or phobic object triggers a problem for the parent. In other cases, the object of the child's phobia begins to restrict the family's freedom by interfering with travel or other family visits. The parents must be actively involved in this treatment. Behavioral techniques, like desensitization, can promote active mastery but require the family to bear some level of the child's distress. Since many simple phobias disappear with maturation, the therapist can help the child and family cope by using some avoidance and helping the parents balance their active support along with limits.

Case 4: Separation Anxiety Disorder

> Katie, a 3-year-old girl with an anxious temperament, responded to beginning day care with tearfulness, difficulty separating, and tantrums when being picked up. The child's difficulties and mother's reactivity were successfully contained by creating a storybook called "My New School," combined with a series of stars for "no more tantrums" that led to a special game playing time for the mother and child, and a calendar that had "purple days" (her favorite color) for school days so that the little girl could check on the calendar herself about whether she had to go to day care.
>
> Because the therapist had intermittent contact with this family, it became clear that during each new school year transition, the little girl asked for her "My New School" book to help her adjust to saying goodbye again. She continued this request until entering third grade when she decided it was time to put her book in her memory box.

Problems with separation anxiety may become manifest when youngsters are placed in day care, when they begin kindergarten, or even in later school years. In addition, moves or changes in family life, especially for the anxious child, may precipitate more clingy or tearful behavior, irritability or stubbornness, and a heightened reactivity to situations that previously were managed well. In these situations, treatment that helps the family manage change while they maintain relationships is indicated. Each component of treatment should reinforce the family relationships to prevent additional stress or any impact on the quality of their connections.

The book-making technique can describe the details of the day, the nature of leave taking, and the routine for being picked up as the basis for the therapeutic intervention. In addition, the therapist's story can define the parameters for managing both the child's and the parent's behavior. It can serve as a platform for the new behavioral contract. The therapist's description of the new routine can contain rewards for the child as well as the newly required parental behavior where the parent has become part of the cycle of reactivity. In this instance, to facilitate the new routine, the therapist suggested that the father be the person to drop off Katie. The mother would pick her up.

In clarifying how "Mommy will say goodbye and get to see Katie again" or "When Daddy drops me off," the story can reinforce parental limit setting and create a new climate of predictability. Even if there is continued tearfulness, the child can earn a star for saying goodbye. *Limits that foster predictability, understanding of the difficult moment, and acceptance of the feelings* are the cornerstone of this cognitive–behavioral intervention which can address the feelings and behavior of both the anxious child and the family while preserving the relationships. In some of these cases, the full-blown picture of all symptoms of a separation anxiety disorder may not be present.

In this instance, the parents' ability to offer structured information in a supportive way helped this child with a series of difficult transitions. In the process, the child consolidated a new set of coping skills and accepted the limit that she had to say goodbye and go to school. In the treatment of the full panoply of symptoms of a separation anxiety disorder, the skills of the therapist are needed to direct and guide the parents' behavior as well as the child's reactions. The parent's abilities to accept and use this direction places this family in zone 1.

Later Treatment of Case 4: Onset of Panic Disorder in Adolescence

When another severe episode of separation anxiety occurred for Katie with her transition to middle school in fifth grade, the therapist again used a combination of individual and family meetings to promote understanding, relationship, and active problem solving. The individual meetings with Katie had again used relaxation techniques. Parent meetings helped the parents set the expectation for school attendance. Because of the severity of some of Katie's symptoms, the parents had discussed whether medication should be considered. A psychiatric consultation had been arranged and medications were discussed that might help Katie manage the ride on the school bus, where her symptoms were the most intense. After some discussion together, Katie and her parents decided to use just their therapy to see if that permitted Katie to adjust and reestablish her previous level of coping.

When Katie reached 16 and was a junior in high school, however, she developed panic disorder. She was able to report recurrent discrete episodes of frightening feelings that were unpredictable to her that included her sense of her heart racing, sweating, tingling, nausea, shortness or breath, and fears that she would die. The therapist recommended that Katie and her parents make a list of Katie's experiences and the frequency and where they occurred as well as the parents' observations. Although Katie was given cognitive-behavioral tools to manage these attacks, she wanted to see if medicine could help.

At this point, Katie's symptoms were severe enough–and she could recognize them clearly as a result of her prior treatment–that the parents also wanted to see if medication could be helpful. Psychiatric consultation was arranged. This next phase of treatment allowed Katie to meet with a psychiatrist and describe her symptoms with her parents' support. She was offered a trial with an antidepressant, which was successful in combination with the continuing work with the therapist and family.

In children who present with anxiety disorders, the treating clinician must be alert for signs of the onset of panic disorder before or during adolescence. The psychotherapy of panic disorder is an important consideration in the treatment of these youngsters. While controlled studies on a large scale are still lacking, and those available are complicated by the high rate of placebo responses in children and adolescents (Popper, 1993), many anecdotal reports suggest positive results of pharmacotherapeutic intervention for panic disorder with use of the antidepressants, the beta blockers, and the antianxiety medications (Steingard, 1993; Joorabchi, 1977; Kutcher & MacKenzie, 1988).

Case 5: Selective Mutism

Belinda was referred to a special after-school support program since she had started first grade and still refused to speak. Her parents reported that she had never spoken outside of the home as a preschooler. She had warmed up and spoken to some familiar relatives, although that had stopped when she began kindergarten. The school had only promoted her to first grade on the condition that the parents agreed to the afternoon school special placement. No learning disabilities or language or speech problems had been identified. They described her as an extremely strong willed child who had wild tantrums when her father set a limit on her. The mother never had limited her behavior since she did not want to destroy her spirit "the way mine had been destroyed."

As the parents gave their family history—slowly over the course of three months—they gradually revealed the level of tension and conflict between them. Their sexual relationship had virtually ceased following the birth of their second child who was now 3 years of age. He had had multiple stitches as a result of Belinda's tantrums in which she would strike him with a toy that he had attempted to use that was hers. "She would rush across the room and grab it from his hands and hit him with it." The mother said she was never able to anticipate these problems or stop her. She said, with a small smile, "Belinda knows what's hers." The father, as a result, spent most of his weekends visiting his own family with the boy and left mother to care for the daughter. Neither acknowledged having any symptoms themselves, although in the first three months of treatment, they had never acknowledged family conflict either.

This family and child are in the mild range of zone 4 families. The degree of severity is mitigated by their willingness to participate actively in a treatment program that has been provided for them by a school system. This family would not have sought outpatient services independently. They needed to be supported in a broader multifaceted program that was paid for by a school system, not the mental health insurance, in order to begin to honestly face the severity of their child's emotional difficulties and the way in which they were enfolded in the family function.

Enhancing Family Relationships. Both maternal and paternal psychopathology are present. There are significant marital issues. The family was, however, able to begin to make a treatment relationship with the school program's family therapist who worked with the teachers. Tentatively, they began to be honest. Had they brought Belinda to an outpatient office, their efforts to continue to disguise their own struggles, within themselves, in the marriage, and with Belinda would have been very strong. These forces would have quickly led to noncompliance. For an outpatient therapist, this is a classic zone 4 problem. In fact, there was a prior history of a failed treatment contact following a pediatrician's referral.

Multiple aspects of troubled relationships within the family had to be addressed. One component was the family therapy, which was focused on the expression of anger appropriately—for all members of the family—which began to alter the family's secret alliances and the way in which withholding was the major form of assertion. The mother's role needed to be addressed separately, and she was referred to the mothers' group that was held as part of the program.

The initial fragile alliance with the family therapist was built on an overt assumption that Belinda's tantrums and striking out "were not the healthiest way for a young girl to build her strength and independence." It was a way to reach the mother and help her consider, in her parenting group, the issues that had led to her choices in managing her life and how she was relating to Belinda. In the family therapy, the therapist knew that the entire family colluded in letting Belinda get her way (her brother now dropped whatever he was playing with when she came into the room). The mother and father's different ways of child rearing had to be addressed.

Promoting Active Mastery/Coping in the Child. In the after-school program, Belinda participated in all activities without ever verbalizing. She was adept at conveying her wishes, completing projects, and getting what she wanted through careful monitoring of situations and enlisting other children in her refusals. Gradually, the teachers were able to use their relationships with the other children to comply with the rule "to use your words" so that when Belinda wanted to share an activity or use or a particular object, she had to speak with the other children. She began to do this at first only when it appeared that adult supervision was not too close. Gradually her tentative verbalizations included her favorite teacher. A combination of behavioral approaches, combined with the therapist–teacher's sensitivity to the child's feelings, led to more verbal expression in the classroom. As more appropriate developmental achievements were supported, symptom reduction began.

Another concern in the treatment of selective mutism is that of longer term outcome. Even if he or she begins to speak in other contexts such as school or on the playground, the child may still exhibit symptoms of social phobia or avoidant disorder or other symptoms of anxiety disorders in the future (Dummit , Klein, Tancer, Asche, Martin, & Fairbanks, 1997). The therapist must prepare the parents for longer term observations of their child. In this case, the mother (as part of the complications of her own history of trauma) did have an avoidant disorder and a social phobia. The mothers' group helped her recognize this obstacle in her own development. The mother's ability to address this for herself will, in the long run, have a real bearing on the role she plays within her family. The health of her relationship with Belinda hangs in the balance.

Case 6: Generalized Anxiety Disorder with Comorbid Phobias, Aggression, and ADHD

> Don was 8 years old and was in second grade when his teacher told his mother that he should have a behavioral evaluation. His teacher was most troubled by his aggressive impulses on the playground. The mother focused on the fact that she had been thinking about bringing Don to see someone because he was generally fearful. The mother had noted how a variety of simple phobias came and went over the years. At some point, he had reported fears of thunder, darkness, spiders, and other animals. She was most concerned about his constant worries, somatic complaints, poor self-esteem, and constant need for reassurance.
>
> In his play interview, Don talked about how other kids didn't like him and wanted to beat him up. He had very little awareness of how his sudden angry reactions affected his playmates. The mother reported that Don's temper had been very reactive since nursery school and had continued when he began public school. The abnormal Conners scale's scores, obtained by both teacher and mother, made apparent Don's difficulty in sustaining attention. This was confirmed by cognitive testing with the WISC-IIIR.

In every case, assessment includes attention to understanding the interplay between the list of problems and symptoms developed by parents and therapist, the suspected diagnostic entities, and the interplay between the child and family dynamics. Careful consideration must also be given to aspects of the child's behavioral regulation, related to constitutional and temperamental factors, the presence of a disorder such as ADDH, ODD, or conduct disorder (Biederman, Newcorn, & Sprich, 1991) and the child's attempts to comply with parental expectations.

In this case, the mother's preoccupations with Don's fears drew attention away from Don's aggressive behavior and lack of control. The therapist needs to ally with the mother's concern and her protective impulses in order to help the mother broaden her frame of reference. The therapist has to let the mother know that a better relationship can exist between herself and her child if she asserts what she knows to be healthy expectations for Don, which include his respect for her family's rules and that of the needs of his peers.

Treatment of Case 6: Generalized Anxiety Disorder with Comorbid Phobias, Aggression, and ADHD

Don's treatment book was focused on noticing his angry feelings. The first book was presented as a "detective story" in which Don had to gather information about when he was asked "to stop and think" about his behavior. This was a phrase that the therapist asked both home and school to employ in helping Don complete his first book of "times when bad things happened." Another book was also started that was called "My Worry Book" to help Don notice when he was anxious. Following these explorations, appropriate limits were incorporated into star charts to help Don be proud about "bossing my mad feelings" and being "brave with my worried feelings." The intervention increased peer awareness and diminished some of his anxiety.

Although the behavioral program enhanced Don's self-control, he continued to be quite impulsive. Once the comorbid problem of an attentional disorder was highlighted, the parents were able to accept the importance of collaborating with a medication consultation. At this point, both Don and his parents knew how the therapist's techniques were helping and what they wanted to discuss as target symptoms with the doctor. Pharmacotherapeutic consultation was sought and resulted in a suggestion for treatment with stimulants, which were quite helpful.

At this point, the therapist has mobilized different treatment approaches to assist in active mastery of "his worries" and better self-control through focusing on his temper. First, behavioral monitoring helped to more clearly identify the frequency of the problem; then behavioral control techniques could be integrated in the care plan. (See suggested readings in chapter 1 under managing children's behavior and in chapter 3 on behavior shaping.) Medication was clearly effective in helping both Don's attention and control of his aggressive impulses, just as the structured approach to his behavior and worries laid the foundation for the intervention. As a result, his anxiety diminished further.

Case 7: Avoidant Disorder with Encopresis

Alfred, age 6, was referred for consultation following his failure to respond to a combined medical and behavioral approach to his encopresis. In the initial consultation, he sat looking wide eyed and worried as his mother reviewed the problems Alfred had been having with his "poops" and what the pediatrician had prescribed, which he wouldn't take.

When the therapist began to focus on what Alfred liked to do, Alfred refused to join the conversation and mother reviewed what she had come to call his "stubbornness." With continued questioning, the mother revealed what she had accepted as Alfred's style: his avoidance of peers, his retreat behind her when new people arrived, and his demands for reassurance.

When Alfred was seen alone, he hesitantly began to draw and his difficulties with fine motor control were apparent. He gradually engaged with the play therapist but only on his own terms. When this controlling style was noted, he quickly became anxious and regressed in his play choices to molding clay or games typically selected by much younger children. He made lots of clay poops and once made a picture of a toilet, which made him so anxious that he finally hid it under the therapist's couch. The Conners scales, both parents' and teacher's form, included items that flagged both attentional disorder features and symptoms of an oppositional disorder. The dominant symptoms, however, indicated the presence of an *avoidant disorder.*

Treatment of Case 7: Avoidant Disorder with Encopresis

Enhancing Relationships. The intensity of Alfred's anxiety and his tendency to regress led the psychotherapist to have a number of unstructured play sessions with Alfred. The treatment relationship had to enhance Alfred's comfort with the developmental challenges he faced and permit him to ally with the therapist's treatment program. Ultimately Alfred would need to engage with his parents in family-based meetings to prepare for a new attempt at the behavioral program.

Associated parent meetings were held to reassure the parents, who were quite focused on getting Alfred trained, that the free play sessions were designed to prepare Alfred to notice his problem. He had to realize that he'd like to overcome his smelly pants problem. The therapist said without Alfred's ability to see the same "worry" that the parents had, he would be much less likely to cooperate with a behavioral plan and the family would just return to enacting a losing battle. This balancing act is wonderfully described in a parent–child intervention in the third chapter of Siskind's (1997) book where she describes an intervention with a mother and a 3-year-old who has developed a toileting problem.

The parents needed to be reminded that Alfred was quite anxious and regressed easily. Alfred would need a lot of family support to begin. The parents were also going to have to monitor and remind Alfred of the early steps of the program. They needed to be more attuned to how he responded so that the way "they loved him wouldn't feel so frustrating." Also, if Alfred ignored any training program that he felt he couldn't do, the parents would again feel a sense of disconnection or anger.

This case, also discussed here in chapter 3 described the parental component: this child's vulnerability brought to the fore the mother's attentional disorder, not simply her own psychological sensitivities. Her ability to manage the "sitting program" and the behavioral reinforcers required a degree of organization on her part that she initially experienced as overwhelming. Integrating both a medical evaluation and treatment component for the encopresis would also be required if Alfred was not able to respond to this initial structure (Levine, 1975, 1976; Hatch, 1988; Howe & Walker, 1992).

Active Mastery. Alfred's considerable anxiety lessened as a result of the play interviews. In this instance, symptom reduction is accomplished through enhancing relationships, and it set the stage for another effort at mastery of toileting. The parents were prepared for the work and how to work together.

The therapist and family wrote a book with Alfred to explain, "the trouble I have with my poops." Alfred was given a simple calendar in which to note "BM days" and "P days" when he lost control of his urine. The calendar, and his faithful cooperation in keeping it, then set the stage to begin a program that combined medications and toilet sitting times with which he could agree. Alfred really wanted to help himself "be a big boy the way he'd like to be." He was ready to face the toilet! In this case, the collaboration with the bowel evaluation and medication program the pediatrician had recommended could then begin to support the child's success.

Symptom Reduction. Desensitization, i.e., the graduated exposure of the child to the feared object, is an active program for managing self-control. It is reviewed by Goldfried (1971) as a cognitively mediated process that behaviorists advocate as one approach to coping with anxiety. Therapeutic books can lay out the steps of the exposure to the concerning situations. After the process of learning to understand the effects of tension and the impact they have, special modifications in the relaxation program may be needed for children. One such behavioral script is illustrated by Koeppen (1974, p. 524) as way to help a child control tension in the neck and associated muscle groups:

> Now pretend you are a turtle. You're sitting out on a rock by a nice, peaceful pond, just relaxing in the warm sun. It feels nice and warm. Uh-oh! You sense danger. Pull your head into your house. Try to pull your shoulders up to your ears and push your head down into your shoulders. Hold in tight. It isn't easy to be a turtle in a shell. The danger is past now. You can come out into the warm sunshine. Okay you can relax now. Bring your head out and let your shoulders relax (repeated several times). Notice how much better it feels to be relaxed than to be all tight. There's no more danger. Nothing to worry about. Nothing to be afraid of. You feel good.

Similar exercises can be incorporated into books or tapes or both to help the child and parents practice at home. There are a variety of cognitive–behavioral techniques that have been adapted for use with children. Once the child and parents are appropriately prepared, these anxiety reduction measures can become another focus in the treatment. Table 5.2 lists many of the approaches that can be used to manage anxiety or change behavioral responses in children.

Case 8: Dysthymic Disorder with Oppositional Defiant Disorder in an Early Adolescent

> Nat was initially referred by his school counselor with whom he had been discussing his wish to be a drug addict, like his big brother, Jim, so he did not have so much work. He had been held back in kindergarten as "immature" so he was already 14 in the seventh grade. Since the start of the school year his grades had been falling. He appeared more pale and lethargic week by week.
>
> The counselor had called the parents to ask them to seek help, but they felt that Nat was always trying to get attention and get out of his doing his work. The mother reported that he had been oppositional from day one and "his pediatrician had told me all about that," and she certainly didn't expect it to change because when they "turn 13 it all gets worse anyway."
>
> The mother told the counselor that they had been to treatment before but that it had done little good. She said Nat liked seeing the therapist but his behavior had not improved. The counselor reported that from the school's point of view Nat had always done his work well enough at school since he was so smart, but this appeared to be the first time his grades were falling off. The mother agreed that she would call the therapist on her insurance list and schedule a meeting.

The mother, father, and Nat came to the initial family meeting in which they agreed that while Nat had always been oppositional at home he had always done well in school. In the separate meeting with Nat, he described depressive symptoms. He said he still had fun, but he no longer had any interest in school. He did not meet the criteria for a major depression. The therapist was impressed by the strength of his identification with his brother's "cause."

The therapist asked about Nat's older brother in both the family meeting and when alone with Nat. The family reported that they thought he was a bad seed and Nat reported liking him but knowing he had a bad problem with drugs and had been thrown out of the house two years ago. Nat denied any drug or alcohol use himself. He said, "that stuff just poisons your brain. I want to be a doctor." Nat reported a good circle of friends and a number of after-school activities. Nat said he wanted to be able to see a therapist because he didn't always get to see the school counselor for as long as he wanted. He said he wanted to get good grades, even though he acknowledged that he "had never had to work this way before."

In the separate parent meeting, an extensive history of drug abuse existed on both sides of the family. The father had had an alcohol problem in his teens when the older brother was conceived, but he had been sober and working ever since. The mother also worked in the same neighborhood dry cleaner. They described Nat as their "golden child" because he was so smart. They admitted they had never disciplined him very well. "Maybe he is oppositional because we let him get his way so often." They agreed that now was the time to watch Nat carefully since he was getting close to high school and needed to keep whatever good school habits he had.

The treatment planning meeting discussed how the family had to support the values they had for Nat. Although he was their "star," he needed to see that the family was worried about him. Enhancing more appropriate family relationships would be complicated. The mother had already decided she couldn't enforce limits. The father had disconnected, rather than lose his temper with "his golden boy," as he had with his older son. The mother and father appeared distant, but neither would agree to parent meetings "without Nat."

The therapist decided that asking the family to enforce limits more consistently was not possible in this first phase of treatment; rather, Nat's attention had to be directed to their love. It would be manifested by their carefully monitoring his school success and other activities. Family therapy would emphasize communication about how worried they were when things went wrong for him. They could review what Nat and his family wanted for his future and what might be involved to reach those goals.

A contract would be developed by the parents, Nat, and the school that specified homework completion, involved after-school catch up meetings with each of his teachers, and targeted grades to reach as goals. The therapist would review this with Nat as well to prepare for further family meetings. Nat needed to reconnect with his parents' concern and look at the barriers he was putting in the way of his connections with his parents and his own success.

Treatment of Case 8: Dysthymic Disorder with Oppositional Defiant Disorder

Nat initially was very eager to come to therapy. He looked better and seemed more energized. He talked a great deal in the following meetings about his brother and about seeing him in the neighborhood. He ventilated his anger with his parents about "dumping Jim when he needed them." He protested that he didn't need them any longer since he had his own gang and didn't need their stupid rules.

He described working with his parents in the neighborhood dry cleaners on weekends. He said he was constantly struggling with his father because he was a "dork" and was easily angered. Nat thought that his father's bowling league friends were "way uncool." Nat appeared to like to impress the therapist with the dramatic failures of his family and the coolness of his own crowd. The therapist encouraged Nat to discuss his impressions that his father was either too angry or too strict in the family meeting. Nat refused.

In the following family meeting, Nat's father did not come and his mother reported that his father had said he thought it was a waste of time because Nat's attitude "stunk." Nat looked disgusted and the therapist spent some time reviewing that the family meetings were to go over issues just like these. When the therapist inquired about how the follow-up meeting with the people at school went, the mother reported that while his grades had improved, the school people were "still all on Nat's side."

Uncovering a Zone 3 Problem: Emergence of Early Substance and Alcohol Abuse

The following week the therapist was called by the emergency room. Nat had just been found behind the school gym intoxicated after lunch. The emergency service had done a drug screen and found evidence of both marijuana and cocaine abuse.

Nat had told the emergency room staff he had just done a "forty" to calm down because he felt all worked up. He did not admit to either the cocaine use or marijuana use until the results of the drug screen had come back. When he acknowledged his use, he claimed it "was no big deal since I have been drinking since I was 10."

His mother had come with him to the emergency room and wanted him admitted. The outpatient therapist agreed that he should be admitted since he had denied all drug and alcohol use to her, tended to externalize his problems, and lied about many issues. The history of drug and alcohol abuse was so extensive in the family that a rapid, intense, and continuing intervention was considered important.

Is This a Zone 4 Problem? At this point, the case needs careful reassessment. The therapist observed that the parents had a seemingly negative attitude toward Nat's goals, many of which were quite reasonable. The father was uncooperative and the mother was passively noncompliant. Was this simply a result of their inkling that something more serious was going on that they did not want to confront? What explained their lack of monitoring Nat's activities in spite of their many complaints about his contact with his older brother and his gang of druggies? What did their tendency to externalize mean in terms of their ability to honestly confront Nat with his behaviors, rather than just be negative about school personnel or his older brother?

In this case, while parental function initially appeared to be marginally "good enough," as did Nat's overall function, the severity of compromise was only beginning to emerge. The therapist would need to collaborate with the inpatient unit and see what further information was uncovered during their intensive intervention in order to delineate the next outpatient treatment plan.

Substance Abuse/Alcoholism in Latency and Adolescence. One of the major concerns for clinicians is the onset of experimentation with drugs and alcohol before adolescence. Studies of young adults with major substance abuse problems indicate that onset of use often begins by fifth grade and continues to escalate. The issue of multiple substance use is not uncommon. It appears that the more rapid the progression of use and abuse, the greater the chance of the evolution of a major substance abuse disorder. In a review, prevalence rates for alcohol abuse in early adolescent males ranged from 5% increasing to 30% in later adolescence; abuse of other drugs in early adolescence for males has been reported at 3%, while older adolescent males can reach a 10% usage rate (Brown, Mott, & Stewart, 1992). These rates appear to increase with the presence of other psychiatric comorbidities and community characteristics, which include high rates of crime, physical deterioration, and low socioeconomic status.

The progression from experimental use to more regular use to daily preoccupation and final dependency is often rapid. When this pattern is uncovered, working with the adolescent and family on total abstinence is an important goal. Many cases of adolescent substance abuse may present with erratic use complicated by high risk bingeing. This pattern can be minimized more readily by some families and teenagers but is also of serious concern.

The stages of engagement of the youth in treatment must be modified from adult models, like that of Prochaska, DiClemente, & Norcross (1992). This model looks at an individual adult's perspective as reflecting one of the following stages: precontemplation, contemplation, preparation, action, and maintenance. The therapist's task in each case is to help the individual to move to the next phase.

The therapist's orientation to the teen and his or her parents must be modified because the adolescent most often links substance abuse to socializing. Often a teen's use may mimic that of a peer group and the level of his or her particular use is initially obscured. A change from experimentation to abuse is often one that a teenager has trouble identifying. As a result, the examination of the teen's use must become a source of concern and directed effort by the family. The family's active participation in the therapy is very important. Parents need to identify their guidelines and values in the family meetings. They must more actively monitor the teen's use and activities. Often the association between certain substance abusing peer groups and the teen must be ruptured. Associated risk factors (other diagnoses, past abuse, or learning problems) must be identified. (When a latent alcohol or substance abuse pattern exists within the family, the treatment will be more complicated.)

The overlap between early substance abuse and other diagnostic categories continues to be studied. Because of the impact of mixed substance abuse on both mood and concentration, as in Nat's case, the mood diagnosis will need to be reassessed when he is clean. However, mood disorders can precede, as well as follow, substance abuse episodes. His psychosocial function, academic, and family functioning are cast in a new light as well. All assessments of child and family function need to be appropriately reexamined. See further discussion and suggested readings in chapter 6.

Case 9: Adjustment Disorder with Anxious and Depressed Mood with "Performance Anxiety" (Background Chronic Family Stress and Alcoholism)

> Charlie, age 8, was brought to therapy as a condition for returning to his regular second grade classroom; otherwise, the family was told, he would need to be placed in a substantially separate classroom, a term often used to describe a classroom for behaviorally challenging and learning disabled children, without mainstream children. The teacher observed a great deal of performance anxiety inhibiting the work of a talented youngster who quickly destroyed projects that showed signs of not being perfect.
>
> When the mother brought Charlie into the room, she looked overtired and anxious. She immediately reported that her husband could not come because he was on the verge

of losing his maintenance job and had to have 100% attendance there. Charlie appeared anxious throughout the discussion and said little. In his individual play interviews, his Draw a Person test and Kinetic Family Drawing were unrevealing and he gravitated to structured games or played with army men who joined opposing teams that wiped each other out, leaving a lone survivor.

In the parenting meeting, Charlie's behavioral difficulties in the classroom led the mother to feel overwhelmed and confused. She just "wanted the school to handle it." Treatment had to focus on making an alliance with the mother so she could feel stronger and less confused in her interactions with Charlie. Treatment would need to include meetings with Charlie and his mother. This frayed relationship needed therapeutic attention, while the therapist also gently reviewed "what was happening with Dad." The therapist suspected more significant trouble with the father since he was on a reporting schedule at work.

Parenting meetings with the mother occurred during each of Charlie's weekly meeting. Charlie's mother, with the structure of the behavioral charts made during therapy with Charlie, was able to reward him appropriately for self-control. At the beginning of Charlie's individual time, he and the therapist briefly reviewed how he was doing with his plan.

During one exercise in which Charlie had to put a nickel of his allowance in a "swear jar" when he cursed, it was revealed that everyone had this problem in the family. The mother was able to get the entire family to join this activity and, at the end of the week, whoever had put in the fewest nickels got to decide how the money would be spent on an activity the family could do together.

Charlie was functioning better in the classroom and his mother reported that her husband had discussed coming to a family meeting. In Charlie's play interview, he revealed that Dad had taken the money from the swear jar and had gone out to drink. Charlie was willing to discuss this problem with his mother, so she joined him and her husband's pattern of episodic alcohol abuse was revealed.

At this point, Charlie's pervasive anxiety associated with his conflicts about anger and self-assertion and concerns about the future became more understandable. However, in a combined parent and child treatment, Charlie and his mother had secured their alliance with each other, they were learning ways together to help Charlie master his impulses, and treatment had reduced some of his symptomatic anxiousness. The combined treatment thrust of enhancing parent–child relationships along with attention being paid to active mastery on the part of both parent and child led to further symptom reduction. It prepared the treatment relationship for another level of disclosure that would lead to a reconsideration of the overall treatment plan.

With his mother's help, Charlie made a book about the bad times and good times in the family that revealed the impact of his father's episodic drinking. After much preparation, both the mother and Charlie were ready to show this book to the father and invite him to a family meeting to discuss it. To their surprise, the father agreed and a new stage of treatment was begun.

In this instance, the child's symptoms and the latent familial conflict are such that they hover at the edge of zone 4. The concealed paternal alcoholism, the stress and impact of the resulting marital conflict and family turmoil, and the level of symptoms of the child are all of major concern. However, the mother was able to mobilize herself to take the risk to begin to work with someone on her child's behalf. This set the stage for the above breakthrough, in which an honest family history was able to be developed, which revealed severe ADHD, alcoholism, anxiety disorders, and bipolar illness present on both sides of the family. The treatment prognosis brightens in the face of the family's ability to help Charlie acknowledge that the problem applies to the parents as well, not just Charlie. They will help him cope while they try to take care of themselves. The therapist can only help the child and family maintain their relationship while attempts are made by the father to seek treatment for his alcoholism.

The child has also been granted the opportunity to have feelings that do not have to be split off from the reality of his father's drinking problem and his mother's despondency. His worries about his family can be validated. The feelings, the reality, and the parents' willingness to acknowledge these with the child enhance the likelihood of a successful outcome. The split-off anger or fear does not have to be acted out elsewhere. The child can have a dialogue with the family that looks toward healing even if the pathway of that process may be bumpy.

Case 10: OCD in an Early Adolescent

Eugene, 12, had been doing well in sixth grade at school and home until he began to worry about a child's germs in the row next to him. As this worry grew, he became preoccupied with thoughts of all the germs that existed in his school, particularly the cafeteria, and his room at home. He began to be unable to concentrate and began failing his tests. When his teacher found him making covers for his desk, she called his mother in for a school conference.

First, the teacher pointed out Eugene's considerable difficulties with completing his work. His abilities were age appropriate and he had above-average language skills. He was so perfectionistic, however, that once he made an error he would not complete his paper. He would scribble on his paper, sprawl across his desk, and mutter, "it's too hard" or "I can't do it." He constantly wanted attention and reassurance. When asked to read out loud, he said, "I can't do it because my voice doesn't have enough expression." He could not tolerate the teacher's praise because he worried he wouldn't do as well the next time, while criticism led him to repetitive negative self-statements. Recently, he had begun to develop little rituals to help soothe his self-esteem following mistakes. All of this, the teacher reported, had been further complicated by his fears of germs.

The therapist discovered that Eugene could discuss all of these issues with his parents in the family meeting. His individual meeting confirmed his perfectionism, as he could not complete the Draw a Person test after five tries. In the parent meeting that followed a few days later, the therapist learned that Eugene had always been easily preoccupied by his worries. When he was a preschooler, he had pulled out so much hair that he created a bald spot. When he had difficulty with something, he would subsequently avoid it. He was very specific about where he placed things in his room, and he became very upset when his mother moved something while cleaning. He would dwell on sad thoughts, obsess over issues of danger, and resist parental attempts to provide comfort. Eugene's parents confided that they had begun to tune him out and experience irritation at his distress since they felt they could not reach him with any reassurance they offered. The family history was negative on the father's side, although the mother's family had many different anxiety disorders. Neither parent appeared to have any other problems and both were committed to treatment.

In the family meeting, the therapist revealed a plan for working together to help Eugene. There would be a lot of work needed so that Eugene could be freed up to think about his schoolwork as well as fun things instead of germs or worries. In addition, she asked that the family plan to have a psychiatric consultation. She explained to Eugene that sometimes medicine can help to get Eugene back in control so he doesn't feel so embarrassed about the things he has felt compelled to do to control the germs.

Eugene's obsessive–compulsive anxiety disorder was complicated by depressive features, reflected by tearfulness and a focus on sad events. His trichotillomania (hair pulling), noted to be associated with OCD (Lenane, Swedo, Rapoport, & Leonard, 1992), had simply been tolerated by his parents. Although Eugene actually met the full criteria for a diagnosis of OCD, milder obsessions and compulsions can also be associated with other forms of anxiety. Medication consultation should be promptly considered in the initial evaluation of OCD. Obsessive–compulsive disorder in children is well treated by pharmacotherapy. It has one of the best response rates among the childhood anxiety disorders (DeVeaugh-Geiss et al., 1992).

In this case, the therapist has ascertained that the family relationships are functioning well, there are no related risk factors, and the child and parents are prepared to learn more about how to manage this condition and reduce its symptoms. Medication approaches need to be set in the context of an overall cognitive–behavioral strategy that stresses mastery of symptoms and improving the child's overall sense of control (March & Leonard, 1996; Rapoport, 1990). There are protocols to help both children and parents work together to regain a better level of function. These are identified in the suggested reading list at the end of the book.

Clinicians should be aware that PDD can be accompanied by regressive catastrophic anxiety reactions even in children who function at a higher level in other contexts (Cohen, Paul, & Volkmar, 1987). Their resistance to change and apparently irrational insistence upon rigid routines may bring them to the attention of clinicians during their early school years rather than sooner, because their parents have accepted their idiosyncrasies without seeking help. While presenting quite similarly in some respects, children with PDD require significantly different treatment approaches and their prognosis, even with treatment, may not be as good.

Case 11: Dysthymic Disorder with Somatic Preoccupations in an Early Adolescent Boy

Jared, age 12, had had a gradually increasing preoccupation with his body. During the eight months that preceded the referral, he had been to the doctor's office on multiple occasions. His parents had brought him for multiple consultations and to medical specialists. The mother was chronically anxious and the father, while employed as an engineer, had a long-standing dysthymic disorder.

Jared complained that nothing was fun anymore and did not want to do anything. He was extremely irritable and would flare into little tantrums in which it was impossible to comfort him. His relationship with his older brother had deteriorated to the point that his brother would no longer play with him. He was easily tearful. In order to get him to do anything, his parents felt like they were constantly pressuring him. He went to school easily enough but was often "inactive and mopey" according to his teacher. The parents believed that the major long-term change they had seen in him was withdrawal.

The assessment did not reveal major parenting or family problems and Jared and his parents had a good relationship. The major stress in the family occurred after Jared provoked fights with his older brother who he felt "got everything" no matter how much his parents reviewed how "equal" things were. The therapist recommended that they begin to include Jared's brother in the family meetings. His individual meetings with Jared would help Jared identify what he felt he most strongly needed to communicate about with his family. Jared and the therapist would also work on noticing what Jared "wanted to get done" as well as when his worries about his body got in the way.

Dysthymic disorder is the most common form of mood disorder in prepubertal children. It carries a major risk for converting to major depression in adolescence. Unfortunately, it may also have a protracted and chronic course (Kovacs, Akiskal, Gatsonis, & Parrone, 1994). As a result, the basic principles of the interventions spelled out above are quite important.

The therapy needed to help the parents, Jared, and his brother have the best relationship they could have "even while Jared was feeling so bad." Some structuring of his interactions with his brother would need to be accomplished in the family therapy to reduce this stress. In addition, his parents would have to learn how to accept Jared's complaining while helping him mobilize and direct himself toward other activities. Their connection needed to be kept alive. Jared's individual therapy would help him see that those habitual somatic complaints were "signs his body was giving him that he did not feel good. He was unhappy." His coping with the active symptoms would need to be supported while the therapist explored whether Jared could redirect his thinking and behavior during his moments of gloom and doom.

Pharmacological consultation was also initiated. Jared used this consultation to further define for himself his concerns about his unhappiness. He even said, "sometimes there is nothing that my brain wants to do, even though I know that there are things that I like." The child psychiatrist was able to confirm this observation that "this was what depression did." The psychiatrist directed Jared to continue to work on his activities with the therapist and his parents. He knew the treatment plan had been designed to get Jared to engage with things as a way to distract and activate him.

When a trial of medication reached a certain dose, it did seem to Jared and his parents that he had more energy and many fewer somatic complaints. Jared and his parents had meanwhile developed a better spirit and had a little more detachment from his many complaints. The "rules for arguing" between Jared and his brother had been defined and were being followed. The spirit of the family's relationships was much improved.

When the clinician identifies depression in a child, seasonal exacerbations of the disorder need to be monitored. In one recent large population study was described in which parents reported that 50% of children manifested at least one winter related symptom, whether sadness, irritability, withdrawal, fatigue, or increased sleep or eating (Carskadon & Acebo, 1993). This difficulty may contribute to some children's difficulty awakening to get to school. Approximately half of the adults with seasonal affective disorder reported that their symptoms began in childhood. The incidence in adults of seasonal affective disorder is estimated to be 6% and current estimates suggest that it may affect from 1.7% to 5.5% of children (Glod, Teicher, Polcari, McGreenery, & Ito, 1997).

Case 12 Major Depressive Disorder in Adolescence

Sheila was referred to the crisis intervention center following her report to her tutor that she wanted to be dead and had held a knife to her wrist. In fact, Sheila had done this more than 18 times since the beginning of the school year, often leaving small marks on her arms. In the individual assessment, she had mentioned these episodes to her mother and her mother had encouraged her to talk to someone at school. Sheila appeared quite able to make a relationship in the initial interview. She denied a plan to kill herself, felt able to tolerate her suicidal thoughts, and appeared ready to have the capacity to request another acute intervention were she to feel more at risk.

> Sheila reported that her grades had steadily dropped since beginning high school last year. At the point of the crisis, she was failing all subjects. She reported depression, tearfulness, a low mood, poor energy, decreased concentration, and a feeling of being tired even though she was sleeping nine hours a night. She also described brief episodes of depersonalization. In the acute episodes when she reacted to family or personal stresses by grabbing a knife, she often heard male voices saying "Do it" or "Don't do it." She denied other psychotic symptoms, drug or alcohol abuse, or a history of physical or sexual abuse. She described herself as generally a worrier and was often preoccupied and nervous.
>
> Adding to the current crisis was the abrupt loss of her best friend who had "just cut her dead" and wasn't talking to her any longer. She did not have a close relationship with either of her two older brothers. She recently learned that her biological father, whom she idealized, had severely abused her mother. Her biological father had left the family when she was 3, and she had had less and less contact with him.
>
> The mother worked two jobs and often left Sheila in the care of her stepfather, who had been in the family for the past eight years, but since his loss of his job over one year ago he had become increasingly critical of Sheila. During the crisis intervention with the mother and Sheila, the mother admitted she had been minimizing her husband's behavior. She felt prepared to address this with the help of counseling.
>
> The mother reported that there were frequent family fights stemming from the stepfather's jealous preoccupation with the mother's increased independence. There had been no overt physical violence. She did not believe her husband would participate in any meetings. She said she would make sure Sheila stayed with her sister until things were straightened out.

Although there are many red flags for a zone 4 problem, there is some ability for the key family member, Sheila's mother, to understand and care for Sheila. She seemed willing to comply with treatment so that a reasonable care plan could be created. However, the therapist noted that Sheila's despondency may have followed in the wake of repeated failed attempts to change the family context. The parent meeting would test the degree to which Sheila's well being might be sacrificed to her mother's need to maintain a relationship with her husband.

In the parent follow-up meeting the next day at the crisis center, the mother acknowledged that the way in which her husband was acting was intolerable. She felt she could confront her husband with what she felt were reasonable expectations. The mother said her own continuing psychotherapy would make this more possible. She acknowledged her history of depression, which she felt made her more distant "at times" from her children.

In the family-based meeting, the mother was able to say to Sheila, "No man's behavior is going to damage my daughter. If he can't change, he is going to have to leave." Sheila's nonverbal response clearly indicated her sense of relief as well as her feeling that she received this as her mother's affirmation of their relationship. This is the key relationship that Sheila needed to feel connected to so that she could continue the process of establishing her own independence without fearing for herself or her mother. The therapist cautioned both mother and daughter that the course of this change would not be easy. As a result, ways to deal with the emotional upheaval had to be defined as well as plans about what services could be used in the event of an emergency. The emergency contact plan to reach the therapist was reviewed. A psychiatric assessment was scheduled for Sheila.

Sheila responded well to a combination of medication and psychotherapy directed toward focusing on her life, her feelings, and her choices. Both active mastery and symptom reduction were prompted as Sheila took more charge of her life as she felt her mother was taking charge of the family life. The treatment plan included twice monthly meetings with her mother to support and enhance that relationship. The family course was, as predicted, very tumultuous. Many supplementary crisis-based meetings were needed. Coordination with the mother's therapist was required. Eventually the stepfather did move out. Sheila found herself having to work after school to help her mother with the rent. They seemed able to work well with this plan in spite of the tensions and resentments it brought up.

In this case, in spite of the factors of maternal depression, periods of rejection or criticism, and an early significant loss (from the girl's point of view the loss of her father was significant), there were may positive signs. No serious comorbidity complicated the picture. The absence of a severe learning disability, attentional disorder, a more severe anxiety disorder, or conduct disorder was important. There was not a history of physical or sexual abuse. The adolescent was not using drugs or alcohol or sexual behaviors to cope with her stress. The evaluation concluded that the voices Sheila heard debating outside her head about her suicidality were symptoms prompted by stress. Monitoring the presence of psychotic features was included in the course of the therapy. She had friends and a mother who could attend to her distress at this time. Within 10 months, they were discussing changing the frequency of the meetings. However, until this time, they used a great many visits which could be supported by only the most flexible managed care plans or a "free care" situation.

At this point, information that needs to be shared with the parent includes the potential risk of further problems. Some studies have suggested that the rate of conversion from major depression to bipolar disorder in adolescents may be as high as 20%. Although the assessment defined key precipitants to the depression, both the adolescent and parent must understand the signs of a recurrence of depression as well as mood shift problems. This psychoeducation can affirm their continuing ability to work together and the mastery they have achieved in the course of therapy.

The clinician must also be comfortable with suicidal risk assessment and be prepared for the process of referral for psychiatric assessment or hospitalization. Even with the treatment contracting and careful assessment, suicidal adolescents are at risk as a result of their sensitivity to relationship shifts, the unpredictable use of drugs and alcohol, or their own impulsivity. Understanding depression (Cytryn & McKnew, 1996) and the special issues in suicidal children and adolescents is important (Hendin, 1991; Schwartz, 1979).

Pharmacotherapy Referrals

Referring a child to a psychiatrist is best accomplished when the therapist and psychiatrist know each other and have an understanding of the way in which each works. The therapist should know and help the family understand that the psychiatrist's orientation will be comprehensive. Although the therapist can refer to a psychiatrist for confirmation or definition of diagnostic issues and identify medications that might be used for treatment, the psychiatrist will be as interested in the makeup of the child and family's emotional life. In addition, since therapists must understand that a psychiatric consultant has both medical and legal responsibility for the treatment (even, indirectly, the component delivered by the therapist), the psychiatrist will be reviewing all facets of the treatment plan and considering whether these are adequate or whether the psychiatrist wishes to suggest changes or additions to the treatment plan. (See Sprenger & Josephson, 1998.)

Pharmacotherapy, used in conjunction with treatment, can contribute to a child's recovery. When well-targeted medications achieve a response, their efficacy can enhance a child's (or adult's) coping skills through diminishing the intensity, frequency, and impact of debilitating symptoms. However, in view of the limited data available at this time to support pharmacological intervention in anxiety and depressive disorders in children as monotherapy (Sylvester & Kruesi, 1994), it is recommended that medications be prescribed within the context of the kind of multimodal approach described in this text. Treatment should include individual and family treatments, along with parent education, which draws upon the insights of dynamic and cognitive–behavioral approaches.

Do Therapists Care about Diagnosis? This book was written to review contemporary perspectives about the treatment of children and families. The emphasis on diagnosis is driven by many factors. The gains in diagnostic clarity and continuing research about child development, psychiatric disorder, and outcomes will continue to shape and change therapeutic practices. To help therapists continue to be able to comfortably use and review this information, the section on treatment is presented within a diagnostic framework. The book's emphasis on the behavioral checklists and symptom surveys is to help the therapist consider these issues quickly and to be able to discuss them with parents.

Another push for diagnosis comes from insurance protocols and constraints about utilization of benefits. Diagnostically based access to services is not about to disappear from the mental health field, whether for children, adolescents, or adults. As a result, it is valuable for the therapist to review current diagnostic terminology and help the parents appreciate that this issue is a major concern for their insurer and will be actively considered by the consulting psychiatrist.

Both authors, as child and adult psychiatric and pharmacotherapy consultants to many therapists, often find that both the level and severity of the diagnosis may have been "softened" by the therapist to decrease parental concern. It also appears that many therapists do not routinely define comorbidities. As a result, therapists should prepare families for the fact that the psychiatrist may use a broader range of terms than the therapist may have discussed.

(1) The First Step: The Diagnostic Appraisal. A psychiatric consultation is suggested, when a child with a given diagnosis and set of problems does not appear to be responding to a treatment plan appropriate for that diagnostic cluster. In some instances, the presenting problems indicates an immediate referral, and the questions and concerns of the parents and therapist should be clearly identified. These are best described and reviewed in a written letter, which includes the therapist's formulation and the details of the treatment plan. A photocopy of the behavioral and symptom checklists can be provided. Just as psychotherapeutic books can help parent, child, and therapist focus on the same goals, so can a well-written referral letter.

(2) What Should a Therapist and Family Expect from a Psychiatrist? The first thing that should be expected is a diagnostic assessment associated with a brief formulation of the problem that will lead to the psychiatrist's recommendations. These may or

may not include medication. (See the following review for some of the current practices in medication use by psychiatrists. It is important to note that psychiatrists, like medical doctors, can use any medication in the current formulary to treat the condition that they define.)

When the recommendation includes medication, the parent should expect some discussion (or handouts) on the common side effects and risks of the medication. These will be discussed in the context of the value the medication may have in reducing the identified symptomatic or behavioral problem or in treating the diagnostic disorder that is defined.

For the patient population who may just want to "take a pill," the therapist can ask the psychiatrist to reinforce the family's need to collaborate with treatment. Some families do not want to pay attention to stresses or issues that are affecting the child. The pharmacotherapist will remind them that a combination of approaches must be utilized in the treatment of their child.

(3) Will the Patient, Family, and Therapist Value What the Psychiatrist Offers? If the therapist is comfortable with the orientation of this book, the therapist is likely to be pleased by diagnostic confirmation or an additional perspective about where to focus treatment efforts with child and family. In addition, since many medication interventions can be clinically helpful to children and adolescents and often permit the treatment to develop more fully without the pressure of active symptoms, the plan of the therapist and child–parent treatment team can often be facilitated in a productive way.

(4) What If the Therapist has Difficulty Identifying a Psychiatrist with whom the Therapist can Work? The American Psychiatric Association and the American Academy of Child and Adolescent Psychiatry can help identify psychiatrists in your area. Many adult psychiatrists will see children as young as 10 to 12, depending upon the availability of child psychiatric consultation in the area, so adult psychiatrists are worth considering as a colleague.

Using the orientation of this book will help the therapist establish a useful working relationship with a psychiatrist. The therapist will know what the psychiatrist needs to do the work and the therapist knows what to expect. In addition, the therapist should be familiar with the time constraints of managed care practices and how the psychiatrist is reimbursed. Helping the family understand these issues in the current mental health care delivery system is as important for the therapist as it is for the consulting psychiatrist.

In those instances in which referrals do not easily work out, a meeting with the psychiatrist is often useful to explore what will make the referral process or the expectations clearer. If the therapist (and family) report that they do not receive clear feedback or that the psychiatrist's manner is abrupt or troublesome, other practitioners may need to be identified. Often the family may need to travel to a location with a larger base of professionals.

Pharmacotherapy. The pharmacotherapy of children with anxiety and depressive disorders is still not fully established with replicated and controlled studies. There are, however, ample case experiences and a number of useful studies that serve as guidelines for the prescribing clinician. As a result of the inconsistency of some of the results of controlled trials with pharmacotherapy, medication is not the sole, or even the first, choice in an intervention for the internalizing disorders of childhood or adolescence. When parents ask if there are long-term risks to taking medication, the answer is that this is not known. However, parents will be reminded that there are potential long-term risks in leaving psychiatric disorders untreated! In treating many anxious and depressed adults, on the other hand, clinically supported studies make medication one of the first clinical considerations.

Until the mid 1990s, the benzodiazepines and the tricyclic antidepressants were the two most carefully researched and were the most frequently prescribed classes of medication for anxiety disorders in children (Popper, 1993). Continuing medication research, including investigation of the role of specific serotonin reuptake inhibitors (SSRIs), will target more and more selectively some of those centers of the brain that are related to affective modulation and anxiety control. As a result, the SSRIs, and newer medications, will be prescribed with increased frequently to children as a result of their lower side effect profiles and good response rates in adults.

At this time, however, given the limited availability of data regarding long-term effects of pharmacotherapy on brain and other bodily tissues, pharmacotherapy is generally to be avoided as a *sole* first approach to the treatment of anxiety or depression in a child. A therapist must prepare parents for the fact that, even if they are interested in pharmacotherapy, their consulting psychiatrist may, in Popper's words, "find it a challenge to disclose full and appropriate information to parents who give informed consent for these treatments" (p. 53).

Psychotherapeutic work must continue to be directed first toward symptom reduction and the development of coping skills in the child that can be supported by the family. Then the treatment process should identify the ways in which symptoms may reappear after the resolution or diminution in the presenting symptom complex so that later treatment may occur, if needed. In that regard, an emerging point of view is that pharmacotherapy may interrupt recurrent cycles of symptomatology and prevent any further decline in function. This point of view is being researched in some long-term studies of some of the more severe and recurrent psychiatric disorders which begin in childhood.

Trials with the older antidepressants in both prepubertal children and adolescents have not yet yielded strongly supportive results for pharmacotherapy. Existing trials, however, are still limited in the numbers and types of antidepressants used, as well as in the small numbers of children and adolescents treated. There is not vigorous evidence that the antidepressants have a statistically significant benefit over placebo, as there is in adults.

There are now two studies demonstrating the efficacy of an SSRI over controls in the treatment of children and adolescents with depression (Rey-Sánchez & Gutiérrez-Casares, 1997; Emslie et al., 1997). Many clinicians believe that antidepressant treatment is warranted and appears to be helpful, especially in the major depressive disorders. Unfortunately, this result is confounded by the shorter duration of the depressive episode in children and that most interventions are combined with an individual and family treatment component.

Interestingly, some of the most convincing evidence of the biological effects of treatment exists for both psychotherapeutic work and psychopharmacotherapy with OCD. Behavioral therapy in adults with OCD has demonstrated the same normalization of the metabolism of glucose in the caudate region of the brain that occurs with successful pharmacotherapy (Baxter et al., 1992). In children and adults, however, even with successful pharmacotherapy, there is mainly a reduction in the range and intensity of symptomatology rather than full remission. As a result, Rapoport, Leonard, Swedo, and Lenane (1993) argue for psychoeducation, a well-defined behavioral treatment plan, and family therapy. An approach that minimizes secondary avoidance or social withdrawal, and one that educates and strengthens the family collaboration, also helps normalize family life. March, Mulle, and Herbel (1994) recommend combining pharmacotherapy (studies suggest SSRIs or an atypical tricycle antidepressant, clomipramine) with a well-defined behavioral therapy in children and adolescents with OCD.

The other four most discussed pharmacotherapeutic approaches to anxiety disorders in children and adolescents exist for the treatment of separation anxiety disorders (school phobia), panic disorder, attentional disorders with comorbid anxiety and depression, and the treatment of elective mutism. A trial with the SSRIs had begun (Black & Uhde, 1994) with elective mutism, which raises the possiblity that there is a potential treatment for social phobia in children (previously referred to as the avoidant disorders of childhood). In many case reports, successful pharmacotherapy has helped ameliorate primary symptoms where psychotherapeutic intervention has not succeeded.

Even if a specific youngster responds well to medication, the child will *still* need parental support and limits. The parents may continue to need guidance and psychoeducation in order to help a child return to school, for instance. The child will need to develop coping skills to manage developmental challenges, such as performance anxieties at school or social fears in peer-based activities. Treatment must consolidate both coping abilities and psychosocial competencies in childhood and adolescence. Research also needs to identify whether an increase in psychosocial functions may also diminish future symptom recurrence. Ultimately, psychotherapeutic enhancement of the management of stress may be illustrated in the same way that behavioral treatment of OCD changes the brain.

6

CHAPTER

Externalizing Disorders: ADHD, ODD, and Conduct Disorder

☐ Child and Family Treatment Challenges

By far the greatest number of treatment referrals for children under 12 come as a result of behavioral disturbances. Unlike the internalizing disorders, the externalizing disorders cannot be treated without a high degree of parental cooperation. When a high level of parental dysfunction is directly linked to externalizing disorder in the child, these conditions often cannot be treated in an office-based setting at all (zone 2 or 4).

Parent guidance work is complicated by the major challenges that result from the stress that the child's poor behavioral, social, and emotional controls can place on the parents. Since these same stresses are felt in many of the other child's settings (scouts, school, in the neighborhood), the level of parental stress is additionally heightened. As the parents deal with the child's teachers or coaches, they will hear how their child is blamed and feel blamed themselves. The result is a destructive spiral of anger, negativity, and maladaptive coping responses between the child, parents, and family.

The zone of care defines the severity of child or parental pathology and is a primary consideration in developing the treatment plan. A careful parent and family assessment is needed in order to understand the best way to mobilize the productive forces within the family so the best possible relationship can exist between parent and child. Psychoeducation may help the parents understand the impact of the child's disorder on self-control and prepare the parents for treatment. The therapist can explain that their child cannot be successful without the parents' understanding of the child's difficulties or being able to tailor some aspects of family life and parental reactions to promote success.

In externalizing disorders, the plan must promote the parents' ability to use healthy behavior-shaping techniques (not inconsistent expectations, threats, or punitive reactions) and support the parents' ability to engage in fostering psychosocial problem solving with the child. The parents' treatment plan must address any adult psychopathology that compromises the parents' ability to support the child's emotional growth. While treatment can enhance the coping skills of the child, some degree of impulsivity (or other externalizing behavior) must be endured by the parent without destroying the parents' ability to care for the child since even with good cognitive–behavioral treatment or psychopharmocology, most symptoms are not abolished, only diminished.

Treatment plans for these children often need the supplementary programming provided by community resources that offer supervised and structured opportunities for learning and play in off-school hours. These depend upon the parents' ability to arrange for them and access them. The therapist cannot control whether these supports are available. Rather, the therapist must understand the community well enough to help the parent utilize what is available. Given the time intensive nature of this work, it is expensive for families to have the therapist do this work, rather than do it themselves. Insurance coverage does not pay for this needed work. Therapists must discuss early in the treatment contract that the externalizing disorders of childhood often require collateral work, and fiscal issues will require some further discussion and planning.

Clinical Assessment

The clinical assessment includes all of the elements described in Part I. The parent checklists, most often corroborated by the symptom profile obtained from the school, will clearly indicate the significant red flags of an externalizing disorder, such as attentional, oppositional, or anger control problems. The diagnosis is made when the *DSM-IV* criteria are met. The teacher's checklist offers important data in the externalizing disorders of childhood. The teacher's observations can help parents understand the child's variable levels of control. These vary with the requirements of the classroom, the difference between recess or lunch times, and the degree to which the child can respond to another adult's caring support or structure.

Although some children may show marked differences between their level of function at school and home, the great majority of the cases tend to exhibit similar problems with impulse control in either setting. These behavioral difficulties are most often manifest in periods of transition, during unstructured times, or in periods of stress associated with performance demands, interpersonal conflict, or inner emotional turmoil.

In the office-based interview setting, the child's problems with impulse control are usually diminished. The therapist should be prepared to hear the parents report that the pediatrician said, "He acted fine with me." The child's poor regulation is often more evident in the family-based interview than in the individual play interview. Integrating some degree of performance challenge during the individual evaluation, like a sample of mathematical or reading tasks, a sentence completion test, or even the Draw a Person test, may help the therapist see some aspects of the child's difficulties with self-control and may suggest if there are any associated learning problems.

Interventions for children with externalizing disorders are composed of the same three basic treatment tenets that are the focus of this book. In comparison with interventions for internalizing disorders, there are some modifications in emphasis as follows.

I. Enhance relationships

A. Family-based obejctives. Treatment should help the parents meet the child's emotional needs and set appropriate limits on the child's behavior. The parent's ability to learn appropriate behavior shaping techniques combined with supportive reassurance *must be at the top of the list of the treatment plan.* The assessment of adult psychopathology that contributes to any parental dysfunction must be identified and appropriate adult/parent treatment plans discussed. Appendix 6.1 follows this chapter and reviews strategies on how to develop behavioral interventions. These are framed in a manner designed to strengthen the alliance between parent and child in support of these goals.

If a cycle of escalating anger or discouragement has developed between parent and child, it should be addressed on both sides. The therapy must facilitate progress toward new ways to express feelings (rather than act out) and build psychosocial problem solving. The family's ability to maintain healthy and flexible relationships must be encouraged. No member of the family should be frozen into an inescapable role. Children with externalizing disorders often become the "clown," the "bad one," or the "scapegoat." It is the belief of the authors that these roles are "chosen" in part as a result of family interactional patterns and in part by the temperamental or biological liability toward impulsivity in the child.

B. Psychoeducation. Psychoeducation is often a key ingredient in helping the zone 1 family adjust its attitude and respond better to the child's needs for structure and containment. This clinically tailored information and education should help the parents foster the child's success, tolerate the inevitable mistakes, and help parent and child keep a positive connection. The clinician can help the child and parent understand the features of the externalizing disorder and the way it has impinged on the child's behavioral controls and the way the child is labeled or labels himself (the parent: "He's just no good"; the child: "I'm a bad kid").

It is important to note that the self-statement by the child does not lead the therapist to offer direct reassurance to the child. The perception that "I'm bad" must be translated into "I have trouble or make mistakes a lot." The therapist must remember that this perception is also part of the child's motivation, which can be directed toward change and cooperation. The parents' perception of the child—"he is bad"—which can lead to either the child or the parent disengaging or having emotional outbursts, must be changed. As a result, both child and parents will need education about the fine line between behavioral control and the loss of behavioral control that these children experience.

Children who are prone to lose control are also prone to secondary anxiety and the silliness sometimes associated with loss of control. This should be identified as part of the potential reaction of one child to a loss of control. Current and future risk behaviors, such as the tendency to gravitate to negative peer relationships in which the child's control or self-esteem are not challenged, should be discussed.

C. Restoration (or futher development) of healthier child and parent emotional connections and problem solving. As behavioral regulation is achieved, the treatment plan can then further enhance social and emotional understanding and the relationship of both parent and child to each other. Problem solving within the family as a whole, which develops the child's skills, should be the focus of the family component of treatment. Once the child's and family's ability to identify the child's symptoms (versus the child's willfulness or avoidance of frustration) are consolidated by the psychoeducational work, they can work on addressing cooperation or task completion.

II. Increased active mastery/coping

The clinician assists in strengthening the child's self-control, problem recognition, and management of feelings in treatment. Often these children have poor insight or awareness of these behaviors. They will often report another person's evaluation as the first indication of success in managing their behavior; e.g., the child may say, "My teacher says I'm better." They may attribute their success to others; e.g., "Nobody is bothering me anymore." Family meetings can help focus the child's awareness on their coping and help them take ownership of the mastery they develop. Because of this vulnerability, however, it is especially important that there are other concrete areas of success that they notice.

Particular attention should be paid to the child's level of frustration and its impact on the child's ability to persevere. The clinician should work with the child's feelings that prompt acting out and identify when their psychological defenses fail.

III. Reduce symptoms

The identification of core symptoms also builds the foundation for any concurrent pharmacotherapeutic consultation. Defining these symptoms will help both parent and child understand what medicine can do, like increase attention span, for instance, while it cannot change a learning disability profile.

Each of these steps is most easily implemented when the child and family are in zone 1. When the child's overall ego function and developmental level is good, the symptoms that define the child's diagnosis will stand out clearly. When the parent and family function has clear strengths, they can mobilize quickly to use diagnostic information and treatment suggestions. Even in those cases in which the child has a severe externalizing disorder, e.g., a severe attentional disorder complicated by, for instance, an expressive or receptive language problem, an anxiety disorder, or a conduct disorder, the strengths of the family and parent are often enough to contain the child and hold the course of prescribed treatment recommendations. In those externalizing disorders in which little positive adaptation or self-control had been established by the child during the premorbid period, extended child treatment may be needed. The individual treatment for those disorders located in zone 3 must establish a secure enough treatment relationship so that parent–child cooperation can be preserved and reinforced. Where there is significant familial disturbance (zone 2—poor parental self-control, addiction, domestic violence) or where the familial disturbance is combined with the child's severe psychiatric disorder (zone 4), the resulting treatment plan must mobilize ancillary supports and intensify the nature of any possible separate parent or family treatment or both. In the face of unaddressed issues in these parents, which the clinician has identified in or near, zone 2 or 4, the entire treatment plan will likely fail. As a result, treatment must focus less on the child's alliance with therapy or the child's psychiatric symptomatology than on the family's ability to function. At times, these parents may be more engageable if some aspect of the child's behavior can be stabilized first.

Making Books for Children and Families with Externalizing Disorders

The same technique described in chapter 5 can be used to establish a treatment plan for children with an externalizing disorder. The book, written by the therapist, can be used to define current stresses which may have led to the child's loss of control. It is a concrete aid to children and their parents so they understand the treatment plan. The book can stress an understanding that helps maintain the parent–child bonds (*enhance relationships*). It can be used to lay out the elements of a behavioral modification plan to help get the parent and child "on the same page" to encourage *active mastery and self-control.* The parent–child relationship will begin to work on *symptom reduction* (e.g., impulsivity) at the same time. The external authority of these therapist-designed books can review what parent and child are working on and why, so that the sense of active mastery is increased. The technique will shore up and enhance the child's social problem solving and support emotional communication between the parent and child.

Impulse Control Disorder, Not Otherwise Specified

Ryan came to the neighborhood clinic when he was 5 because his mother felt he was just too active. In the initial family meeting, the mother explained that it had never bothered her before. Now that he was 5, however, when he was walking with her to the store he just kept running when she wanted him to wait for her at the corners. The family meeting established that the mother and child had appropriate communication, and the mother was responsive to the child's cues. The interviewer noted that there was an avoidance of feeling terms in the exchange, but the mother geared her language and expectations appropriately to the child's developmental level.

Ryan played silently until his mother became angry in talking with him about his running behavior, then Ryan crashed his trucks into each other so loudly that it was hard to hear. The interviewer helped the mother and child talk about "good listening" and safety and the child engaged again in the interview. The child's behavioral checklists, from both mother and his preschool were subsymptomatic for ADHD.

In the child's meeting, the therapist did not identify any concerns. Ryan showed a range of normal play themes and related easily to the examiner. The process of the mother and child's separation for the interview and the reunion was normal. Ryan appeared clearly sensitive to his mother's cues and was eager to reunite with his mother.

In the parent meeting, the mother reported she had become frightened about Ryan's behavior. As a result, she had begun to have more arguments with Ryan and deprived him of some of his favorite activities. As he became more sullen, she became preoccupied that he did not love her and she became more withdrawn. It was this preoccupation that was, in fact, most painful for her. He was her only child and she was vulnerable to feeling abandoned. These feelings were related to her experience with her own cold and rejecting mother. She did not mind having an exuberant and motorically active child. He was not distractible and engaged in many extended play activities at home and at his preschool.

The diagnostic meetings had not identified any developmental difficulties, the relationship of Ryan and his mother was secure, and his mother did not present with any complicating psychopathology, other than the psychological echoes identified. The therapist's formulation suggested that the treatment needed to reaffirm the love between parent and child as well as to address the impulse control issue. An exercise designed to help Ryan learn how to stop would be employed as well as highlighting the mother and child's positive relationship in each session. A book that reinforced both elements of the treatment focus would be made.

The following six sessions were focused on making a book about the life and special times that Ryan and his mother had. In addition, each session involved 15 minutes of playing red light, green light. First the therapist and then the mother would play this game with Ryan. Ryan would be rewarded for stopping really fast when "red light" was called out. First this was practiced in the hallway and then the practice extended to the sidewalk.

To help Ryan understand the overall nature of the problem and the direction of the therapy, a book was written by the therapist. The therapist also had the plan to use the structure of the book to reinforce the positive relationship between the mother and child. Mother needed to know how important her love really was, even if Ryan was having trouble listening.

Each session included time set aside for working on two pages. The therapist had prepared the pages with the words, and then on large sheets of paper Ryan and his mother made the pictures together and added other ideas both in the session and then, later, at home together. The therapist wanted the book to provide the incentive and the structure for a regular "talking time" between the parent and child.

"Ryan's Book about Me!"

Page 1: This is my family.
Mom and Ryan! I love Mom and she loves me!

Page 2: Here is where we live.

Page 3: These are all my streets. Here is how we get to the corner store and here is how to get to school. Sometimes we visit Grandma but then we take a bus.

Page 4: STOP is one of Mom's biggest rules. I need to stop to help keep me safe from cars. Mom has other rules that help me to be proud of myself, too.

Page 5: Here are some of Mom's other rules.

Page 6: Special times for Ryan and his Mom.

Page 7: How Ryan shows his Mom he loves her.

Page 8: How Mom shows Ryan she loves him.

The last four pages are designed to heighten the dialogue in the therapy room between the mother and the child. The therapist's sentences are a cue, rather than a description, so that the therapist can guide the mother and child in sharing rules as well as memories and daily events that show their mutual love. The book can be used to focus on the special moments that they can recognize as part of their relationship.

At the fourth session, as Ryan was responding well to the "stop" game, the mother and Ryan were encouraged to go back to the map they had made of their neighborhood and put in all the stop signs. In the following sessions, Ryan and mother were instructed to bring the game of red light into the neighborhood and practice stopping at all their stop signs. They reported their success to the therapist in the following meetings. Ryan's mother reported her relief and increased comfort with Ryan and was comfortable with the last meeting coming up.

As in most cases of externalizing disorders, the treatment is a blend of family-based and parenting meetings. An individual component is added for the child when his or her collaboration with his or her parents' rules is needed or to help the child reach clear objectives. When trust between parent and child has been stretched by the child's oppositionalism, the goal of the individual component with the child is to help the child use the parents' limits. When that is possible, the child's abilities to exercise self-control and recognize feelings often increases accordingly. Simultaneously, the therapist's work inside the family is to make the parent's rules more visible, more consistent, and simple enough for the child to utilize. The therapist wants to heighten the parents' awareness of the way children use structure and consistency to contain their behavior. Finally, all parents will tire of being the "one who nags" and can expend more effort when they feel loved in return by their child.

Adjustment Disorder with Mixed Disturbance of Emotions and Conduct

Waleka, age 9, had arrived in the city approximately one year ago. As a result of Waleka's surly attitude and being reported for a minor theft, Waleka's aunt had requested an evaluation. She reported that prior to joining his aunt's household, he had lived with his mother in South Carolina. She had died of ovarian cancer. Since Waleka had often visited his aunt in the summer, she took him in.

He had started third grade and begun to develop a new set of friends. Many of the young people were known to the aunt since she volunteered in her church's tutoring program for youth. Waleka had initially adjusted well. Because Waleka was in her home for the first time, Waleka's aunt did not register him for the church's after-school program but allowed him to stay home after school at a neighbor's house "because I wanted him to feel more like he had a home since he had just lost his mother. He was from a small town in South Carolina and isn't used to all these programs and stuff."

After his first report card in which he received mostly Cs and one D, he had seemed more resentful. He complained that he had "no money" and that his aunt's neighbor was too strict. The neighbor told his aunt that she was getting ready to "whop his butt" because of everything he got into around her house. His aunt knew that his peers were more distant, too. She became even more alarmed when she learned that Waleka had kept the money from the church envelope she had given him for Sunday school.

All of these issues were discussed in the initial family meeting with the therapist. Waleka appeared sullen and withdrawn although he did not deny the problems that his aunt was defining. He cried when she talked about his mother and his hometown. As his aunt put her arm around him and said she knew things had been sad for him, he began to engage more. He told her that he "hated the dumb neighbor" and accused his aunt of not wanting to have him around her after-school program. His aunt appeared surprised; she explained that she was very busy there and worried he would be mad that she wouldn't be able to pay attention to him because her lessons were with the older children. Waleka just looked downcast.

The therapist gave the aunt the checklists for her to complete at home and for his teacher to return to her. The therapist explained to Waleka that she wanted to meet with him alone to hear his ideas about the problems, listen to his feelings, and get to know him a little better so that she might help things get better.

In his interview, he told the therapist that he had to save up "in case something happened to his aunt." He also described how the work was too hard "up here" and that he never had gotten a D before. "I just hate how cold it is up here, too." These remarks were interspersed in the game of Sorry they were playing together in which he was delighted when he got to "sorry" the therapist and send her "home." He explained that at the neighbor's house they never had time to play because she expected the kids to do their homework and then they had chores to do.

In a later meeting, Waleka's aunt, described how she had chosen to decrease Waleka's contact with his grandmother from South Carolina following the aunt's observation that after each phone call he was more depressed and withdrawn. She thought he needed to

> have more time to settle in here in the North before calling Down South so often. She also explained that she wanted him to have loving adults up here. Even though she knew her neighbor was a little rigid, she thought she had a good heart and that "nobody made Waleka happy anymore."

The therapist's formulation was that Waleka continued to suffer from a grief reaction that was prompting resentful acting out. His stories to her about "the cold," "the meanness" of his aunt's neighbor, and his feeling of being further removed from his grandmother had led him to begin to plan how to get money to go back home "just in case." Waleka's need for some grief work was complicated for Waleka's aunt to bear and the therapist felt this process should be initiated in therapy. In addition, the therapist felt more regular phone contact with family and familiar people from his former town would help this process.

The task the therapist would work on with Waleka would be to write a book about the loss of his mother to share with his aunt. Although the therapist understood the rationale for his aunt's decisions, she felt that if the aunt reevaluated these decisions, Waleka could be more comfortable. She wanted to help increase the empathy and understanding between them so that Waleka could be free to form a new relationship with his aunt after he had processed this loss.

To encourage further mastery and pride, Waleka could work with the therapist on how to discuss with the aunt how he could get some money "to save for warm things in the North." Waleka also needed to be in an after-school homework club to support his catching up. Both of these objectives could only be accomplished with the aunt's cooperation. She also wanted the aunt to request a learning evaluation from the school since the teacher had noted at the bottom of her checklist her concerns about Waleka's reading level.

Since Waleka did not enjoy writing, the therapist told Waleka that half their time would be for playing Sorry or another game and the other half would be for him to dictate a story about his last year in the South. An evaluation at school did not identify a classic learning disorder but did find a need for Title I reading support. New friendships blossomed at the after-school program. And Waleka continued to beat the therapist at the board games at every opportunity.

Each meeting also included a period in which Waleka dictated a fantastic tale of loss and confusion that had elements of Waleka's story in it but was transformed into a tale of high adventure and adversity. At its completion, an agreement was reached to read it to Waleka's aunt. She intuitively felt the pain and despair in the story and as the therapist read it (Waleka still felt uncomfortable reading aloud), she began to cry. Waleka went over and sat in her lap and in comforting her, began to cry, too. By the eighth meeting, both Waleka and his aunt felt that things were going much better and requested that they meet in one month. The therapist agreed.

Currently Defined Externalizing Disorders in Children and Adolescents in *DSM-IV*

The externalizing disorders include attention deficit disorders, both hyperactive and inattentive types; oppositional defiant disorder; conduct disorder; and intermittent explosive disorder. Each of these may be associated with various learning disorder profiles. A history of neurological disorder, head injury, fetal alcohol syndrome, or other brain-based disorder also should be considered. An *adjustment disorder with disturbance of emotions and conduct* or an *impulse control disorder NOS* may be the most common initial diagnoses in an office-based practice where the child's symptoms are neither severe nor fit criteria for any other disorder. These disorders may respond to treatment promptly unless there are familial factors that continue to keep the child stressed and poorly contained. When either of these disorders persists past six months, a diagnostic review should reexamine the case looking for the presence of individual-, psychological-, or family-based problems that were not clearly identified.

Attention deficit hyperactivity disorder is currently classified as having a hyperactive–impulsive subtype, or an inattentive subtype, or as combined. While the overall prevalence of this category has been reported as between 3% to 5%, some reports suggest there may be up to a 10% incidence, especially if attentional problems associated with learning problems are included. The inattentive subtype has also been reported to have a much higher representation in girls, while the hyperactive impulsive subtype has a more than a 4:1 boy to girl ratio. Comorbidities with oppositional defiant disorder, conduct disorder, and learning problems must be considered.

The clusters of behaviors that currently make up the diagnosis of *oppositional defiant disorder* are still a source of much debate. The category itself is somewhat diffuse, but most clinicians recognize the cluster of poor temper control, poor response to rules, provocative and blaming behaviors, along with easily triggered negative responses and interpersonal sensitivity. Defining this cluster of symptoms is important as it can help the clinician focus on the interpersonal and parent–child issues while helping the child find other ways to manage emotions and behavior.

Conduct disorder can have its onset during the latency years or in adolescence. There is some suggestion that the presence of the early onset of conduct disorder with ADHD may increase the incidence of a sociopathic disorder in adulthood. Features of the disorder include physical aggression, destruction of property or theft, and serious violations of rules. Characteristics such as poor empathy, the misperception of other's intentions, and aggressivity with little associated guilt are of concern in this population.

While the interpersonal problem of managing anger is common to all of the above categories, *intermittent explosive disorder* is not a category that is specific to childhood. It is listed under impulse control disorders not elsewhere classified in *DSM-IV*. It is a diagnosis to use when none of the criteria for the above disorders are met. Often the individual feels a sense of relief following the release of anger but is also upset and remorseful about its impact.

Comorbidities with *substance abuse disorders* must be considered as issues with this population and may present as early as 10 to 12 years of age. Children with externalizing disorders can also present with symptoms of an internalizing disorder. In one subset of young women referred to counseling, the incidence of substance abuse disorders increased when a depressive disorder was associated with features of a conduct disorder. Other diagnostic syndromes, such as Tourette's and autistic spectrum disorders, can also present with issues of behavioral control.

Issues to Consider in the Course of the Diagnostic Assessment

All of these factors are reviewed to help therapists be aware of the many potential contributions that may complicate the treatment of the presenting problem. The more of these issues that the therapist identifies, the more severe the presenting problem in the child and the family. Their place in the zone of care will be adjusted accordingly.

Biological and Temperamental Factors. There are two main avenues of recent research about early signals for externalizing disorders. One line of research has looked at the category that Thomas and Chess called the "difficult" child, while another group of researchers has looked at those preschoolers who seem to be novelty seeking with a low harm avoidance. These latter children have often been noted to have more accidents as a result of their fearless behavior and impulsivity rather than as a problem with motor clumsiness or incoordination.

Thomas and Chess's (1977) classic studies of temperament were particularly interested in features that persisted over time. Their findings suggested that the variables that have the most persistence over the first five years were approach–withdrawal, adaptability, mood, and intensity. It was on this basis that they described the behavioral vulnerability of the "difficult child." These children were characterized by "an excessive frequency of high activity, irregularity, low threshold, non adaptability, intensity, persistence and distractibility" (p. 34). These features became most prominent by years 4 and 5. However, Thomas and Chess are equally emphatic that negative outcome, or deviant development, was "always the result of the *interaction* between a child's individual make up and significant features of the environment." In addition, temperament, which represents only one aspect of a child's characteristics, also "reacted with abilities and motives, the two other facets of individuality, in determining the specific behavior patterns that evolved in the course of development" (p. 38).

The work of Cloninger (1987) has suggested that there are three personality dimensions that are related to specific negative behavioral outcomes. He described novelty seeking, harm avoidance, and reward dependence. He proposes that each of these relate to the central nervous system's ability to activate, inhibit, and maintain behavioral systems. Masse and Tremblay (1997) reported a longitudinal study that described youngsters who were high in novelty seeking and low in harm avoidance were more vulnerable to cigarette use, excessive alcohol consumption, and other drug use. Reward dependence, in their study, did not appear predictive.

The early identification of the presentation of ADHD in preschoolers is confounded by the normal active exuberance of this age group. Many preschool children may be described as overactive or inattentive, although the children of most concern may also be noted to have frequent temper tantrums, be argumentative, and have fewer aggressive controls, which may be predictive of an ADHD diagnosis. These complications result in more frequent impulsive hitting or grabbing other's possessions in play (Cantwell, 1996), which can lead to their referral to a therapist.

Most researchers agree that the diagnostic category of ADHD is somewhat nonspecific and can represent the end-point symptom of many different etiologic pathways. For instance, children whose brains have been shaken (shaken baby syndrome), whose nutrition has been poor (neglect or deprivation of resources), or whose care has been violent (traumatic abuse) may all show signs of attentional problems and have poor behavioral controls as a result of both organic and psychological factors. Compounding the discrimination is that traits of ADHD appear in some form in all children's function. In addition, an impairment of attention can be seen in many disorders (borderline personality, psychosis, Tourette's syndrome, depression, various forms of learning disabilities, and brain damage).

The brain-based systems that contribute to the maintenance of attention are widely represented throughout the central nervous system. These include the limbic region, the reticular activating system, orbito-frontal cortex, cerebellum, and other areas. Indeed, one researcher at the Children's Hospital in Boston (Cavazutti, personal communication, 1985) noted that in her studies of new head injured children who presented to the neurology service, there was often clear indication that the recent brain injury was superimposed onto prior dysfunction. She felt these prior problems of attentional control and impulsivity had been a central risk factor in the child's vulnerability to injury.

Attachment. As some researchers have pointed out, it is difficult to separate temperamental factors from the influences of early parent–infant interaction (Lyons-Ruth, Alpern, & Repacholi, 1993). Children with disorganized or disoriented attachment responses may be more vulnerable to the development of externalizing disorders. However, large population-based studies have yet to be completed. Many of these children may present a history of disrupted attachments that result from parental vulnerability at key points in their development. This disruption, combined with the child's natural grief and anger, may take the form of behavioral dyscontrol.

There is growing evidence from other lines of research that documents the influence of adverse parental circumstance on the externalizing disorders, just as Thomas and Chess noted in their follow-up studies of temperament. In the zone 4 family, with high levels of parental psychopathology, addiction, or family disorganization, the child's externalizing disorder can appear purely reactive. Biederman's group studied the degree to which the level of parental conflict or parental psychopathology can play a role in the etiology as well as the expression of the externalizing (ADHD) disorder. This group felt they were able to demonstrate a significant association between the nature of parental conflict and parental psychopathology on the psychosocial and externalizing symptoms in the function of the children they studied with ADHD (Biederman et al., 1995).

Just as the impact of adverse family circumstances has been documented, the positive influence of the family's ability to monitor their child's activities and promote their engagement in healthy community-based activities is also reported. From a treatment perspective, the use of management training for parents, combined with greater attentiveness to where the child goes and what the child does, has been noted to restore positive functioning in children with conduct disordered and other disruptive behavioral disorders.

Normal Cognitive–Development Issues. The stages in the development of a moral sense and the child's acquisition of social skills have been described in the child developmental literature. Both developmental lines influence a child's behavioral controls. In his research, Kohlberg (1985) described the evolving levels of moral development, and other researchers have expanded his work to look at the level of moral development in juvenile offenders. Another application of this work has been to examine the relationship between the nature of the child's attachment and the stage of moral development achieved (Stillwell, Galvin, Kopta, Padgett, & Holt, 1997).

The stepwise development of social skills has been examined in the work of Selman (1990). Child therapists must understand that cognitive abilities, such as sequencing, influence a child's ability to use certain social skills, such as turn taking.

Learning and Developmental Disorders. Impairments of executive function have often been described in relation to ADHD. These most often refer to the work of the central nervous system, which includes planning, self-regulation, selective inhibition, set maintenance, and organization. These deficits have been studied in nearly every externalizing disorder and are often present.

There has been further developmental study of speech and language skills and performance deficits in the population that suffers from impulse control. Follow-up studies suggest that speech and language difficulties at age 5 tend to persist, although articulation errors decline (Beitchman, Wilson, Brownlie, Walters, & Lancee, 1996). The language impairments were most associated with poor linguistic and academic outcome. In addition, associated behavioral disturbances were greatest in those children with receptive and pervasive speech and language problems (Beitchman, Wilson, Brownlie, Walters, Inglis, & Lancee, 1996). Auditory comprehension or auditory processing problems may be associated with both hyperactive behavior and aggressivity.

Left-sided brain dysfunction can present as a disruptive behavioral disorder (Dinklage, 1994). ADHD, conduct disorder, and oppositional defiant disorder may all be considered diagnoses in these cases. In the absence of solid language function, a child adapts by focusing on action. Behaviors that parents or school personnel may feel are willful often represent the child's failure to understand or process language. So much of schoolwork is language based that the child will appear inattentive and distractible since he may be responding to something incomprehensible.

Fetal alcoholism is a diagnosis made by history, i.e., that maternal alcoholism has led to exposure during the pregnancy. The threshold and the timing of alcohol exposure necessary for damage is not clear. These children may manifest trouble with attention and hyperactivity as well as have learning problems. Their ability to make cause and effect connections may be damaged so that their social–emotional learning is quite impaired. (See Dorris, 1989, for a personalized account.) The diagnosis is difficult to make in the absence of good historical information, and these histories are often difficult to elicit.

Psychodynamic Factors. The emotional problems that are finally expressed by externalizing behaviors tend to be a reflection of the failure of the family environment to nurture, protect, or limit the child. The child's angry responses lead to the constellation of primitive defenses, like denial, splitting , projection, acting out, or identification with the aggressor, which diminish the child's behavioral controls. Mature patterns of defense (see Table 5.1, drawn from Erickson, Feldman, & Steiner, 1996) are associated with better global adjustment in adolescence. This work needs to be extended to the school-age child. Age norms for the development of particular defenses, as well as common arrays of defenses that a child may employ to manage stress, will help child clinicians develop better assessments.

Often these psychological reactions are difficult to separate from genetic factors. There may be a higher incidence of impulse control or conduct problems by history (sometimes suggested by a history of family members in jail), alcohol or drug abuse in the family, and attentional disorders. There is some evidence that even in those children who are not directly exposed to violence, but who have witnessed violence in the home, may be more vulnerable to impulsive and aggressive behaviors.

Even in the family in which there appears to be reasonable care and protection, some children may have difficulty tolerating feelings and act out or may have more specific difficulty mastering the management of their angry affects. Some children may be particularly sensitive to control issues, prone to feeling a loss of control or feeling overcontrolled. Vaillant (1975) has written a paper suggesting that some aspects of sociopathic behavior function as a defense against sadness, shame, and guilt, just as earlier theorists saw these children as suffering from a very primitive superego or "the pathology of a sick conscience" (Redl & Wineman, 1951).

From another point of view, many presentations of externalizing behavior disorders appear to represent an exacerbation of an underlying temperamental vulnerability where the child is stressed by life events, family conflict, or diminished resources. They cannot manage their emotional reactions except through acting-out behaviors.

Parental, Familial, and Environmental Factors. Later in this chapter a series of zone 2 problems that can lead to externalizing behavioral problems will be described. These include the fragile family, the split family, and the blaming (scapegoating or triangulating) family. Externalizing behaviors may also be exaggerated in dysfunctional families because the child's foundation of love and care is compromised. While the obvious impact of poor limits can manifest itself in impulsive behavior disorders, an assessment of the family's ability to care and contain and to provide predictable structures should be made. The foundation of love and supportive care may do much to ameliorate the course of an externalizing disorder of childhood.

Four other specific functions of parenting should be considered. (1) the ability to self-soothe may need to be learned and acting out may be seen when the parent has not been able to offer the child effective care to help him or her calm tensions. (2) Parents who discipline in a harsh way, are prone to repetitive conflict with their child, and appear to dislike the child tend to have children with conduct problems (Eron, Huesmann, & Zelli, 1991). (3) The dimension of overcontrol versus undercontrol in parenting should be gauged. This dimension is often a factor in those families in which there is marital conflict or violence. (4) The inability of the parents to monitor their children's activities has been cited as well (Farrington, 1983).

Where issues of parental addiction lead to chaos, poor behavioral containment of the child can be seen that has multiple determinants. Positive involvement is often absent (an essential ingredient of love in behavioral containment). The level of language stimulation in the home should also be considered since, as noted above, one impact of diminished language can be poor self-regulation. In families where resources are limited, high levels of motor activity may be the method children use to stimulate themselves. Finally, aspects of the conflicted family can be acted out by the child. The child can attempt to draw anger toward himself to protect one parent from another, and can become the scapegoat.

Cultural factors in levels of motor activity, problem solving, and emotional communication must be considered from within the cultural context. The form of discipline families may use must be culturally assessed. One way to heighten a cultural perspective about the nature of child rearing practices is to look at other countrys' points of view about Americans. From the point of view of many Europeans, Americans tend to use too much violence in child rearing and expose children to too high a level of violent stimuli on television and in computer games. Scandinavian countries have more severe legal prohibitions against the use of physical discipline in child rearing.

Foundation of Treatment Planning: Six Principles

The child and family therapy model proposed here for the treatment of children with externalizing disorders has six major goals. (See Table 6.1.) Each of these goals relates to the triad of therapeutic goals: enhancing relationships, achieving active mastery, and symptom reduction. Parents and children are taught to distinguish between the impact of the various aspects of the child's diagnoses on the child's behavior or resulting emotions and other aspects of his or her personality. These goals are managed within an educational, family-based model that integrates behavioral strategies and an appreciation for how the feelings between parent and child will influence any outcome. These goals can be used as a platform for any insurer.

(1) *Self-control.* The parents must provide the structure that helps these children master specified behavioral goals. Therapy for the externalizing child must reinforce these goals and help parents learn behavioral skills. In order to help the children develop a sense of self-control, therapy can clarify that children can stop and think even though it is hard to do so. They can "boss" themselves by working with parents and with the behavior chart, and it is possible to discuss mistakes without denial or distortion. This objective is particularly complicated by the presence of an oppositional defiant disorder. The degree to which the presence of these negative traits, the influence of attentional problems, and the failure of aspects of parenting or family function will be illustrated in Table 6.2 in the discussion of zone 4 families.

(2) *Self-esteem.* The therapist must help the parents and child identify the strengths, as well as the weaknesses, that the externalizing child may have. The child's sense of his or her parents' pride is as important as parental support to motivate the child's efforts to compensate for the disability. The child must come to terms with the fact that some things are, indeed, "hard to do." Grieving can help both the child and parents accept their problems while they still experience love and hope.

(3) *Frustration tolerance and anger management.* These children must use both the parents' and the therapists' understanding to manage the frustration associated with weak skills, distractibility, impulsivity, and short attention spans. Unless they can accept the disability and manage the consequent anger, they will become further alienated from educational goals as frustration impedes their ability to persevere and achieve any kind of success (Ziegler, 1981).

(4) *Identification of emotions.* Most children with externalizing disorders have difficulty recognizing and labeling their feelings. As a result, their ability to use feelings as a guide to successful behavior is impeded. In fact, for many children and adolescents with externalizing behavior disorders their feelings (often angry defensiveness or sadness associated with self-pity) need to be identified as feelings not to be listened to. They are neither a guide for good communication nor provide appropriate motivation for action. These children are often extremely vulnerable to disappointment and a sense of sadness, which they have difficulty tolerating. As Vaillant (1975) indicates in his classic article on sociopathy, helping these patients tolerate their own inner sadness is a key to their ultimate self-control and success.

(5) *Social and emotional problem solving: Promoting family dialogue.* As a result of the long-term course of externalizing disorders, the ability to face problems, discuss

TABLE 6.1. Child and family model to promote positive adaptation in children with externalizing disorders with or without learning disabilities

Step in Process	Goals 1	2	3
Therapeutic objective	Increase behavioral controls.	Define realistic behavioral and educational goals while anticipating progress (realistic grieving).	Support tolerance for frustration while maintaining effort and and developing new compensations.
Task for child	Accept behavior charts and discuss problem areas. "I can boss myself."	Accurate but positive acceptance of self. "Some things are hard for me." "I can still do OK."	Recognize anger and the wish to quit. "This makes me mad." "I can try." "I can ask for help and learn new ways to do it and other jobs."
Task for parent	Learn behavior shaping skills. Provide structure. Discuss problems in neutral way. Increase developmental awareness and empathy.	Accurate but positive acceptance of child. Manage grief. Accept disability. Be respectful of child's efforts.	Tolerate frustration. Support new and varied effort. Provide new opportunities.
Desired outcome	Self-control. Increased trust between parent and child. Increased ability to communicate and to identify ways to increase child's control.	Increased self-esteem. Decreased anxiety. Increased flexibility. Consolidate basic skills.	Positive management of frustration. Promote compensations. Support for new avenues of competence. Learn perseverance.
	4	**5**	**6**
Therapeutic objective	Increase recognition and labeling of emotions. Increase family dialogue.	Increase social and emotional problem solving.	Support love and attachment.
Task for child	Learn to identify feeling: scared, mad, glad, sad, and bad (guilt or internal confusion). Share feelings.	Accept responsibility. Listen to others calmly. "I can talk about my mistakes."	Recognize parents' love. Accept praise, affection, and give thanks. Be able to say, "I love you."
Task for parent	Label child's feelings in a neutral empathic way. Accept child's feelings. Understand child's developmental level.	Accept responsibility. Avoid blaming. Define age appropriate emotional solutions. Avoid black and white ideas. Accept different approaches.	Give love and praise. "Three compliments a day." Give physical care and comfort.
Desired outcome	Ability to recognize internal states and their influence on choices and actions.	Dialogue, rather than conflict, in enhanced positive problem solving.	Solid, reliable belief in relationships with give and take.

Note. Drawn from "Family Therapy for Learning Disabled and Attention-Deficit Disordered Children," Ziegler, R., and Holden, L., 1987, *Amer. J. Orthopsychiat., 58*, 196–210.

TABLE 6.2. Child and family vulnerabilities exacerbating negative outcomes

	Interacting Variables	
Deficits in Skill Sets (ODD-like problems)	**Neurobiological Components (ADHD-like problems)**	**Family Problems**
Skill deficit		
Poor perspective taking.	Poor sustained attention to external stimuli.	Poor understanding of child's developmental needs.
Poor knowledge of steps of conflict resolution.	Poor ability to sequence.	Unpredictable or erratic interactions. Poor processing of disagreements.
Performance deficit (Child knows skill)		
Inability to use social cues for skill	Poor short-term memory; erratic retrieval functions.	Mixed messages. Poor cueing and reminders to child. Extremely varied responses on the part of the parent.
Poor motivation to exhibit behavior.	Decreased function of dopaminergic CNS which links behavior and rewards.	Inconsistency of reward. Poor systems of praise. Erratic or extreme punishments. Neglect of child's bad behavior.
Emotional/dynamic deficits		
Decreased ability to function during heightened emotions. (Failures in "critical moment.")	Poor inhibition of action or of emotion.	History of trauma in family. Child recipient of exaggerated emotional responses.
Immature defenses.	Poor regulation of arousal.	Inconsistent/insecure attachment between parent and child.

potential resolutions, and proceed toward a solution in a calm consistent way needs constant attention, relearning, and reinforcement. Often the families, as well as the youngster, tend to have more than their fair share of inconsistency, reactivity, split opinions, and negative blaming as a response to difficulties in the environment. New forms of listening, tolerating feeling, and problem resolution need to be fostered.

(6) *Support, love, and attachment.* Children with impulse control disorders are likely to erode relationships as well as to take them for granted. As a result, securing the value of care in the foundation of the relationships within families is extremely important. This goal is a key component of all treatment interventions in this volume.

Treating externalizing disorders requires a long-term perspective. A child may have more difficulty with the achievement of one goal rather than another during different phases of development, depending upon the demands of the environment. At each phase of development or in a symptomatic recurrence, the specific behavioral goals or skills to be developed can be more specifically defined in one of the above domains. The degree to which early goals are achieved impacts on the attainment of the others. For example, the first goal is behavioral self-control. Active mastery must be promoted within caring relationships. This goal must occur within the context of a loving, secure, and reasonably consistent environment. Unless this goal is reached to some degree, the second and third goals of self-esteem and frustration tolerance cannot be reached. Children who feel out of control cannot feel very good about themselves. Children who cannot contain themselves cannot begin to raise their level of frustration tolerance.

Unfortunately, many of these children's problems are not confined to the home. As a result of their misunderstanding of verbal or nonverbal communication, the social skills of these children are often poor. Their difficulty in maintaining the sequence of various behavioral repertoires means they can be "out of step" with the neighborhood or school peer group. Their distractibility during task completion disrupts chores as well as games. Failure faces these children at home and with peers.

School problems must also be identified. Over half of the children with attentional problems have some associated learning difficulty. School nurses and nurse clinicians are often asked about this diagnosis (Shealy, 1994). They become part of the team that can ensure that therapeutic followup occurs. All practitioners need to help parents insist that educational plans be updated. The therapist can help the parents continue their advocacy for the child. For example, a child who has been performing adequately with moderate visual motor supports from first through fourth grades may begin to encounter additional frustration and failure in the fifth grade: deficits in the area of attention, encoding, or language processing may be highlighted as these functions are increasingly called upon to perform higher level academic tasks (Levine & Zallen, 1984). A new team meeting of parents and school specialists may need coordination.

Secondary problems, such as depression, performance anxiety, or angry devaluations of school, may represent comorbidities of the problem. These, too, can be better evaluated and handled when the therapist has a continuing relationship with both parents and child. In addition, since schoolteachers or coaches may confuse fear of failure or poor attention with laziness or lack of motivation, the therapist's intervention must include external systems consultation, e.g., school planning or consultation to coaches or activity leaders, to prevent further child–teacher or parent–child conflicts.

Medication can be used to support and reinforce the other objectives of the treatment program. Symptom reduction is a central goal. Medication may help abate motor restlessness, lengthen attention span, decrease impulsivity, or all of these. In the

United States, most prescriptions for stimulants are written by pediatricians. But, as the pediatric literature points out, while stimulants can be quite useful in treating attentional disorders (with or without hyperactivity), medication alone is not sufficient (Whalen & Henker, 1984). However, it must be noted that there has even been some discussion in the literature that medication alone may provide as many benefits as a multimodal therapy (Popper, 1997). Research is needed that uses long–term outcomes–work, successful relationships, legal involvement, drug and alcohol use–as well as looks more closely at the ability of the individual to understand his or her condition and to use treatment appropriately.

Once the foundation of a treatment relationship is established between therapist and family, the treatment objectives can be maintained over the course of intermittent therapeutic contacts (once a month) or by periodic short-term contacts. Using an intermittent, or short-term but continuous, family-based model for the zone 1 family has the following advantages:

(1) The therapist benefits from finding something "new" to offer in each visit since the visits are spread out over time.
(2) Realistic optimism can be preserved in a way that is impossible in weekly appointments, since progress takes time.
(3) The burdens of frequent appointments or financial hardship are lessened.
(4) A long-term view of ongoing contact can be more easily maintained, a view made necessary by the fact that some aspects of the learning disability or attentional disorder may persist throughout the child's middle school years and adolescence.
(5) Both the child and parent's efforts can be reinforced.

Zone 1: Children with Mild to Moderate Externalizing Disorders within the Healthy Family

In the healthy family, the mild to moderate deficits in a child's self-control are the only problems that impair family functioning. The parents have generally demonstrated sound parental skills with other unaffected children and often with the index child as well. The assessment points to emotional stability of individual family members and the family unit. Their self-esteem is adequate. The parents are capable of insight and abstract thinking; they are able to convert verbally presented concepts into behaviors they use at home to foster the child's growth; they do not have problems with their own loss of control; and the child's problems do not overwhelm them with grief or frustration.

Not surprisingly, the healthy family of a child with an externalizing disorder is likely to fare well with good treatment and cooperation among the involved professionals. The influence of organic factors can be forcibly modified by family life. One recent report found that the later presence of psychiatric disorder following brain injury related to the injury's severity, presence of preinjury psychiatric disorder, and preinjury level of family functioning (Max et al., 1997). The level of family function can either take a severe toll on the child's attempts to function or support a positive outcome. Biological factors, such as the nature and extent of hyperactivity, the degree of aggressivity, the presence of sociopathic features, the level of concurrent depression, or all of these, can certainly affect outcome (Hechtman, 1985; Weiss, Hechtman, Milroy,

& Perlman, 1985). Nevertheless, the nature of family life provides an ongoing opportunity for a positive resolution of these issues for the child.

Children and adolescents with externalizing disorders seem to do best in families whose lives reflect several related traits: the child is expected to function with normal children; concerted efforts at compensation in both learning and self-control are reinforced; aspects of the child's difficulty are accepted as bologically determined and not fully under the control of either the child or family; and the parents are commited and concerned for the child at the same time as able to maintain a certain detachment from "the problem," so that none of the family members is overwhelmed by frustration. Their ability to love, limit, and appreciate the real life struggle of the child is clear.

In addition, the grieving process over the loss of a "normal" child is always in the background. Problems with such loss can impair the parents' ability to face the child's disability, heighten denial, and decrease the motivation to alter their parental style. The parents' feelings of guilt may interfere with the family's ability to grieve or set limits about the child's handicap. When parents feel powerless to change themselves ("he's just like I was"), they cannot expect much from their child. If an overly sympathetic response leads the parents to expect less than normal functioning, the child's efforts to create a compensation can be undermined.

Good descriptions of the nature of the subset of children with ADHD or learning disabilities are currently available (Silver, 1984; Smith, 1981) to help parents understand and gain perspective on what their child is experiencing and how they must help their children manage these issues. In addition, making sure that parents can connect to national resources like CHADDER or local programs that can supplement treatment. There are increasing numbers of parents who access web pages that carry information about childhood disorders, and therapists should be familiar with the particular biases or orientations that exist on some of the networks, just as familiarity with current parent texts is important.

ADHD with Mild Learning Problems and Anxious Features

Brian, 8, and his parents were referred following a consultation with their pediatrician. At school, Brian's parents had already requested an individualized education plan (IEP) and the testing had identified both a visual motor delay and attentional difficulties. In addition, Brian suffered from considerable anxiety, manifested by multiple trips to the bathroom at points of stress, quiet withdrawal, and resistance to making any effort when tasks were frustrating. He cried readily following a "bad report." Brian was the middle child, with older and younger sisters. His older sister functioned well at school, but, later in treatment, his younger sister, would be identified as having a reading delay for which Title I assistance would be provided.

In the parent meeting the parents described a busy schedule that was, nevertheless, marked by a great deal of support and commitment to the children. Both of Brian's parents worked full time. They varied their work schedules so that the children would not be unattended at home during the day. Although this imposed some stress on their relationship, they were united in their financial, emotional, and parental goals. They found ways to maintain mutual contact and support. Both shared similar child rearing values and were able to nurture, set limits, and structure their children's activities.

However, the burden of Brian's disability had begun to take a toll. His difficulties at school and his anxious responses had made his parents feel guilty and uncertain. They

> had begun to vacillate in their expectations and limit setting. They wanted to let him "off the hook" so that his self-esteem would not be further damaged. The mother and father found themselves arguing when they had different approaches to the problem. There were moments when they blamed each other for his trouble adjusting. At times, his mother felt guilty and confused when one of Brian's outbursts of anger and tears would be directed at her since she "made him go to school." While she tried to rebut these attacks, she had begun to feel more unsure of herself.

The Family Work. In this instance, the positive tenets, values, and connectedness of this family system needed to be reinforced. Even during the parent assessment, the therapist tried to decrease the parents' guilt through education about the learning disability. It was explained to them that learning functions depend on the brain's maturation as well as on differences in the structure of each child's brain. Thus, the parents were offered absolution.

Each of the first three of the six basic goals for the management of an externalizing child was then reinforced. In the family discussions, which included all three children, the basic limits and structure for each child were clarified to reinforce Brian's self-control. Extra time was spent helping Brian to understand that he got "extra reminders," not "extra work," so he could better accept his frustrations. In addition, the supports that helped him function at home and at school needed to be defined as aids, rather than as markers of his underlying badness, in order to help his self-esteem. *Here, the definition of a zone 1 family suggests that the natural strengths of the family will support reasonable and accurate attention to the social–emotional goals 4–6 without a great deal of therapeutic direction or support.* The family's care and loving concern was evident throughout the treatment.

When his sister's learning disability was diagnosed six months after the work began, Brian's perspective on the family discussions improved enormously. In each family discussion, the meetings were begun with the good things that had happened and with new signs of each child's maturation and increased abilities. The trouble spots were reviewed next.

The Child Work. The child therapy with Brian was task focused. In the time devoted to play, games were chosen that offered opportunities to identify and review Brian's learning problems; for example, in the card game, "War," the confusion between the numbers 9 and 6 was a natural point for intervention. On the other hand, a walk through the hospital's corridors to get a snack gave an opportunity, on the return trip, to underline Brian's excellent visual memory for the route and items passed going the other way. This ability, it was explained, was one of the reasons he was so frustrated with some of his numbers and penmanship: he was very smart and he noticed when he did badly, feeling angry and sad. He wanted to do the letters as nicely as other children, but getting them "just right" was not simple for his brain. Brian needed to learn patience was important while he made new efforts and his brain learned new ways to handle difficult tasks. Later, a game of checkers could underline the use of patience and planning: persistence and effort would be rewarded.

Each of these therapeutic interventions was designed to help Brian deal better with his self-appraisal, handle the acceptance of difficulty, and see the efforts of the "team" (parents, school, tutor, and therapists) as ways to help him over a developmental hurdle. The first three central tasks for the child permeated the various activities of his therapy:

(1) keeping behavior on target (self-control), (2) maintaining self-esteem while accurate assessment and acceptance of problem areas continued, and (3) defining compensations while tolerating the frustration of the disability. Brian could readily identify feelings. His parents and he were able to engage in productive problem solving in calm moments. His parents were clearly committed to his support and Brian knew that their rules and structures were designed to "help me do my best and be proud of myself."

Treatment Planning. The healthy family can usually benefit from meetings that start out with all the members and, halfway through, separate the child; this is especially true during the assessment and early treatment phase. Thus, family meetings are used to assess interactions and to explain the disability to the entire family in a way that offers support to the child. Aspects of the child's in-session behavior that reflect learning problems or attention deficit disorder can be pointed out to parents as they appear. Discussions about school failure, home discipline, or social problems can be reframed in the context of the dysfunction they represent, for the benefit of both parents and child. Their relationship is adjusted for these difficulties and their love and care for each other preserved.

Separating parents and child for part of the session allows the parents to make detailed inquiries about the nature of the dysfunction and to ventilate their frustration in ways that, if the child were present, might damage his or her self-esteem further. Separate meetings with the child provide opportunities to build a therapeutic alliance that fosters collaboration with any behavioral modification program the therapist designs. Individual meetings also allow a closer-range assessment by the therapist and the expression of any personal concerns the child might find difficult to share otherwise. In the zone 1 "good enough" parent–child relationship, it is important to remember that most of the child's concerns are communicated to the parent. More often than not, the parent wants to share these with the therapist so that the parent can review how best to respond to the child's needs.

After the first few meetings, more time could be spent meeting separately, with brief family discussions at the end of each session. These primarily separate treatment sessions allow parents to work on the details of behavioral techniques (e.g., charting, the use of "time out," structures, and positive reinforcers) and to proceed with work on grief. (See Suggested Readings on discipline under chapter 3 as well as Appendix 6.1.) In some of the current literature, this is described as parent management treatment. For the child, treatment sessions allow work with the therapist toward understanding and acceptance of limitations and how to compensate for them.

Gradually, as the family teamwork is reconstituted as the child's anger dissolves, the therapy sessions can begin to be more intermittent and then adjourn for a while. In most externalizing disorders, it is rare to reach a state of no problems. Rather, a state of manageable problems is defined as a goal. In most instances, this is signaled by the presence of increased family communication and comfort as well as by the child's ability to more easily comply with the structures developed at home.

ADHD, Inattentive Type

Melissa was an 8-year-old girl who was preoccupied with Barbies. Each day started with a check of her outfit and an attempt to coordinate it with that of her Barbie of the day.

> Her parents had accommodated to her demands, although often her inability to make a decision, swings in her mood, and a tenacious resistance to her parent's suggestions got the day off to a bad start.
>
> The evaluation was triggered by what the teacher called her "hypersocial" behavior. She could not settle down to work. She was easily distracted. She impulsively called out to her friends when she was having trouble attending to the task at hand. Gradually her friends had begun to ignore her since they were unable to complete their papers in the midst of Melissa's pestering.

Melissa did not like the family meeting at all. She felt she was being deprived of a playdate, angrily rejected her parents concern, and thought the therapist was "old and stupid." Her parents appeared quite embarrassed. Melissa was better able to engage when she was told that the therapist had a very special Barbie in a drawer. While hoping to continue the dialogue about the presenting problem longer, the result was that Melissa jumped off her chair and began trying to go through every drawer in the therapist's office. The parents' tension escalated and they began to angrily call her back to the chair. The therapist decided to end the family-based portion of the meeting early and went over to help Melissa with her search after the parents left the room.

The subsequent child interview verified Melissa's preoccupation with Barbies and, in every other task, a short attention span, easy distractibility, and the attributes of an inattentive attentional disorder. No other symptoms were elicited; Melissa did not report any recent or past trauma, and her draw a person test and kinetic family drawing, while hastily completed, were not indicative of other concerns. The inattentive subtype of attentional disorder is more commonly seen in girls. These girls are often characterized as being hypersocial and hyperverbal. These are the symptoms that often bring the girls to a therapist's attention because their schoolwork is disrupted by their social needs. While these issues often interfere with work, it is the underlying attentional problem that needs to be uncovered.

The parents' checklists, completed while the child interview proceeded, confirmed the evaluator's impressions. The subsequent parent evaluation was also used as a feedback session, and a pharmacotherapy evaluation was recommended. In addition, the therapist decided that the main value of treatment right now was to help Melissa be more successful with peer relationships outside of the classroom. The parents needed to work with her so that her classroom disruptions were not alienating her friends. It was easy to use Barbie materials as reinforcers!

The Family Work. In this instance, the parents were receptive to and understanding of the diagnosis. Each parent had a sister who was "flighty" and whom he or she now felt also had an attentional disorder. Each sister had some talent that they were able to use so that their outcome was positive. As a result, the parents were not intimidated by the diagnosis and were not discouraged about Melissa's outcome. They readily understood how Melissa's self-control and self-esteem were linked. They knew that when she did not control herself with her peers that she wound up feeling angry and rejected. While she more often complained about them "hating her," sometimes they had heard her tell her older sister that she hated herself.

They realized she had no tolerance for frustration, and they needed to support the teacher's efforts to help Melissa complete some tasks. They were prepared for the fact that Melissa would complain of being bored after two seconds of frustration. Melissa did not seem to care about her grades, but playing with her older sister did matter to her. The parents felt comfortable arranging that Melissa's older sister could give her more attention after the completion of several kinds of study sheets that were like those used at school. They felt they could accomplish most of these objectives on their own.

They eagerly accepted a child psychiatric consultation and were open to medication trials. One of their sisters was currently being medicated. She had reported to them a great sense of relief with the degree of function she had attained with medication that had not been possible previously.

The Child Work. Melissa was not very interested in anything the therapist had to say. She had discovered what she wanted to do when in the office—"old-fashioned Barbies" as she said—and did not appear interested in any other activity. She told a long and complicated story about her girlfriends but did not want to answer the therapist's questions about her friends. It was a one-way conversation. She rejected "Blast-OFF" (a directed cognitive–behavioral problem solving, story telling, and feelings exploration game)[8] and other avenues of play exploration. She gave one-word answers to the sentence completion test. She easily named all the feelings on the feelings chart with an attitude of "Why are you making me do this?" The therapist decided to have another play interview following her medication trial.

The therapist noted a great deal more flexibility in her play and in her interests when Melissa began her stimulant. She was happy with the new plans that her parents had for her work, reported less distress about her friends, and could explain what her parents were helping her with in their talks with the therapist. "They tell me everything, you silly," she said pointedly.

After the next visit, the therapist saw that Melissa's attitude about herself and her schoolwork was decidedly better. The parents reported experiencing more success with her. The therapist decided it was not necessary for individual meetings at this time, but she would continue with periodic parent meetings.

Treatment Planning. Given the parents ready acceptance of the diagnosis and their rapid and successful implementation of the treatment suggestions, the therapist and family agreed to a yearly checkin model that would follow one of the psychopharmacology visits. This way, they knew that the topic of how Melissa was doing would be in the forefront of her mind when they met. They understood what the risk factors might be and were comfortable calling again if any concerns developed.

ADHD, ODD with Tics

The therapist invited Kevin, 9, and his mother into the office right after the child had tried to kick his mother. They had been having an argument over who got to sit on which side of the couch in the waiting room. The therapist had overheard Kevin threaten to run away before she came out and saw the child sitting where he wanted.

The therapist asked mother and son to come into the office for a brief meeting. Given what she had observed, she decided to keep this initial contact quite structured to see if the mother and child could manage with that help. Both the mother and child seemed

---

[8]"Blast-OFF" was developed by R. Ziegler and W. Gresser in 1992. It is available from Toys for a Reason, c/o Otter Creek Associates, 86 Lake Street, Burlington, VT 05401 (www.toysand reasons.com).

slightly sullen and answered curtly but contained their behavior. The therapist asked the mother to fill out checklists while she had a play session. Kevin immediately went to a game of Sorry and the therapist noted how his facial tics increased every time he was close to getting home or "sorrying" her. He was quite attentive in the game but would not respond to any other requests for information or engage in other suggested activities. The therapist felt relieved that he was willing to leave the playroom at the defined time to let his mother "have a turn." He made the therapist promise she would not play Sorry with his mother.

Mother came in to review her insurance and her concerns and readily agreed to a separate parent meeting. "I think I need help," she said upon leaving.

Is This Zone 1, 2, 3, or 4? The diagnostic evaluation conducted over the course of the three initial meetings that have been outlined in Part I should permit the therapist to answer that question. The more complex questions surrounding contemporary understanding of Tourette's syndrome are well addressed by Cohen, Detlor, Shagwitz, & Lechman (1982). In this case, the therapist was able to identify the poor relationship patterns that both mother and child exhibited. Kevin had little capacity to identify emotions and his mother tended to focus in the parent meeting on all the unhappy ones in her own life. Together identifying and labeling a problem was impossible without a major fracas.

The roots of this difficult family discourse were complex. Although the mother did not have either an axis I or axis II disorder, her relationships growing up had been neither caring nor helpful. Her parents did not abuse her, although she recalled a pass her father made at her when she was a teenager when he had one of his drinking binges. She never felt truly cared for or valued. She had made a commitment to make sure Kevin felt loved and wanted. She would get him what he needed. She struggled to set limits but was readily defeated by Kevin's behavior. Being a single mother, she did not have other supports to help her appreciate the difference between typical struggles of childhood and his oppositionality or attentional problems. She was very worried about his transient and changing tics. She had brought him to three neurologists already. All had reassured her that he was just a "normal boy."

The therapist felt that for both mother and child a 1 to 2 year course of individual therapy would be needed. The mother's therapy would need to begin as monthly parent meetings since, as she said, "there's no point in discussing my life. The past sucks and now I'm just getting by. I need you to help my kid. My insurance isn't going to last forever." She was willing to begin the process of parent education and to attempt to learn new management skills. It was the only way to help her rebuild a positive relationship with her child.

Occasional family meetings were necessary to begin to create a basis for self-control, emotional communication, and a collaborative relationship within the family. They needed to be short so that neither child nor parent was overwhelmed and so both could experience brief moments of positive exchange and success. As the treatment continued and mother and child were more stable, the length of the family-based meetings could be increased.

The Family Work. The first year of work followed a traditional supportive parent guidance model and parent management model. The therapist's attention was directed both at helping the mother to get the child to comply and finding ways to support their relationship so that each could enjoy the other. The mother followed through on most suggestions as well as she was able, but the anger she felt as she did everything "as well as she could" only began to diminish after the first nine months of Kevin's therapy. She was able to have better moments with her child "because of you" she said to the therapist and felt the help the child received was genuine.

Up until this point, she had totally rejected pharmacotherapy for her child and herself. She reported her own history of familial alcoholism and felt that the biological father of the child had had a drinking problem as well. She didn't want "another one of those in her family." The therapist reassured her that medication use in children with externalizing disorders does not increase their risk of substance abuse. There was no clear evidence that it prevented the high incidence of substance abuse in these youth, but she pointed out to the mother, "success is what we all count on." It was explained that if Kevin could take some medicine and listen a little better to his mother and to his teacher, control his temper better, and feel like he can trust his own choices a little more, it could only benefit him. The therapist then added, "the same goes for you." The mother said that might be so, but she was not agreeable to have her child take medication, despite her gratitude toward the therapist. "Besides," she said, "I looked it up in the pill book and it said it gave tics and he has them already. I won't tell you what else it said, but you probably already know."

Her gratitude to the therapist was expressed in another way. She went for a medication consultation for herself. Her medication response diminished her underlying dysthymia and the easily aroused irritability that she always felt in danger of expressing. This improvement allowed her to talk further about the lack of support she had felt in growing up. Her "wild years, drinking, partying, and finding fun men" came to an end with her pregnancy. Although she harbored resentment about the abandonment she experienced by the child's father, the worst of it by far was the final rejection from her own family. "Not that I was surprised, mind you," she said.

The Child Work. The therapist spent the first few months focusing totally on the child's feelings, whims, and choices. In the background, she dreaded the moment in which the boy would kick her, as he had his mother. The moment came eight months into the weekly therapy. The therapist gave him a time out. The child accepted a time out and then guiltily apologized. The child's receptivity to a fuller exchange began after that outburst. He began to be able to listen to, although not accept, a play suggestion or idea. His collaboration in the joint family meetings became more manageable.

Treatment Planning. In cases like these, the relational obstacles to the work are the ones that must be treated first. The therapist must walk the tightrope of forming a relationship with both parent and child within their conflicted relationship. At the same time, the therapist must reassure both parent and child, in the intermittent family meetings, that the therapist is on *both* their sides. The therapist's understanding should help create a bridge between parent and child. A cognitive–behavioral approach is bound to founder on the shoals of the affect that is constantly intruding on the transactions and poisoning the ability of the behavioral paradigm to be experienced positively. The therapist must always have an eye on the essential relationship between the parent and child. Pharmacotherapy must be considered and integrated into the care.

The therapist had decided the initial presentation of the case hovered on the edge of a zone 4 problem but was still in the zone 1 continuum. The child's intelligence, reasonable function in school, and ability to engage kept her from thinking of him as in zone 3. His oppositionality was not intractable, which could have led to another approach to the behavioral management (see Greene, 1998) if direct management techniques had failed.

Mother's clear ability to love, support, and provide for Kevin kept the therapist from thinking of the parent falling into a zone 2 classification. She had consistently provided Kevin with stability and had not permitted the men in her life to affect the routines she had gauged were important to Kevin's life. No man had made enough of a commitment to her to allow "any date to act like he owned my kid." The therapist recognized that many of her traits were "good enough" in spite of the obstacles mother faced in setting limits.

Risk Issues for Substance Abuse/Alcoholism in Latency and Adolescence in ADHD and Externalizing Disorders. The issue of the evolution of polysubstance abuse and alcoholism is a clinical issue for families whose children have externalizing disorders, although it is a risk factor in adolescent depression as well. Indeed, many parents refuse to have their children medicated on the mistaken assumption that using medication to treat them will heighten their risk of substance abuse, although there is no substantiation of this finding in the clinical literature. There is indeed a higher rate of polysubstance abuse and alcoholism in adults with ADHD, as there is a high incidence of comorbidity with antisocial traits and character disorder. The role of treatment, whether individual or family treatment or pharmacotherapy, has not yet been demonstrated to influence these unfortunate outcomes, although the reader should be advised that the existing studies are limited in their design and completeness of data collection.

A four-year follow-up study conducted at Massachusetts General Hospital (MGH) was unable to demonstrate any increased use of polysubstances in adolescents diagnosed with ADHD (Biederman et al., 1997). There was a higher correlation of substance abuse with conduct disorder and bipolar disorder during adolescence. The evolution of this risk may be heightened in the transition to adulthood, since the incidence of alcoholism and substance abuse has been consistently elevated in the studies of adults with histories of ADHD. The authors suspect this change may relate to the higher rate of conflicts with authority at work, higher job turnover, and relationship instability, which all accompany the ADHD diagnosis. The large population with ADHD studied at MGH sheds additional light on these outcomes by identifying the subgroup of youngsters with ADHD who have a significant social disability, i.e., traits of poor social function, which are more prominent in some youngsters than others (Greene, Biederman, Faraone, & Ouellette, 1996). This social disability includes a decreased ability to understand the impact of their actions on others, decreased perspective taking, a limited social repertoire, and an insufficient ability to hold the process of an ongoing social interaction in mind.

Conduct Disorder in an Early Adolescent

The initial family meeting followed Warren's court appearance in which the judge told the parents that a condition of his probation was therapy. Warren would be assigned a parole officer who would follow up on his compliance with the recommendations of the court. Warren had been arrested after he shoplifted a hooded sweatshirt at the neighborhood mall that was popular with his peers. He was 12 years old.

Warren's parents were surprised that "he had gone so far." They were aware that he had often been disruptive or made errors in judgment over the course of his school years. They felt they had dealt with these effectively. He had never been a great student, but the parents noted that in the past year his buddies in sixth grade "had begun to leave him in the dust." They reported that as a result of the court action, they had gone to school to meet with his counselor and found out that he had been skipping days of school. When Warren's parents said this in front of him, he looked tearful. He yelled at his father that his father didn't know anything and they should stay out of his business.

In the individual meeting, Warren was quite taciturn. The therapist was able to draw him out about his friends and Warren described how no one seemed to want to hang out with him anymore. He said that he thought he could show them that he could look as good as they did since they had recently teased him about the kind of shirts he had been wearing. The therapist told him she would be working with his parents to help him get back on track with some buddies but he had some real work to do and so did his parents. She told him that she was going to ask his parents to get him involved in some after-school activities and also to keep a closer eye on his schoolwork. She was going to make sure that Warren brought up his concerns in family meetings and would be getting reports from teachers, the leaders of his activity groups, and his parents.

In the meeting with his parents, an honest look at Warren's history, his relationships in the family, and his vulnerability to perceived slights by his peers helped to mobilize his parents. They saw that this pattern of lying and his truancy had just begun. They were able to investigate with the therapist what kind of supervision and support they could provide for him. They also needed to work with the school to make sure he could feel more successful.

Unlike some cases of conduct disorder, there are several bright spots in this history. There have been consistent attempts by the parents to help Warren learn better problem solving and monitor his activities. They do not deny his academic difficulties and appear to be aware of his loss of a circle of friends. Warren himself cares about having some peers to relate to and he does not have a long history of negative relationships with authority. His current poor judgment appears to have been exacerbated by a loss of peer status and little ability to identify where or how he might realistically recover. Treatment will need to support his parents' management skills and how they work to monitor his activities and peer contacts closely. More appropriate activities will need to be provided with the hope that he can develop another peer group. The parents must recognize that his prognosis will worsen if he turns to the more detached and antisocial teens that hang out in the town center.

The more serious forms of childhood and adolescent conduct disorder includes those youth who manifest compromises in multiple domains of function. There are often deficits in social competence associated with poor social problem solving and temper control. Academic function is often compromised. Many youngsters may have had a prior diagnosis of attentional disorder or oppositional disorder. Attachment to parents may be poor and complemented by a family that has multiple risk factors. Socioeconomic factors often compound these issues.

No single intervention is usually effective for the treatment of conduct disorder. Conditions associated with conduct disorder, such as ADHD, or the presence of impulsive aggressivity, should receive consideration for psychopharmacological trials.

Just as these symptom complexes must be identified, the adolescent's difficulties with problem solving, interpersonal skills, situational perceptions, anger control, stress management, and empathy also need to be evaluated. When these skills are poor, specific cognitive–behavioral training modules can be integrated into the basic adolescent–family therapy. (See Goldstein, 1988.)

Aggressive long-term treatment is needed in addition to case management and collaboration with courts. When risks factors such as substance abuse problems evolve or additional violations of societal rules and the rights of others intensify, the prognosis worsens. Forty percent of adolescents with conduct disorder may go on to develop antisocial personality disorder.

The Edge of Zone 2: Poor Parental Function in Externalizing Disorders. The Fragile Family, the Split Family, and the Blaming Family where the Family can still be Engaged in Treatment

In all of these cases, treatment can be initiated when an alliance can be forged with the parents. Treatment often requires multiple sessions over the course of the first year or two since the deficits in each parent, as well as in the family as a whole, do not yield readily to intervention. The child's difficulties are significant but not to the degree that the child would be seen as "impossible to treat" or unresponsive to environmental and parental care (i.e., not zone 3). Often these cases benefit from well-coordinated therapy with two therapists. The case material emphasizes the essential role of the concurrent treatment of the parents, which blends elements of adult therapy, couples work, and parenting education that is mindful of the nature of the individual adults and couple.

The factors that keep the parental or familial dysfunction from being classified in the most severe reaches of zone 2 include the presence of *all* of the following:

(1) The parents ability *to love* the child appears clear.

There may be difficulties in the smoothness of the attachment or some poor emotional attunement, but the therapist judges that the parents do love the child and the child recognizes the presence of that love.

The third component of love is commitment. These parents are willing to commit themselves to working for the child's benefit.

(2) The parents have the ability to comply with treatment. At the first and most basic level, it means that they will attend therapy. They will keep their appointments and try to follow the therapist's directives. They also accept responsibility for managing the costs of the psychotherapy or working with their insurance company.

(3) The therapist also believes that as the treatment alliance strengthens, the parents will be able to undertake any work that they need to do on their own issues.

While the ability to limit a child or to take full account of the real life nature of the child's struggles may be limited or even absent, neither of these deficits necessarily means the family falls into zone 2. With a clear foundation of love, parents can learn in therapy to limit their child—or at least consistently monitor their activities and whereabouts—and commit to making sure they are appropriately engaged in prosocial activities. In addition, the therapist can help them understand and empathize with the child's struggles.

Just as therapeutic support for the child must be based on a thorough understanding of the child, the family work requires understanding the interface of particular aspects of family functioning and the child's difficulties. The special vulnerabilities of the acting-out child in the areas of self-control, self-esteem, and frustration tolerance need to be investigated in the way they are manifested in the family and how the family handles them. If the parents' ability to control their temper or their own lives is impaired, the child's risk is increased. If the parents' self-esteem is fragile, the difficulties their child faces may trigger a defensive response. Parents must be able to tolerate the frustration of having to tell their child "one more time" and to continue to provide structure or support past an age when most children need less supervision.

The major focus of treatment is on the parent milieu, although often this approach may begin "through the child" for the parent to be willing to collaborate with treatment. The caring relationship and healthy connections in the family must be supported. The children in these instances are as victimized by their parents' lack of parenting skills and relationship as they are by the effects of their externalizing disorder. The parenting function, and the adult (or couple) psychopathology that determines it, becomes a major focus of attention in the evolving parent–adult psychotherapy. When necessary, other community supports for parents or children are mobilized.

ADHD and Developmental Delays in the Fragile Family. In the fragile family, communication and child-rearing skills are marginal, even before the externalizing disorder is recognized or diagnosed. The parents' self-esteem may be low. Their intellectual sophistication and capacity for insight and abstraction are limited. There is no major debilitating psychopathology or family systems imbalance, merely an insufficiency of coping skills. The parents manage adequately, although follow-through may be poor. Loss of control is infrequent, but it occurs, often with negative results. As a result, frustrating situations are dealt with more frequently by ignoring them or by helpless complaining. The child's impairment is significant but not to the degree to require residential placement or to the degree that daily function in the context of adequate care is not possible. The task of therapy for this kind of family is both educational and supportive of the best possible relationship. Treatment may involve filing for neglect in regard to the child's safety or overall medical compliance, as in the following case example:

> Regina was developmentally delayed in speech and language, her motor skills were immature, and her impulses were poorly controlled at home, although she managed at school with appropriate supports. In one set of tests, her IQ was in the borderline retarded region. In addition, Regina was extremely hyperactive. Her social skills were limited and she often resorted to hitting or throwing whatever was nearby whenever she was frustrated with her younger sister. Her younger sister was born with birth defects, which included the absence of a left hand.
>
> The mother was a childhood diabetic and had long-standing back problems, which limited her ability to set limits on the children as well as to help them care for themselves. The mother was in and out of the hospital, often appeared depressed, and in addition to her medical problems had a somatizing disorder. Within the family, however, she was characterized as the "army sergeant." The father was a postal clerk who worked hard but was chronically exhausted and overtaxed. He could not refuse his family much. When the girls needed clothes, he would get the most expensive and fancy dresses. It was one of the few things that his wife enjoyed as well.

For holidays, he would buy big stuffed animals appropriate to the season that the children would enjoy for only a few days. He was the cook in the family and was continually in a state of dismay because the children would not eat their supper. He could never refuse them snacks beforehand or desserts after so they had learned that supper was not necessary. His schizoidal adaptation lessened his ability to receive supports from any area apart from the therapy. As a result of his difficulties, the family was chronically on the verge of bankruptcy.

There was little difficulty in establishing the diagnosis from the checklists and ancillary testing. The challenge was in developing a treatment plan. While the stimulant medication seemed to work that the pediatrician had previously prescribed, the parents often forgot to administer it. In addition, their insurance plan did not cover the full cost of the stimulant, and they often owed the pharmacy money for the mother's medications, which had a copayment. As a result, the pharmacist often decided to wait for them to catch up on their other copayments before giving them Regina's prescription.

Parental communication was minimal; each harbored deep feelings of insecurity and low self-worth and felt unable to expose their neediness to the other. After supper, the family would collapse in exhaustion on the big couch in front of the television set. There, the girls watched the special child cable shows for which the gas money had paid. Then the therapist had to write letters to the gas company to make sure that the heat was not turned off. The girls would squabble, with little parental intervention until the mother or father exploded. Nevertheless, the children felt loved and cared for and their parents paid attention as best they could to medical appointments and school obligations; but their overall adjustment was marginal.

The Family Work. As these basic concerns were identified, the therapist decided to request that another colleague in the practice join her in the treatment. The therapists discussed who would work best with the children and who could best manage the countertransference to the parents' inadequacies. The conjoint work was always conducted in a language that even the youngest child (aged 4) could understand. Everyone had to agree what they were working together on so that the family could stop complaining and focus on a "good choice" and the rules that could help to make them all feel just "a little" better. The father's employment by the post office meant that they had the federal insurance plan that had reasonable mental health benefits to permit each therapist to bill for the twice monthly meetings. Often the parents could barely organize themselves to come to these.

Basic parenting rules were taught: the cotherapists modeled communication and limit setting, the children were expected to listen and to take their turn, and appropriate expectations were defined. The father had to be reminded that the girls could not sit still, but they could talk and "listen to the doctors" for part of each meeting. Miniature play structures, which could alternate with periods of discussion and family play, were created for the girls within the interview. When the girls were given structured play activities, the adults talked and reinforced their good behavior. Interruptions by the girls during these parental discussions were treated firmly, though kindly. Parents had to have a turn, too, the girls were reminded, and the therapists and parents helped define how they could entertain themselves until everyone could listen to them.

The cotherapists took turns managing certain tasks. When it was clear that the children were too restless to stay, one therapist took the children out of the room while the other continued the important discussion at hand, thus underlining the value of the time for the parents. In addition, the kinds of resources and supports that the children needed were defined clearly and simply. Progress was slow but occurred steadily, although crisis points led to tension in the treatment when the mother's resources were failing.

The therapists decided to file with a child welfare agency. This was done in the family's presence to underline the open communication and to have them hear that it was a way to establish more supports for the children, including a therapeutic afterschool program for Regina when her mother was debilitated. The girls began to fight more. In addition, the youngest had finally learned to hit Regina back. Regina then left the house and no one could go after her. She was at risk in the neighborhood by herself. While the parents were able to accept this intervention at this point without fleeing from treatment or feeling betrayed, they had missed three sessions and denied their anger had anything to do with it. They again began to minimize their difficulties, but the social worker's home visit documented the marginal organization and care in the household. A homemaker was put on the treatment plan to support mother's home function.

The initial behavioral contracts with the girls were made by the therapists, and behavior charts were made and given to the parents to check off each day. Once these initial contracts were settled, the parents were quite able to follow through on what was needed. Little by little, they began to keep a basic list of the tasks that they would face with each of the children. The army sergeant aspect of the mother was identified as a strength that had its place in the collaboration. The parents' tendency to denigrate each other was elucidated as showing their own weak points. It was explained that parents had them, too, just as their children did, but that there were lots of things to respect in each other and in both girls.

The Child Work. The children in this family were seen separately for part of each family meeting. Because of the family's level of functioning, the family-based messages were given in front of the children and the parents. In this way, the parents themselves would have a message that they could use repeatedly in their exchanges with the girls. The therapists could follow this interaction separately to see if the girls or parents reported similarly when they were not together. At times, each therapist saw a different girl. Communication was supportive and conveyed in basic language.

Treatment Planning. In this fragile type of family, conjoint meetings with a cotherapist and all family members can be ideal. The children can be seen at the same time the parent work is done. It decreases the problems the children may have in the waiting room while the parent work is done, and the parents do not have to get babysitters that they can neither find nor afford. However, it is rare to be able to develop this kind of care within the current constraints of many insurance plans.

Cotherapy includes opportunities for the parents to observe the therapists' modeling, limit-setting techniques, positive reinforcement, and the communication skills used for problem solving. Simultaneously, the parents can be supported and their authority and demands reinforced for the children. The therapists reinforce the children's connections to their parents as they help the parents tell the children of their love and care in more direct (and often less sarcastic) ways.

Child welfare services may need to be integrated with the treatment and prepared for early on as "support" for the family needs. Didactic efforts can be kept simple and experiential. Disciplinary issues or academic questions that arise between sessions can be reviewed and discussed in specific terms. When the cotherapist can be a child psychiatrist, the reinforcement of medical authority, medication management, and the medical model may help these families maintain their efforts and contact.

Intermittent Explosive Disorder in the Split Family. In split families there is a profound difference between the parents in point of view and approach to the index child. Much family therapy and literature has reviewed techniques for the inclusion of fathers in treatment (Wylder, 1982) and for working with families divided in opinion and actions (Haley, 1976). Additional complications occur when the child in such a family has either a learning disorder or behavioral problems or both. The therapy must then provide the family with an additional perspective. A middle ground must be formed between the father's typical denial and the mother's typical overreaction.

The treatment of the split family focuses on how to deal with the problem of the child's lack of self-control. The mother often feels extra nurturing is called for since the child must be angry for some reason; the father may resort to denial, claiming that change will come of its own accord or that punishment (e.g., grounding the child for a month) is all that is necessary. The way in which the family identifies and communicates about angry feelings is impaired. (See Table 6.3: Anger management.)

Billy was 8 years old when his parents brought him for an evaluation His preschool years had been marked by a difficult temperament. He reacted poorly to changes, had frequent tantrums, and was overreactive and immature. His weak motor skills had been noted throughout his preschool experiences and he actively avoided many large motor tasks. He had repeated first grade in order to give him time to "catch up."

His mother, a psychiatric nurse, and father, a computer programmer, felt helpless about managing his behavior. They felt they had tried everything and that Billy's moods dominated the household. When his parents discussed Billy's temper in the family meeting, Billy began to pout. His mother sympathized with him (it was "hard to talk about sad things"), whereas his father asked Billy to shape up. Billy was told by the therapist that "it's hard to be proud of yourself when you can't boss your temper." He was told that the therapy would try to help the family so that he would feel better.

The therapist suggested initial detective work for Billy and his parents to keep a chart of "his good days and his bad days." He stomped out of the meeting room. The parents asked if there was a medicine to help "change his mood" and were told that this question would be considered later. The therapist explained that the next step was to have a parent meeting and follow up on Billy's chart.

For the two weeks before the parents were able to schedule the parent evaluation, Billy kept a chart that had all good days. The following week, when the therapist asked for the chart, the mother looked to the father for it and thus was introduced to the serious struggle existing between the parents. The specifics of the argument, in this instance, were about whose responsibility it was to keep the chart. The mother controlled her anger about being left "holding the bag" of Billy's problems; the father complained that she always gave in to Billy, never followed through with limits, and got hysterical. The therapist had to work very hard to contain this argument and move to eliciting a family history and to evaluate the question of whether there existed any underlying symptomatology in either parent.

Before the close of the meeting, the instruction to help Billy keep his chart was maintained with the additional instruction that both mother and father were to keep their own to make sure they were aware of what they each thought was happening as the

TABLE 6.3. Anger management

Internal (child)	External (family)
Recognize physiological cue that indicates onset of anger.	Calm responding feedback and observation.
Containment of arousal of emotions.	Low-key instructions for time out. Physical soothing. Continued acceptance of child.
Verbalization skills. (Identify presence of language deficits in child or parents.)	Promoting dialogue. Use simple phrases. Consistent terms.
Problem Classification	**Objective of intervention**
When anger appears to be	
Predatory violence in the service of power	Methods of control are most important.
Reactive-impulsive hostile-emotional	Methods of calming are most important.

treatment proceeded. The therapist decided it was not time for the use of any consequences since the parents had already made it clear that they could not follow through. As a diagnostic test, they were also asked to define in the next parent meeting about which behavior they would most like to see changed at home. The therapist suggested that the plan for treatment would involve a meeting with Billy that would be followed by a meeting with them. The parent work would continue to help them define their objectives and parenting strategies.

By the end of the month before Billy's next individual meeting, he was ripping up his own chart and his parents' charts each week. At this point, his parents gave up keeping theirs. The therapist suggested to the parents that it was still desirable to keep up their charts. They could be put away in a safe place. Both child and parent meetings focused on helping Billy and his parents try to understand that charting these events could help him to function better.

The Parent Work. By the next meeting the split between the parents was even more apparent. Their inability to accept direction was further illustrated. In spite of the therapist's direction to the contrary, the mother had selected a particular behavior for their son to change. She had begun rewarding Billy when he succeeded. The father acted out his part by punishing him when he failed. The underlying difficulty in their communication surfaced. The therapist showed them how they shared only aspects of their feelings or plans and never completed their dialogue or listened carefully to each other.

At this point, it was possible to review these difficulties in terms of Billy's uncertainty about what would be expected of him. Both communication skills and behavior shaping skills became the focus of the parents' therapy with the marital conflict issues still below the surface. The therapist felt the tightrope that had to be walked was in the marital relationship, which was acted out in their parenting relationship with Billy. Medicine was no longer seen as a "quick fix."

The treatment shifted to include more conjoint couple's work when the mother found an e-mail message from one of father's female colleagues at work. This led to a relationship crisis in which each member of the couple had to decide if they were committed to each other. This work took another 10 sessions. As it began to resolve, their level of cooperation about Billy had begun to improve and Billy's behavior was more settled.

The Child Work. Billy's charts, even ripped, were accepted each week as a reminder that he "wished" he never lost his temper. His parents' charts were received without comment in Billy's presence. Discussion focused on how good children can feel when they can choose their own actions; Billy pretended not to listen. Billy's only chosen activity in the playroom was the card game "go fish," an activity that did not expose any learning weakness. Feeling he was very lucky in this game, he refused to attempt any other activity; in fact, he would not even shuffle the cards because of his motor coordination problem.

By the fifteenth meeting, with each session split between Billy and his parents, Billy had achieved one week of temper control that was confirmed by his parents' charts. He ventured a question to the therapist about what his parents were fighting about. The therapist explained that would be a question that could be asked in the family meeting. Billy did not address this again until after the major marital fight had erupted.

As the parents became more contained, he was more willing to shuffle the cards and could comment that "some things are hard for me to do." He tolerated supportive discussions about his areas of learning difficulties, as illustrated by his problem with shuffling cards and with riding a bicycle at home. Billy was beginning to recognize these problems and to believe that he would get some help with them.

Severe ADHD in the Blaming Family. The blaming family creates a context in which it is the child who is made responsible for the pain, anger, and deprivation that is felt within the family. There is most often severe character pathology present in the parent or parents. The more the child is abused, the greater the likelihood of a poor outcome. The child's self-image is more dramatically and negatively affected in this family type. Like the scapegoat in the alcoholic family (Wegsheider, 1981), or the child whose attentional disorder prompts an adaptation as the class clown (Gardner, 1971), the child who is blamed for behavioral or learning problems over which he or she has little control suffers greatly.

The pain and grief already present in a dysfunctional family is projected onto the child; the child, in turn, identifies with the aggressor. Frustration cannot be contained. When it is possible to help the parents develop some self-esteem, distancing from the child can be created. This task is often affected by the presence of major character pathology in the parents. There are times when their pathology is too extreme to permit them to enter into a therapeutic contract. Often these families are seen in the courts where bitter enactments over control (rather than the child's well being) are being fought in different and malicious ways by one or both parents. If a clear structure for self-control and can extend it to the child, the prognosis may be better, as is evident in the following case example:

> When Jamie was 5, his mother brought him to the division of neurology to see if there was something wrong with his brain, "just like his father." His father had been an alcoholic and drug addict. The mother had escaped from him by the time Jamie was 2 years old. She managed to care for Jamie, her only child, with the help of Aid to Families with Dependent Children (AFDC) and working occasional stints as a waitress, "if I can get somebody to stay with him." At the time she brought Jamie in, his mother felt that his bad reputation had spread throughout the neighborhood. Nobody could stand to be with him: when he couldn't get his way, he would throw a tantrum and hit his mother; his attention span was so short that he could not play with anything for more than five minutes. Most of his toys, bought with the arrival of a new check, would be broken by the end of the month. She felt that her loneliness was his fault, that he chased everybody away. He had ruined her life from the moment he started to grow inside her.
>
> Although Jamie's mother felt dismayed by his behavior, she had not resorted to beating him. He got his share of spankings, but more often than not she wrote him off. She felt there was nothing she could do with him. The more she ignored what he did, the worse he behaved. She did not believe that her behavior affected him. She was pleased that, to stop herself from hitting him when she lost her temper, she had begun to lock herself in her bedroom for extended periods. When he kicked and cried against the door in order to get to see her, she felt it was evidence of his nastiness and lack of understanding. Jamie's mother had already been seen in a child guidance clinic in her section of the city when Jamie was 3. She was sure that we were going to tell her the "same old things." Nothing made any difference in Jamie's behavior; he was just bad.
>
> The parent evaluation revealed that mother had had a long history of early child sexual abuse, which was then compounded by a series of conflicted and violent relationships with men. Her own drug abuse had ended two years before having Jamie, but she continued to entreat her abusive partner to return. When that failed, she decided to "dedicate" herself to Jamie and make sure he was a male "fit to live with." She was not sure whether she hated Jamie or herself more. She had never been in treatment herself or used a recovery program. The therapist concluded that she had borderline features in the context of an early history of PTSD and an alcohol and substance abuse problem in remission. She was not interested in treatment but was willing to bring in Jamie and to accept that half of the meeting would be with her and another therapist about parenting solutions and, at times, some interviews with both her and her child would be on the agenda.

The Family Work. The first step in the brief conjoint interviews was to reestablish some positive connection between this dyad. Jamie's need for his mother's affection had to be underscored as a way to define how much she had already given him. It indicated that Jamie, unlike his father, cared very much about what his mother expected of him, even if he couldn't "do it right" yet. However, like another mother whose child's father had been severely abusive to her, she exclaimed, "I see this child; I see his father; and I just start screaming."

In this instance, treatment by two therapists was critical. Since Jamie's behavioral controls were very poor, only brief periods of time could be spent in conjoint work. Jamie had to be removed from the room so that he could complete a project to give to his mother. In addition, Jamie's response to medication was vital in dispelling his mother's projections. Medical treatment enabled him to extend his attention span and bring his behavior into better conformity with his mother's demands. While one therapist could have been able to begin to work with Jamie and his mother, transferential and countertransferential issues would need to be monitored very closely in order to balance the varying relational demands.

The Parent Work. Jamie's mother needed someone to care for and be concerned about her before she could mobilize herself to implement plans for Jamie. She needed empathy and support. Jamie's treatment was her entry to her own therapy. Initially she could accept this only in a derivative way. The focus had to be on how difficult it was to care for Jamie (without asking her to do more or different) and gradually allow her to describe more her own losses. She had to grieve for her own lost childhood and the negative parenting she had received, her lost hopes of getting love from a drug addicted man, and her grief at having had a baby who did not repair her feelings of emptiness.

She needed to assess her losses even while she began to recognize what she had accomplished for herself. Attending Alanon and then AA as she owned her own alcohol and drug history, provided a much needed support. Both this recovery work and her receptivity to advocate for her child and bring him to treatment are the factors that made the clinician see, as treatment progressed, that this mother's behavior no longer constituted a zone 2 problem. The extended long-term outpatient treatment that involved both mother and child gradually permitted increased amounts of family work.

Only after her individual work had progressed could she begin to receive the gifts that Jamie brought her. When her treatment permitted the possibility of conjoint work, she could see that Jamie was able to do better in the family meeting. It was then possible to engage her in learning more effective limit setting. The stage was set for a long course of steady meetings before intermittent work could be focused on the six goals of treatment defined in this chapter.

The Child Work. Play sessions with Jamie were oriented to creating positive free play experiences. Tasks and games needed to be completed so that some positive exchange could be felt or a product created that could be offered to his mother. These times gave ample opportunity to help Jamie understand that it was hard for him to finish things, but he could do it if he listened to his helper. Success was programmed into the type of activities selected for play.

Once these initial activities had established an alliance and some good feelings between the therapist and Jamie, some nice products were made. The child portion of the behavior modification program began. The rules that helped Jamie to play and to finish things were made into a list. His experience had prepared him to understand that these were aids. Jamie had already been instructed that the medication was a "helper," but he was not really aware of its effects. The goal of the rules and of the stars that he would get on his chart was to help his mother to play with him and like him better (there was little mystery about her feelings when the therapy started). Enough stars would help him pick a special food that he could have at snack time or dessert the following day. He could even earn a "special time" with his mother.

The "stop and think" idea was established as a key term to be used in all phases of the child's therapy and the parent's therapy, and in the conjoint sessions. The phrase was underlined in block play. Jamie had wonderful ideas, but his constructive analysis of what was needed to complete his structures was destroyed by his impulsivity. Eventually, after the therapist had stopped his hand often enough, he was able to use the stop and think model with just a verbal cue. Most of the work of the first year related to the first goal of therapy: helping Jamie find ways of keeping his behavior on target. Once this base was established by medication, work at school, and in therapy, the next phase of therapy would be better able to address the other aims of the treatment plan to consolidate Jamie's more reasonable function and a less volatile connection between mother and son.

Zone 3: The Emergence of a Bipolar Disorder in the Context of Treating Severe ADHD with Temper Tantrums or Severe Conduct Disorder

The case described above could take an entirely different course were Jamie's pathology to evolve and worsen rather than respond to both the treatment and his mother's new efforts. There is increased awareness of the small percentage of children who present with ADHD symptoms that are compounded by violent temper tantrums, where episodes of irritability are sometimes combined with silliness and inflated mood. Noted intermittently in these children are the depiction of graphic sexual or violent scenes or both, at times combined with thought distortions or poor reality testing. Often there are periods of depressive affect combined with negative statements about the self, expressed wishes to die, and a negative perspective about all caretakers. These periods may alternate over the course of a year or manifest themselves in mixed states in which the child often appears depressed and agitated simultaneously (Wozniak et al., 1995; Geller & Luby, 1997). Thorough research must continue to carefully elucidate this syndrome as well as the impact of early pharmacological interventions and their risks as well as their benefits.

That said, the presentation of these cases may often require aggressive pharmacological management along with the other treatments described above. Stimulant medications may be temporarily helpful but rarely hold the child's symptoms in check. These children are at high risk for repetitive hospitalizations and are often referred for a residential program when the combination of outpatient support, parent containment, and educational systems cannot help the child maintain a level of function.

Another zone 3 problem can be the presentation of more virulent forms of conduct disorder, particularly when associated with interpersonal violence. Conduct disordered youth with concurrent substance abuse, who may also manifest other comorbidities, are extremely difficult to treat. Their tendency to minimize symptoms, conceal current behaviors, and lie makes individual dynamic treatment a poor approach. These youngsters may also be at high risk for suicide when they are in lockup treatment facilities. Far reaching issues of socioeconomic disadvantage, racial issues, and poor community supports compound the difficulty of caring for this population. The treatment requires vigorous case management, family supports, and court supervision along with appropriate school and environmental choices.

Zone 4: ADHD, Conduct Disorder, Expressive and Receptive Language Disorder with Medical Complications in the Disorganized, Destructive, and Noncompliant Family

Bart's neurologist had referred him for psychotherapy when he was 6 years old. His aggressive, impulsive, and destructive behavior was noted, as were the ineffectual limit setting of his mother and the instability of the entire family network. Over the years to come, he was repeatedly referred for treatment after various medical followups or after emergency room contacts.

The initial workup revealed expressive and receptive language-based learning disabilities, an attentional disorder with hyperactivity, and the presence of an inoperable brain tumor, which led to poorly controlled seizures. Erratic medical compliance further complicated his care, and protective services were contacted on several occasions.

Bart lived at home with his younger brother, his mother, and, frequently, other members of the extended family. His mother alternated periods of work with periods of staying home as a result of her anxieties, Bart's condition, or a new relationship. She remained married to the boy's father although he was often out of the home. When he was away, both boys' behavior was worse.

When Bart was first evaluated by the team, at the age of 6, structured residential placement was recommended. His mother rejected this idea. An alternative treatment plan was made, but Bart's mother never followed through with outpatient visits and could not implement the team's recommendations for structure, care, or consistency.

Case Unfolding. Since no child or family treatment was possible, there is no discussion of the child or family treatment. Outpatient treatment planning was irrelevant. Over the next 10 years, the agency had brief contacts with Bart and his family. His mother would bring Bart in as a result of escalating behavioral problems, or she was sent in following crises in the emergency room. School staff would be in touch with the clinic to raise questions about educational placement or concerns about the family. Once Bart reached adolescence, DSS became involved because the family conflict was out of control and neighbors reported domestic violence. Frequent contacts between the therapists, DSS, and other community agencies were necessary to coordinate services.

Throughout the years of sporadic contact with the family, his mother often called with frantic requests for residential placement for Bart. She just as frequently decided against it, once the process got under way. Her frequent reversals in attitude reflected her intense, but ambivalent, tie to Bart and tended to alienate other professionals. Contact with the father was occasionally helpful.

With this family there was little opportunity to make use of cotherapy or, for that matter, any therapy at all. Once or twice a year, Bart met with a child psychiatrist for a reevaluation of his needs or the possible role of medications, while the parents' therapist met with the parents to reassess the family system, but the family was never able to follow through on any recommendations. Medication was suggested but was never prescribed since the family never met criteria for appropriate followup. The parents' therapist took on the role of providing crisis intervention and liaison work with the multiple professionals and agencies involved.

Ultimately, when Bart was 17 years old, the family was able, with the help of intensive efforts by the team, DSS, and another community agency, to go through with placing Bart in an appropriate residential setting.

Zone 4 Treatment of the Disorganized and Disrupted Family/Future Treatment Possibilities: The Child and Adolescent Support Services Program (CASSP) Model. For the disorganized family, often described as the multiproblem family, the prognosis depends on the degree of disorganization (Minuchin, Montalvo, Guerney, Rosman, & Schumer, 1967). If the family is highly disorganized, there is a strong likelihood of treatment failure: appointments will be missed, behavior management programs will not be followed, school and medical professionals will be alienated, and medication may be mismanaged. Structure, the most critical element of support for children with externalizing disorders, is the very element lacking in the family system. Consequently, the treatment goals defined in this chapter, because of their consistency, become an anchor for the coordination of work with other agencies in the community that have dealings with the family. The prognosis is particularly guarded where either or both parents have serious problems with impulse control and periodic violent eruptions. As in the blaming family, the experience of aggression or abuse fosters the child's identification of the "out-of-control" self with the parent. The poor impulse control and aggressivity become more ego syntonic and are then used to mask the child's low self-esteem, fear, and insecurity. Straightforward discussion and problem solving are impossible.

Therapeutic investigations are often thwarted by denial and evasion on the part of both child and family. Crisis situations may prompt some therapeutic contact but the family rarely follows it up. These emergency contacts may lead to a child disclose abuse or neglect.

Much of the work with this type of family depends upon case consultation with the school and social service agencies. The school personnel, in order to protect their alliance with the child, often need to know that other professionals are involved. They can be helped by a realistic review of the problem in terms of both child and family and by an emphasis on the importance of the support they themselves offer the child. Behavioral charts that can be implemented by the teacher are designed. Medication adjustment and administration may depend on the school nurse. The resource room teacher may become an ancillary therapist and help identify issues of self-esteem, frustration, and self-image for the child.

The treatment must be planned to cover an extended period. Whether one therapist maintains consistent, although intermittent, contact with the family or whether this is done by various professionals within the same agency, the constancy of the supportive goals provide a holding environment for the child, family, and other community services. In fact, there may be times, especially during crises, when a series of three or four office visits occur, which both child and family will recall in later contacts. As the above case shows, any steady therapeutic course is difficult to chart with such families. Often the final solution will be to place the child in an alternate residence in spite of the lack of conclusive evidence that exists to support the effectiveness of these services over other interventions for most at-risk children (Kutasch & Rivera, 1996).

Home-based teams have been developed to help children and families stay together and function better. These teams often represent the effort of certain communities to pool funds from the different state agencies that are responsible for education, mental health resources, and child and family welfare (CASSP model, Stroul, Lourie, Goldman, & Katz-Leavy, 1992). These teams rely on the pioneering work of the family therapists (Ackerman, 1966). The concrete services, therapeutic opportunities, or parental support can encourage and support the parents in helping themselves and their child. These models will provide direction for child and family policies that may succeed with these zone 4 families. These interventions are impossible for individual therapists or in general outpatient child psychiatric practices or clinics.

The alliance that the parents can establish with the team sets the tone for the child to participate in treatment. Once the parents maintain a positive alliance with the team they may be able to engage the child more collaboratively. Of course, the child must establish a connection with their parents that the team can support. Often the relationship is based on cycles of defiance, heightened emotional connection, and absence. Although the ability of the therapist to form a working alliance with the child is affected by the degree to which the child can trust, a factor moderated by the child's level of exposure to trauma, the child will form a relationship only as the family indicates it is acceptable to do so. Particularly for younger children, it can be unsafe to challenge the parent's view of "the problem" and thus also the parent's solutions. Children will most often not move ahead of the parents in their ability to work toward solutions.

The multidisciplinary team, through the incentives they can offer by making resources available, can facilitate the alliance with the parents and their belief that "something can help." A bridge can be built to help facilitate the parents' understanding of the child's difficulties in a nonblaming way. The team must help the parents to conceptualize a solution to the family's current difficulties with the child that go beyond "fixing" the child. There must be a willingness within the family to hold responsibility for facilitating change and finding the solutions to care within the family. The treatment team then becomes a mechanism to support the family's own efforts to change their relationships to manage the nature of the child.

At times, court mandates are needed to require the family to be involved in treatment planning. In these cases, it is only with the potential threat of the child being removed after noncollaboration that the family will make another effort. In this challenging context, the therapeutic home-based team must find a way to develop a working alliance with the parenting system.

Flexible funding is a key ingredient in the "new" outreach and home-based teams. It can permit them to help families find the kind of material resources and community supports that they need. The family's access to reasonable food, clothing, and shelter enables the parents to have more time and energy to devote to caring for the child. Basic survival issues understandably take priority over the mental health issues of the children and families. The team must be able to find ways to help them identify and then access these resources for basic needs. Often these resources help parents overcome their own distrust in relationships, which has been exacerbated through their experience of previous mandated treatments that were unsuccessful. As emphasized in chapter 3, the parents' own mental illness, substance abuse, or experience of family violence (current or past) will all play a role in the manner in which the parent can collaborate with treatment.

The degree to which the primary caretakers of the child have relationships with their extended family is important. Does the family network share the view of the nature of the child's difficulties? Can they provide alternate supportive relationships for the parent or child? These other figures can support the authority of the parental system or help to make decisions about the child. They may help "translate" these decisions to the child. They are potentially available as respite for the family. They may decrease the need of the family to look to the treatment team to provide respite services or out-of-home placement for the child. The degree to which the team can fund these caretakers keeps these resources available.

The availability of supportive resources in the community (after-school programs, support groups, recreational services, etc.) to which the child and family can be connected is important. They allow the team to further its treatment alliance with the family. However, the family needs to be willing to utilize these resources. They may initially require multiple supports to be able to access these resources or to bring the child to them regularly. Again, the treatment team's ability to offer transportation or vouchers can help the family to engage and eventually follow through on their own. (The authors thank the effort of Paul Reinert, director of the FASST project, for providing these insights.)

☐ Pharmacotherapy Referrals

There is a wider range of medication options in the treatment of externalizing disorders for children and adolescents than for the internalizing disorders.

The foundation of pharmacotherapy for attentional disorders still involves the stimulants. They have been well documented in test–retest situations with academic measures. The stimulants increase length and quality of attention, decrease distractibility, and improve aspects of academic function, including improving visual motor performance. Stimulants also improve psychosocial function, decreasing the severity of aggressive responses and improving social behaviors.

Two of these stimulants, methylphenidate and dexedrine (both of which exist in extended release forms), are the most frequently used compounds. Both stimulants have been used since the 1940s and no long-term troublesome side effects have been discovered. They are most often prescribed by pediatricians. Although recent discussion has focused concern on the frequency of their use in children, the evidence suggests that given the high incidence of attentional problems in children (5%–10%) they are not being overprescribed. The third stimulant used to treat this population is the long-acting compound, pemoline.

Additional medications used to treat attentional disorder include the alpha agonists (e.g., clonidine or guanfacine) and beta blockers (e.g., propanolol). These have been used to minimize the rebound in hyperactivity that may follow as the child's treatment with a stimulant wears off, as well as prescribed for the sole threatment for ADHD. They have also been used to treat impulsive, anxious, and post-traumatic symptoms. They have been noted to reduce the frequency of some children's aggressive responses.

Trials with tricyclic antidepressants have been defined in their role in the treatment of attentional disorders which are compounded by internalizing symptoms, such as anxiety and depression (Biederman, Baldesarini, Wright, Keenan, & Faraone, 1993). Newer antidepressants, such as bupropion and others, currently are being investigated for their potential role in the treatment of this population. Bupropion has had two well-documented studies of its efficacy in the treatment of ADHD (Barrickman et al., 1995; Connors, Casat, Gualtieri, & Weller, 1996).

There have been few trials that report solely on medication approaches to ODD. For the most part, behavioral approaches have been used to modify these children's oppositionality. When underlying irritability and mood instability appear to contribute to the oppositonal and tantruming behaviors, they have been treated with antidepressants as well as mood stabilizers (see Greene, 1998). In some instances, severe aggressivity is treated with low doses of major tranquilizers.

There have been few reports that indicate that pharmacotherapy can modify the conduct disorder. Psychiatric referral in conduct disorder is still indicated. Most psychiatrists attempt to identify either a symptom or a comorbid condition (such as ADHD or an underlying mood disorder) that might respond to medication.

Finally, the treatment of bipolar disorder in children relies on the same mood stabilizers that are currently used in the treatment of adults with bipolar disorder: the mood stabilizers include lithium, sodium valproate, and carbamezapine. These latter two medications have a long track record in the treatment of juvenile epilepsy, and so information about long-term use in a large population of children is available. Now other antiepileptic medications are being studied for their potential efficacy in the treatment of mood instability, as are some of the new generation of antipsychotic medications.

Like other complex conditions, any medication can be integrated into the care of a child with multiple symptoms to offer relief. These medications may include the antidepressants, the major tranquilizers used to treat psychotic symptoms, minor tranquilizers, and stimulants.

☐ Appendix 6.1. Basic Principles for Behavioral Contacting with Children and Families

1. Assess the quality of the relationship between parent and child.
   a. If poor, therapeutic efforts should be directed toward increasing the warmth, comfort, and positive contact between parent and child through conjoint therapy meetings, prescriptive suggestions (i.e., spend at least 30 minutes per day in a pleasant activity with the child, three compliments a day, etc.) to individual treatment meetings with parent and child that direct their attention to their feelings about their relationship with each other.
   b. If good, confirm and support these as the most important and enduring aspect of experience for the development of the child. The behavior shaping contract should be seen as an extension of the love and regard the parent has for the child and the child's success within and outside the family. This perspective should be generously repeated in the behavioral contracting reviews.
2. Assess the quality of the parents' ability to be consistent (which may vary across time periods of the day or week or in regard to particular topics).
   a. If poor, help parents define weakness, how it may be corrected, and then target behavioral goals toward the areas in which the parents can be most consistent.
   b. If good, help the parents identify their underlying values/meaning of what they are attempting to accomplish with their child so the child understands the consistent feedback as an effort to build "good habits" in the child.
3. Assess the quality of the child's behavioral controls.
   a. If poor, identify clearly learning (e.g., language processing problems, concreteness), developmental, impulse control problems, or all of these that bear on the child's success. Make sure the parents understand these and the degree of improvement to be expected (e.g., from a 40% success rate toward a 75% success rate—perfection is not to be expected). Target behaviors and techniques that may most readily succeed.
   b. If good, help the child understand his or her own feelings ("Dad gets too mad, so I won't listen") or reactions to other family members ("nobody thinks I'm as good as my brother"), which bear on the child's willingness to make efforts toward success.
4. Start small.
5. Stay specific.
6. Frame the goal positively.
7. Accomplish one goal as a way to define the way in which the parent–child–therapist team works together in discussing, defining, implementing, and then monitoring and evaluating the success of the intervention.
8. Build on this success.
9. Identify public space for noting goal and tracking reward system—refrigerator, outside door of child's room.
10. Parent must be in control of stars or points.
11. Have the child be in charge of placing "splotch" marks for mistakes, which will heighten child's awareness, sense of responsibility, and increase neutral communication about mistakes.

12. Investigate the realities of "sustainable" reinforcers.
    a. Do not exceed a family's budget.
    b. Use extra parent contact in positive ways as a reinforcer (which will also strengthen the relationship).
    c. Use naturally occurring daily activities for rewards, e.g., choosing a special breakfast food, having a 15 minute later curfew for playtime or bedtime, tie into the existing allowance structure.
13. Make sure to discuss issues of anger or negative reinforcers (hitting) that may occur in the family so that the parent and child know the therapist is aware of the realities of these exchanges between parent and child. Acknowledge that these are dramatic and often have a short-term impact. Remind the family that the therapy with the child–parent team is designed to produce long-term learning.
14. Build a "tier" of reinforcers.
    a. First tier: Immediate reinforcer: praise, placement of star (create a ritual of acknowledgment that strengthens child's self-esteem and builds positive moments between parent and child).
    b. Second tier: Daily reward at end of day.
    c. Third tier: Weekly goal reward.
    d. Fourth tier: In selected instances, parent and child can be working toward special vacation or weekend event.
15. Understand the use of "negative reinforcers" (in behavioral terms: overcorrection).
    a. Discuss error.
    b. Write apology notes.
    c. "Fix" what was broken when possible.
16. Understand the law of natural consequences.
    a. The child not locking his or her bike so it gets stolen means it is stolen. The process between parent and child should involve how the child works with the parent to replace it. A new bike should not appear miraculously.
    b. Interactional trouble with peer or teacher should lead to parent having a meeting with child, with teacher, or with other family members and child to discuss event. This should help the child build skills and corrections, not humiliations.
    c. Not completing homework leads to a bad grade, not a parent having a temper tantrum with a teacher for "not supporting my child."
17. Keep consequences connected to the problem.
    a. Incomplete homework should lead to homework time or homework club after school to get the job done.
    b. Riding bike beyond designated perimeter of acceptable neighborhood locales should alter biking privileges.
18. Extend reinforcement to other sites and family members—get the child's significant relationships on board.
    a. Share point system with after-school program.
    b. Have reinforcement come from outside the nuclear family relationship—special aunt, grandmother, or family friend.
19. The therapist should accept responsibility for failures of program. Acknowledgment can be made in the following ways:
    a. "I didn't design this right."
    b. "I need to know more about how you and Johnny work together."
    c. "You're helping me see how tough things are sometimes."
    d. "We can make this better, but it may take more time and energy than we thought. It's a good thing we have parent meetings!"

7

CHAPTER

Problem or Solution: Complications in the Treatment Plan in Zone 1

In zone 1 problems, children and families often respond well to focused interventions using an integrated combination of treatment approaches. These interventions maintain a flexible focus on the triad of therapeutic goals defined here: supporting healthy relationships within the family, developing a way to achieve active mastery of the difficulty within the child and family, and suggesting methods to lessen the experience of symptoms. Each therapist will use his or her own personality and trained instincts to develop a creative mix of exploration, psychoeducation, behavioral management training, family therapy, the insight into underlying dynamic or emotional conflicts, or all of these to resolve the problem and prompt new solutions. Even when the therapist uses a model that constantly reassesses the movement promoted by the use of each of the three approaches, there will be cases in which there may be little progress seen.

The most striking example is noted in most zone 2 or 4 contacts. These tend to be brief, not because of the rapid resolution of the child's difficulty, but because these families shy away from most treatments or are noncompliant. Other approaches must be developed, as discussed in chapters 4, 5, and 6, depending upon the nature of the presenting problem and other agencies that may be involved.

Brief therapy is rarely indicated in zone 3. Here, severely affected children have competent parents and treatment is most appropriately dedicated to the use of long-term care through multiple modalities. The parents recognize that maintaining a therapeutic relationship with the child is essential. They want to make sure their child is coping with the developmental challenges posed by his or her illness and the feelings associated with it (as well as their own) as best as possible.

Models of brief treatment all rely upon assumptions that require the patient or family to have some skill and resources. As the introduction to this book mentioned, most zone 1 *families* are within managed care plans because they are employed. The skills that permit them to work are the ones they will need to complete a brief treatment. There is a variety of brief treatment models (Sifneos, 1992; Mann, 1980; Friedman &

Fanger, 1991). Common elements of these therapies include a focus on the here and now or an orientation to the future, even if the problem is seen as a result of a past trauma.

These approaches specify limited treatment goals. The restoration of premorbid functioning is emphasized (meaning that the client does not "grow" beyond his or her baseline). The active collaboration of the patients is expected and, when not forthcoming, requires the rapid and active reevaluation of what the patients "will" dedicate themselves to achieve. Treatment plans that reflect this point of view are developed in Jongsma, Peterson, & McInnis's work, *The Child and Adolescent Treatment Planner* (1996), and illustrate how this approach is formalized in the paperwork many MCOs expect.

In one review of solution-oriented therapy, the outcome is defined as changes "in the client," not in the family, the school, or other parts of the client's life. This statement highlights the conflict that many child therapists experience. In order for many children to function, changes must be made within the family, in the parents' approach to the child, in school settings, or elsewhere. The MCOs, for the most part, do not wish to pay for the expensive function of child advocacy or indirect case management time. For this reason, many HMOs are ill suited to provide care for the more compromised children and families with poor resources (the Medicaid population).

As a result, the therapist who works with managed care resources for zone 1 families must classify the parental level of function promptly, as Part I suggests. The health of the parents is integral to sharing the care plan developed for the child. The parents must be willing and able to change their own style of parenting, advocate for their child, and find other supportive systems to help their child function. The therapist will not find these functions insurance reimbursable and must discuss self-pay options with parents if the parents want this additional service. Many families in zone 1 are willing to do this work themselves or bear the expense of the support they wish from a child expert.

However, in some cases in zone 1, the therapist may face complications. The therapist may begin a focused approach, which seems to start well and then flounders. The therapist then must distinguish those cases that are moving along in a predictable fashion, but at a slow rate, from those in which another complication exists. This is similar to certain sprained ankles that will respond to rest, ice, compression, and elevation but will require more time to heal in order to reestablish motion and function. A slow healing ankle must be distinguished from a ligamentous tear, which requires a very different treatment.

In the cases to be discussed in this chapter, the course of treatment is complicated by information or aspects of the child or family that—belatedly—is revealed. This information may require the therapist to alter the assessment of the zone of care. At other times, it may simply move either the child or family (or both) further along the continuum of severity of dysfunction. (See Figure 7.1, which will be discussed below.) An entirely new formulation may be required. Treatment techniques need to be reassessed and treatment goals reevaluated.

In zone 1, the initial assessment sets the stage for the therapist to implement a solution-focused approach that enhances existing relationships, promotes mastery, and reduces symptoms. These goals can all be spelled out neatly in a "managed care" format. However, the course of all zone 1 treatments is not necessarily smooth. Furthermore, when these complications arise in the course of treatment, they may not be simply described in cognitive–behavioral terms. Comorbidities, complex parental psychopathology, underlying unconscious conflicts or resistances, or family systems complications may emerge that block the straightforward pathway of problem resolution. These complications may be revealed only during the course of the treatment. Their emergence may take the therapist by surprise or gradually unfold.

Simply put, the therapist's proactive, multidimensional approach has not changed or resolved the presenting problem. In the instance described below, the initial treatment plan had been to treat the appearance of a panic disorder. The adolescent and her family described it as their chief concern. The evaluation revealed that the panic attacks had occurred after 17-year-old Tammy stopped using marijuana. Neither the girl nor her parents could be pinned down on the extent of the girl's use, which they staunchly maintained was "in remission." Both Tammy and her parents had participated in the assessment and appeared initially compliant. They understood the diagnosis of panic disorder and accepted a psychiatric referral for medication assessment, as well as agreed to the therapist's plan to use two strategies: one to continue to support the girl staying straight (increased coping) and the other to acquire tools to manage the panic (symptom reduction). The parents agreed to support both prongs of the intervention and by doing so accomplish the third goal of strengthening relationships.

Since the onset of anxiety symptoms early in the course of recovery from substance abuse is not an uncommon problem, the therapist set to work developing this framework for treatment. A focused relaxation program was wrapped within a relapse prevention model. Continued education about recovery work would be included for Tammy along with the directive education of her parents. Both Narcotics Anonymous (NA) and Alanon were recommended.

The therapist had adopted a symptom-based approach given the girl's lack of psychological insight or interest in introspection. No one in the family seemed too psychologically minded. The therapist focused on helping the girl use techniques of self-calming (the fourth and fifth sessions). Participation in NA was reported, and the parents had gone to Alanon. Both the mother and father had agreed with the initial treatment plan, although the mother seemed to be more appropriately alarmed by Tammy's drug abuse, whereas her father was more minimizing. All had agreed that a major treatment goal was for the girl to stay straight. It wasn't until the fifth individual session that Tammy revealed she had regularly used many over-the-counter drugs and had gone to many primary care doctors to get other prescriptions for migraines or other somatic complaints.

The way the girl and family had obscured the girl's level of drug use had been a red flag in the initial evaluation, but there had also been the seeming commitment of the parents and their daughter to recovery. Following Tammy's revelation, a family meeting was held (the sixth family session and the end of their benefits) in which the parents discussed their acceptance of their daughter's "drug-based" approach to her somatic reactions. Mother said, "I've always had terrible menstrual problems and the doctor was always willing to prescribe something to help me. I didn't think it was unusual." The mother reported that she had always experienced more concern about the girl's somatic complaints. As she spoke, she even seemed fearful of them. In this regard, she had been very invested in Tammy's medicalization of her need for "something" to help with her pain. The family agreed to continue treatment on a self-pay basis. Neither the mother nor father wanted to use their own mental health benefits for parent and family meetings. The therapist scheduled an appointment with the parents together to review further their perspective on their daughter's difficulties and what they defined as "a problem."

The full extent of these complications burst upon the therapist with a midnight phone call to the therapist. Neither the case's therapist nor the consulting psychiatrist was totally surprised at the turn of events when they later reviewed their initial assessment, but the intensity of the complication unfolded suddenly.

> Tammy said, "I can't sit still. I feel so anxious. I don't know what to do with myself. This is how I felt when I used to abuse drugs. What medicine can you get for me?"
>
> All of this was said between sobs, gasps, and with a whining regressed tone that suggested there was no ego available for an alliance. Tammy had recently begun treatment for a panic disorder and had been drug free, supposedly, for three months before the treatment had started. After the therapist had conducted the initial diagnostic meetings, she added a psychopharmacological consultation in which an antipanic drug had been added and brought to therapeutic level.
>
> As Tammy and the therapist explored her suicidal potential, her level of impulse control around drug taking, whether she had been to an NA meeting recently, what had happened to her work on her relaxation program and what efforts she could make to calm herself. Every answer was framed in a tone of desperation. She admitted that she had not gone to another NA meeting after the first and shouted that she felt the therapist was as stupid as those meditation exercises, which "you had to be a genius to remember, anyway."
>
> She denied anything had ever been helpful and that even the knowledge that she had survived other anxiety episodes was no comfort to her. In the background the therapist could hear her anxious mother asking if she was explaining herself well enough to "get the doctor to do something." She steadfastly refused any suggestion other than the need for more or a different medication that would affect her condition immediately. (Tammy had a preferred list of drugs on the top of which had been Valium-like compounds that she had abused before.) She denied any thoughts of harm to herself or others. When the therapist asked to interview the mother, the patient objected, but her mother heard the exchange and got on another line. The mother reported that she felt capable of staying with her.
>
> The therapist suggested that they would need to travel to the nearby emergency room to be observed, to have her physical symptoms monitored and to be reassured about them, and to have the presence of professionals available who could support her. They might decide to use some medication, but they could only gauge that in seeing her. As she started to talk about the trip to the emergency room, her mother started to complain about the weather, that she couldn't drive her, and that a cab was too expensive at this hour and they would have to wait.
>
> The girl agreed that she could make her own arrangements, that she had her own cab fare, and that she would get off the phone and argue with her "stupid" mother. The next morning in a call to see how she had managed that evening, she replied in a very nonchalant tone that she had made a cup of tea and found something to read.

There are several complications. Each member of the family is involved. The addictive disorder was not truly in remission. The girl's apparent engagement in recovery work was a veneer. This behavior could be labeled as lying, resistance, or noncompliance with treatment, and the therapist must decide how to label it and manage it. In the crisis, the girl also reveals she has not been attending meetings. Neither Tammy nor her parents had previously reported the girl's continued drug-seeking behaviors with other doctors or her continued use of over-the-counter medications. They had only recently been able to identify this as a "past" behavior.

While active illegal drug abuse had not continued, the girl's characterological and emotional problems had become more evident and were being acted out within the treatment, with the parent's support. How the mother and father's ambivalence and differences in approach and feeling to the girl's past drug problem, versus her somatic disorder, has become more prominent. How they plan to manage her current problems will exaggerate their differences. The mother wavers back and forth in the face of the girl's demands but sends her to doctors for medication for her somatic complaints, whereas the father insisted that their daughter should do something "to help herself and stop all this doctor stuff." Each parent effectively negates the role of the other.

Although the therapist was beginning to witness (not treat) the obstacles posed by the underlying character of the patient and the underlying makeup of the family, there was now no clarity about what either Tammy or her parents would commit to in terms of treating these newly revealed issues. A light has been cast on their relationship with each other and their different approaches to problem solving. The girl's impatience (and the family's latent support) for anything other than a medical "quick fix" has moved to center stage. Their alternating disparagement or acceptance of the support available in the recovery community had led to many conflicts between both parents and also with their daughter. They had denied, minimized, or not discussed any of the therapy issues. The psychiatrist and therapist needed to review all of this information.

The therapist now had to bring the entire treatment contract to the table again with the girl and parents separately and then with the family together. Limits and closer monitoring of this teenager's drug-seeking behavior was indicated. Both Tammy and her family had to confront that *more* effort *of their own* was going to have to be expended to manage "this problem." The symptom at this point was an "agitated wanting," and both Tammy and her family felt it was their right to have this need filled.

The girl and family hovered at the more dysfunctional edge of zone 1. At the first assessment, neither family nor the girl was seen to be severely compromised and the comorbid diagnostic disorder, substance abuse, had been defined as in remission. However, the family's ability to manage certain emotions, separately and together, was quite compromised. The family functioned reasonably well in other areas of interaction. There was no lethality or issue of potential self-harm. The anxiety disorder diagnosis was unchanged but now was clearly most manifest as this child and family faced "wanting." The issue of wanting led to a complex collusion between different family members that had ramifications in each member's psychological makeup. The resolution of these intersecting problems was not going to be straightforward.

Another aspect of the interface of "wanting" and accepting responsibility would be tested when they had to face accepting responsibility for the payment of the emergency phone call intervention. These responsibilities were discussed during the initial fiscal informed consent component of the evaluation. They had agreed that they were to be billed directly for phone-based services, since these were not covered by their MCO.

Whatever their insurance, whatever their resources, a review of the treatment goals must occur in light of the additional information. The number of sessions needed must be redefined as it is apparent that there will be a slow, and potentially erratic, rate of treatment response, which may include dramatic relapses of substance (or medication) abuse. The therapist, as well as the psychiatrist, will need to explicitly redefine the treatment contract and the anticipated costs. The *girl's* attitudes toward substances, medical care, and her own goals need to be reappraised. The *parent's* attitudes must be reviewed. The mother's covert support of the girl's medicalization and her seeming "fear" of her medical complaints needs exploration. The father's minimization and apparent lack of empathy needs discussion. How the parents work together as parents must be reexamined. The process through which the *family* reaches consensus and establishes directions needs to be tested further.

Central to this case, and many others that do not resolve quickly in zone 1, is the issue of the family's "ownership" of the problem or the way in which they take responsibility for their emotional conduct. Their behavior together as they face the problem becomes a task the therapist must focus on and this is not a task the girl or family wishes to discuss! This is the complex territory where "consumer driven goals in mental health" are the source of much debate. The parents may not believe that they are exercising choices or have any ability to direct or control their thoughts, feelings, or actions or those of their daughter. "I can't help it," or "These feelings just come over me," are common complaints in these more complex cases. Their goals may have as much to do with maintaining the problem as treating it, "If only the doctor could find the right medicine so she'll feel better. She really liked those valiums." Since their ambivalence and conflict about control is unconscious, it is difficult to simply tell a child and a family that "you don't want to get well" or "you aren't cooperating." Often, from their base of perceptions, they think they are.

Although few therapists will argue that all emotion and experience fall into a conscious domain, the holding environment that the therapist creates in the relationship with child and family must be strong enough to help them take another step. The family must be helped to recognize the choices they face once aspects of the problem are more exposed and the therapist commits to working with them to improve their experience. The ability to take ownership and confront their own ambivalence is an ego domain that is often dangerously weak in these adolescents and their families and requires consistent support. They need to choose to use their energies to make a change; something that people who have traumatic histories or poor supports cannot easily do.

These issues are not easily captured by common rating scales that focus on risk factors (such as substance abuse, lethality) or even the severity of diagnostic category or the person's level of function. Often the stresses the family faces and their impairment in interaction are deeply intertwined with the very nature of the problem being presented. In areas of function that do not involve the core conflict or character element, they may do quite well.

In *zone 1*, the therapist must remember that in some way most symptoms are both problems and solutions. As such, when these solutions are intensely held, even when they result in symptoms or other problems, these strategies are difficult to relinquish. Consequently, they affect the resolution of the presenting problem. Understanding the dynamics of conflict helps in this work. Some solutions are part of a character problem that requires as much confrontation as support. As in the case above, *the problem* (I want something) and *the symptom* (the anxious affect of waiting or frustration) and *the solution* ("Give me what I want immediately") were the same in the child and family's mind. Wanting and getting were an anxious jumble in their lives.

The therapist's solution—tolerating the affect of waiting, wanting, and its associated frustration—was unacceptable at this stage in the treatment alliance.

If the therapist had conceded to a strategy of appeasement, the alliance would be gained at the cost of an effective intervention. The therapist must learn to tolerate a family's anger or disappointment as part of their confrontation with the issue and the limits that need to be set in treatment when they are not set in the family. It is hard to hold one's ground in the face of angry people and to still reflect on these tensions in the therapy. Early in one's clinical work this is not easy to do and requires consultation about the strategies that can be used and the countertransference that is elicited. These cases require all of the skills and knowledge from training in psychopathology, personality development, and the dynamic issues that relate to affect and defense. (See Cummings and Sayana, 1995, for a distinction between cases that reflect "garlic" verus "onion" problems.)

Looking at Figure 7.1, we see that these cases fall into the area defined by the oval on the figure. While this area is predominantly within zone 1, there are overlaps with zones 2, 3, and 4. Stresses, or fluctuations in symptom levels, or both; ability to take responsibility; or lack of social, emotional, or financial resources can push the family and child further along the continuum of severity. Dysfuntion is not simply defined by the intensity of the symptoms: it includes psychological factors, the level and nature of connectedness, available resources, other stress factors, and the availability of other supportive relationships. These cases are often time intensive and involve multiple collaborations. Unfortunately, the current system of mental health reimbursements does not make these cases easier for therapists. With the additional availability of resources, however, the treatment of these cases can often be quite rewarding as dramatic progress in the level of function in all the subsystems of the family can be improved with continued care.

There are other treatment cases, which, on review, may present a zone 3 or 4 level of severity. For instance, a patient who is actively suicidal or self-harming, or who has continued issues of safety, requires other treatment supports. Although a focused treatment can often diminish the level of acuity, most suicidal adolescents have poor coping mechanisms and complex defenses that make it difficult for them to know what they feel. As a result, spelling out a specifically behavioral or goal-oriented treatment (other than safety contracting) is difficult. Identifying some goals explicitly with the adolescent often gives rise to greater denial or resistance to treatment, so often these discussions are best handled within the parent meetings.

Depending upon the severity of symptomatology of the index patient and the emotional and behavioral characteristics of the parents, these parents and adolescents can fall into zone 4. The issues of zones 2 or 4 need to be identified promptly, as these are cases in which traditional outpatient resources are rarely enough. The family's lack of resources and style of interaction are difficult to manage. When the flavor of the entire family system is like that of a character disorder, the adolescent or child's makeup may be a less relevant factor in the treatment. The family's behaviors, which may take some time to reveal as a repetitive pattern, must be confronted so that the therapist does not become incorporated into the system's status quo.

As noted above, symptoms in children, adolescents, and their families can be solutions to internal or external challenges. A symptom in a particular child can distract the family focus from stresses within the family system. These times include when parents are struggling with marital conflict or in response to other pressures in the environment that other family members may be attempting to deny in order to cope. At other times, the symptoms that school counselors may identify (the black clothes, body piercing, reckless drug or alcohol abuse) are part of the adolescent's struggle for identity and differentiation from a traumatizing family. It may represent their resolu-

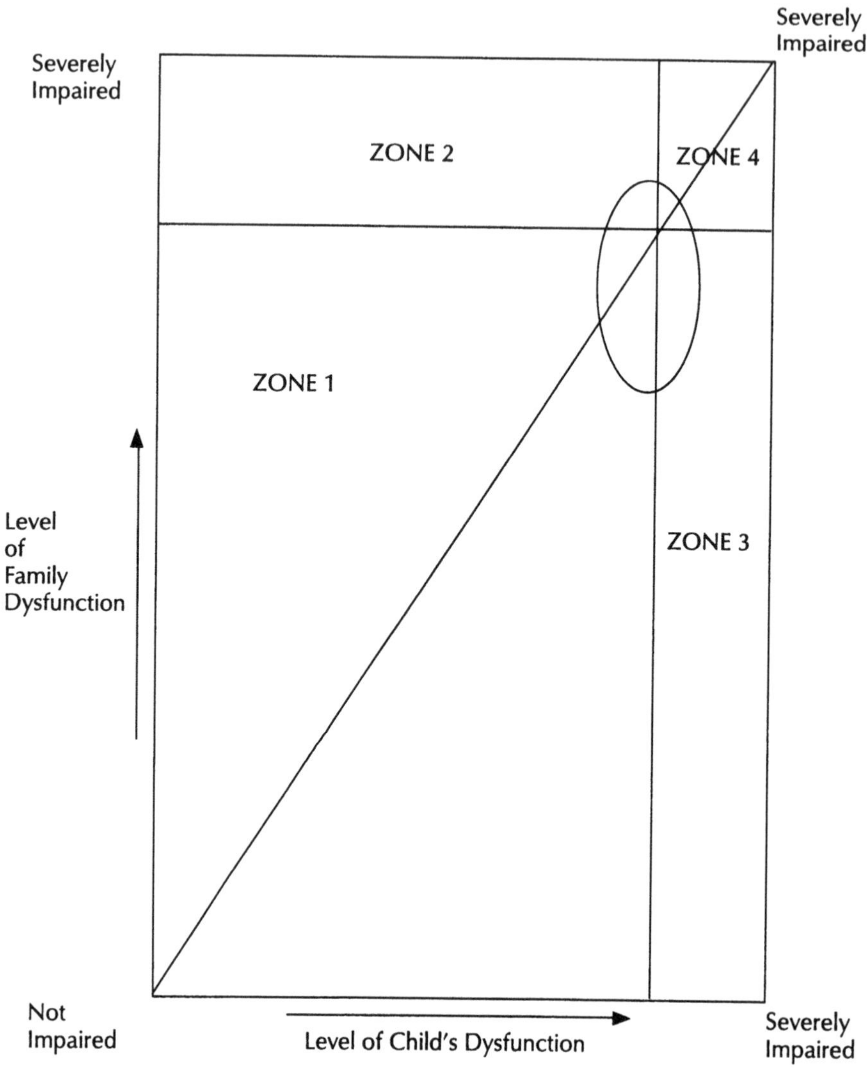

FIGURE 7.1.

tion of some despair triggered by failure and rejection. The episodic suicidality of some adolescents is often best treated by a continuous, stable, relationally based dynamic therapy. The limits of the patient's insurance, the degree of investment or concern of the parents, and their resources all make staying on the tightrope of a continuing care plan difficult.

In the cases that follow, a diagnosis of an adjustment disorder or a single *DSM-IV* disorder had been made. The child and family have been defined as zone 1. (The previous chapters have already reviewed that the presence of additional comorbidities represented by more than one diagnosis will pose additional treatment obstacles. Most often, these can be identified early on.) Personality impediments to the treatment plan often emerge in the course of the therapy. Initially, all members of the family may have appeared quite amenable to the work defined in the mutually developed (therapist–family–parents–patient) care plan. In zone 1, a way of working together had been established. The alliance seemed satisfactory. When the stubborn persistence of the chief complaint continues, new issues arise. Reappraisal is needed.

These cases elicit countertransferential issues toward both the child and family, as well as toward gatekeeping of the MCO or limited mental health insurance, school accommodations, or other resources. Even when the family wishes to be able to work on issues and there are limited resources, frustration ensues. Usually the child continues to express pain and discomfort and the therapist feels the treatment needs to continue. Often the family may agree but "only for what the insurance company will pay for."

These are the cases where therapists often feel they may fall off the tightrope, between the pull of the family's perceptions and the push of the patient's or parents' covert undermining behaviors or vice versa. This countertransference is diagnostic. Often the position of the MCO is that they will provide sessions for "medically necessary" conditions, and that does not include the despair of a child. The MCO may wish to have the patient and family's problem fit within the length of their rope, their "customary" utilization pattern. When the family may have few other resources available, the therapist is driven toward a further identification with the child and feels a great deal of inner conflict, which can be displaced onto the parents.

☐ Adolescent Issues

The dilemmas presented by limited resources are nowhere more compelling than in the problems presented by suicidal adolescents. While therapists may engage in focused teaching about safety steps, define alternate ways to handle risk, or strengthen the adolescent's ability to manage his or her impulsivity, these interventions rarely "take" rapidly. The unconscious processes that underlie the way adolescents come to handle motivation, emotion, or thoughts about themselves are not readily summarized in a behavioral contract, yet they have a dramatic effect on the unfolding treatment.

Although a clinician can focus on aspects of the behavioral presentation, the process of the establishment of a trusting relationship with an adolescent is not fast. Adolescents are as ambivalent about therapists as they are about their parents (Wolf, 1991). Suicidal adolescents hedge. They make most therapists appreciate the complexity of character, relationship, and the ways in which a youngster's history can shape his or her self-image and self-esteem. Nevertheless, the task lies in the present and future, aspects of which the suicidal adolescent usually feels are impossible to control. The therapist must lead the adolescent toward the belief that he or she can influence his or her destiny without the drama of the black and white control struggle they frame as leading to their wish to die.

The therapist must be alert to the constellation of characteristics that may mark an early borderline presentation. Although adolescents can have borderline features, the marked sense of aloneness, sensitivity to loss and abandonment, as well as the persistence of the use of primitive defenses, should alert the therapist to a zone 3 issue that requires further parental education and increased support for the adolescent. Understanding the common defenses that adolescents use (see Table 5.1 on adolescent defenses) and their place in the "hierarchy of health" can permit the therapist to more clearly assess the level of function of the adolescent.

Although the responsibility for the child's safety can be shared with the family, the nature of the family has a tremendous influence. Covert rejection, lack of empathy, and the demands of other children can be covered over during an acute hospitalization, especially as the length of stay continues to decrease; these may begin to emerge more clearly in the continuing treatment of the adolescent. These zone 2 factors must further influence the structure of the treatment plan. However, even a well-connected and caring family cannot control the emotions of an adolescent who is in intense psychological distress or control the impact of peers' attitudes, a special boyfriend or girlfriend, or the issues of self-esteem or underlying guilt and shame that can suddenly activate impulsive self-harm.

> Bill was brought to treatment after he took a handful of pills. His parents had been called from the prep school he attended and had brought him home. An underachiever for many years, he was in the middle of his junior year and his school performance was "adequate." He had few overt problems and was rarely angry or defiant. His family enjoyed him. A passionate reader of history and philosophy, he tended to be a bit of a loner, even though he had a small group of friends.
>
> In the extended treatment assessment (five sessions), he was able to recognize that he had taken pills as a result of feeling rejected by a girl he thought "liked him." He had few skills in reading other people's cues and had become more and more focused on her behavior and interactions with his group. He never revealed to his friends that he liked her. He was not inclined to psychologize about his difficulties and spent much of his time in therapy talking about teachers, their expectations, and what was wrong with his generation. He mocked the "preppies," "jocks," and "rats."
>
> His parents were warm and supportive and had frequently searched for avenues through which Bill could connect with schoolwork so that he could have more confidence about his intelligence. (Actually, Bill had conveyed to the therapist that he thought most teachers were "dumber than he," so he usually ignored what they expected of him. When he had to produce a paper or project, he procrastinated and then did it poorly, excusing his behavior and resulting grade by denigrating the task. He kept most of these feelings to himself.)
>
> His parents found it difficult to talk with Bill since they didn't want to pressure him about friends or schoolwork. They had found that when they pressured him, he did worse. In addition, he shut down most often in direct discussion and was more likely to open up during a car ride or other activity, although there were few he ever admitted enjoying. In the parent assessment they seemed attuned to Bill's needs and difficulties and no underlying personality or marital issues appeared to complicate the parents' relationship with Bill. Their other son was doing well and actually was, in their words, "probably Bill's best friend."
>
> The therapist found this same pattern in treatment. Bill came to the therapist's office. It took him a while to start to talk. He rarely answered the therapist's questions or made jokes about being "shrunk." He had returned to school and was back in his routine. He refused to discuss his thoughts or feelings about the girl "since that was over." He would not talk about other girls he had been attracted to or how he was handling those feelings. When the therapist talked about "what other guys did," Bill appeared disinterested but seemed to listen.
>
> He did not meet criteria for a dysthymic disorder, academic and psychological testing had been done in the past and learning problems had been ruled out. So his diagnosis at

the end of the assessment and after another four sessions was an adjustment disorder. At this point, at session eight, there was neither a specific behavioral nor emotional goal on which Bill could commit to work. He did not refuse to come to therapy, but he did not have a risk profile of symptoms that could warrant extended care by the MCO's criteria. (They required three active symptoms to extend care.)

Bill denied any suicidal ideation or intent. At times, he had made innuendoes about "someone having to pay for his having to come to therapy," but this appeared consistent with his sarcastic approach. The statement unnerved the therapist a bit. Bill was not especially comfortable with his anger, and the therapist was fearful that Bill could brood over this issue and potentially pose a risk. The therapist could not pin down other thoughts, so he could only advise Bill's parents that Bill had work to do on his emotional makeup. He shared this as a potential risk the parents should monitor in their own way. He again recommended continued therapy. Bill's parents were ambivalent about treatment, because Bill usually made fun of the therapist, although they acknowledged "he had talked about few other teachers or grownups as much." Bill was willing to continue in therapy if his parents "made him," but would not say he wanted to.

In this instance, the therapist felt strongly that Bill should continue in therapy. The parents were willing to agree even though they had reached the end of their insurance benefits. They were not "therapy oriented" but believed that Bill should have an opportunity to see if he can contend more directly with his feelings and how he does his work. They felt prep school could give him a boost in getting into college but did not feel he will get into the kind of school that will challenge him. As a result, they were willing to support his being in therapy for the rest of the school year and then reevaluating with the therapist. Arrangements were easily enough made for Bill to come from school to see the therapist on a weekly basis.

Were this case to be uncovered in a family with fewer resources, the therapist would have to focus strongly on the issue of providing avenues of communication to minimize the risk of Bill's impulsive reaction to harm himself. His parents would need to monitor more closely issues that might bear on another interpersonal crisis. Meetings between the parents and the school staff and discovering resources there could provide some backup as well as another source of observations. This is a case in which a relationally based therapy that is a "bridge" to better real world relationships is important. It is not a treatment that is always possible to implement.

☐ Child-Based Issues

Some of the most difficult symptoms to resolve can represent a child's resolution for a difficulty that he or she cannot manage otherwise. These may require more time in treatment, rather than present an emerging complication. The psychological resources of children are limited when they face a dilemma that leads them to conclusions they cannot tolerate or that makes them feel inadequate. One of the most common of these presentations involves the treatment of children with learning disabilities. While many of the children may have some attentional features, the primary problem is the challenge that the learning disability poses for the child's self-concept and self-esteem.

Lydia was referred by her second grade teacher following a parent conference in which she explained to the parents that she could not engage Lydia in any of her work unless it involved cats or her favorite comic book character, Catwoman. The teacher felt that as the school year had continued she was falling more and more into her own world.

The therapeutic assessment revealed a warm parental relationship, reasonable family communication, and no defined parental pathology. The greatest difficulty in the family meeting arose when they discussed the trouble there was with homework completion, which mirrored the teacher's observations. The parents, in their separate meeting, defined this as an intense emotional dilemma for them since they kept vacillating about how much to "force her to do what she couldn't."

Lydia had a well-defined visual motor learning disability, which made writing a very labored task. Her phonic abilities were poor so that in addition to the struggle she had with writing, most of her words were misspelled. When the therapist asked Lydia to draw a person and write her name, her face fell. She reacted to what the therapist felt was her sense of incompetence by writing what she called "Spanish hieroglyphics" and said that was how she and Catwoman communicated.

Individual treatment progressed very slowly. Lydia gradually brought the therapist into her world with Catwoman where they could "do everything" together. Nothing was impossible or hard. In scene after scene, she and Catwoman surmounted impossible odds. In these moments, Lydia was alive and cheerful. Often when these scenes ended, and the therapist raised a question about what else they might do together, "a game, another play choice?" Lydia appeared perplexed and sad.

The parenting work focused on beginning to help the parents manage their sadness about Lydia's learning challenge. They knew they had to confront their feelings and adopt a better way to be consistent about her work. They knew it could be a long-term issue and they had to balance their attitudes.

By the end of the eighth individual and family sessions, both therapist and parents understood that Lydia needed more time in therapy to gain further mastery over her feelings about the "somethings I can't do." They had to review their insurance plan and see what family resources they could use to continue her therapy. The parents understood better how to talk with Lydia about her school problems and how to support her. They felt that she needed continued therapy to be better engaged with her work at school and to accept their support.

Many of these cases require an extended individual treatment and family treatment. All must be planned considering fiscal resources, the regulations of an MCO when there is one, and the family. The best possible treatment plan must be developed even as the therapist must bear the pain of the child and the potentially limited resources.

□ Parent-Based Issues

Some symptoms are signals that the expectations of the parents' demands for the child's development need to change. In some cases of encopresis, for instance, the issue may be that the child's own defenses are not mature enough to contain their emotions about this developmental step, which may trigger some anxiety or some aspect of further separation from his or her parents which the parent has trouble bearing. At other times, a learning or peer challenge or aspects of his or her sexual or aggressive feelings may trigger a regression in the child that is not readily resolved and the parents need to redefine their expectations.

Modifying these demands requires that the parents accept a change in their own concept of their child; the problem is not resolved simply by supporting, demanding, or cajoling the child to "move ahead." Here the parents' own identification with the child's achievement, their own latent sense of "badness," or an aspect of their past history may emerge. It is the parents' psychology that poses an impediment to the work. The work for the parents to create a holding environment for the child's pain, maintain a behavioral structure, or discuss emotions and loss may trigger a regression that although manifesting in some way in the child, requires parenting therapy. The issues of learning disabilities, in otherwise bright children, are common triggers.

> A teenager was brought to therapy following his second sophomore year report card that was filled with C's. He was a perfectionist about his dress and worked hard to have a cool guy look. He was, as his mother affirmed "one of the in crowd." He was a good athlete and on the football and basketball teams. As the mother and son talked together, the mother revealed that Al had a learning disability. His reading was on grade level but his written expression test results from last semester hovered at the fifth-grade mark. Al said he knew this and was working with the learning center even though it was a bother.
>
> In the individual component of the initial meeting, Al was angry about his mother's expectations, had little to talk about with the therapist, and said that if he wasn't so worried about his mother he wouldn't be there at all. The therapist was able to help Al see that his mother was working very hard to give him the best shot at a school she thought he would like. The therapist acknowledged that his mother was very tense about his performance and the therapist would review how the two of them set reasonable goals using the school's feedback.
>
> The parent meeting with mother replicated the tearfulness that the counselor reported she had seen during the teacher conference. The mother had requested a meeting with the guidance counselor following the release of Al's report card. She demanded that he remain in the mainstream college bound classes, which the school supported as well, but felt his grades should be altered. The school had again reviewed how Al's curriculum was modified and the support that he was given in all writing assignments in the learning center. The counselor reported that Al was completing his work and was involved with the resource center. She focused over and over on contradictory ideas about what the school should or shouldn't do. She reported that Al's father was a busy successful executive and couldn't be involved and this was "her job."
>
> The therapist continued the treatment trial using the split session model where Al and his mother could discuss his current work and then the therapist would meet with the mother alone to focus on her feelings about Al, his work, herself, and how she gauged how "she was doing with her executive task." After the sixth session Al refused to come and mother came alone. She spent much of the meeting complaining about the therapist. Still the therapist was able to observe again that she appeared very anxious about Al even though, as the therapist reminded her, Al's described himself as "doing OK," "even better than her," he added at one point.
>
> Mother conceded she was indeed quite anxious. This meeting set the stage for a more extended parent therapy. The mother was able to request sessions in her own name, although she worried about her husband's opinion of this. This issue would become more prominent when her sessions were exhausted!

Al's mother's ability to engage in treatment required the cover of her son, who obliged initially. The mother's self-esteem, her sense of her own competence, and the judgment she experienced (or projected) onto her husband was intense. She had a long history of feeling that she had not measured up, complicated by a diffuse anxiousness. She had always felt that therapy was one more situation in which she would be judged—just like in her school meetings about Al—so she admitted that "a good offense was the best defense." Once this work began and exhausted her insurance benefit, the therapist would be tested to see how she could deal with the issue of continued treatment, its cost, and whether in the transference she would be angry about not being fixed faster, just like she had harbored many angry feelings about the school not fixing Al.

In the case that follows, the child's symptoms evolve from the parents' reduced financial circumstances. Their guilt and confusion do not emerge until a family meeting–late in the treatment–reveals this underlying conflict. The "original" presenting problem had been about the boy's management of his anger. Over the past year, he had become more and more volatile. He seemed to "want everything" and would not take "no" for an answer. The family seemed to respond to his declared needs, but his anger flared again triggering a new family crisis.

> In the eighth session, 8-year-old Mikey was focused on his anger about his parents not getting him a new computer game system. His parents had decided to bring him without his siblings who had participated in earlier family meetings. He was both angry and oppositional, even though in the preceding sessions the treatment plan for family-based discussions about "how to express anger and make plans" had been working quite well. The mother's tactic was to appease Mikey and explain how long it would take to plan to get it. The father was more adamant about saying no. Mikey kept pushing.
>
> Suddenly the dammed up feelings in the family broke. Both the mother and father attacked Mikey for "wanting too much." They described how everybody had to sacrifice and that no one else complained. They told him that his brother and sister also wanted things and they hadn't gotten them. In fact, they had joined previous family meetings and a "turn-taking" system had been discussed for how each member of the family could get things that he or she wanted. The other siblings had, in fact, appeared quite accepting of the rule and participated well in the family meetings they joined.
>
> Then the mother began yelling at Mikey that he was stupid, "How come he didn't understand that his father had a new bad job that didn't pay what he used to get paid?" This piece of information had never been shared before. In fact, the parents had decided not to tell the children that the father had become "underemployed," following the downsizing of his company. He had accepted a huge pay cut and a lower position so that the family did not have to move. The father had been unable to find a more competitive position locally. The parents liked the good school district, and they did not want to make the kids feel guilty about the new financial pressures.
>
> The mother was dedicated to being a good mother and being home for the children. She had decided she would not work while the children were young, because she had felt so alone growing up as an only child in a professional family. Her husband had agreed with her wishes. In this explosion, a major family secret was revealed. Mikey had been the channel through which a great deal of parental tension and pain had been funneled. They had not told the therapist about this dilemma, because they each felt ashamed of their choices for different reasons. This crisis set the stage for another examination of the equilibrium of the demands in the family system.

Mikey had not been able to understand why he couldn't have "all the neat stuff" his friends have since they "were all the same." The parents wanted to protect their reputation in the community and not become second-class citizens. As a result, Mikey became the focus through which the conflict between wants, guilt, and resentment was played out.

In this case, no major diagnosis was established for either child or parents. As suddenly revealed, there would be no easy solution for this dilemma. Although the family had few resources for treatment, the parents were willing to request further visits for them from their MCO, which, by state law, granted eight visits per family member per year. Were the law to change so that these benefits were also managed, this family might face further difficulties in maintaining their relationships without the support of family therapy to help them negotiate this source of shame and pain in their lives, the kind of shame that would make it emotionally difficult for them to request services from a managed care reviewer, "because it would expose that they were down and out."

In cases of parental character pathology as described in chapter 3, working with the way the character problem manifests itself in the parenting relationship would be a major challenge for a long-term therapy. Other illustrations of character pathology (and past trauma) were presented in the zone 2 treatments of externalizing disorders in chapter 6. Without enough parental recovery to help the parent create a containing environment for the child, the treatment will not succeed. A reassessment of the zone of the case is needed to begin to reappraise the other supports the child may need.

☐ Family-Based Issues

Those issues that are found in the "interpersonal space" between family members may be revealed as treatment proceeds. The parents' initial presentation of a cooperative approach to the child may have only been sustained by "the problem," and, as it diminishes, marital conflict may emerge that keeps the problem from being resolved. Other times the case may begin to reveal a covert alliance between one parent and the child, which sustains the problem. In another, the roles in the family may be so rigid that as the child's role as "problem maker" begins to diminish, other family members resist. They may place added stress on the identified patient so that their own roles will not have to alter. Often communication and problem solving strategies within the family are quite poor. The therapist's ability to address these can be increased through the use of learning communications techniques and conflict resolution (Robin & Foster, 1989). Many of these complications are not immediately apparent in the assessment phase, because they are not what the family wishes to accept, or show, as "the problem."

> Tommy, age 13, was referred following a charge of breaking and entering. This was his first offense, which had been preceded by some difficulties with school authorities. The assessment defined an adjustment disorder with conduct problems as the working diagnosis and found the parents eager to participate. The parents were willing to cooperate by more carefully monitoring Tommy's behavior and more actively involving themselves with his peer group.
>
> As the treatment plan was implemented there was a growing tension in the meetings that related to whether or not the father had been on time to pick him up after his games or whether he was just going "through the motions" in his activities with Tommy on Saturdays when the mother worked. Tommy tended to roll his eyes when this tension surfaced between his parents. After the sixth meeting, the therapist planned to have two more follow-up meetings with Tommy and his family a month apart to make sure the plan was being well maintained and that Tommy was doing better.
>
> The following month the parents appeared without Tommy. The mother finally had evidence of her husband's affair. This revelation had led to a great deal of family turmoil, but Tommy was still doing all right. The mother wondered about whether she should ask Tommy's father to leave. She had found out that the father had not been staying at the

> boy's games on Saturday and only dropped him off and picked him up. One of her neighbors had seen the father with another "soccer Mom" on two different Saturday afternoons. When father had been confronted with this, he acknowledged the affair. Neither parent believed that the children know about this, although Tommy might know, because he was a friend of the other woman's son. The father admitted that the affair began some time before Tommy got in trouble. Both parents were apprehensive that he will get in trouble again.

At this point, the therapist reformulated the case and considered whether the boy's acting out (problem) was a solution to a potential family split. Father did get more involved in the family to set limits, but his affair continued. The therapist recommended marriage counseling, although the parents said their health insurance policy did not cover that. Other options needed to be considered. Both parents felt they needed someone to help them with their relationship and to help them decide how to "tell the kids, if they have to."

The large body of family therapy literature and study will help the therapist address how to conduct therapy in which the family-based elements pose the major dilemma for the child or adolescent. See the Suggested Readings section of this book.

Is It Really Zone 2?

In a similar case, the level of conflict and disenchantment of the parents with each other, along with a long history of a poor marital relationship, led the therapist to reclassify the following treatment case as a zone 2 problem and begin the search for other resources and relationships for the adolescent patient.

> Janet was 16 and a junior in high school when she asked her parents to bring her to a therapist. She was an honor student and a popular member of her class. She had begun to skip school and said, "I don't know what I want anymore." She expressed a kind of amorphous discomfort, without clear symptoms of anxiety or depression.
>
> The family accepted that individual therapy and a support plan was reasonable. Janet agreed to return to school and the school agreed to send a weekly attendance report to the parents. Shortly after Janet's return to school, she broke off her relationship with her best girlfriend. She called her a "druggie who has nasty things to say about everyone." By the sixth session, her truancy began again.
>
> The therapist requested a family meeting. Both parents appeared disengaged and said they thought "Janet was just going to do what Janet wanted to do." They felt that the problem resumed again after the mother took a week off from work. Janet maintained a stony silence. The mother said Janet hung around the house all the time and acted like "my jail keeper." This phrase struck the therapist and she asked to meet with the parents alone.
>
> When the parents came in for a conference, they seemed as silent as Janet in the meeting before. The mother then glared at her husband and said he was poisoning Janet's mind. Besides, he had not been willing to get up to drive Janet to school in the past two weeks. At that point, the father looked enraged and said to the therapist, "If my wife wasn't up all night on the Internet with her admirers, perhaps *she* could get up to bring Janet to school." The father said he had no interest in doing two jobs in the family, "being the wage earner and ferrying the kids around." When the therapist inquired if the marriage was on the rocks and might break up, they said they knew that neither wanted to get divorced, but they thought their marriage was over.
>
> The parents confessed there had been physical outbursts between them. Neither the

mother nor father was interested in treatment. The mother felt her contacts on the Internet were "her own business" and nobody was going to label her obsessive or addictive. She felt she had a right to her own life and was not just the servant of her husband. "He can drink every night, can't he?" she asked. The father simply said yes and left the treatment room. Before the mother left, the therapist asked if he could discuss these issues with Janet. The mother agreed.

At this point, the therapist could conjecture that "the problem," Janet staying home (truancy), was her solution to the fear she had about her mother's behavior and the family's dissolution. She may have hoped that therapy could engage her mother with the family. Janet may also have been fearful that her father's anger would be acted out against her mother if she was not home. The therapist also wondered if Janet's best friend had said something about her mother or father's behavior that had ruptured their relationship. With all these concerns in mind, the therapist prepared for what may be the final contact with Janet.

Neither parent wanted to change and they have seemed to disconnect from Janet as well. Their apathy about Janet's leaving school or her change in her grades seemed to not matter to them. Each was quite absorbed in their own needs and defenses. The therapist also conjectured if there was no family connection to treatment or support for Janet to continue therapy that she would stop attending, too. As a result he wanted to discuss what he had learned and what other choices she might have. He would discuss with her whether there were other resources at school she could use.

In chapter 6, we reviewed the factors that a therapist should consider to determine whether a case is zone 2 including the degree to which the parents love and concern for the child are affected. In this case, the parents are so involved in their own struggles that neither has much emotional energy for maintaining a connection with their child. They seem neither attached nor attuned. In addition, their brief commitment to helping her was quickly exhausted. Neither of the parents was willing to commit themselves to working (even outside of treatment) on behalf of the child.

At this point, neither parent has the wish to comply with treatment, for their marriage, their individual needs, or the issues that affect their daughter. They will not show up. It then follows that it will be impossible to get the parents to undertake the work that they need to do on their own issues.

Is It Really Zone 3?

Rhonda, a 17-year-old junior in high school, was admitted to the inpatient unit of a child and adolescent unit after she was medically cleared in the emergency room where she had been brought by ambulance from her aunt's house. Rhonda had been discovered on the floor of the living room where she had fallen asleep. When her aunt returned home from her afternoon shift as a nurse's aide, she promptly called an ambulance.

Rhonda had had a previous psychiatric admission in another state three years before. She had attempted suicide following her mother's anger and disappointment with her after Rhonda had made numerous expensive phone calls to her cousin, the daughter of her aunt. She had been in the hospital for 10 days and had not received any outpatient treatment following that discharge.

The mother then decided to allow Rhonda to move to her aunt's house and live with her cousin so she could have a close friend and a better life. The extended family had grown up in one of the French-speaking Caribbean islands where this practice was not uncommon. Rhonda had been born in New York. Mother reported that she felt badly that she had not gotten treatment for Rhonda before but that there were not many therapists in their neighborhood. In addition, she said, people in our culture don't use therapy. She felt a move would help Rhonda a lot more that a therapist. "You know, she's never been very talkative." Rhonda, following her move to her aunt's, called her mother every week. Her mother never felt she was troubled or depressed.

In reviewing Rhonda's history, mother reported she had done well in school, although her mother did recall a period of time in the fourth grade when her grades fell for no apparent reason. The mother thought she seemed withdrawn at this time but the mother was also breaking up with her boyfriend. Rhonda made some increased effort after this and her grades returned to above average. They had remained so at the high school while she lived with her aunt, and teacher's reports were positive.

Mother also said that Rhonda always had a circle of acquaintances, but she never appeared to have a best friend other than her cousin. Since this relationship was so important to her, the mother's sister had welcomed Rhonda into her home. Her aunt felt Rhonda could benefit from her daughter helping Rhonda make new friends. She did not have any inkling that Rhonda was having any adjustment difficulties with her. This was the second year that Rhonda lived with her aunt and cousin.

Rhonda explained that she had gotten depressed for "no reason." She wrote a note saying goodbye to everyone and took the various pills she found in her aunt's medicine cabinet. Her cousin was on a school trip. Rhonda said she changed her mind about dying but felt tired and dizzy. She lay down on the living room floor where she fell asleep. She denied other suicidal thoughts, drug or alcohol abuse, or any other symptoms. Her mental status examination was normal. She said that her suicide act had just been an impulse. When pressed about writing the note she had no response. Then she said, "it was all so fast—maybe it was because my cousin was away with her class." Diagnostically she fit the category of adjustment disorder with depressed mood.

There was no family history of psychiatric disorder or drug and alcohol problems. Rhonda's father had been in their lives until she was 8, but once he left he was never seen again and they knew little about his family. When Rhonda and her mother, aunt, and cousin were interviewed together there were no apparent interactional difficulties. Rhonda maintained she didn't like being in the hospital because she missed time with her cousin and missed her work at school. She was somewhat withdrawn but interacted positively with the staff and her family in planning her outpatient discharge.

In outpatient therapy, she appeared to make a connection with the therapist. She described few other friends and explained that her cousin was the only one she could "trust with my secrets because we are so much alike." She said she felt "blue" when she wasn't with her cousin and that there was an emptiness in her heart. The treatment plan was to have weekly meetings with Rhonda and, initially, have an additional family meeting with the aunt and her daughter, Rhonda's cousin.

As her therapy continued, her primary focus was talking about her cousin. In the eighth session, nearly two months after discharge, she drew a picture of her cousin inside her heart but then added a dagger into it. While she did not appear overtly psychotic, she had a strange little smile when she talked about her cousin. She explained that the dagger is what stabs her heart when her cousin goes out. She denied feeling angry or jealous.

In the next month, in the family therapy, Rhonda's aunt noted that her daughter had some concerns about her relationship with Rhonda and how they "had to be together." Rhonda's cousin said she wanted Rhonda to hang with her own friends more. She explained to Rhonda that Rhonda wasn't "her best friend; she was her cousin." She said she did want to help her, but her mother "shouldn't put all this stuff on me." She said she liked talking with Rhonda about her problems but "not all the time." In the therapy session, she reported that Rhonda's conversations were about perceptions of schoolmates "cutting her" (which she felt didn't happen) and about boys doing disgusting things. She didn't understand what Rhonda meant but told her which boys to stay away from. She wanted Rhonda to talk with the therapist more about these things and the cousin said she would share her ideas more in family therapy. She appeared concerned about Rhonda and said she was glad she had a therapist and other friends. Rhonda became silent when she listened to her cousin. Her aunt responded to the anxiety by reminding Rhonda of all the different friends she did have and how well she was doing at school. The therapist and aunt and cousin all asked Rhonda repeatedly how she felt and Rhonda just said, "Well, I guess it has to be OK."

That night when the aunt went in to say goodnight to Rhonda, she discovered her with a plastic bag over her head. She was still conscious, but her aunt had her brought to the emergency room.

At discharge from the first hospitalization, the case could be made that this is a previously untreated adolescent, with a number of strengths and with adequate family supports, who fell in the first zone of care. By the third suicidal act, it is definitely a zone 3 case. Rhonda's reaction to the psychological injury of her cousin telling her she wasn't her best friend underlines a zone 3 problem. Rhonda's underlying thought distortions—hinted at in her picture of her heart—combined with her lack of insight or awareness of her anger and jealousy, indicate significant deficits. Her repeated potentially lethal impulsive responses to perceived hurts (which were never disclosed to either therapist or family) require even closer followup and more frequent meetings. While the current diagnosis is still uncertain, there are warning signs of a potentially emerging borderline or psychotic disorder. Although no physical or sexual trauma has been uncovered, the possibility that Rhonda's mother's boyfriend was an offender exists, given Rhonda's decline in functioning during that breakup. She no longer "had to" hold herself together.

These are cases that challenge therapists who work with families whose resources are limited or when managed care companies have stringent criteria. The level of available resources in a lower-class community further impacts on the availability of care. Even though Rhonda's mother is employed, she is employed in another state, which does not grant benefits for out-of-state treatment. Even after three months of treatment, the nature of the alliance between the outpatient therapist and the adolescent is uncertain. The adolescent's inability to tell her aunt and her cousin of her hurt and anger suggests the fragility of Rhonda's trust in relationships. The risk is high and the problem difficult to contain.

This discomfort is further increased in an atmosphere in which therapists feel their use of sessions is monitored and their own survival as a practitioner threatened. In the case above, the freedom provided by the availability of a service and training program that provided free care and was well connected to more intensive resources helped this therapist take on this case. In other circumstances, the lack of resources would prompt inpatient providers to search for residential options.

Is It Really Zone 4?

Some cases that are referred by the child welfare agency often have great potential to improve their level of functioning, especially when the child, parent, and family are dedicated to receiving care and can access it easily. Other cases, however, prove to be zone 4 problems. The clinician should at this point be able to identify the red flags of a zone 4 problem: disrupted family relationships, conflicted parental caretaking styles, overt hostility between parent and child, and the scars of past emotional disorder and substance abuse sprinkled generously in the family's history. Instances of zone 4 problems are unlikely to sneak up on a clinician. Immediate problems in compliance and keeping appointments will surface. The more quickly the therapist makes the classification of a zone 4 problem, the more quickly the therapist can turn attention to mounting a systemic approach that mobilizes other agencies or caretakers who may be involved in the family's care.

8

CHAPTER

Enhancing Parental Care, Family Structure, and Coping in Children: Long-Term Contact in Zone 1 Children, Parents, and Families

The long-term (potentially intermittent) treatment for children with internalizing or externalizing disorders and their families continues to follow the same broad principles emphasized throughout this volume. The respect the family experiences as the therapist emphasizes and supports the health within the family relationships is remembered. The practical suggestions that build mastery or reduce symptoms always help the child and family recognize that the therapist has a knowledge base that can help them. Mastering this way of working will provide the therapist with a sense of satisfaction as well as provide assistance that is greatly appreciated by the families with whom the therapist works.

Families then often return for further care. Another piece of work may be requested, whether as a result of some exacerbation of symptoms, a challenge or stress that impacts family life, or as a result of the child reaching another developmental level of understanding. Well-directed family-based treatment creates a respectful space for each family member. Many children will, as adolescents, request some contact with the therapist to review an issue or concern about their life or changes in family life. Their parents may return to do a piece of individual work or use therapy to improve their function in their marriage.

Being able to work with children and families in zone 1 over the course of several years is among the most enjoyable and productive experiences a therapist can have. The therapist's understanding of family function and support for child development is affirmed and valued by all members of the family. As the societal debate continues about the validity of mental illness and the worth of any therapeutic intervention, a therapist can find his of her own self-worth validated in these contacts. The relationships that the therapist has supported within the family lead to the development of new possibilities for each family member. Active mastery is extended in child and family, and symptoms are managed well, if any continue.

The relationships, over time, help counteract the sense of having been devalued by insurance carriers and society in general. This perspective that mental health providers are less important than other health care workers was again accentuated by the insurance "revolution." Mental health was carved out of the medical benefit. Historically, the long-standing lack of parity for mental health care in comparison with other medical benefits was a backdrop for this latest effort to save money (which it has). Therapists have seen insurers exclude payment for important work, decrease revenues for therapeutic time, and demand additional administrative time and coordination in the face of those same decreased revenues.

In addition to zone 1, zone 3 is the other zone of care in which long-term relationships and continuing care can be a source of satisfaction for the committed therapist. Although there may be more problems finding additional resources to support the child and family and more case management work than the therapist would face in zone 1, these families appreciate the way the treatment can anchor their care for the child. Because the child's (and then the adolescent's) symptoms can be daunting and, at times, progressive, the relationship that is built by the therapist with the family needs to be made of reinforced concrete.

This foundation will be used so that the therapist can balance parenting education and family systems meetings along with the support, advocacy, and individual treatment that the child needs over time. The therapy creates an opportunity for both child and parent to become attuned to those issues that may trigger symptoms and how to manage them. A long-term involvement can permit the therapist and family to carefully examine what creates successful experiences and how to continue to improve the relationships within the family, even with the stress of the illness. The therapist is always mindful of the need to identify paths through which new avenues of active mastery can be found.

Frustrations inevitably arise within the zone 3 treatment during periods in which symptoms are out of control or frightening, with repeated inpatient stays or the need to identify school resources that take the child out of the mainstream. All of these events underline the severity of the child's condition but permit the family an opportunity for reevaluation, second opinions, and a chance to regroup and reexamine additional supports. Often these events mobilize extended family for a time. If the alliance in treatment is strong, planning for the child's needs can go forward while managing the sadness, fear, and frustration that arises for all. The focus of this book has not been on the management of these most challenging cases, but for many child adolescent and family therapists these cases will come to mind in considering issues of long-term care.

There are, however, many zone 1 families who will return for different types of intervention once the first treatment has been successful and a relationship established. The two cases that follow describe work that has continued over two decades. One case involves problems that represent an internalizing disorder; the second involves a case in which the initial presentation of an externalizing disorder in a child is complicated by later substance abuse. This second case also illustrates how the child intervention creates a foundation for later treatment in the family as they all face life challenges.

Internalizing Disorder

One previously presented example of an enduring relationship over time is the clinical case of Katie in chapter 5. Three treatment episodes were described. The child and family consistently presented as a zone 1 treatment problem. The first occurred with the onset of her separation anxiety disorder in preschool, the next when she had a severe recurrence in fifth grade, and the last when she was a high school student and experienced the onset of a panic disorder. Here, the strength of the family's relationships was good, and the psychoeducational work of the family in the first episode prepared them for the possibility of recurrences. Neither blame nor shame was mobilized in these later episodes, and the family understood that therapy helped them find ways to master a challenge and to minimize symptoms during their earlier encounters. Their periodic access to the therapist included phone contact when they had a question about the nature of an observation they had about their child. They would occasionally seek consultation when they were debating about how to discuss a particular level of family stress with the children.

The following case spans two decades. The contact involved extended periods of care, intermittent contact, and future episodes of care which were extended in duration. The treatment began with individual therapy, later involved couple's work, and then child and family work. Each episode of treatment was successfully accomplished using a flexible focus on enhancing relationships, promoting active mastery, and diminishing symptoms.

First Episode of Care: Individual Therapy of a Young Adult

The treatment relationship was established with a 24-year-old woman, Gretchen, who presented with anxious symptoms that included obsessive features and mild depression. Her own family environment was supportive but was not highly emotionally attuned. Her father had a drinking problem and her mother was often automatically critical.

Gretchen's feelings about control and privacy interacted so that a continuous treatment was needed to permit her to examine successfully the emotional constraints that had affected in her life. Her anxious preoccupations diminished and she was better able to define her own needs and personal objectives. Her ability to manage anger and self-assertion improved. Her tendency to create impossible standards for herself or others diminished. After an extended individual treatment of four years, her sense of freedom and new possibilities were sustained through periodic contact. Brief visits were made when stress was particularly high or as she progressed in her career and faced new challenges.

Gretchen felt she had a positive and successful long-term therapy. This psychotherapy was highly valued by the patient, just as 4,000 individuals in other long-term therapies have reported (Consumers Union, 1995). For these respondents, longer psychotherapy was associated with better outcomes. In comparison with people who left therapy before six months, those people who entered therapy and stayed in treatment for more than six months reported greater gains. The three ways in which people said therapy was helpful were

(1) They felt their presenting problems were relieved.
(2) They felt they were better able to function in relationships as well as at work.
(3) Most people reported growth in self-confidence, self-esteem, and enjoyment of life.

Like these individuals, treatment for Gretchen was terminated when she felt she had reached her goals. Eventually, she undertook further graduate work in another city where she met her future husband.

Because this client was able to dedicate her own resources to this work, the therapist did not need to focus the work through a need to ration sessions or develop forms for an MCO. Some patients experience this process of resource managment as making "the holding environment of the therapy unstable and often causes the patients to feel unsafe" (Stadter, 1996). The fiscal stigmatization of mental health care heightens individual's inability to accept care for emotional reasons.

Second Episode of Care: Couple's Therapy

Gretchen met Arthur in graduate school. Each were interested in research, his interests more scientific, hers more sociological. They dated for a year and then moved in together. A year later they were married. They did well together until they graduated. At the point at which each had to seek a job, define where in the country they wanted to settle, and how to more closely share finances, a new level of struggle emerged between them.

The issue of power had to be contended with in a new way. Prior to this, the context—graduate school—had dictated much of the frame of their lives. When both had to face their different needs and priorities for employment, finances, and the development of their own family, the control of final decision making was up for grabs. Gretchen yielded to Arthur over the location of their next home since his professional expertise was in a narrow scientific field . Employment was possible for him in only a select number of locations around the country. Gretchen gave up her dream job in order to move to another city with Arthur.

Their struggle moved to a new level of intensity when Arthur revealed that he hated his new job and that it was making him extremely anxious. Her disappointment and anger about what she had given up for him, and "he wasn't even happy," fueled many contentious arguments between them. They began to disengage, communicate less, and avoid each other. They felt they were just trying to get through while Arthur found another job. After one bitter argument in which Gretchen threatened to move out, Arthur agreed to couple's therapy.

In spite of the therapist's concerns, Gretchen's prior treatment did not bother Arthur. He didn't believe much in therapy and felt if Gretchen thought the therapist was good enough, he would go along "since she was kind of a perfectionist anyway." The initial interactions between Gretchen and Arthur seemed to involve his putting on a good front and accepting her anger while simultaneously not taking in what she was telling him. As she calmed down, he began to seem less guarded and began a more open dialogue.

At this point, the therapist was able to take a more formal history with Arthur—asking them to be curious about each other. For both, independence from their families had been hard won and both were careful about the degree of connectedness they permitted that might affect their level of control. His family history involved a more dramatic problem of maternal alcoholism whose impact on the family he described through high humor and wry sarcasm. He had not discussed these issues much before with Gretchen because "they were history" and each had "more interesting projects in their lives now."

Gretchen responded with more disclosure about her own experience in her family "which she had hoped she left behind with the therapist." By the fifth couples meeting, they each became somewhat softer with the other. The therapist supported their independent strengths as part of what could make their connectedness stronger. It already had, as they were reminded of how they had shared many of the challenges of graduate school, dissertations, and oral examinations as well as their initial job search. It was in this context that Arthur revealed his panic disorder. He reported that he felt so insecure that he felt no job would truly accept him and had been extremely grateful when a company he liked had accepted him. Now, however, in the presence of a demanding supervisor, he felt vulnerable and that all of his inadequacies were "up in lights."

Arthur was asked if he wanted an individual appointment in order to discuss how he might manage some of these issues and not be as anxious. He agreed to come in for individual meetings.

Third Episode of Care: Panic Disorder in the Husband

Arthur reported feeling very relieved about acknowledging his panic attacks. He said he had tried to hide them from Gretchen because she was so angry about his being so worried and negative about his work. He didn't believe she "could stand to hear about one more thing that was wrong with me." The following treatment covered six sessions.

The therapist reviewed Arthur's insurance and discovered a stress management program was listed under his medical benefit that was not part of his mental health benefits. Arthur was extremely worried about being fired, decompensating, and becoming financially dependent on Gretchen or destitute. He needed Gretchen's support, as well as the therapist's, to work out how to access treatment for himself. He completed the stress management program and was continuing to experience episodic panic attacks.

The therapist then identified how Arthur could get a psychiatric assessment and possibly some medication. Arthur agreed to follow up on these things "without procrastinating so that you won't have to complain about me the way Gretchen does already." The therapist reviewed that Arthur had his own negative feelings about procrastination and that he found it easier to motivate himself if he turned some negative judgment over to his superiors—now Gretchen, the therapist, and his boss were all qualified to take this role! Arthur was able to laugh and said that by the time they had their next couple's meeting he would be able to report about how far he had gotten.

Arthur responded well to medication and was able to continue to use the stress management skills he had learned. As he was relieved of these symptoms and began to believe he could manage life, his discussions with Gretchen began to take on a more assertive flavor. The therapist had to help Arthur understand the impact of his symptoms and how he managed them within the relationship. Arthur's decreased symptoms and increased coping were a key to helping Gretchen and Arthur reach of new level of connectedness and empathy. Gretchen tolerated Arthur's complaints of feeling that she had let him down and then she gradually reviewed all she had done to support him before she gave up. Arthur could see that it was difficult for him to remember all that support because while it was happening he had been so symptomatic, and it felt like nothing was being given to him.

In the follow-up couple's meetings, they clarified their renewed alliance with each other as well as their ability to be more intimate (and to disagree more clearly). They began to turn their attention together to their work worlds and what choices were available there. Gretchen helped Arthur begin to identify what he could ask for at work. First, he asked for a current job review in writing so that he could assess his current function. Gretchen reminded him that it was not unusual to do a three- or a six-month review of someone in a new job. Arthur was able to pursue this strategy and together they reviewed the report, first before therapy and then in therapy.

Their teamwork was commended and each began to reach a new level of certainty about what they contributed to each other even if the work world was uncertain. They then began to tackle their interface with each of their families of origin and how to orchestrate those visits. By the time they accomplished these discussions, it was six months from the first contact and they decided it was time to space out their appointments. Periodic contact continued over the following year while each evaluated new work opportunities and consolidated their partnership.

Fourth Episode of Care: Separation Anxiety Disorder in Their First Child in Preschool

Gretchen and Arthur had called periodically after their last couple's meeting. They had sent a baby announcement when their first child, Samuel, was delivered and a picture of themselves together at his first birthday party. Arthur had a new job and was quite pleased with the challenges there. He reported that he felt appreciated, too, and when he didn't feel valued he was better able to ask for more feedback. Gretchen was working part time and delighted in being a mother, although they didn't have "an easy" first child. Samuel's sleep and eating patterns were hard to establish and he became fussy easily. At times, he was inconsolable. But by age 1, he was easier, more outgoing, and eager to explore the world.

In the second year that Samuel was in preschool, he began to complain about having to go to school. His favorite teacher had just been out sick for a week but had now returned. Both Gretchen and Arthur talked with him about his feelings about his teacher. They reassured him that he could tell the teacher he missed her and was even "a little mad" when she wasn't there. They reminded Samuel of his other friends and the other staff that he liked there. They generally cajoled, supported, and set the limits on him about having to be at preschool each day. This persisted for approximately two months. Then Samuel began to have temper tantrums when he was dropped off by Arthur. He would cry uncontrollably when he had to get into the car after saying goodbye to Gretchen. Gretchen and Arthur called and a focused intervention for a separation anxiety disorder began. (See chapter 5, Case Example 4, for a similar intervention.)

Fifth Episode of Care: Panic Disorder and OCD in Their Latency-Age Child

In fifth grade, Samuel began to struggle more and more over getting his homework done. These struggles were a reflection of his chronic uncertainty about getting things done perfectly or avoiding them altogether. In the middle of the year, he began to develop panic attacks in which his throat would close up. He felt he couldn't eat. Both his mother and father recognized these as reminiscent of panic symptoms they had experienced themselves. They requested a consultation.

In therapy, they learned how they could teach Samuel what these anxiety attacks were. They practiced talking him through an attack while individual therapy focused on helping Samuel learn how to manage these episodes as well. The panic attacks abated, but Samuel continued to have anxious preoccupations at night. He often complained of disrupted sleep.

Five months later, a new preoccupation arose for Samuel. He became fearful of germs and often felt worried after he had put food in his mouth. Sometimes he would need to spit it out or rush to the bathroom and throw up. He repetitively questioned his parents about whether he would catch something and anxiously washed his hands over and over. These events led to a family meeting in which Samuel discussed his anger and his fears. Some of these centered on people who coughed and spread germs, others on how his teachers would never give him enough time to get things "exactly right." The diagnosis of childhood onset OCD was made.

Individual and family-based treatment was recommended along with a medication consultation (see March & Leonard, 1996). Focused treatment combined with medication led to a gradual reduction in his symptoms and obsessions. Samuel was then better able to talk about his frustrations, fears, and how he wanted "things to be" in the family with less bossiness and anger. Since Samuel's approach to most things tended to be somewhat rigid, the therapist was able to help him more calmly address the fact that "sometimes not everything is possible." Therapy helped him focus on more attainable goals.

The therapist was able to help Samuel develop a continuing art project, a collage, in which he could put together all the different elements that he felt would make a perfect world. He encouraged Samuel to have his best friend make one, too, since "everybody's perfect world is a little bit different." The therapist felt this could be another way that Samuel's parents could continue to support his few but special friendships. Samuel also had to become more comfortable with differences and relax some control.

☐ Externalizing Disorder

The pattern of long-term care in the externalizing disorders offers some contrast to that of the internalizing disorders. More often these clients have a limited degree of insight. Their awareness of their symptoms usually results only from the impact they have on their parents first. For example, problems emerge as the client's behavior impacts on the intimate relationships at home, or results in conflicts with authority at school or work. Often the identified patient's perspective is focused on the behavior of others, not their own. As a result, it is often the positive relationship that the therapist has with the extended family that helps to maintain the treatment contact. The therapy must work with these significant relationships to focus a continuing intervention and to minimize the damage the child's symptoms may produce.

First Episode of Care: P.J. Is Failing Seventh Grade

Mrs. Peters called for an appointment after her son had been told that he might have to repeat seventh grade. She reported that he had been promising all quarter to bring up his grades, but she guessed he hadn't. Mrs. Peters brought P.J. to their first appointment. They were able to talk reasonably well together about his school performance, less so when P.J. complained about his father's lack of involvement. At this point, Mrs. Peters became somewhat defensive. P.J. was the oldest of six children. Her husband worked long hours in an accounting firm to support them and he "couldn't do everything."

The therapist inquired further about the father's ability to participate in the therapy. Mrs. Peters said her husband didn't believe in therapy, but he would "consider" any suggestions that the therapist made. At that point, P.J. asked if his father would have to know that he had been caught shoplifting at the mall. Mrs. Peters looked shocked that P.J. had revealed this and said, "You know that was going to be our secret unless you did something again." The therapist recommended that his father should be told now so that the family could really begin working together. Although P.J. protested, the therapist thought he saw a look of relief on P.J.'s face

The assessment revealed that, in addition to his father's remoteness from the family, P.J. had an attentional problem. It had gradually been impacting more and more on his functioning as the demands increased for him to organize and manage more tasks at school. The therapist was concerned about the of signs of conduct disordered behavior. While these were currently less prominent, they were a troublesome risk factor. On the positive side, P.J.'s innate intelligence had permitted him to perform reasonably well in earlier grades, although he had never performed "up to his potential." As the school's demands had increased, his efforts had flagged. He was somewhat depressed about whether he could catch up. Socially, P.J. was a bit of a loner and his favorite activity was fishing. His father had introduced him to fishing, but they fished together less and less as the family size grew.

The parenting evaluation led the therapist to the conclusion that Mrs. Peters was suffering from both anxiety and depression. She was extremely attached to her first child and felt very responsible for his performance. She said this was the first quarter that she hadn't been nagging him. Previously, she visited the school all the time. However, P.J. had told her he was becoming more embarrassed and he would just quit altogether if she kept it up. She had worked very hard at being less intrusive and heightened her involvement with the other five children—all of whom were doing well. The youngest was now 2 years old. Mrs. Peters said she had planned to have another baby when she realized how depressed she would be when P.J. went to junior high school. All her life, she said, the only thing that had really made her happy was a baby. The therapist recommended individual treatment for Mrs. Peters with a colleague. Mrs. Peters declined.

The treatment plan that could be negotiated included the therapist working with both P.J. and his mother on P.J.'s problems. His father had agreed to go fishing with

P.J. every other Saturday. He had thanked the therapist for the idea but declined to join the therapy meetings. Medication assessment was recommended, but the family declined. Mrs. Peters did discuss this suggestion with P.J.'s pediatrician. The therapist also recommended that Mrs. Peters work with the school. She could advocate for the school to develop some resource room supports for P.J. that would help him organize and more carefully monitor his homework assignments. The school was quite responsive.

A family-based treatment was developed in which the therapy meeting would be split between an individual meeting with P.J. and time for P.J. and his mother together. The meetings were scheduled on a weekly basis until the school quarter ended and P.J.'s grades were turned in. At that time, P.J. and Mr. and Mrs. Peters would review P.J.'s success. If he had not met his goals, the therapist said that father should again consider joining the therapy. If P.J. had reached his goals, the result of the family's conclusions in their meeting at home would be brought to the therapist. The follow-up appointment would review the treatment contract. P.J. was successful in the third quarter. Mrs. Peters apologetically requested that the visit frequency be reduced since there were many other things she needed to do. The therapist, along with Mrs. Peters and P.J., reached an agreement to have monthly meetings. When P.J. completed seventh grade, Mrs. Peters and P.J. requested to terminate.

Second Episode of Care: P.J. Steals the Family Car

When P.J. was in the ninth grade, the therapist got an emergency call. Mrs. Peters reported that P.J. had taken the family car. When he was stopped by the police, they gave him a Breathalyzer test since he appeared intoxicated. He was. The therapist recommended a family meeting that would involve Mr. and Mrs. Peters and P.J. Mrs. Peters said she would talk with her husband.

All three arrived for the appointment. The father took control of the meeting and began to run it as if his staff members were assembled to plan a project. Half the meeting was completed before the therapist could thank the father for organizing all the things that needed to be done. The therapist suggested that P.J. thank his father and ask what his father was feeling about him, given the seriousness of the event. P.J. thanked the father for coming and acknowledged that "therapy wasn't Dad's thing, or mine either." The therapist repeated his thought that a father's feelings for his son were quite crucial at this junction. The father seemed comfortable enough. The therapist continued by asking P.J. what he thought his father was feeling, since his father hadn't said. P.J. shrugged but then after a few moments of silence said, "Scared, I guess." The therapist then actively elicited how each member of the family could tell each other what they were feeling.

A plan was made for the therapist to meet with P.J. alone and then have another family meeting. Mrs. Peters hesitantly asked if she could meet with the therapist alone before that meeting, too. The therapist set another appointment time for Mrs. Peters. At this point, the therapist was following the basic principles for a crisis intervention. These tenets include a mix of structured reality planning, emotional debriefing about the crisis, and continued efforts to support the family's connectedness and collaboration to restore baseline function. P.J. projected his usual air of detachment, relief, and defensiveness. He accepted that he was grounded for the coming month and that his bank account would be the source of some of the money needed to pay the fines and other court costs.

The family completed a series of eight family-based visits. These were supplemented by P.J. being put on probation. He was mandated to an adolescent drug and alcohol education program sponsored by the district court. P.J.'s father drove him there and back. Their travels were a mixture of diverting conversation, silence, and lecture. Both father and son discussed these in family therapy with a mixture of amusement, aggravation, and acceptance of each other. The mother appeared more remote and there was some discussion that the family was going through a new life stage. Each kid's activities, performance in school, and relationships were reviewed. P.J. was asked to act as the master of ceremonies for this exercise since he was the oldest son and could comment on "what his parents still didn't know."

P.J. had maintained his grades and was still working with the resource room. He never reported making a special connection with any subject or teacher, but therapy continued to put some emphasis on his finding his "place" or "niche" in something that captured his interest, his intelligence, and helped him think about the future. He was somewhat less isolated at this point and his mother and father approved of most of his peer relationships. He was able to thank his parents for helping him out after he had "made a mess of things."

Third Episode of Care: Mrs. Peters Gets Severely Depressed

Mrs. Peters began to get depressed when her youngest daughter, Kathy, age 5, started kindergarten. P.J. was doing well. Although there had been some difficulties in the past year with a couple of the other children, she found that she and her husband worked reasonably well together on the issues. He was still a workaholic, and now she was facing an empty nest. She called the therapist when she found that she could barely get out of bed in the morning to get Kathy off to school. Once she did, she returned to bed to weep, or sleep, or have anxious fantasies about her children dying.

This round of therapy was extended. Mrs. Peters had a major depression with many anxious features. She was referred for a psychiatric consultation and began taking an antidepressant. Her response was minimal and she had three trials over the course of the coming year to see if a medication was available that she could tolerate and that had some effect.

Mrs. Peters' therapy focused on her current sense of emptiness. She felt alone and incompetent. She felt she no longer had a place in the world. She dreamed of being pregnant but knew it was unacceptable to her husband. She had just turned 40. The first six months of therapy supported her managing her feelings, accomplishing what she needed to do as a homemaker, and reviewing her life experience. She began to relate some of the more traumatic elements of her childhood and adolescence. She was unable to consider other alternatives for her time—school or work—during that period. She conveyed aspects of her concerns to her husband but felt she could not expose how horrible she felt to him.

As the depression mitigated, she was able to begin to review what she liked, her skills, and her interests and to review possible occupational opportunities. In the meantime, she became involved with the town's advocacy program for youth and the high school substance abuse education program. She felt strongly that the court intervention had been extremely useful to P.J. and she wanted it available for other youth. After another six months of therapy and successful volunteer work where she received a lot of positive feedback, she got a job working as a legal secretary, which she had done previously.

She felt stronger and more directed. She began monthly meetings in therapy and began to plan for termination. She felt her children were happy for her and since the older children could help the younger ones, she had no trouble working from 8:00 to 3:00, a schedule she had worked out with the law firm. At times she mentioned her husband seemed more preoccupied, but whenever she asked him, he said he was okay. Other aspects of their relationship appeared unchanged with her return to work. He did say he appreciated how she used the extra money to help with the things the children needed. She left treatment, after two years, feeling relieved and optimistic about the future.

Fourth Episode of Care: Mr. and Mrs. Peters Referred for Couple's Therapy

Two years later, Mrs. Peters called. Her husband had been laid off and he was home now and was drinking every night. She was alarmed and concerned. He rejected treatment contact. She came in for a consultation. As she described the events that had transpired at his company, she clearly felt her husband had been abandoned by a company to which he had devoted 25 years. He had been told that for him to stay with the company, which had merged with a larger accounting firm based in the Midwest, he would have to be relocated to the Midwest. When he discussed this issue with the family, everyone rejected the idea of a move. He thought he could make a lateral move, and when he proposed this, he was laid off.

The therapist suggested that Mrs. Peters tell her husband that she couldn't cope with the changes and demands in the family without his help. She had to remind him that problem solving discussions didn't come easily to them. She wanted to be able to get his advice and make plans in the presence of a therapist who could just be "for them" without talking about the kids. He reluctantly agreed since he felt it would keep them focused on what they needed to do together, rather just blaming each other for their decisions.

The therapist arranged for a colleague to see the couple and advised her of some tactics that might be helpful since he knew the nature of the relationship style Mr. and Mrs. Peters had established. (Mr. Peters was "in charge" and Mrs. Peters was the "detail" person.) He suggested that Mr. Peter's self-esteem had been seriously assaulted and that if she could position herself to work with Mr. Peters as a consultant to Mrs. Peters and the family that he might more easily open up about his own concerns.

This couple's work continued for six months. Mr. Peters began to control his drinking. The couple achieved a new balance in the manner in which they shared power and solved problems. Three months after the couple's therapy had begun, Mr. Peters was called by his previous employer and asked to return to a new position. He accepted. Mr. Peters was able to tell his wife that the loss of his job and their work together as a couple had been good for them. It helped him reevaluate his priorities and see that he may have had "a flaw or two in his approach." Mr. and Mrs. Peters continued in couple's work during his initial return to work and were able to manage to maintain their new orientation and spirit of collaboration.

Fifth Episode of Care: P.J. Gets his Girlfriend Pregnant

Mrs. Peters contacted the therapist again when P.J.'s girlfriend told her she was pregnant. P.J., now 21, was on an assembly line for a local electronics firm. He had been dating Melanie for a year. Her family had been quite abusive to her. She spent a great deal of time at the Peters house, which Mrs. Peters has enjoyed. Now, Mrs. Peters felt quite confused and anxious. She was—she confided—terribly excited to be a grandmother. She wanted so much to have a baby in the house again. Although she knew it wasn't her place to make a decision, P.J. and Melanie both counted on her advice.

She knew she had to consider her feelings carefully so that she could discuss their options with them reasonably. She wanted to feel some emotional balance as she examined their potential choices without prejudice. She also told them to talk with their local pastor who knew them both, and they had agreed. They did not want to see a therapist. P.J.'s job did not have health insurance, and Melanie was in her last year in high school. They did not want another financial burden and did not want to feel further obligated to the Peters family's generosity.

Sixth Episode of Care: P.J.'s Alcohol Abuse Worsens

When P.J. and Melanie's second child was 3 and their first was 5, P.J. had begun drinking more. Mrs. Peters suspected that he was also smoking marijuana. He had become more volatile and negative, and several times the children told their grandmother they were scared. She was alarmed and upset since she hated seeing the impact on both of the children. At this point, she requested contact with the therapist. Melanie had turned to her faith and was working with a pastoral counselor. Mrs. Peters had assumed the role of frequently caring for the children as Melanie was working part time.

Mrs. Peters had already asked P.J. if he wanted to see the therapist again and he had refused. He denied that his drinking was a problem. Mrs. Peters was able to accept the therapist's suggestion to begin to go to Alanon with Melanie. Melanie was able to accept Mrs. Peters' support in confronting P.J.'s drinking (Edwards & Steinglass, 1995). When they began to do this on a regular basis, P.J. becaume angry and went on a drinking binge. At the therapist's suggestion, Mr. Peters was drawn into a family conference about how to support Melanie and P.J.

Both of P.J.'s and Melanie's children were voicing their worries about the family. Mrs. Peters told Melanie that this was part of the strength of their family. The children didn't need to be silenced about their feelings and Melanie could help them. The therapist suggested that Mrs. Peters work with Melanie to make a book about what the children were telling her. Melanie accepted this idea and made books for the kids about "When Mommies and Daddies Have Hard Times." When P.J. returned home, the kids showed him the book and he was able to acknowledge that he had made some mistakes. He told them that they would try to have fewer hard times and he would try not to lose his temper.

Contact with Mrs. Peters was intermittent while she helped support her son, her daughter-in-law, and the grandchildren in getting their lives back in control. Fortunately, P.J. did not lose his job and could continue to support the family.

Conclusions

As is evident from the above cases, the skills of a child therapist depend upon their additional training as both adult and family therapists. One therapy format is not rigidly adhered to, but types of interventions are used flexibly to enhance and support existing relationships.[9] The therapist invariably attempts to understand the relational field and helps the individual in treatment make their relationships "work" for him or her as successfully as possible. The key role parents play in the resolution of any child difficulty (as well as the times in which they are part of its source) must be actively addressed.

Good family relationships and available community supports, especially in the form of schooling opportunities and assistance with special needs, available employment, a court system that is oriented to youth and has substance abuse education services at its disposal, and a community and work context that destigmatizes mental health care, are important elements for successful treatment. Unfortunately, the availability of these is not in the control of the therapist. Extended family can both support alternative positive relationships for a child and provide respite for parents. The systems of care that exist for children and families in certain communities are not found in others, whether it is the quality of schooling, supplementary supports, or after-school activities and supervision.

The varying availability of resources for families in different communities that reflect class and fiscal issues highlights the role of political–social and cultural attitudes that continue to impact on children and families (Shaw, Winslow, Owens, & Hood, 1998). The Family Leave Act supports those who work within larger corporations that often offer better wages. It does not help those employees who are paid hourly rates or who have no union support where management penalizes lower level employees for missed hours or days. Finally, the issue of hunger in children and its pervasive destabilizing effects cannot be underestimated (Murphy, Wehler, Pagano, Little, Kleinman, & Jellinek, 1998).

Americans have made choices about broad social policies, such as school supports, decisions about funding Head Start and other early intervention programs, or after-school programs. Some policies, such as managed care initiatives, appear to have mixed results and seem to benefit one part of society at the expense of others. A therapist who is faced with the overwhelming need of some children and families works with the systems of care that have been put into place as a result of these policies. While these are political issues over which therapists have little control, they have broad ramifications on the ability of therapy to help parents make change for their children and themselves. These grow in importance as the zone of care moves toward 2, 3, and 4.

These are families that have asked for help in managing situations that have overwhelmed their own resources. They are often not in a position to advocate for themselves, let alone advocate for broader social recognition and change. Life stresses and family dilemmas, internalizing or externalizing disorders, or more significant mental and developmental illness, are not likely to disappear, but the context in which we address them can continue to improve as it has across the 20th century.

---

[9]This is not to say there are not treatments in which the goal is setting limits on intolerable behaviors that, if not addressed, may lead to the dissolution of a relationship.

References

Achenbach, T. M. (1991a). *Manual for the child behavior checklist/4–18 and 1991 profile.* Burlington: Department of Psychiatry, University of Vermont.

Achenbach, T. M. (1991b). *Manual for the teachers report form and 1991 profile.* Burlington: Department of Psychiatry, University of Vermont.

Ackerman, N. (1966). *Treating the troubled family.* New York Basic Books.

Ainsworth, M. D. S., Blehar, M. C., Waters, E., & Wall, S. (1978). *Patterns of attachment: A psychological study of the strange situation.* Hillsdale, NJ: Erlbaum.

Aponte, H. J., Zarski, J. J., Bixenstine, C., & Cibik, P. (1991). Home/community based services: A two-tier approach. *Am J Orthopsychiatry, 61,* 403–408.

Barkley, R. A. (1997). *Defiant children: A clinician's manual for assessment and parent training* (2nd ed.). New York: Guilford Press.

Barlow, D. H. (1992). Cognitive-behavioral approaches to panic disorder and social phobia. *Bull. Menninger Clin, 56* (Suppl.), A14–A28.

Barrickman, L., Perry, P., Allen, A. J., Kuperman, S., Arndt, S., Hermann, K. J., & Schumacher, E. (1995). Bupropion versus methylphenidate in the treatment of attention-deficit hyperactivity disorder. *J Amer Acad Child Adolesc Psychiatry, 34,* 649–657.

Bateson, G., Jackson, J., Haley, I., & Weakland, J. H. (1956). Toward a theory of schizophrenia. *Behav Sci, 1,* 251–264.

Baxter, L. R., Schwartz, J. M., Bergman, K. S., Szuba, M., Guze, B. Mazziotta, J. C., Alazrahi, A., Selin, C. E., Ferng, H. K., & Phelps, M. E. (1992). Caudate glucose metabolic rate changes with both drug and behavior therapy for obsessive-compulsive disorder. *Arch Gen Psychiatry, 49,* 681–689.

Beck, A. (1972). *Depression: Causes and treatment.* Philadelphia: University of Pennsylvania Press.

Beitchman, J. H., Wilson, B., Brownlie, E. B., Walters, H., Inglis, A., & Lancee, W. (1996). Long term consistency in speech/language profiles: II. Behavioral, emotional, and social outcomes. *J Am Acad Child Adolesc Psychiatry, 35,* 815–825.

Beitchman, J. H., Wilson, B., Brownlie, E. B., Walters, H., & Lancee, W. (1996). Long term consistency in speech/language profiles: I. Developmental and academic outcomes. *J Am Acad Child Adolesc Psychiatry, 35,* 804–814.

Bernstein, G., & Garfinkel, B. (1986). School phobia, the overlap of affective and anxiety disorders. *J American Academy of Child Psychiatry, 25,* 235–241.

Biederman, J., Baldesarini, R. J., Wright, V., Keenan, K., & Faraone, S. (1993). A double-blind placebo controlled study of dopamine in the treatment of ADD: III. Lack of impact comorbidity and family history factors on clinical response. *J Amer Acad Child Adolesc Psychiatry, 32,* 199–204.

Biederman, J., Faraone, S., Mick, E., Wozniak, J., Chen, L., Ouellette, C., Marrs, A., Moore, P., Garcia, J., Mennin, D., & Lelon, A. (1996). Attention deficit hyperactivity disorder and juvenile mania: An overlooked comorbidity? *J Am Acad Child Adolesc Psychiatry, 35,* 997–1008.

Biederman, J., Milberger, S., Faraone, S., Kiely, K., Guite, J., Mick, E., Ablon, S., Warburton, R., & Reed, E. (1995). Family environment risk factors for attention-deficit hyperactivity disorder. *Arch Gen Psychiatry, 52,* 464–470.

Biederman, J., Newcorn, J., & Sprich, S. (1991). Comorbidity of attention-deficit hyperactivity disorder with conduct, depressive, anxiety, and other disorders. *Am J Psychiatry, 148,* 564–577.

Biederman, J., Rosenbaum, J., Bolduc-Murphy, E., Faraone, S. V., Chaloff, J., Hirshfeld, D., & Kagan, J. (1993). A 3-year follow-up of children with and without behavioral inhibition. *J Am Acad Child Adolesc Psychiatry, 32,* 814–821.

Biederman, J., Wilens, T., Mich, E., Faraone, S., Weber, W., Curtis, S., Thornell, A., Pfister, K., Jetton, J. G., & Soriano, J. (1997). Is ADHD a risk factor for psychoactive substance use disorders? Findings from a four-year prospective follow-up study. *J Am Acad Child Adolesc Psychiatry, 36,* 21–29.

Black, B., & Uhde, T. (1994). Treatment of elective mutism with fluoxetine: A double-blind, placebo-controlled study. *J Am Acad Child Adolesc Psychiatry, 33,* 1000–1006.

Boris, N. W., Fueyo, M., & Zeanah, H. (1997). The clinical assessment of attachment in children under five. *J Am Acad Child Adolesc Psychiatry, 36,* 291–293.

Boszormenyi-Nagy, I. (1962). The concept of schizophrenia from the perspective of family treatment. *Family Process, 1,* 103–113.

Bowen, M. (1978). *Family therapy in clinical practice.* New York: Jason Aronson.

Bowlby, J. (1971). *Attachment and loss* (Vol. 1). London: Penguin Books.

Brent, D. A., Holder, D., & Kolko, D. (1997). A clinical psychotherapy trial for adolescent depression comparing cognitive, family and supportive therapy. *Arch Gen Psychiatry, 54,* 877–885.

Brown, R., Kaslow, N., Hazzard, A., Madan-Swain, A., Sexson, S., Lambert, R., & Baldwin, K. (1992). Psychiatric and family functioning in children with leukemia and their parents. *J Am Acad Child Adolesc Psychiatry, 31,* 495–502.

Brown, S. A., Mott, M. A., & Stewart, M. A. (1992). Adolescent alcohol and drug abuse. In C. E. Walker & M. C. Roberts (Eds.), *Handbook of clinical child psychology* (2nd ed., pp. 677–693). New York: Wiley.

Burns, D. (1990). *The feeling good handbook.* New York: Plume.

Butzlaff, R. L., & Hooley, J. M. (1998). Expressed emotion and psychiatric relapse, a meta-analysis. *Arch Gen Psychiatry, 55,* 547–552.

Canals, J. (1997). Prevalence of depression in Europe [letter to the editor]. *J Am Acad Child Adolesc Psychiatry, 36,* 1325–1326.

Cantwell, D. P. (1996). Attention deficit disorder: A review of the past 10 years. *J Am Acad Child Adolesc Psychiatry, 35,* 978–987.

Carlson, C., Figueroa, R., & Lahey, B. (1986). Behavior therapy for childhood anxiety disorders. In R. Gittleman (Ed.), *Anxiety disorders of childhood.* New York: Guilford.

Carskadon, M. A., & Acebo, C. (1993). Parental reports of seasonal mood and behavior changes in children. *J Am Acad Child Adolesc Psychiatry, 32,* 264–269.

Caspi, A., Moffitt, T. E., Newman, D. L., & Silva, P. A. (1996). Behavioral observations at age 3 years predict adult psychiatric disorders: Longitudinal evidence from a birth cohort. *Arch Gen Psychiatry, 53,* 1033–1039.

Chilcoat, H. D., & Breslau, N. B. (1997). Does psychiatric history bias mothers' reports? An application of a new analytic approach. *J Am Acad Child Adolesc Psychiatry, 36,* 971–979.

Cloninger, C. R. (1987). A systematic method for clinical description and classification of personality variants. *Arch Gen Psychiatry, 44,* 573–588.

Cohen, D., Detlor, J., Shagwitz, B., & Lechman, J. (1982). Interaction of biological and psychological factors in the natural history of Tourette Syndrome: A paradigm for childhood neuropsychiatric disorders. In A. Friedhoff & T. Chase (Eds.), *Giles de la Tourette Syndrome* (Advances in Neurology, 35, pp. 31–40). New York: Raven Press.

Cohen, D. J., Paul, R., & Volkmar, F. R. (1987). Issues in the classification of pervasive developmental disorders and associated conditions. In D. J. Cohen & A. Donellan (Eds.), *Handbook of autism and pervasive developmental disorders* (pp. 20–40). New York: Wiley.

Cohen, H., & Weil, G. (1971). *Tasks of emotional development test manual.* Lexington, MA: Lexington Books.

Conners, C. K. (1973). Rating scales for use in drug studies with children. *Psychopharmacology Bulletin Special Issue,* 24–29.

Connors, C., Casat, C. D., Gualtieri, C. T., & Weller, E. (1996). Bupropion hydrochloride in attention deficit disorder with hyperactivity. *J Amer Acad Child Adolesc Psychiatry, 35,* 1314–1321.

Consumers Union. (1995, November). Mental health, does therapy help? (Our ground-breaking survey shows psychotherapy usually works. This report can help you find the best care). *Consumer Reports, 60,* 734–739.

Corkhum, P., Tannock, R., & Moldofsky, H. (1998). Sleep disturbances in children with attention-deficit/hyperactivity disorder. *J Am Acad Child Adolesc Psychiatry, 37,* 637–646.

Cotton, N. (1993). *Lessons from the lion's den.* San Francisco: Jossey-Bass.

Cotton, N. (1994, February). *The deadly combination: Adolescence and mental illness.* Paper presented at the Harvard Medical School Continuing Education Conference, Cambridge, MA.

Cummings, N., & Sayana, M. (1995). *Focused psychotherapy: A casebook of brief intermittent psychotherapy throughout the life cycle.* New York: Brunner/Mazel.

Cytryn, L., & McKnew, D. (1996). *Growing up sad: Childhood depression and its treatment.* New York, London: Norton.

Dawson, G., Frey, K., Patagiotides, H., Osterling, J., & Hessl, D. (1997). Infants of depressed mothers exhibit activation in their electroencephalographic atypical frontal brain activity: A replication and extension of previous findings. *J of Child Psychol Psychiatry, 38,* 179–186.

DeVeaugh-Geiss, J., Moroz, G., Biederman, J., Cantwell, D., Fontaine, R., Greist, J., Reichler, R., Katz, R., & Landau, P. (1992). Clomipramine hydrochloride in childhood and adolescent obesssive compulsive disorder: A multicenter trial. *J Am Acad Child Adolesc Psychiatry, 31,* 45–49.

DiLeo, J. H. (1973). *Children's drawings as diagnostic aids.* New York: Brunner/Mazel.

Dinklage, D. (1994). Neurodevelopmental disorders and psychotherapeutic interventions in children. In J. Ellison, C. Weinstein, & T. Hodel-Malinofsky (Eds.), *The psychotherapist's guide to neuropsychiatric patients: Diagnostic and treatment issues.* Washington, DC: American Psychiatric Press.

Dorris, M. (1989). *The broken cord.* New York: Harper and Row.

Dummit, E. S., Klein, R. G., Tancer, N. K., Asche, B., Martin, J., & Fairbanks, J. A. (1997). Systematic assessment of 50 children with selective mutism. *J Am Acad Child Adolesc Psychiatry, 36,* 653–660.

Edwards, M. E., & Steinglass, P. (1995). Family therapy treatment outcomes for alcoholism. *Journal of Marital and Family Therapy, 21,* 475–509.

Emslie, G. J., Rush, J., Weinberg, W. A., Kowatch, C. A., Hughes, C. W., Carmody, T., & Rintelmann, J. (1997). A double-blind, randomized, placebo-controlled trial of fluoxetine in children and adolescents with depression. *Arch Gen Psychiatry, 54,* 1031–1037.

Englander, L. (1994). *Necessary confrontations: Women's dilemmas exercising authority in the parental role.* Unpublished doctoral dissertation, Antioch/New England Graduate School, Keene, NH.

Erickson, S. J., Feldman, S. S., & Steiner, H. (1996). Defense mechanisms and adjustment in normal adolescents. *Am J Psych, 153,* 826–828.

Eron, L. D., Huesmann, L. R., & Zelli, A. (1991). The role of parental variables in the learning of aggression. In D. Pepler & K. H. Rubin (Eds.), *The development and treatment of childhood aggression.* Hillsdale, NJ: Erlbaum.

Eysenck, H. J. (1967). *The biological basis of personality.* Springfield, IL: Thomas.

Farrington, D. P. (1983). Offending from 10 to 25 years of age. In K. T. Van Dusen & S. A. Mednick (Eds.), *Prospective studies of crime and delinquency.* Boston: Klumer-Nijhoff.

Fava, M., Alpert, J. E., Borus, J. S., Nierenberg, A. A., Pava, J. A., & Rosenbaum, J. C. (1996). Patterns of personality disorder comorbidity in early-onset versus late-onset major depression. *Am J Psychiatry, 153,* 1308–1312.

Ferber, R. (1985). *Solve your child's sleep problem.* New York: Simon and Schuster.

Fine, S., & Forth, A. (1991). Group therapy for adolescent depressive disorder: A comparison of social skills and therapeutic support. *J Am Acad Child Adolesc Psychiatry, 30,* 79–85.

Free, K., Alechina, I., &, Zahn-Waxler, C. (1996). Affective language between depressed mothers and their children: The potential impact of psychotherapy. *J Am Acad Child Adolesc Psychiatry, 35,* 783–790.

Free, N., Winget, C., & Whitman, R. (1993). Separation anxiety in panic disorder. *Am J Psychiatry, 150,* 595–599.

Friedman, S., & Fanger, M. (1991). *Expanding therapeutic possibilities: Getting results in brief psychotherapy.* Lexington, MA: Lexington Books.

Garcia-O'Hearn, H., Margolin, J., & John, R. S. (1997). Mothers' and fathers' reports of children's reactions to naturalistic marital conflict. *J Am Acad Adolesc Psychiatry, 36,* 1366–1373.

Gardner, R. (1971). *Therapeutic communication with children: The mutual story telling technique.* New York: Science House.

Geller, B., & Luby, J. (1997). Child and adolescent bipolar disorder: A review of the past 10 years. *J Am Acad Child Adolesc Psychiatry, 36,* 1168–1176.

Gerber, P. J., Reiff, H. B., & Ginsberg, R. (1996). Reframing the learning disability experience. *J Learn Disabil, 29,* 98–101.

Gil, E. (1991). *Healing power of play.* New York: Guilford Press.

Gilham, R. (1990). Refractory epilepsy: An evaluation of psychological methods in outpatient management. *Epilepsia, 31,* 427–432.

Glasser, W. (1965). *Reality therapy, A new approach to psychiatry.* New York: Harper and Row.

Glod, C. A., Teicher, M. H., Polcari, A., McGreenery, C. E., & Ito, Y. (1997). Circadian rest-activity disturbances in children with seasonal affective disorder. *J Am Acad Child Adolesc Psychiatry, 36,* 188–194.

Goldfried, M. (1971). Systematic desensitization as training in self-control. *J Consult Clin Psychol, 37,* 228–234.

Goldstein, A. P. (1988). *The prepare curriculum: Teaching presocial competencies.* Champaign, IL: Research Press.

Goodyer, I. M., Herbert, J., Tamplin, A., Secher, S., & Pearson, J. (1997). Short-term outcome of major depression: II. Life events, family dysfunction, and friendship difficulties as predictors of persistent disorder. *J Am Acad Child Adolesc Psychiatry, 36,* 474–479.

Greene, R. (1998). *The explosive child: Understanding and helping inflexible, easily frustrated children.* New York: Harper Collins.

Greene, R., Biederman, J., Faraone, S., & Ouellette, C. A. (1996). Toward a new psychometric definition of social disability in children with attention deficit disorder. *J Am Acad Child Adolesc Psychiatry, 35,* 571–578.

Gunderson, J. (1984). *Borderline personality disorder.* Washington, DC: American Psychiatric Press.

Gutheil, T. (1997). *Fiscal informed consent.* Presented at Continuing Medical Education: Caribbean Clinical Update.

Haley, J. (1976). *Problem solving therapy: New strategies for effective family therapy.* San Francisco: Jossey-Bass.

Harris, D. B. (1988). *Children's drawings as measures of intellectual maturity.* New York: Harcourt, Brace and World.

Hatch, T. F. (1988). Encopresis and constipation in children. *Pediatric Clinics of North America, 35,* 257–279.

Haugaard, J., Reppucci, N., & Feerick, M. (1997). Children coping with maltreatment. In S. Wolchink & I. Sandler (Eds.), *Handbook of children's coping: Linking theory and intervention.* New York: Plenum Press.

Havens, L. (1989). *A safe place.* New York: Ballantine.

Havens, L. (1997). *Suicide: Critical issues in assessment and treatment.* Presented and discussed at Continuing Medical Education: Harvard Medical School, Boston.

Hechtman, L. (1985). Adolescent outcome of hyperactive children treated with stimulants in childhood: A review. *Psychopharmacology Bulletin, 21,* 178–191.

Helfer, R. E. (1975). *Child abuse and neglect: The diagnostic process and treatment programs* (DHEW Publication No. OHD-75-69). Washington, DC: U.S. Department of Health, Education, and Welfare.

Hendin, H. (1991). Psychodynamics of suicide with particular reference to the young. *Am J Psychiatry, 148,* 1150–1158.

Herman, J. (1992). *Trauma and recovery.* New York: Basic Books.

Herman, J. L., Perry, J. C., & van der Kolk, B. (1989). Childhood trauma in borderline personality disorder. *Am J Psych, 146,* 490–495.

Herzog, J. (1995). Men in the psychoanalytic situation: Encountering father hunger. *Psychoanalysis & Psychotherapy, 12,* 46–59.

Himelein, M. J., & McElrath, J. A. (1996). Resilient child sexual abuse survivors: Cognitive coping and illusion. *Child Abuse Negl, 20,* 747–758.

Hirshfeld, D. R., Biederman, J., Brody, L., Faraone, S., & Rosenbaum, J. (1997a). Associations between expressed emotion and child behavioral inhibition and psychopathology. *J Am Acad Child Adolesc Psychiatry, 36,* 205–213.

Hirshfeld, D. R., Biederman, J., Brody, L., Faraone, S., & Rosenbaum, J. (1997b). Expressed emotion toward children with behavioral inhibition: Associations with maternal anxiety disorder. *J Am Acad Child Adolesc Psychiatry, 36,* 910–917.

Holden, L. (1985). *Parenting children with epilepsy.* Presented at the Epilepsy Association of Massachusetts Conference, Waltham, MA.

Hooper, C. (1992). *Mothers surviving child sexual abuse.* London: Tavistock/Routledge.

Horner, A. J. (1978). *Being and loving.* New York: Jason Aronson.

Howe, A. C., & Walker, C. E. (1992). Behavioral management of toilet training, enuresis, and encopresis. *Pediatric Clinics of North America, 39,* 413–431.

Hyman, S. (1996). Addiction to cocaine and amphetamine. *Neuron, 16,* 901–904.

Jan, J. E., Ziegler, R. G., & Erba, G. (1991). *Does your child have epilepsy?* (2nd ed.). Austin, TX: Pro-Ed.

Jones, M. C. (1924). The elimination of children's fears. *J Experimental Psychology, 7,* 382–390.

Jongsma, A. E., Peterson, L. M., & McInnis, W. P. (1996). *The child and adolescent treatment planner.* New York: John Wiley and Sons.

Joorabchi, B. (1977). Expressions of the hyperventilation syndrome in childhood: Studies in the management, including an evaluation of the effectiveness of propranolol. *Clin Pediatr, 16,* 1110–1115.

Kagan, J., Resnick, J. S., & Sniedman, N. (1988). Biological basis of childhood shyness. *Science, 240,* 167–171.

Kashani, J. H., Daniel, A. E., Dandoy, A. C., & Holcomb, W. R. (1992). Family violence: Impact on children. *J Am Acad Child Adolesc Psychiatry, 31,* 181–189.

Kestenbaum, C. (1997). *Affective disorders in children.* Presented at the NECCAP meeting, McLean Hospital, Boston.

Koeppen, A. S. (1974). Relaxation training for children. *Elementary School Guidance and Counseling, 9,* 521–528.

Kohlberg, L. (1985). *The psychology of moral development.* New York: Harper.

Kottmeier-Leandro, C. (1995). *Appraised meanings and ways of coping: Their relationships to the psychological adjustment of homeless young adults.* Unpublished doctoral dissertation, University of Vermont, Burlington, VT.

Kovacs, M. (1996). Presentation and course of major depressive disorder during childhood and later years of the life span. *J Am Acad Child Adolesc Psychiatry, 35,* 705–715.

Kovacs, M., Akiskal, H. S., Gatsonis, C., & Parrone, P. (1994). Childhood onset dysthymic disorder. Clinical features and prospective naturalistic outcome. *Arch Gen Psychiatry, 51,* 365–374.

Kutasch, K., & Rivera, V. R. (1996). *What works in children's mental health services: Uncovering answers to critical questions.* Baltimore: Paul H. Brooks.

Kutcher, S. P., & MacKenzie, S. (1988). Successful clonazepam treatment of adolescents with panic disorder. *J Clin Psychopharmacol, 8,* 922–924.

LaClave, I. J., & Brack, G. (1989). Reframing to deal with patient resistance: A practical application. *Am J Psychother, 43,* 68–76.

Laing, R. D. (1965). *The divided self.* Baltimore: Pelican Books.

Leimkuhler, M. E. (1994). Attention deficit disorder in adults and adolescents: Cognitive behavioral and personality styles. In J. Ellison, C. Weinstein, & T. Hodel-Malinofsky (Eds.), *The psychotherapist's guide to neuropsychiatric patients: Diagnostic and treatment issues.* Washington, DC: American Psychiatric Press.

Lenane, M. C., Swedo, S. E., Rapoport, J. G., & Leonard, H. (1992). Rates of obsessive-compulsive disorder in first-degree relatives of patients with trichotillomania: A research note. *J Clinical Psychology and Psychiatry and Allied Disciplines, 33,* 925–933.

Levine, M. D. (1975). Children with encopresis: A descriptive analysis. *Pediatrics, 56,* 412–416.

Levine, M. D. (1976). Children with encopresis: A study of treatment outcomes. *Pediatrics, 58,* 845–852.

Levine, M., & Zallen, G. (1984). The learning disorder of adolescent organic and nonorganic failure to strive. *Pediatric Clinics of North America, 3,* 345–370.

Lewinsohn, P. M., Klein, D. N., & Seeley, J. R. (1995). Bipolar disorders in a community sample of older adolescents: Prevalence, phenomenology, comorbidity, and course. *J Am Acad Child Adolesc Psychiatry, 34,* 454–463.

Lewis, J. (1998). For better or worse: Interpersonal relationships and individual outcome. *Am J Psychiatry, 155,* 582–589.

Livingston, R. (1991). Anxiety disorders. In M. Lewis (Ed.). *A comprehensive textbook of child psychiatry* (pp. 673–684). Baltimore: Williams Wilkins.

Lothman, D., & Pianta, R. (1993). Role of child-mother interaction in predicting competence of children with epilepsy. *Epilepsia, 34,* 658–669.

Lumley, M. A., Mader, C., Gramzow, J., & Papineau, K. (1996). Family factors related to alexithymia characteristics. *Psychosom Med, 58,* 214–216.

Lydon, J. (1997). *Daughter of the Queen of Sheba.* Boston: Houghton Mifflin.

Lyman, D. R., & Selman, R. L. (1985). Peer conflict in pair therapy: Clinical and developmental analyses. *New Dir Child Dev, 29,* 85–102.

Lyons-Ruth, K. (1997, February 19). *Recent attachment research and its implications for psychotherapy.* Paper presented at the Grand Rounds Conference, The Cambridge Hospital, Cambridge, MA.

Lyons-Ruth, K., Alpern, L., & Repacholi, B. (1993). Disorganized infant attachment classification and maternal psychosocial problems as predictors of hostile-aggressive behavior in the preschool classroom. *Child Dev, 64,* 572–585.

Main, M. (1994). *A move to the level of representation in the study of attachment organization: Implications for psychoanalysis.* Annual research lecture to the British Psycho-Analytical Society, London.

Mann, B. J., & Borduin, C. M. (1991). A critical review of psychotherapy outcome studies with adolescents: 1978–1988. *Adolescence, 26,* 505–541.

Mann, J. (1980). *Time limited psychotherapy.* Boston: Commonwealth Fund Publications.

March, J. S., & Leonard, H. L. (1996). Obsessive-compulsive disorder in children and adolescents: A review of the past 10 years. *J Am Acad Child Adolesc Psychiatry, 35,* 1265–1273.

March, J. S., Mulle, K., & Herbel, B. (1994). Behavioral psychotherapy for children and adolescents with obsessive-compulsive disorder: An open trial of a new protocol-driven treatment package. *J Am Acad Child Adolesc Psychiatry, 33,* 333–341.

Margalit, M., & Heiman, T. (1987). Family climate and anxiety in families with learning disabled boys. *J Am Acad Child Psychiatry, 25,* 841–846.

Masse, L. C., & Tremblay, R. E. (1997). Behavior of boys in kindergarten and the onset of substance use during adolescence. *Arch Gen Psychiatry, 54,* 62–68.

Max, J. E., & Lindgren, S. D. (1997). Child and adolescent brain injury: Psychiatric findings from a pediatric outpatient specialty clinic. *Brain Inj, 11,* 699–711.

Max, J. E., Robin, D. A., Lindgren, S. D., Smith, W. L., Sato, Y., Matthies, P. J., Stierwalt, J., & Castillo, C. S. (1997). Traumatic brain injury in children and adolescents: Psychiatric disorders at two years. *J Am Acad Child Adolesc Psychiatry, 36,* 1278–1285.

Miller, A. (1981). *The drama of the gifted child and the search for the true self.* New York: Basic Books.

Miller, L. (1998, November). *Effects of major mental illness on parenting: Assessment and intervention.* Presented at the 11th Annual U.S. Psychiatric and Mental Health Congress, San Francisco, CA.

Miller, S. J. (1998). *Never let me down.* New York: Henry Holt.

Minuchin, S., & Fishman, H. C. (1974). *Families and family therapy.* Cambridge: Harvard University Press.

Minuchin, S., Montalvo, B., Guerney, Jr., B. G., Rosman, B. L., & Schumer, F. (1967). *Families of the slums. An exploration of their structure and treatment.* New York: Basic Books.

Mischkulnig, M. (1989). [Infant characteristics and anger reduction.] *Z Exp Angew Psycholo, 36,* 567–578.

Morse, G. G. (1997). Effect of positive reframing and social support on perception of perimenstrual changes among women with premenstrual syndrome. *Health Care Women Int, 18,* 175–193.

Murphy, J. M., Wehler, C. A., Pagano, M. E., Little, M., Kleinman, R. E., & Jellinek, M. S. (1998). Relationship between hunger and psychosocial functioning in low-income American children. *J Am Acad Child Adolesc Psychiatry, 37,* 163–170.

Murray, H. A. (1943). *Thematic apperception test manual.* Cambridge: Harvard University Press.

National Institute of Mental Health. (1993). *Understanding panic disorder* (NIH Publication No. 93-3509). Rockville, MD: U.S. Department of Health and Human Services.

Oates, R., O'Toole, B. I., Lynch, D. L., Stern, A., & Cooney, G. (1994). Stability and change in outcomes for sexually abused children. *J Am Acad Child Adolesc Psychiatry, 33,* 945–953.

Papp, P., & Imber-Black, E. (1996). Family themes: Transmission and transformation. *Family Process, 35,* 5–20.

Parke, R. (1981). *Fathers.* Cambridge: Harvard University Press.

Pfefferbaum, B. (1997). Posttraumatic stress disorder in children: A review of the past 10 years. *J Am Acad Child Adolesc Psychiatry, 36,* 1503–1511.

Pisterman, S., McGrath, P., Firestone, P., Goodman, J. T., Webster, I., & Mallory, R. (1992). Outcome of parent-mediated treatment of preschoolers with attention deficit disorder with hyperactivity. *J Consult Clin Psychol, 57,* 628–635.

Plizka, S. R. (1992). Comorbidity of attention-deficit hyperactivity disorder and overanxious disorder. *J Am Acad Child Adolesc Psychiatry, 31,* 197–203.

Popper, C. W. (1993). Psychopharmacologic treatment of anxiety disorders in adolescents and children. *J Clin Psychiatry, 54* (Suppl. 5), 52–63.

Popper, C. W. (1997). Antidepressants in the treatment of attention-deficit/hyperactivity disorder. *J Clin Psychiatry, 58* (Suppl. 14), 14–29.

Prochaska, J. O., DiClemente, C. C., & Norcross, J. C. (1992). In search of how people change: Applications to addictive behaviors. *Amercian Psychologist, 47,* 1102–1114.

Rank, B. (1955). Intensive study and treatment of preschool children who show marked personality deviations or "atypical development" and their parents. In G. Caplan (Ed.), *Emotional problems in early childhood.* New York: Basic Books.

Rapoport, J. (1990). *The boy who couldn't stop washing: The experience and treatment of obsessive-compulsive disorder.* New York: Dutton.

Rapoport, J., Leonard, H., Swedo, S., & Lenane, M. C. (1993). Obsessive-compulsive disorder in children and adolescents: Issues in management. *J Clin Psychiatry, 54* (Suppl. 6), 24–29.

Rayner, R. (1992). *The elephant.* New York: Random House, Turtle Press.

Redl, F., & Wineman, D. (1951). *Children who hate.* New York: The Free Press.

Reiss, D., Hetherington, E. M., Plomin, R., Howe, G., Simmens, S., Henderson, S. H., O'Connor, T. J., Bussell, D. A., Anderson, E. R., & Law, T. (1995). Genetic questions for environmental studies: Differential parenting and psychopathology in adolescence. *Arch of Gen Psychiatry, 52,* 925–936.

Rey-Sánchez, F., & Gutiérrez-Casares, J. R. (1997). Paroxetine in children with major depressive disorder: An open trial. *J Am Acad Child Adolesc Psychiatry, 36,* 1443–1447.

Robin, A., & Foster, S. (1989). *Negotiating parent adolescent conflict.* New York: Guilford Press.

Rosenbaum, J. F., Biederman, J., Bolduc, E. A., Hirshfeld, D., Faraone, S., & Kagan, J. (1992). Comorbidity of parental anxiety disorders as risk for childhood-onset anxiety in inhibited children. *Am J Psychiatry, 149,* 475–481.

Sattler, J. (1988). *Assessment of children* (3rd ed.). San Diego: Jerome M. Sattler.

Schaefer, C. E. (Ed.) (1976). *Therapeutic use of child's play.* New York: Jason Aronson.

Schultheis, G. M. (1998). *Brief therapy homework planner: A skill-building sourcebook.* Washington, DC: American Psychiatric Press.

Schwartz, D. (1979, Spring). The suicidal character. *Psych Quarterly, 51,* 64–70.

Segroi, S. (1988). *Handbook on sexual assault.* New York: Springer.

Seleckman, M. (1997). *Solution focused therapy with children: Harnessing family strengths for change.* New York: Guilford Press.

Seligman, L. (1975). *Helplessness.* San Francisco: Freeman.

Selman, R. L. (1990). *The growth of interpersonal understanding: Developmental and clinical analyses.* New York: Academic.

Shaw, D. S., Keenan, K., Vondra, J. I., Delliquadri, E., & Giovanelli, J. (1997). Antecedents of preschool children's internalizing problems: A longitudinal study of low-income families. *J Am Acad Child Adolesc Psychiatry, 36,* 1760–1767.

Shaw, D. S., Winslow, E. B., Owens, E. B., & Hood, N. (1998). Young children's adjustment to chronic family adversity: A longitudinal study of low-income families. *J Am Acad Child Adolesc Psychiatry, 37,* 545–553.

Shealy, A. (1994). Attention-deficit hyperactivity disorder–Etiology, diagnosis and management. *J Child Adolesc Psychiatric Nursing, 7,* 24–35.

Siegel, B. (1996, November). Simple questionnaire helps screen for autism. *Clinical Psychiatry News.*

Sifneos, P. (1992). *Short term anxiety provoking therapy: A treatment manual.* New York: Basic Books.

Silver, L. (1984). *The misunderstood child. A guide for parents of learning disabled children.* New York: McGraw-Hill.

Siskind, D. (1997). *Working with parents.* New York: Jason Aronson.

Smith, J., & Beck, J. (1998, May). *Panel discussion.* Department of Psychiatry. The Cambridge Hospital, Cambridge, MA.

Smith, S. (1981). *No easy answers: The learning disabled child at home and at school.* New York: Bantam Books.

Spitzer, R., Gibbon, M., Skodol, A., Williams, J., & First, M. (1994). *DSM-IV casebook.* Washington, DC: American Psychiatric Press.

Sprenger, D. L., & Josephson, A. M. (1998). Integration of pharmacotherapy and family therapy in the treatment of children and adolescents. *J Am Acad Child Adolesc Psychiatry, 37,* 887–889.

Stadter, M. (1996). *Object relations brief therapy: The therapeutic relationship in short term work.* New York: Aronson.

Steingard, R. (1993, June). *Psychopharmacology perspectives.* Response to case presentations in Child Psychotherapy Conference, Harvard Medical School Department of Continuing Education, Boston, MA.

Stewart, M. (1996, April). *Haitian culture and child rearing,* The Cambridge Hospital Department of Child Psychiatry Ambulatory Treatment Seminar, Cambridge, MA.

Stillwell, B., Galvin, M., Kopta, S. M., Padgett, R. J., & Holt, J. (1997). Moralization of attachment: A fourth domain of conscience functioning. *J Am Acad Child Adolesc Psychiatry, 36,* 1140–1147

Stroul, B., Lourie, I. S., Goldman, S. K., & Katz-Leavy, J. W. (1992). *Profiles of local systems of care for children and adolescents with severe emotional disturbances.* Washington: Georgetown University Child Development Center, CASSP Technical Assistance Center.

Sullivan, H. S. (1953). *The interpersonal theory of psychiatry.* New York: W. W. Norton.

Swedo, S. E., & Leonard, H. L. (1994). Childhood movement disorders and obsessive–compulsive disorder. *J Clin Psychiatry, 55* (Suppl. 3), 32–37.

Sylvester, C., & Kruesi, M. (1994). Child and adolescent psychopharmaco-therapy: Progress and pitfalls. *Psychiatric Annals, 24,* 83–90.

Terr, L. (1990). *Too scared to cry: Psychic trauma in childhood.* New York: Harper and Row.

Thomas, A., & Chess, S. (1977). *Temperament and development.* New York: Brunner/Mazel.

Tureki, S., & Tonner, L. (1985). *The difficult child.* New York: Bantam Books.

Vaillant, G. E. (1975). Sociopathy as a human process. *Archives of Gen Psych, 32,* 178.

Vaillant, G. E. (1993). *Wisdom of the ego.* Cambridge, MA: Harvard University Press.

Vogel, S. (1996). Urban middle-class Japanese family life, 1958–1966: A personal and evolving perspective. In D. Shwalb & B. J. Shwalb (Eds.), *Japanese childrearing: Two generations of scholarship. Culture and human development.* New York: Guilford Press.

Warren, S., Oppenheim, D., & Emde, R. (1996). Can emotions and themes in children's play predict behavior problems. *J Am Acad Child Adolesc Psychiatry, 34,* 1331–1337.

Watson, J. B., & Rayner, R. (1920). Conditioned emotional reaction. *J Experimental Psychology, 3,* 1–14.

Wegsheider, S. (1981). *Another chance: Hope and health for alcoholic families.* New York: Science and Behavior Press.

Weiss, G., Hechtman, L., Milroy, T., & Perlman, T. (1985). Psychiatric status of hyperactives as adults: A controlled prospective 15 year follow-up of 63 hyperactive children. *J American Academy of Child Psychiatry, 24,* 11–20.

Whalen, C., & Henker, B. (1984). Hyperactivity and the attention deficit disorders: Experimental frontiers. *Pediatric Clinics of North America, 3,* 397–442.

Wind, J. W., & Silvern, L. (1994). Parenting and family stress as mediators of long term effects of child abuse. *Child Abuse Negl, 18,* 890–902.

Winnicott, D. (1958). Hate in the countertransference. In D. W. Winnicott, *Collected papers: Through pediatrics to psychoanalysis* (pp. 194–203). London: Tavistoch.

Winnicott, D. W. (1965). *The maturational processes and the facilitating environment.* New York: International Universities Press.

Woititz, J. (1983). *Adult children of alcoholics.* Hollywood, FL: Health Communications.

Wolf, A. E. (1991). *Get out of my life, but first could you drive me and Cheryl to the mall.* New York: Noonday Press.

Wozniak, J., Biederman, J., Kiely, K., Ablon, S., Faraone, S., Mundy, E., & Mennin, D. (1995). Mania-like symptoms suggestive of childhood-onset bipolar disorder in clinically referred children. *J Am Acad Child Adolesc Psychiatry, 34,* 867–876.

Wylder, J. (1982). Including the divorced father in family therapy. *Social Work, 27,* 479–482.

Ziegler, R. (1981). Child and context: Reactive adaptations of learning disabled children. *J Learning Disabilities, 22,* 339–346.

Ziegler, R. (1992). *Homemade books to help kids cope: A guide for parents and professionals.* New York: Magination Press (Brunner/Mazel).

Ziegler, R., & Holden, L. (1987). Family therapy for learning disabled and attention-deficit disordered children. *Amer. J. Orthopsychiat., 58,* 196–210.

Ziegler, R., & Musliner, P. (1977). Persistent themes: A naturalistic study of personality development in the family. *Fam. Proc., 16,* 293–305.

SUGGESTED READINGS

☐ Introduction, Part I

Lewis, J. (1998). For better or worse: Interpersonal relationships and individual outcome. *Am J Psychiatry, 155,* 582–589.

Dr. Lewis' review of basic relationship mechanisms (attachment, connection, separation, negotiation, unconscious fears, power, and issues of balance) gives the reader a sense of the concerns that are a dynamic aspect of any intimate couple's relationship. Reviewing this article will help the reader bring these same ideas to the richness and complexity of the child–parent relationship.

Safety in Life—Safety in Therapy

Herman, J. (1992). *Trauma and recovery.* New York: Basic Books.

This text helps the reader understand the complexity of the impact of trauma, the multiple steps that can contribute to recovery. It will prepare the reader for working with the parent who has a trauma history and who, for instance, fears limit setting as a form of abuse of the power in relationship to a child.

Havens, L. (1989). *A safe place* (pp. 53–65). New York: Ballantine Books.

Dr. Havens' books suggest how the therapist may develop "a way of being" in treatment. Dr. Havens explains the function of receptive empathy. He stresses the respect that must be present in psychotherapy in order to create a condition for the client's self to emerge in all its complexities. The mysteriousness of the process he describes with adults is not unlike that experienced by child therapists as they attempt to join the child in the complex and often opaque aspects of a play exchange. While *Sharing Care* relies on both directive and diagnostic aspects of treatment, the therapist must find a way to "be with" the complexity of a child and his family in the face of uncertainty and ambiguity.

Rogers, A. G. (1995). *A shining affliction.* New York: Penguin Books.

The importance of safety and being heard in therapy and in life is described in a "novelized" form by Annie G. Rogers that is both moving and informative. This is a classic tale of a zone 2 to 3 switch. A child is placed in foster care after horrendous early experiences. The family's love and care cannot restore health to this child without intensive treatment. The story of that residential and psychotherapeutic treatment asks the reader to marvel at the strength of children's survival mechanisms and the complexity of healing relationships. In addition, during the parallel story of the author's treatment, her own history and intensive symptomatology is portrayed as a zone 4 child and family, until her family dissolves.

Communication with Children and Adolescents

Glasser, W. (1965). *Reality therapy, A new approach to psychiatry.* New York: Harper and Row.
Cotton, N. (1993). *Lessons from the lion's den* (pp. 69–129). San Francisco: Jossey-Bass.

Both of these books help the child and adolescent therapist find ways of being real with children and adolescents in the context of some of their most difficult presentations and most shocking histories or behavior. They are necessary reading for those who must attend to the child issues in a family-based treatment. Chapters 2 and 3 in Cotton's writing will help the therapist guide parents as they model respectful, yet painful, conversations about life problems with children and adolescents. Glasser helps the therapist appreciate the techniques needed for directly addressing issues with adolescents.

☐ Chapter 1

Accepting and Understanding Families

Comer, J. P., & Poussaint, A. F. (1992). *Raising Black children: Questions and answers for parents and teachers.* New York: Plume.

This work helps therapists talk with children who face the different family and societal challenges that are created by issues of race in America. The authors' suggested readings include Gibbs, J. T., and Huang, L. H. (1990). *Children of color: Psychological interventions with minority youth.* San Francisco: Jossey-Bass.

McGoldrick, M., Giordano, J., & Pearce, J. (1996). *Ethnicity and family therapy* (2nd ed.). New York: Guilford Press.

The therapist's ability to understand different cultures and their impact on an individual's emotional style, manner of self-revelation, or anticipated patterns of intimacy and communication is enhanced by this book. Another important book that brings the reader into the lifespace of children and families is Oscar Lewis' *La Vida: A Puerto Rican Family in the Culture of Poverty–San Juan and New York* (New York: Random House, 1965). This book will help the reader understand the many material and resource challenges that children and parents face in the context of poverty. The fact that America has continued to decide to have an underclass with women and children in poverty is described in a more recent work, Jonathan Kozol's *Amazing Grace* (New York: Harper Collins, 1996), which describes contemporary dilemmas in the lives of Black and Hispanic families.

Haley, J. (1974). *Uncommon therapy: The psychiatric techniques of Milton Erickson* (pp. 24–46). New York: Ballantine.

Chapter 2 focuses on the family's life cycle and the influence of relationships on the developmental challenges that can lead to symptoms or stress. This interesting and provocative work reviews Milton Erickson's therapy. It continues to challenge a clinician's thinking (as well as any *DSM* orientation) after three decades.

Visher, E. B., & Visher, J. S. (1996). *Therapy with stepfamilies.* New York: Brunner/Mazel.

Understanding the presentation of issues within stepfamilies (a more common occurrence now) will be useful in the diagnostic assessment of child and stepfamily constellations. Treatment approaches are well defined.

The Holding Environment

Winnicott, D. W. (1965). *The maturational processes and the facilitating environment.* New York. International Universities Press.

Winnicott was a pioneering pediatrician and psychoanalyst. He directed the field's attention to the nature of the parental relationship and how it facilitates the child's emotional and psychological development within the "holding environment" that the parents create.

Understanding Children's Styles

Thomas, A., & Chess, S. (1977). *Temperament and development*. New York: Brunner/Mazel.

A seminal work in the development of understanding temperament. Thomas and Chess place the child's long-term outcome within the perspective that highlights the importance of the way parents can adjust their relationship to the needs of their child. Their review of the degree of match versus mismatch between parent and child focused attention on this topic. For an application of these concepts, see Tureki's *The Difficult Child* (New York: Bantam Books, 1985), which is also recommended in Part II.

Play Therapy

Schaefer, C. (Ed.) (1976). *Therapeutic use of child's play*. Northvale, NJ: Jason Aronson.

This volume includes a wide selection of readings that introduce a child therapist to the many facets of play and ways to use play in treatment.

Two additional articles well worth reading are:
Hartman, L., & Hanson, G. (1986). Child psychotherapy. In J. Masserman (Ed.), *Current psychiatric therapies.* New York: Grune and Stratton.
Brooks, R. (1985). The beginning sessions of child therapy: Messages and metaphors. *Psychotherapy, 22*, 761–769.

Managing Children's Behavior

Barkley, R. A. (1997). *Defiant children: A clinician's manual for assessment and parent training* (2nd ed.). New York: Guilford Press.

This more advanced behavioral text will be referenced again in discussing the treatment of externalizing disorders. Barkley's work has been a useful guide for child clinicians for many years. His focus helps place the child's behavior in a broader context. He looks carefully at parental issues (see chapter 3 of this book) and provides some guidelines for focused behavioral interventions.

Working Quickly with Families and the Use of Homework in Therapy

Seleckman, M. (1997). *Solution focused therapy with children: Harnessing family strengths for change.* New York: The Guilford Press.
Schultheis, G. M. (1998). *Brief therapy homework planner: A skill-building sourcebook*. Washington, DC: American Psychiatric Press.

Both these texts give the reader a variety of ideas about how to quickly make use of the strengths families may have and how to put them "to the test" through the use of homework. The *Brief Therapy Homework Planner* will offer basic suggestions, and then the therapist will need to make creative adaptations of the material.

☐ Chapter 2

Addressing Troublesome Thinking and Feeling

Burns, D. (1990). *The feeling good handbook*. New York: Plume.

In an easy to read manner, Dr. Burns leads the reader through ways to identify their clients' thought processes. He shows how to reshape the patterns of thinking that accentuate or deepen hopelessness, depression, and anxiety. His work follows the pioneering studies of Dr. Beck and others in cognitive–behavioral research.

Considering Organic (Brain-Based) Impacts on Experience

Dinklage, D. (1994). Neurodevelopmental disorders and psychotherapeutic interventions in children. In J. Ellison, C. Weinstein, & T. Hodel-Malinofsky (Eds.), *The psychotherapist's guide to neuropsychiatric patients: Diagnostic and treatment issues.* Washington, DC: American Psychiatric Press.

Leimkuhler, M. E. (1994). Attention deficit disorder in adults and adolescents: Cognitive, behavioral and personality styles. In J. Ellison, C. Weinstein, & T. Hodel-Malinofsky (Eds.), *The psychotherapist's guide to neuropsychiatric patients: Diagnostic and treatment issues.* Washington, DC: American Psychiatric Press.

These two chapters help the child clinician appreciate the degree to which a child's (adolescent's or adult's) learning problems can impact on their psychological development and presentation. These works will help the reader anticipate the discussions in chapters 5 and 6 and the role of comorbid learning problems in the internalizing and externalizing disorders.

☐ Chapter 3

Difficult Families

Minuchin, S., Montalvo, B., Guerney, Jr., B. G., Rosman, B. L., & Schumer, F. (1967). *Families of the slums. An exploration of their structure and treatment.* New York: Basic Books.

Minuchin, S., Rosman, B., & Baker, L. (1978). *Psychosomatic families: Anorexia nervosa in context.* Cambridge: Harvard University Press.

Both of these volumes are a value to the reader because they illustrate the world of the zone 4 family. Each volume shows different distortions in family life that can lead to child-based symptoms. For treatment approaches, see Minuchin and Fishman's *Families and Family Therapy.* (Cambridge: Harvard University Press, 1974) for a description of his family therapy interventions.

Respect in the Approach to the Clinical Interview (Even with Difficult People)

Sullivan, H. S. (1953). *The interpersonal theory of psychiatry.* New York: W. W. Norton.

Sullivan's clinical and theoretical work stresses the importance of relationships in experience and the delicate sensitivities that engage one individual with another. He suggested that love evolves as the child gains the ability to treat another individual's needs with the same importance that one regards one's own. A forerunner of Dr. Leston Havens, Sullivan is able to convey the respectfulness with which he engages even the most dramatically impaired individual. The child and adolescent therapist must recognize the added challenge of managing this in the "group" context of the family.

Gunderson, J. (1984). *Borderline personality disorder.* Washington, DC: American Psychiatric Press.

While not every character disorder is a borderline, understanding how to work with this complex disorder will enrich the therapist's work with all character problems. See chapter 4, Table 3, for a clear representation of the levels of development between impaired or primitive ego and emotional defenses and more mature function.

The Importance of Attachment

Bowlby, J. (1971). *Attachment and loss* (Vol. 1). London: Penguin Books.

Bowlby's seminal contributions to attachment theory have influenced much current developmental research and treatment.

To Work with a Child Is to Work with the Parent

Siskind, D. (1997). *Working with parents.* New York: Jason Aronson.

This book presents an empathic, yet incisive, view of the role of parental difficulties in both the origin and solution of children's difficulties. When combined with Daniel Stern's *The Motherhood Constellation* (New York: Basic Books, 1995) and Selma Fraiberg's classic paper, "Ghosts in the Nursery" (*J Am Acad Child Psychiatry, 14,* 387–421, 1975), the book offers the therapist a broad and psychologically attuned approach to parenting.

Issues of Behavior Modification and Discipline

Dodson, F. (1978). *How to discipline with love.* New York: Signet Books.
Cotton, N. (1993). *Lessons from the lion's den* (pp. 130–185). San Francisco: Jossey-Bass.

Every child clinician needs to understand the rudiments of behavior-shaping techniques and plans that can help parents be successful with their children. (They may also wish to make sure they have some skills in managing the potential uproar a child may create in the office.) Chapters 4 and 5 of Cotton's book show how structure is maintained in a child psychiatric inpatient unit.

Conceptualizations of the "True Self" and the Impact of the "Disordered Self" on Individual and Family Member's Experiences

Laing, R. D. (1965). *The divided self.* Baltimore: Pelican Books.
Miller, A. (1981). *Prisoners of childhood: The drama of the gifted child and the search for the true self.* New York: Basic Books.
Winnicott, D. W. (1971). *Therapeutic consultations in child psychiatry.* New York: Basic Books.

These works reveal the complexity of the nature of the self and multiple influences that the child absorbs from the behavior and emotions of the family. The damage that can be done to the inner world of a child by a self -involved parent is well described by Miller.

Lydon, J. (1997). *Daughter of the Queen of Sheba.* Boston: Houghton Mifflin.

Lydon gives a child's eye view into the impact of parental and family disturbance on a child's emotions and the way children's expectations in relationships are shaped. The author presents the experiences of a child growing up with a parent with manic-depressive illness. The relationship with the stepfather helps the reader appreciate the further impact of a stepparent's unpredictability and self-absorption. Another moving and "wickedly funny account of an apolcalytic childhood" is presented in Mary Kerr's *The Liars's Club* (New York: Penguin Books, 1995). She quotes R. D. Laing: "We have our secrets and our needs to confess. We may remember how, in childhood, adults were able at first to look right through us, and into us, and what an accomplishment it was when we, in fear and trembling, could tell our first lie, and make, for ourselves, the discovery that we are irredeemably alone in certain respects, and know that within the territory of ourselves, there can be only our footprints." (*The Divided Self;* see above.)

☐ Chapter 4

Child and Family Therapy with Trauma Survivors

Terr, L. (1990). *Too scared to cry: Psychic trauma in childhood.* New York: Harper and Row.
Gil, E. (1991). *Healing power of play.* New York: Guilford Press.

Both works help the reader develop an approach to managing the impact of child trauma or sexual abuse or both with a child and within the family. The many portraits developed in novels, which are vividly described in ways that clinical portraits cannot, include Maya Angelou's *I Know Why the Caged Bird Sings* (New York: Bantam, 1997) and Dorothy Allison's *Bastard Out of Carolina* (New York: Plume, 1993).

A Model for a Behavioral/Parent Based-Approach to Symptom Resolution

Ferber, R. (1985). *Solve your child's sleep problem.* New York: Simon and Schuster.

A nice approach to clarifying how, even in one aspect of early infant regulation (sleep), the behavior of parents can lead to unanticipated results. The author clarifies how to address sleep issues in a straightforward manner. The text provides a model that the clinician can adapt to working with any behavioral disorder.

Working with Zone 2, 3, and 4 Families: Relational Approaches

Combrinck-Graham, L. (Ed.). (1995). *Children in families at risk: Maintaining the connections.* New York: Guilford.

Multiple chapters describe approaches that are occurring in different regions of the country, which attempt to help families at risk help their children. Sections include chapters on family preservation, families of children placed in institutions, foster care options, and reunification.

☐ Introduction, Part II

Vaillant, G. E. (1995). *The wisdom of the ego.* Cambridge: Harvard University Press.

The author's many years of research and careful thought about the development of the mind makes a wonderful book. It describes the ways in which the mind can both create or destroy itself in its efforts to protect its emotional equilibrium. Vaillant discusses how, through the use of emotional defenses, the mind can deal with internal conflict, intense emotions, and the context in which an individual functions. These defenses begin in childhood (see the seminal work of Anna Freud, *The Ego and the Mechanisms of Defenses,* New York: International University Press, 1946) and their use is currently being studied in adolescents (see Erickson, S. J., Feldman, S. S., & Steiner, H. (1996). Defense mechanisms and adjustment in normal adolescents. *Am J Psychiatry, 153,* 826–828).

☐ Chapter 5

Difficult Temperament/Internalizing or Externalizing

Tureki, S., & Tonner, L. (1985). *The difficult child.* New York: Bantam Books.

This is an excellent "how to" description, which uses the concepts of temperament in parent education and parent training. The book, when offered to parents to read while working with a therapist, can help parents accommodate their styles to the needs of the child.

Readings on Anxiety Disorders

Carlson, C., Figueroa, R., & Lahey, B. (1986). Behavior therapy for childhood anxiety disorders. In R. Gittlemen (Ed.), *Anxiety disorders of childhood.* New York: Guilford.

This volume helps child therapists become familiar with current cognitive-behavioral approaches to the treatment of anxiety in children.

Management of Stress and Change

Ziegler, R. (1992). *Homemade books to help kids cope: A guide for parents and professionals.* New York: Magination Press (Brunner/Mazel).

The reader is introduced to a process of developing therapeutic books for children. The basic principles can be applied to extremely difficult clinical case problems as long as the context of the child's development (the nature of family or school where the book will be developed and read) is carefully considered. This can be combined then, for children in certain diagnostic categories, with generally available books for children on certain topics. For instance, for children with ADHD, there is Galvin and Ferarro's *Otto Learns About His Medicine* (New York: Brunner/Mazel, 1988) or Gehret's *Eagle Eyes* (New York: Verbal Images Press, 1991).

Gardner, R. (1971). *Therapeutic communication with children: The mutual story telling technique.* New York: Science House.

Dr. Gardner's work has always looked for new ways for the therapist to connect with children. His writing is clear and easy to digest.

Substance Abuse/Alcoholism

Substance abuse and alcoholism can complicate the course of any mental illness, internalizing or externalizing disorder, or response to stress or family conflict. As a result, understanding the elements of the management of alcoholism and substance abuse is needed in treating internalizing and externalizing anxiety disorders in adolescents, and in approaching families where substance abuse or alcoholism may be a complicating factor.

Mooney, A. J., & Eisenberg, A. (1992). *The recovery book.* New York: Workman Publishing.
Miller, W., & Rollnick, S. (1991). *Motivational interviewing: Preparing people to change addictive behavior.* New York: Guilford.

These two books provide the clinician with tools to begin to develop a treatment plan to address the issues of alcoholism and drug abuse.

Wegsheider, S. (1981). *Another chance: Hope and health for alcoholic families.* New York: Science and Behavior Press.

This book is an important contribution to the understanding how children's roles can evolve in alcoholic families.

Specifically for Adolescent Substance Abuse and Alcoholism

Jaffe, S. (1990). *Step workbook for adolescent chemical dependency recovery: A guide to the first five steps.* Washington, DC: American Academy of Child and Adolescent Psychiatry.
Fanning, P., & O'Neill, J. T. (1996). *The addiction workbook: A step by step guide for quitting alcohol and drugs.* Oakland, CA: New Harbinger Publishers.

This workbook may be useful to facilitate the therapist's work with parents to complement the work with the adolescent.

Encopresis/Enuresis

Siskind, D. (1997). *Working with parents.* New York: Jason Aronson.

In chapter 3, "Brief Treatment of a Bowel Retention Problem," Siskind uses clear and direct exposition to help the clinician understand how a toilet training issue can exist between the parents' psychology and that of the child. Not all problems of encopresis or enuresis, however, are so simple. The reader must have some background in the complex determinants of toileting disorders and their treatment. See below.

Levine, M. D. (1975). Children with encopresis: A descriptive analysis. *Pediatrics, 56,* 412–416.
Levine, M. D. (1976). Children with encopresis: A study of treatment outcomes. *Pediatrics, 58,* 845–852.
Hatch, T. F. (1988). Encopresis and constipation in children. *Pediatric Clinics of North America, 35,* 257–279.
Howe, A. C., & Walker, C. E. (1992). Behavioral management of toilet training, enuresis, and encopresis. *Pediatric Clinics of North America, 39,* 413–431.

On High Functioning Autism (PDD)

Grandin, T. (1996). *Thinking in pictures and other reports from my life with autism.* New York: Vintage Books.

This book, along with Oliver Sacks's last two chapters in *An Anthropologist on Mars* (New York: Knopf, 1965), will help the therapist appreciate many of the complex issues in autism. Grandin's book, and Sacks' other collection of essays, *The Man Who Mistook His Wife for a Hat* (New York: Summit Books, 1985), also helps the therapist gain some perspective on what it means to be "differently brained." Grandin's book and Sachs's work explore the impact of a developmental disorder (such as autism) or the result of psychiatric/neurological disorder (such as Tourette's syndrome or stroke).

Cohen, D. J., Paul, R., & Volkmar, F. R. (1987). Issues in the classification of pervasive developmental disorders and associated conditions. In D. J. Cohen & A. Donellan (Eds.), *Handbook of autism and pervasive developmental disorders* (pp. 20–40). New York: Wiley.

An excellent review chapter.

OCD

Rapoport, J. (1990). *The boy who couldn't stop washing: The experience and treatment of obsessive-compulsive disorder.* New York: Dutton.

This book is a thorough clinical introduction to the issues of OCD in childhood and adolescence.

March, J. S., Mulle, K., & Herbel, B. (1994). Behavioral psychotherapy for children and adolescents with obsessive-compulsive disorder: An open trial of a new protocol-driven treatment package. *J Am Acad Child Adolesc Psychiatry, 33,* 333–341.

Once the therapist understands the broad issues of OCD and its impact on children's function, a detailed multimodal treatment plan can be mounted—as described above—which includes psychoeducation for the parents and child, behavioral interventions that are psychologically and contextually attuned, and the role of medication.

Depression

Cytryn, L., & McKnew, D. (1996). *Growing up sad: Childhood depression and its treatment.* New York, London: Norton.

A balanced and lucid review of state-of-the-art research into the multiple determinants of depression in children and adolescents. Issues of developmental psychopathology are aired as well as current considerations that inform treatment and intervention strategies. Efforts on prevention and policy formation are discussed in a book that can be read by both professionals and parents. For an "inside view" of a complex and suicidal adolescent, read Green's novel, *I Never Promised You a Rose Garden* (New York: Signet, 1964), which provides an interesting contrast to Plath's *The Bell Jar* (New York, Harper & Row, 1971). Green's novel portrays a wonderful adolescent psychotherapist (some say modeled after Frieda Fromm-Reichman) in action.

Articles of interest include:

Hendin, H. (1991). Psychodynamics of suicide with particular reference to the young. *Am J Psychiatry, 148,* 1150–1158.
Schwartz, D. (1979, Spring). The suicidal character. *Psych Quarterly, 51,* 64–70.

☐ Chapter 6

ADHD

Barkely, R. (1990). *Attention deficit disorder handbook for diagnosis and treatment.* New York: Guilford Press.
Barkely, R. (1996). *Taking charge of ADHD.* New York: Guilford Press.

Both of Barkely's books, the first addressed to the professional and the second to parents, are useful reading given the prevalence of this problem in children and adolescents.

In addition, therapists should be familiar with works that are written to help parents with different approaches to ADHD (Parker, H. C., *The ADD hyperactivity workbook for parents, teacher and kids.* Plantation, FL: Impact, 1988). Parenting books about discipline in young children (Clark, L., *SOS: Help for parents.* Bowling Green, KY: Parents Press, 1996; Phelan, T., *1-2-3 Magic: Training your preschoolers and preteens to do what you want.* Glen Ellyn, IL: Child Management, 1990) or those that support "tough love" in adolescence can help some parents.

Other books describe "a basic family legal system, a family economy, and family traditions" (Eyre, L., & Eyre, R., *Three steps to a strong family.* New York: Simon and Shuster, 1994) to ground parents in their thinking. Love and discipline are balanced in Samalin's work (Samalin, N., *Loving your child is not enough: Positive approaches to discipline.* New York: Penguin Books, 1987). The issues that parents must face in looking at their different styles or examining their anger is described in a later volume (Samalin, N., *Love and anger: The parental dilemma.* New York: Viking Penguin, 1991). Parents inevitably face differences in style as they attempt to coordinate their parenting and can benefit from other reading, such as R. Taffel's *Why Parents Disagree: How Women and Men Parent Differently and How We Can Work Together* (New York: William Morrow, 1994).

Therapists should be familiar with the full range of currently available parenting texts. These books range in subject from nonconfrontational acceptance to more punitive styles. Knowing the resources available from a national organization, such as CHADD, as well as local support groups can be very helpful to parents.

CHADD (Children with Attention Deficit Disorder), 499 Northwest 70th Ave., Suite 308, Plantation, Florida 33317.

ODD

Barkley, R. A. (1997). *Defiant children: A clinician's manual for assessment and parent training* (2nd ed.). New York: Guildford Press.

This behavioral text was referenced in Part I as a guide to structured behavioral interventions. This is a "first-order" approach, which means that many oppositional children's behavior can be improved by consistency, clarity, and behavioral rewards. Direct intervention should always be attempted first. There are, however, children with extreme regulatory difficulties who respond poorly to these interventions. In that case, a second-order approach (such as the one described by Greene, below) can be used to minimize the impact of behaviors that neither the child can control nor can the parents help the child control.

Greene, R. (1998). *The explosive child: Understanding and helping inflexible, easily frustrated children.* New York: Harper Collins.

Dr. Greene's behavioral approach to an out-of-control child can be integrated into any treatment intervention. The text will support the parents' understanding of the triggers that prompt a child's behavioral and emotional "meltdown." The text defines how to focus on the precipitants of the child's reactivity and then how to help child and family recover from the loss of control.

Learning Disabilities

Silver, L. (1984). *The misunderstood child. A guide for parents of learning disabled children.* New York: McGraw-Hill.

Smith, S. (1981). *No easy answers: The learning disabled child at home and at school.* New York: Bantam Books.

The general influence of learning disabilities, as well as the complex processing problems that may be associated with ADHD, must be understood by therapists who work with children and families. The impact of LD issues at school may be somewhat different than those at home. The therapist should be prepared to discuss these issues and help refine the parents' approach and what they can expect from their local school system and community.

Dinklage, D. (1994). Neurodevelopmental disorders and psychotherapeutic interventions in children. In J. Ellison, C. Weinstein, & T. Hodel-Malinofsky (Eds.), *The psychotherapist's guide to neuropsychiatric patients: Diagnostic and treatment issues.* Washington, DC: American Psychiatric Press.

Leimkuhler, M. E. (1994). Attention deficit disorder in adults and adolescents: Cognitive, behavioral and personality styles. In J. Ellison, C. Weinstein, & T. Hodel-Malinofsky (Eds.), *The psychotherapist's guide to neuropsychiatric patients: Diagnostic and treatment issues.* Washington, DC: American Psychiatric Press.

The impact of learning disabilities, developmental language disorders, and issues of "executive control" are presented to help a therapist gain a neurodevelopmental understanding of the cluster of behavioral dyscontrol problems that characterize ADHD and many of the externalizing disorders.

Fetal Alcoholism

Dorris, M. (1989). *The broken cord.* New York: Harper and Row.

This book paints a dramatic picture of a father and an affected child. It shows how a parent struggles with the grief and denial that can be associated with facing a developmental disorder in a child. It illustrates many facets of the challenge of single parenting. It sensitively describes the parent's processes of acceptance, fear, and the struggle to compensate for the child's difficulties. It raises the issue of race and racism, which affect the life of the child because community supports may not be mobilized to address the needs of minority cultures in America.

Conduct Disorder

Vaillant, G. E. (1975). Sociopathy as a human process. *Archives of Gen Psych, 32,* 178.

Redl, F., & Wineman, D. (1951). *Children who hate.* New York: The Free Press.

These are two early works that introduce the reader to the challenges of sociopathy. The first focuses on the complex emotions that can be the underpinning of sociopathic or delinquent behavior, whereas the second looks at what both workers and children face when children cannot control their behavior.

Kohlberg, L. (1985). *The psychology of moral development.* New York: Harper.

This book addresses the developmental processes that contribute to the creation of a conscience. These processes need to be placed within the context of the child's evolving understanding of peer relationships. An excellent introduction to this body of work is by Selman.

Selman, R. L. (1980). *The growth of interpersonal understanding: Developmental and clinical analyses.* New York: Academic.

One result of research on interpersonal understanding is that it has permitted other researchers to break down the stepwise development of these skills and then to look at how to foster their development. One approach to conduct disorder (such as the psychopharmacological approach that focuses on facets of symptoms) is to highlight the adolescent's skill deficits and attempt to modify these with cognitive behavioral interventions. This body of work is reviewed in Goldstein's book cited below.

Goldstein, A. P. (1988). *The prepare curriculum: Teaching prosocial competencies.* Champaign, IL: Research Press.

This text includes training on problem solving, interpersonal skills, situational perceptions, anger control, stress management, and empathy. These are presented so that the modules can be used for individual or group treatment.

Focused Game for Social-Emotional Exploration

"Blast-OFF" The Kids' Game about Feelings. Designed by R. Ziegler & W. Gresser.

This is a therapeutic game that helps explore feelings and solve problems, designed for children ages 4 to 12. It uses the structure of the board to help the child approach the instruction, "Tell a story about a character from a book, movie, one made up by your imagination, or one about you, where the character feels_____ (the square the therapist or child lands on). It then moves on to more directed cognitive-behavioral problem solving and social emotional discussion along the separate trails of school, family, or friends. The final steps of the game help children develop their thoughts and feelings about their hopes, pride, and dreams. It can be ordered through Toys and Reasons, c/o Otter Creek Associates, 86 Lake Street, Burlington, VT 05401 (www.toysandreasons.com).

Other games similar to this one are available from psychological and behavioral catalogues such as Childswork/Childsplay (P. O. Box 61586, King of Prussia, PA 19406).

Difficult Families

Haley, J. (1976). *Problem solving therapy: New strategies for effective family therapy.* San Francisco: Jossey-Bass.

Haley's work, including *Uncommon Therapy* (New York: Ballantine, 1974), is a must read for most therapists. His flexibility and creativity can inspire therapists to continue to find ways to use their perceptions about family interactions.

☐ Chapter 7

Approaches to Brief Treatment

Friedman, S., & Fanger, M. (1991). *Expanding therapeutic possibilities: Getting results in brief psychotherapy*. Lexington, MA: Lexington Books.

This volume describes a variety of approaches that help therapists develop effective brief treatments. Chapter 7 of this book is on clinical strategies with children and families.

Normal Adolescent Issues

Wolf, A. E. (1991). *Get out of my life, but first could you drive me and Cheryl to the mall.* New York: Noonday Press.

The author presents an entertaining overview of the developmental issues of adolescents, which can be read by parents and professionals. This current approach should be compared with that of the more classic volume by Irene Josselyn (*The adolescent and his world*. New York: Family Service Association of America, 1952). An excellent text on psychotherapy with the adolescent is by Donald Holmes (*The adolescent in psychotherapy*. Boston: Little, Brown, 1964).

Adolescent-Parent Conflict

Robin, A., & Foster, S. (1989). *Negotiating parent and adolescent conflict.* New York: Guilford Press.

This is an excellent text, which helps therapists identify communicative and problem solving failures between adolescent and parent. It provides concrete techniques for structuring and improving communication. It offers specific suggestions to help families continue to focus on problem solving.

Family Breakdown and Divorce Issues

Wallerstein, J., & Kelly, J. B. (1984). *Surviving the break-up: How children and parents cope with divorce.* New York: Basic Books.
Wallerstein, J., & Blakeslee, S. (1989). *Second chances: Men, women and children, a decade after divorce.* New York: Ticknor and Fields.
Ricci, I. (1982). *Mom's house, dad's house: Making shared custody work.* New York: Collier Books.
Ives, S. B. (1985). *The divorce workbook: A guide for kids and families.* Waterfront Books.

Besides the texts for professionals and parents, there are a number of books that children and adolescents can read to help them with the breakdown of the family and divorce issues. These range from books specifically for preschool-age children (Brown, L., & Brown, M., *Dinosaurs divorce,* Boston: Atlantic Monthly Press, 1986) to ones for schoolage children (Krementz, J., *How it feels when parents divorce.* New York: Knopf, 1984) and those for teenagers (Rofes, E. (Ed.). *The kid's book of divorce–By, for and about kids.* New York: Vintage Books, 1982).

INDEX

S

T

For Product Safety Concerns and Information please contact our EU representative GPSR@taylorandfrancis.com
Taylor & Francis Verlag GmbH, Kaufingerstraße 24, 80331 München, Germany

www.ingramcontent.com/pod-product-compliance
Ingram Content Group UK Ltd.
Pitfield, Milton Keynes, MK11 3LW, UK
UKHW022003180926
475701UK00003B/175

* 9 7 8 1 1 3 8 0 0 9 7 0 7 *